Social Darwinism
Science and Myth in
Anglo-American Social
Thought

American Civilization
A Series Edited by Allen F. Davis

Gospel Hymns and Social Religion:
The Rhetoric of Nineteenth-Century Revivalism
by Sandra S. Sizer (1978)

Social Darwinism:
Science and Myth in Anglo-American
Social Thought
by Robert C. Bannister (1979)

Twentieth Century Limited:
Industrial Design in America, 1925-1939
by Jeffrey L. Meikle (1979)

Social Darwinism
Science and Myth in Anglo-American Social Thought

ROBERT C. BANNISTER

Temple University Press *Philadelphia*

Temple University Press, Philadelphia 19122
© 1979 by Temple University. All rights reserved
Published 1979
Printed in the United States of America

Library of Congress Cataloging in Publication Data

Bannister, Robert C.
  Social Darwinism.

  (American civilization)
  Includes bibliographical references and index.
  1. Social Darwinism—History. I. Title.
II. Series.
HM106.B255   301'.0424   79-615
ISBN 0-87722-155-3

For Joan

Contents

Acknowledgments

The idea for this study developed initially during a year of reading on British Intellectual History from 1880 to 1920 at the British Library in London, supported by a Study Fellowship from the American Council of Learned Societies. During 1970-71 and 1974-75 I was able to work intermittently on the project in connection with a more general study of the origins of American sociology (forthcoming) under grants from the National Endowment for the Humanities and the Andrew Mellon Foundation. In addition, Swarthmore College has supported the work through a generous sabbatical policy and grants to cover secretarial costs.

Two chapters previously appeared in slightly altered form. Chapter 6 incorporates " 'The Survival of the Fittest Is our Doctrine': History or Histrionics?" (*Journal of the History of Ideas,* 31 [1970], 377-98), and is reprinted with the permission of the editors. Chapter 5 appeared in slightly different form as "William Graham Sumner's 'Social Darwinism' " (*History of Political Economy,* 5 [1973], 89-109), copyright by Duke University Press, which grants permission for republication.

My quest for the elusive Snark of "social Darwinism" placed a special strain on the patience and good will of many librarians. The incomparable resources of the British Library in London and the Bodelian at Oxford proved invaluable. I am also indebted to many libraries in this country for help in tracing often obscure publications, in particular the Library of Congress, the New York Public Library, and the university libraries at Cornell, Columbia, Chicago, Northwestern, Penn, Yale, and Wisconsin. I want especially to thank Ms. Judith Schiff at Yale, and Ms. Josephine L. Harper at the State Historical Society of Wisconsin for assistance with the William Graham Sumner and Henry Demarest Lloyd Papers respectively.

My colleagues and students at Swarthmore College have provided a receptive audience from the start. I wish especially to thank Professor James A. Field, Jr., of the History Department for his interest and critical acumen. Professor Allen F. Davis of Temple University, and general editor of the Temple University Press series, American Civilization, has been supportive at various stages of the project. Finally, I want to thank my associates in the General History Department of the University of Helsinki —where I served as visiting professor in 1977-78—for providing through scholarly example and personal kindness so ideal an environment for completing the final draft.

Social Darwinism
Science and Myth in
Anglo-American Social
Thought

Introduction
The Idea of Social Darwinism

*It is difficult to put one's finger on the expressions of belief
in evolution as determining our political action, but the opponents of liberalism of the twentieth century continually
declared that the measures they opposed would deny the
free play of the struggle for existence and the survival of the
fittest.*
  Edward R. Lewis, A History of American Political
  Thought *(1937), p. 391.*

*It is perhaps unfortunate that so misleading a term as "social
Darwinism" has become accepted terminology, but if it is in
the language to stay, one can at least try to use it always
with the necessary qualifications.*
  Emily Grace, Science and Society, 6 *(1942), 74.*

One

Social Darwinism, as almost everyone knows, is a Bad Thing.
On a national American history examination, a high school senior asked
"how could a democratic society . . . profess to be the land of opportunity
[in the 1880s] when poverty, disease, and social Darwinism were
rampant?" Also speaking of the Gilded Age, another student added,
"Social Darwinism made us very snobbish about what we read or watched
or constructed." In a newspaper *Youth Forum* at the height of the Viet-
nam war, a college student warned readers "not to adhere to a fascist worship of war and to one-sided Darwinism." "Survival of the fittest," he
lectured, "is a concept most applicable to a portion of the animal kingdom
to which civilization is an unknown phenomenon."[1]
  Behind these lessons stood the authority of America's leading textbooks
and numerous scholarly studies. In the post-Civil War decades, so the
story goes, misapplied Darwinism bolstered laissez faire, individualism,
and Horatio Algerism. For defenders of the industrial order, such phrases
as *the struggle for existence, natural selection,* and *survival of the fittest*
provided explanation and excuse for poverty and exploitation. By the
1890s imperialists, racists, and militarists also appropriated Darwinism.

"When Darwinian individualism declined," wrote Richard Hofstadter, foremost authority on the subject, "Darwinian collectivism of the nationalist or racist variety was beginning to take hold." At the same time, progressive reformers turned the new biology to their own advantage in calling for industrial regulation and social welfare. In this *reform Darwinism*, as Eric Goldman termed it in *Rendezvous with Destiny* (1952), the new catchwords were *adaptation, mutual aid,* and *struggle for the life of others.* So much is familiar.[2]

Agreement on the use of the term, however, was not always so clear. Appearing first on the Continent about 1880, the phrase *social Darwinism* described a variety of evils by the time it crossed the Atlantic two decades later. To Achille Loria and Emile de Laveleye, two distinguished European sociologists, *Darwinisme sociale* meant brutal individualism, such as Herbert Spencer advocated. For others it was a new rationale for socialism and the class struggle. In the 1890s, the Russian-born pacifist Jacques Novicow used *le Darwinisme social* to describe a rising tide of imperialist and militarist sentiment. When in 1906 the American sociologist Lester Ward accepted an invitation to discuss social Darwinism, he discovered to his surprise yet another meaning—eugenics. Since Ward hoped to repeat some remarks he had earlier prepared on the Novicow thesis he found himself, as he confessed, "in a position not unlike that of the widow who kept her husband's door plate because, as she said, she might possibly marry another man whose name was also John Brown."[3]

In the *Development of Sociology* (1936), Floyd N. House attempted to find a common denominator in these many definitions:

> Not every sociological writer has attached precisely the same meaning to this phrase, but it will be understood here as the type of theory that attempts to describe and explain social phenomena chiefly in terms of competition and conflict, especially the competition of group with group and the equilibrium and adjustment that ensue upon such struggles.

In most scholarly studies during the interwar years this definition held. As late as 1940, an American sociologist defined social Darwinism as "a technical term [used] to designate a group of writers, sociologists, and eugenicists, who ignore the all important distinction between man and the lower animals, i.e. the former's possession of culture." No less an authority than the Soviet philosophical dictionary agreed: "Social Darwinian:—is an incorrect transference of the law of the struggle for existence in the world of animals and plants . . . to the sphere of social relationships."[4]

Since the *Origin of Species* spoke to a range of issues in biology, there was always opportunity for confusion however. The definition of *biologi-*

cal analogy was a case in point. Did social Darwinism refer to analogies drawn only from evolutionism, or were *organic analogies* of the body physical/body politic sort also included? The latter, of course, had a distinct history within social thought from Aristotle through Hobbes and Spencer. Spencer confounded critics in the 1850s by placing organicism at the service, not of central direction and the established orders, but of his own version of mid-Victorian individualism and liberty—just as he used evolutionism in the same cause. Furthermore, where evolutionism was concerned, did social Darwinism refer to all development theory? For example, did it encompass everyone who held that *social development* or *evolution* was a time-consuming process? Finally, was the crucial determinant the failure to distinguish men from animals (through *culture*), or were all forms of cultural evolutionism and selectionism included?

During the 1940s, historians cut these Gordian knots. The result was a vastly expanded definition of social Darwinism. The term, wrote Merle Curti, was "the name loosely given to the application to society of the doctrine of the struggle for existence and survival of the fittest." In *Social Darwinism in American Thought*, Richard Hofstadter went even further. The phrase did "not refer to a concept limited to the technical provinces of philosophy," he wrote. Rather it referred to "the more general adaptation of Darwinian, and related biological concepts to social ideologies." In this seminal work, related concepts included *social organicism*, general *evolutionism*, and even belief in the power of heredity. Certain arguments became evidence ipso facto. If social Darwinists defended competition, or argued that blacks were inferior, then any who agreed on whatever basis were so labeled.[5]

Although reviewers generally praised *Social Darwinism*, several objected to Hofstadter's definitions, particularly as related to the *conservative Darwinism* of Spencer and Sumner. "The term 'social Darwinism' is not clearly defined," wrote the sociologist Frank Hankins; "in fact, Spencer's ideas hold the center of attention." Bert J. Loewenberg, author of several studies of Darwin's impact, argued that to understand the convergence of Darwinism and Spencerianism one first had "to distinguish between them." In this and other ways, Hofstadter's study lacked conceptual discrimination. "I find a scattering of social scientists, as contrasted with social Darwinists on this Hofstadter roster," complained Albert Keller, William Graham Sumner's successor at Yale. Although he did not name names, Keller thought "some persons hopelessly allergic to 'isms' and 'ismics' [who else but Sumner] . . . have been ushered in the wrong pew." Several years later, Edward S. Corwin, the distinguished constitutionalist, insisted that historians distinguish between Spencerianism and Darwinism.[6]

Meanwhile, however, the social Darwinian hypothesis was transforming American scholarship. Absent from the classic syntheses of Charles Beard and Vernon Parrington,[7] the idea received definitive statement in a series of works during the early 1940s: Carlton J. H. Hayes's *A Generation of Materialism* (1941); Jacques Barzun's *Darwin, Marx, and Wagner* (1941); Thomas Cochran and William Miller's *Age of Enterprise* (1943); and Merle Curti's *The Growth of American Thought* (1943). As their prefaces revealed, these authors' association with one another at Columbia University played a prominent role in this reevaluation. Barzun traced his interest in his subject to Hayes's seminar; Hayes commended the "particular brilliance" of Barzun's analysis. Richard Hofstadter noted his debt to Barzun and Curti and worked closely with William Miller. Curti, in turn, drew on the yet unpublished work of the two younger men. The new terminology stuck. Several years later, J. Bartlett Brebner, also at Columbia, identified "a ruthless form of laissez faire that it has become fashionable to call 'social Darwinism.'" Soon afterward, he launched Bernard Semmel on an important study of *Imperialism and Social Reform* (1960), which developed the thesis for British thought.[8]

Scholars elsewhere confirmed these findings. In *Constitutional Revolution Ltd.* (1941), Edward Corwin announced his own version of conservative Darwinism and contributed to the work of Benjamin Twiss, whose *Lawyers and the Constitution* (1942) traced the impact of Darwinism on legal thought. In 1946, Princeton hosted an American Studies Conference on evolutionary thought, to which Corwin contributed a modified version of the Hofstadter thesis. In 1952, Eric Goldman of Princeton presented a spirited account on the subject in *Rendezvous with Destiny*. At Harvard, doctoral candidates and others incorporated these insights into a series of distinguished monographs. In 1950, Stow Persons (Yale Ph. D. 1940) edited the results of the Princeton conference.[9]

For the past two decades, however, historians of science, social theory, and American history have raised doubts, directly or indirectly, concerning the accuracy of this portrait of late nineteenth-century thought. Among American historians, the best known critic of the thesis as it pertains to conservative thought has been Irvin G. Wyllie. In *The Self-Made Man in America* (1954) Wyllie argued that businessmen during the Gilded Age defended and interpreted their activities in light of a rags-to-riches mythology with deep roots in Christianity and Enlightenment thought. A Darwinian version of success—if it existed—would have differed markedly from this traditional myth: first, in emphasizing struggle among individuals rather than one man's fight against evil in himself; second, in suggesting that room at the top was limited to an elite of survivors; and third, in prescribing (if only covertly) modes of behavior tabooed in the Alger stories. Turning specifically to the Hofstadter thesis in a study of "Social Darwinism and the Businessman," Wyllie found that the little existing evidence was flawed in a variety of ways.[10]

Wyllie was appropriately cautious. Examples of alleged conservative Darwinism did not bear scrutiny, but "it would be folly to deny that such evidence exists." Shifting the onus from businessmen, he proposed instead that the original social Darwinists were misanthropic intellectuals, such as Yale's William Graham Sumner, whose views only later trickled down to the masses. Future historians, Wyllie predicted, "will distinguish between representative and unrepresentative views, between the ideas of an intellectually unsophisticated majority and those of an educated bookish minority."[11]

Other historians replaced wholesale condemnation with retail pardon. One by one such figures as Andrew Carnegie, John Fiske, and Josiah Strong were excused from the social Darwinist ranks.[12] By the late 1960s the suspicion grew that very few Americans were actually social Darwinists. "It is true that in the last half of the 19th century great numbers of Americans were ideologically committed to the notions of competition, merited success, and deserved failure," R. J. Wilson wrote. "But it is not true that this commitment was grounded on Darwinian premises. No more than a small handful of American business leaders or intellectuals were 'social Darwinists' in any sense precise enough to have useful meaning."[13] Thus, while the numbers dwindled, the species remained intact.

These revisions also tended to narrow the definition of social Darwinism. Wyllie made the concepts of struggle and survival—with overtones of brute force and cunning—the hallmarks of the "positive social Darwinist" as distinct from "mere biological or religious evolutionists."[14] While not limiting the term to any "technical" meaning, the present study likewise focuses on the specifically Darwinian concepts of struggle for existence, natural selection, and survival of the fittest—the latter Spencer's contribution, which Darwin accepted. Darwinism is thus distinguished from social organicism, an interesting topic that is omitted entirely. It is also distinguished from evolutionism generally, while not ignoring the fact that during its first three decades Darwinism was a complex blend of Lamarckian environmentalism and a faith in cumulative progress. Here the relationship between Darwin and Spencer is crucial. The fact that Darwin and Spencer shared common intellectual debts, including the assumption that the direct action of environment upon organisms had a role in the *transmutation of the species,* is not itself reason to call Spencer's pre-Darwinian evolutionism, Darwinian. For despite their common grounding in mid-Victorian thought, it is possible to trace the impact of Darwin's idea of selection through struggle on Spencer's cosmic evolutionism.

This narrowing is justified because the term social Darwinism, although applied ubiquitously, consistently derived its sting from the implication that the struggle and selection of the animal realm were also agents of change (and progress) in human society—the governing assumption being that men shared *natural laws* with the rest of Creation. Since the concept of natural laws was the backbone of eighteenth-century thought, the charge amounted to saying that the latter-day classical economists or utilitarians had perverted and undermined the basic American commitment to equality, natural rights, self-evident truths, and self-regulating natural laws—and had, in effect, restated Hobbes against the prevailing Lockeanism. The basic questions for any study of social Darwinism in American thought are: did such a change occur in postbellum American thought, and if it did, when and where did it occur, and who was responsible for it?

Two

My own thinking on this subject has gone through several stages. Attempting to study social Darwinism in British thought more than a decade ago, I was struck not only by the paucity of examples of conservative Darwinism but also by the almost total silence on the issue among British historians. Agreeing with Wyllie's assessment of the evidence in the American case, I was tempted to blame elite intellectuals and start counting heads. At the same time, I was puzzled by the apparently unanimous agreement of American reformers, who from the 1880s onward testified to the widespread grip of such thinking among their opponents. At that stage, I came close to concluding that someone had made the whole thing up—partisans initially, and later, historians.[15]

More study convinced me, however, that head-counting alone could never explain the complexity and significance of social Darwinism in American thought. Even if Spencer was not known to most businessmen, the fact that the *Origin of Species* (1859) had implications for social development was suspected and widely discussed before Darwin broke his self-imposed silence on the issue in *The Descent of Man* (1871). Since British theorists led the discussion, its peculiarly American appeal seemed implausible.[16] Upon closer inspection, even William Graham Sumner, the dean of social Darwinists, seemed not to deserve the label, at least as usually applied.[17]

More intriguing than social Darwinism itself is what one might term the *myth of social Darwinism*—the charge, usually unsubstantiated or quite out of proportion to the evidence, that Darwinism was widely and wantonly abused by forces of reaction. While not a deliberate deception, this myth was important in itself. And as a prelude to the "correct" readings of Darwin, it invariably prefaced the many varieties of so-called reform Darwinism.

Although effective in debate, this tactic was ironical in view of the fact that the reformers, not their laissez faire opponents, were the Darwinians in any precise meaning of the term. Acceptance of the evolutionary framework meant, not simply that ideas and institutions must adapt to new circumstances (as stressed in older accounts of reform Darwinism), but that the situation demanded measures to control an increasingly chaotic "natural" order. This perception of disorder was a common thread in the otherwise apparently disparate reforms of the progressive era—from the regulation of monopoly, to eugenics and Jim Crow. Pre-Darwinian evolutionists, cherishing the Enlightenment faith in beneficent laws of nature, continued to argue that society ought best be left to develop without central direction or controls. But to those who saw nature through Darwinian lenses, this option seemed intolerable.[18]

More specifically, the argument of this study consists of a series of interrelated propositions:

(1) The *Origin of Species*, from the start, fatally undermined social speculation based on the assumptions of harmonious, mechanical, self-regulating laws of nature, which in one form or another have dominated Anglo-American thought since Newton. For Darwin's generation this conclusion could be avoided—although with difficulty. Equivocations in Darwin's own work concerning natural selection, struggle for existence, and survival of the fittest—based in part on honest ignorance concerning the effects of environment and heredity—made it possible for others to reinterpret the *Origin of Species* within the framework of the mechanistic causation just then being confirmed by developments in geology, thermodynamics, and biology. Nonetheless, Darwin, A. Russel Wallace, and Thomas Henry Huxley, the three leading spokesmen of the new view, together supported the theory that nature provided no guide to ethics or social policy—a conclusion Huxley dramatized in his Romanes address at Oxford three decades later (ch. 1). Herbert Spencer resisted this conclusion and attempted to incorporate natural selection within a Synthetic Philosophy framed initially in terms of mechanical concepts derived from thermodynamics. His initial success and subsequent failure was a case study of the collapse of a cluster of pre-Darwinian assumptions concerning nature and society and a clue to the causes of Spencer's final years of

disillusionment and despair (ch. 2). Attracted to Spencer's early writings, his American disciples shared his youthful optimism (ch. 3) but during the 1880s and 1890s had similar problems coming to terms with a world grown increasingly Darwinian (ch. 4). The most notable of these was William Graham Sumner, whose pilgrimage from positivism and classical economics to naturalism and sociology was one measure of a significant crisis in late nineteenth-century liberalism (ch. 5).

(2) Darwinism affected social thought in two ways: directly, in fostering the idea that men must transcend nature rather than following her dictates; and indirectly, as a weapon—in the myth of social Darwinism—against laissez faire and utilitarianism. This stereotype first surfaced in New Liberal writings of the 1880s (ch. 6) and developed in debates over *neo-Darwinism* the following decade (ch. 7). After the turn of the century it played an important role in debates over race relations and eugenics, two attempts to impose new forms of social control (ch. 8 and 9); in the work of Nietzscheans (ch. 10) and the Literary Naturalists (ch. 11); and in discussions of international policy and war (ch. 12). As social myth, it distorted reality in the interest of traditional values, Christian and secular. But its recurrence was no cynical tactic. Modern America seemed to many a jungle in which human purpose and effort played an ever smaller part. If some defended the situation or even explained it in terms of "science," then the science in question *must* be the jungle law of Darwinism. This logic presumably had special appeal to a generation whose own embrace of science masked a covert fear of its "logical" implications. So viewed, the social Darwinian stereotype represented an anti-utopian blueprint of a world guided solely by scientific considerations, a recurring motif in the Anglo-American reaction against scientism.

(3) Although it was generally agreed that Darwinian struggle was brutish, the rhetoric of Darwinism for this very reason provided a tiny minority with the language of cynicism and disillusionment—whether as the Victorian equivalent of modern references to the "rat-race" or as neo-Calvinist warnings to the perils of abandoning individualism, private property, and other "natural rights." These jeremiads were measures of frustration not conviction, alienation not a dominant consensus. Spencer's cranky references to the survival of the fittest in *Man vs. the State* (1884), for example, far from increasing his popularity, set him against "all England," as he put it. Nine out of ten of his readers would say his principles were the "laws of brutes," he predicted.[19] Two decades later Henry Louis Mencken, making similar remarks, reveled in thus disturbing bourgeois sensibilities. Superficially resembling "textbook social Darwinism," these few exceptions again proved the rule: social Darwinism was nasty business and was recognized as such.

(4) The principal legacy of the *Origin of Species,* however, was the reform Darwinism that flourished in various forms from the 1880s onward. Stressing the importance of "intellect" and "culture" in human evolution, activists demanded increased governmental regulation; new efforts of social welfare and control; and a more positive role for America abroad. Attacking the "brutal laws of social Darwinism," they grounded their activism in the nervous perception that natural forces, if left alone, were evil and destructive. Socially, this perception helped generate a decade of progressive reform. Intellectually, it fostered significant departures in sociology and social science. After the war, of course, serious thinkers almost universally abandoned the evolutionary framework entirely in favor of *cultural, ecological,* or *behavioristic* models.[20] While it is too much to claim that attacks on social Darwinism alone brought this major shift in American social science, its continuing role in sociological debate in the interwar years suggests that it was a contributing factor. Its vitality in these years—from the Scopes trial to attacks on the Nazis—in any case provided the immediate impetus to the historical flowering of the 1940s (Epilogue).

Three

In light of the general direction of American scholarship in the past two decades, a revision of the traditional account of social Darwinism is long overdue. Although in some respects the thesis was itself a revision of progressive historiography, in others it simply reversed progressive assumptions while leaving little changed. Vernon Parrington's *The Beginnings of Critical Realism* (1930) and Charles Beard's *The Rise of American Civilization* (1927) pictured Spencer and Darwin as liberating Americans from a variety of outworn orthodoxies, an extension of the "warfare-of-science-with-theology" theme that was at the heart of nineteenth-century Whig history. Reversing this view, the social Darwinist thesis kept science on center stage, but implied that it was at best a mixed blessing, feeding reaction as well as reform. In other respects the older view of a benighted Gilded Age vs. an enlightened progressivism remained. In *The Age of Enterprise,* for example, Cochran and Miller wed social Darwinism to a Beardian vision of rapacious "Robber Barons" and political skullduggery. Likewise, in *Rendezvous with Destiny,* Eric Goldman pitted reform Darwinism against the conservatives, "steel chain of ideas." Older textbooks, *The Growth of the American Republic* for example, easily found a place for the new view.[21]

The Gilded Age and progressivism look different now. In politics, the crude but effective rule of bosses; the structural reforms of the progressives; and the acceptance of interest-group politics nationally appear as successive—and often complementary—responses to the disorder resulting from the breakdown of traditional institutions and party structures. In their quest for nationwide production and marketing, businessmen sought corporate stability through a series of devices that included the trust, pools, and finally government regulation. Privately these same businessmen, as Edward Kirkland has shown,[22] expressed anxieties that resulted from extreme responsibility coupled with financial uncertainties beyond their control. In their daily lives, ordinary citizens sought substitutes for community traditions disrupted by immigration, westward migration, or the move to the cities—in granges and farmers' alliances; in immigrant aid associations and settlement houses; and in labor unions.

Failing to achieve these ends privately, and shocked and bewildered by the social and financial cataclysm of the 1890s, these disparate groups turned finally to government during the progressive era. American reform, an historian-colleague of mine once remarked, boils down to a simple formula: "Help me get what I want, and I'll help you back." Perhaps less remarkable than the reforms of the progressive era were the willingness and ability of so many groups to forge political alliances across economic and social lines.[23]

In their search for order,[24] the generation of the Gilded Age was unlikely to take comfort in a Darwinized version of individualism or competition. The Horatio Alger tales themselves, as Michael Zuckerman has suggested,[25] coupled praise of individual initiative with longings for security and material indulgence and the covert promise of a benevolent patron to supply them. Although some academic economists refurbished classical economics as a weapon against the giveaways of the Grant years, businessmen and others fled the rigors of competition. If life increasingly seemed a Hobbesian *bellum omnium contra omnes*, few wanted it that way. Samuel Dodd, the legal architect of the Standard Oil Trust, expressed this mood in remarking that competition "carried to the furthest extreme without cooperation or compromise . . . would be a fit mode for savages, not for civilized men." So in another way did Henry Demarest Lloyd, one of the trust's chief critics, in observing rather bitterly that "the 'survival of the fittest' is our doctrine."[26]

Work in American intellectual history since the 1940s also suggests the need to revise the social Darwinist thesis. A Janus-faced Darwinism mirrored perennial tensions between Protestant pietism and democratic sensibilities, on the one hand, and science on the other. During the eighteenth century, Americans took refuge from the chilling possibilities of Lockean empiricism, first in the native idealism of Jonathan Edwards and the Great Awakening and later in the Common Sense moralism of the Scottish philosophers. Similarly, in the nineteenth century others found a congenial blend of science and sentiment in the work of William Paley, whose *Principles of Mental and Moral Philosophy* (1785) and other works were well known in the young Republic. A moderate utilitarian, Paley placed religion and ethics squarely on the grounds of observation. Typical was his famous example of the pocketwatch that opened his *Natural Theology* (1802). A man, upon first encountering a watch and observing its workings, would inevitably conclude that it was the work of a skilled artificer, Paley reasoned. So by analogy the perfect operation of the laws of nature was proof of God's existence.

When in the 1850s Paley's philosophy fell victim to transcendental idealism and a second Great Awakening, his "natural theology" made an easy target. Paley taught that "morality is expediency, nothing more," charged Theodore Parker in a lecture on "Transcendentalism": "Nothing is good of itself, right of itself, just of itself." Lumping Paley with Bentham, a college president similarly warned his students against the teaching that "Whatever is expedient is right." Likewise later in the century, Herbert Spencer's restatement of Paley in light of evolution drew similar charges—now packaged under the label of social Darwinism.[27]

Describing the decline of Paleyite utility, the historian Wilson Smith has observed that the antebellum generation thus rejected "practicality at a fatally inopportune time for the nation."[28] In similar fashion one might argue, as the Spencerians certainly believed, assaults on Spencer from the 1880s onward heralded a new irrationalism in religion and social thought (albeit in the name of reform) and an eventual struggle between democratic ideals and aristocratic *Kultur* in a bloody war the Spencerians said never would happen.

From another perspective however, the charge of social Darwinism, a mirror of Christian and democratic values, served as an effective reminder that economic power and social privilege had limits, and material well-being and social efficiency, no matter how sanctified by science, were not the soul of the American experiment. It is the peculiar paradox of nineteenth-century American history that a nation hellbent on personal gain and national power was perennially bothered by the role. Like other social myths—the "Monster Bank" or the money-grubbing "Yankee," for example—social Darwinism was a reflection of this fact.

1.   The Scientific Background

For the place vacated by Paley's theological and metaphysical explanation has simply been occupied by that suggested to Darwin and Wallace by Malthus in terms of the prevalent severity of industrial competition, and these phenomena of the struggle for existence . . . have thus come to be temporarily exalted into a complete explanation of organic progress.
   Patrick Geddes, "Biology," Chambers Encyclopedia *(1882)*.

I too was struck . . . with the remarkable likeness between [Darwin's] account of plant and animal life and the Malthusian theory. Only I came to a different conclusion from yours: namely, that nothing discredits modern bourgeois development so much as the fact that it has not succeeded in getting beyond the economic forces of the animal world.
   F. Engels to F. A. Lange, March 29, 1865, Vladimir Adoratskii, ed. The Selected Correspondence of Karl Marx and Friedrich Engels *(1942), pp. 198-199.*

My views have been often grossly misrepresented, bitterly opposed and ridiculed, but this has been generally done, as I believe, in good faith.
   Charles Darwin, Autobiography, ed. George Gaylord Simpson *(Collier ed.; New York, 1961), p. 62.*

One

      "I have received in a Manchester newspaper, rather a good squib," Charles Darwin wrote to the geologist Charles Lyell, shortly after the appearance of the *Origin of Species*, "showing that I have proved 'might is right' and therefore that Napoleon is right, and every cheating tradesman is also right." Although Darwin ridiculed the charge, it would not go away. "It is splendid that Darwin again discovers among plants and animals his English society with its division of labour, competition, opening up of new markets, 'inventions' and Malthusian 'struggle for existence'," wrote Karl Marx to his associate Engels in 1862: "This is Hobbes's *bellum omnium contra omnes.*" In his *Dialectics of Nature* (ca. 1873-1883) Engels reproduced the charge almost exactly: "The whole Darwinian theory of the struggle for life is simply the transformation from society to organic nature of Hobbes' theory . . . and the bourgeois economic theory of competition." From a quite different quarter, a variation of the same assertion came later in the century. "Over the whole of English Darwinism," wrote Friedrich Nietzsche, "there hovers something of the suffocating air of over-crowded England, something of the odour of humble people in need and in straits."[1]

As the debate over social Darwinism developed, however, most early observers tended to exonerate Darwin himself. Ultra-Darwinists or pseudo-Darwinists twisted and misrepresented the *Origin of Species* and his remarks in *The Descent of Man*. Since Darwin meant pigeons not people in referring to struggle, all applications to human society were nonsense. Historians likewise assumed that Darwin's scientific theory was neutral as to its social applications and was therefore capable of supporting quite opposite ideologies.[2]

The notion that the *Origin of Species* was really or inherently conservative in underwriting Manchesterian economics or Napoleonic militarism nonetheless persisted. Although Darwin could not be held personally responsible, the historian James Rogers argued, natural selection was *not* simply "another discovery in the natural sciences misused to rationalize social preconceptions." Malthus, after all, inspired Darwin's concept of the struggle for existence; and the members of Darwin's circle assumed that his theory was relevant to human society, at least in a general way. Moreover, Darwin shared with Malthus certain assumptions that led him to accept Herbert Spencer's alternative formulation of natural selection—the survival of the fittest. Since *fittest* inevitably connoted *best*, this translation linked struggle and survival to the doctrine of progress. This unfortunate marriage set tongues wagging, Rogers continued, as partisans of industrial competition and *machtpolitik* made struggle the engine of progress. The result was a harsh social Darwinism that Darwin was the last to want. "Spencer's phrase in Darwin's theory," he concluded, "consequently reinforced the Social Darwinians tendency to think of the struggle for existence in social rather than biological terms."[3]

In fact, Darwinism was neither neutral nor inherently conservative. On this point the reform Darwinists were correct: their theory that human control must replace the laws of nature was the accurate reading of Darwin's theory. In the words of the psychologist-historian Howard Gruber:

> It would be entirely in harmony with [Darwin's] thinking to insist that the struggle for survival of the human species must be, in the years to come, a struggle to develop social forms that enhance cooperation and rational, long-term planning for collective ends rather than shortsighted, individualistic efforts for private gain.[4]

This conclusion was implicit not only in Darwin's social speculations but those of Thomas Henry Huxley and Alfred Russel Wallace, fellow biologists who best understood the revolutionary aspects of the new view of nature. Scientists and laymen alike often misrepresented the *Origin of Species*. But the most common distortions involved, not the facile application of such concepts as struggle for existence and natural selection, but the muting of these very ideas. Early interpreters in particular blurred the difference between Darwin and other evolutionists, and subordinated his theory to older concepts of natural law.

These distortions in turn were a measure of the complexity of the scientific revolution of which the *Origin of Species* was a part. Two aspects in particular demand attention: (1) developments in geology, thermodynamics, and biology that by the 1850s marked the culmination of the mechanists' quest for a law-bound universe; and (2) the separate histories of the transmutation of species, the struggle for existence, and natural selection —the principal elements of Darwin's theory.

The scientific background has special bearing on Darwin's reception in the United States. Translated as evolution, pure and simple, Darwinism was received sympathetically and accepted within a relatively brief time. But scientists and laymen alike, claiming to accept Darwinism, effectively downplayed critical parts of the *Origin*. Darwinism did not breed theories of social struggle and selection in part because these aspects of Darwin's work were hotly disputed and widely ignored. The few who best understood the new theory studiously avoided applying concepts of struggle and selection to contemporary society. In contrast to older natural-law theorists—including the followers of Herbert Spencer—Darwin, Huxley, and Wallace insisted that men must find guides to social policy elsewhere than in nature. In short, the early Darwinians were not social Darwinists; likewise, many so-called social Darwinists (such as Spencer) were not Darwinians.

Two

On the eve of the publication of the *Origin of Species*, "science" seemed to have routed "special providences" from the universe once and for all. The *mechanical philosophy*, born in the scientific revolution of the seventeenth century, successively transformed the natural sciences into recognizably modern shapes—astronomy, physics, and finally chemistry, with the overthrow of the phlogiston theory at the close of the eighteenth century. During the next sixty years, developments in geology, physics, and biology etched more deeply the mechanists' image of a universe in which nothing happened spontaneously, a cosmos as regulated and decorous as the Victorian parlor. This climate shaped Darwin's theory and its reception.

Discoveries in geology, culminating in the so-called Uniformitarian-Catastrophist debate of the 1840s, were especially crucial since Darwin himself became personally involved. This debate was long in the making. In the seventeenth century, Descartes and Leibnitz proposed that the earth had evolved from a molten mass. A century later, G. L. L. Buffon, drawing on more detailed knowledge of the fossil record, worked out a cooling scheme, while continuing to adhere to the notion that a special agency had at some point deposited the fossils on a universal ocean floor. Challenging this view, James Hutton's *Theory of the Earth* (1795) maintained that the forces operating in the past were identical to those working in the present. This view became the fundamental tenet of the Uniformitarian position. Synthesizing this previous work, Sir Charles Lyell's *Principles of Geology* (3 vols., 1830-33) launched a debate that continued for two decades.

The argument turned on two key issues. First, concerning geological causes, the Uniformitarians held not only that similar agencies operated at all times (rain, rivers, earthquakes) but that the quantity and intensity of these forces did not vary from one epoch to another. Catastrophists, led by Adam Sedgwick and William Whewell, believed, in contrast, that vast discrepancies in the geological record argued for the operation of extraordinary, perhaps even supernatural, forces in certain epochs. Second, concerning evolution, Lyell denied that geology could discern development in any particular direction. That is, until the appearance of Darwin's work, he was frankly antievolutionary. Catastrophists in opposition held, in Sedgwick's words "that there has been a progressive development of organic structure subservient to the purposes of life."[5]

Lyell's antievolutionary position, as Walter Cannon has observed, was no mere "logical pecadillo," but the essence of the theory. Uniformitarianism was, in Cannon's words, "an anti-evolutionary creed, postulating repetition rather than cumulative development as the net result of eons of geological time." Nor was the issue simply a disagreement over the evidence. While the Uniformitarians presented a broad challenge to the Biblical account of the Creation, Catastrophism easily slipped into a defense of religious orthodoxy—as for example in the conclusion of one partisan that his account would "compel us to conclude, that the earth can alone have been fashioned into a fit abode for Man by the ordinance of INFINITE WISDOM." When in later years Lyell capitulated to Darwin's theory, he confessed with some feeling: "It cost me a struggle to renounce my old creed."[6]

Although Darwin was an early recruit to the Uniformitarian creed, he finally broke from its leading tenet. Without recounting his role in these geological debates, it is important to note both the nature of his debt to the Uniformitarians and his departure from their position. His most general debt, as Maurice Mandelbaum has noted,[7] was to the entire debate itself—since the geologists, in stressing the fossil record, directed attention to living as well as nonliving forces. Furthermore, Darwin accepted from Lyell what Cannon has described as "the method of accounting for large changes by summing up small changes over immense periods of time,"[8] an intellectual predeliction rather than a fixed procedure. This method in turn disposed Darwin to accept Lamarck's account of the mechanism of evolution through direct adaptation to the environment and with it to accept his idea that the accumulation of changes worked to some pattern. This final point marked Darwin's departure from the Uniformitarians, since evolution through natural selection at least implied some sort of cumulative development within the geological and biological record, if not necessarily a progressive one.

In physics, the law of the *conservation of force* (energy) as propounded in the 1840s, provided further basis for assuming immutable continuity within nature. Announced in Hermann von Helmholtz's *Uber die Erhaltung der Kraft* (1847), and later extended in the work of Lord Kelvin, J. R. von Mayer, and James P. Joule, the laws of the conservation of energy and matter put the seal on the notion that nothing was lost in nature. Nor were seemingly new elements the result of special interventions. In the long run, as Alfred North Whitehead wrote in *Science and the Modern World* (1925), this theory undermined assumptions concerning the ultimate permanency of matter that were the basis of mechanistic materialism.[9] So also, as the American philosopher Charles S. Peirce noted, later developments in thermodynamics suggested, as did Darwin himself, that the laws of nature were statistical rather than mechanical, that is were approximations concerning probabilities rather than fixed rules from which one could deduce certain consequences.[10] But in the climate of the mid-nineteenth century, thermodynamics reinforced the idea that the universe was governed by immutable laws of cause and effect, which it was the business of science to uncover.

The advances in thermodynamics became important in debates over biological evolution in large part because Herbert Spencer made conservation of force the starting point of his *First Principles* (1861) and the basis of his conviction that a Synthetic Philosophy could trace the operation of similar laws in the natural, biological, psychological, and social spheres.

Since the time of Newton the lessons of physics or astronomy provided both a guarantee of cosmic order and also a vocabulary for expressing it. In nineteenth-century America, it continued to do so, as demonstrated in the characteristic statement that the "laws of trade" were as "immutable" as those of "gravitation." Defining *force* to suit his own purposes, Spencer translated Darwinian biology into the language of physics.

Finally, developments within biology itself contributed to the mechanistic conception of universal law. The *Origin of Species* was in fact one of three works in the 1850s to establish what Walter Wilson has termed the *law of genetic continuity*, wherein all life is seen to derive from previous life. A second was Rudolf Virchow's *Die Cellularpathologie* (1858), which demonstrated that all cells derive from preceding cells. A third was the writing of Louis Pasteur, who in disproving the doctrine of spontaneous generation likewise showed that organisms derive from pre-existing organisms. These simultaneous announcements, an observer noted later in the century, provided biology with an equivalent of the law of conservation in physics. Gone were the special providences that in the history of biology had worn various guises—from the "Will of the Diety" to "Vis Creatrix." Thanks to the revolution of the 1850s, the study of life, no less than the rest of the universe, was put on a thoroughly naturalistic basis.[11]

The identification of evolution with mechanistic causation—whether material or spiritual—speeded Darwin's acceptance in America, while impeding appreciation of the theory's implications. Interpreting natural selection within the general framework of the *redistribution of matter and motion*, the Spencerians (as will appear in the next chapter) obscured the difference between this doctrine and the Lamarckian mechanism of change through direct action of the environment.

The Cosmic Theists, led by the scientist Asa Gray (1810-1888), similarly interpreted the *Origin* within a framework of spiritual mechanism, whereby God stood behind and ultimately determined the evolutionary process. "It is not surprising that the doctrine of the book should be announced as atheistical," Gray wrote in his initial review of the *Origin*. "What does surprise and concern us is, that it should be so denounced . . . on the broad assumption that a material connection between the members of a series of organized beings is inconsistent with the idea of their being intellectually connected with one another through the Diety, i.e. as products of one mind, as indicating and realizing a preconceived plan." Although admitting that Darwin left readers in the dark concerning his views of "philosophy and theology," Gray suggested that the *Origin* merely updated Paley in postulating a "watch which sometimes produces better watches, and contrivances adapted to successive conditions, and so at length turns out a chronometer, a town clock, or a series of organisms of the same type."[12]

Such interpretations plunged Darwin into the midst of an ongoing debate between *natural* and *supernatural* theology. Identifying Darwinism with mechanistic causation, opponents of natural theology denied that any mechanistic explanation could, in the words of the *Methodist Quarterly Review,* "get over the threshold of vital existence without a miracle." Turning developments in biology against Darwin, this same critic wrote:

> The experiments in "Spontaneous Generation" at every repetition confirm the doctrine that *from life only can life proceed.* How then, without a new creation . . . could our pedigree take its primordial start?

Explicitly criticizing the Cosmic Theists, Enoch Burr, an old-line Congregationalist, first defined evolution as "the Law Scheme," and then insisted that the Development Hypothesis was inimical to traditional Christianity. "The Law Scheme crowds God away until his great orb loses all sensible diameter," he wrote. "It contradicts the whole idea of a personal Divine interference in the affairs of the world, of which our Scriptures are full . . . . Let men say what they will, evolutionism means *materialism.*"[13] Transferred from religion to reform, this theme became a recurring motif in later attacks on social Darwinism.

Three

The immediate background of the *Origin* was the history of the three major elements of Darwin's theory: (1) transmutation of species; (2) the struggle for existence; and (3) natural selection. These issues raise a variety of questions. What was Darwin's relation to earlier evolutionists, particularly Lamarck, his most prominent forerunner? How did his use of the struggle for existence compare to Malthus's? What were the implications of equating natural selection with survival of the fittest? Although difficult to answer briefly, these questions involve an issue related to the question of mechanistic causation and ultimately Darwin's impact on Enlightenment social thought: in what sense if any did the *Origin* undermine conceptions of a natural order and natural laws in the universe?

During the eighteenth century, speculation concerning the relationship of species to one another focused on the *Scala Naturae* or *Great Chain of Being,* a concept which, as Arthur O. Lovejoy has noted, derived from the ancient world. Although recognizing gradations from lowest to highest, this Scala Naturae was initially nonhistorical. Different forms of life, that is, were not conceived as having been created in sequence. The eighteenth century saw, in Lovejoy's phrase, the "temporalization" of the Great Chain of Being, most notably in Carolus Linnaeus's celebrated binomial classification. Unanswered however, was the relation of beings in this ascending hierarchy of genus and species. From simpler to more complex, beings were presumably created in sequence—the Creator as it were changing His mind as He proceeded. Such a view blended naturally with the growing faith in progress. During the late eighteenth and early nineteenth century, the Nebular Hypothesis and Lyell's Uniformitarianism further supported the notion that the Great Chain of Being was the result of an ongoing historical process.[14]

While Linnaeus contributed to the temporalization of the Scala Naturae, he also helped confirm the idea that species represented fixed groupings. Development theory, however paradoxical it may appear, required fixed species as a precondition for orderly change. This idea, as Conway Zirkle has shown, was itself relatively modern. Derived from the Latin, the term *species* referred to appearance rather than inner essence. Viewed in light of the philosophical dualism of classical and Christian thought, species was thus less important than some internal ideal. Neither Aristotle nor Theophrastus, the fathers of zoology and botany respectively, assumed the existence of stable or unchanging species. Medieval and Renaissance science reaffirmed this mutability, citing the failure of animals and plants to "breed true." Only in the eighteenth century, in Buffon's *Histoire Naturelle* (1787) and in the work of Linnaeus, did the concept of fixed species gain new authority—ironically in part thanks to churchmen who now took comfort in the fact that species remained just as God made them in the six days of creation. Although neither the ancient doctrine of mutability nor Linnaeus's fixed hierarchy implied evolution or the transmutation of species, the groundwork was laid.[15]

In biology, the pre-Darwinian development theory of Erasmus Darwin (1731-1802) and Jean Baptiste de Monet, Chevalier de Lamarck (1744-1829) completed the temporalization of the Scala Naturae. Of the two men, the enigmatic Lamarck is more easily misunderstood, his relation to Charles Darwin more complex.

A celebrated botanist, Lamarck turned to zoology relatively late in his life. Wedded to the notion of the immutability of species as late as 1797, he developed his ideas on evolution in a series of essays, culminating in his multi-volume *Histoire naturelle des animaux sans vertèbres* (1815-1822). Influenced by Buffon, Lamarck described the process whereby more complex forms of life developed from simpler ones. Four basic laws explained the origin of animals and the formation of their various organs: (1) the tendency of life "by its proper forces" to increase the volume of "every body possessing it"; (2) the production of new organs as the result of "a new want" that in turn gives rise to "a new movement"; (3) the development of organs through continued use; and (4) the transmission to offspring of all changes undergone by the parent generation. In the second law, Lamarck expressed his conviction that desire or *sentiment interieur* could produce changes in structure through altered habits. The fourth law contained his famous law of the inheritance of acquired characteristics.

Lamarck's theories, in a sense part of the romantic reaction against Newtonian mechanism, were rooted in profoundly reactionary scientific assumptions. The laws of use and disuse, and the inheritance of acquired characteristics were corollaries of the view that "living nature" is the only creative force, seeking perfection of organization through progressive differentiation. Discontinuities in nature result when "the dead hand of inorganic matter" blocks this striving toward perfection. As Charles Gillispie has put it: "Nature in his eyes was cinder and stone, the granite of the tomb, death itself. Life intervenes only accidentally, as a strange but singularly industrious intruder, fighting a perpetual battle with some little success, achieving here and there a certain equilibrium but always vanquished in the end." Sustaining this view were theories concerning the primacy of fire and of a world in constant flux—a view then recently challenged by chemists with the overthrow of the phlogiston theory. Strictly speaking, as Gillispie also has noted, Lamarck was not a "vitalist" since he posited the primacy of living nature, not the obliteration of the dualism between organic and inorganic.[16]

By whatever name, Darwin rejected as nonsense Lamarck's idea that organisms could "will" changes in structure, a popular if inaccurate reading of the second law. To admit as much was to lapse into "vitalism" wrote Darwin, true to the mechanistic principles of mid-Victorian science. But the rest of Lamarck's theory, stripped of the *sentiment interieur*, had great influence on him. He read Lamarck's work extensively in his student days, and accepted the Frenchman's account of *direct adaptation* (the laws of use and disuse and the inheritance of acquired characteristics), if only because his ignorance of modern genetics allowed no alternative explanation of the source of variations upon which natural selection relied. In successive editions of the *Origin of Species*, as Loren Eiseley and others have shown, he even gave these Lamarckian factors increasing weight, not only as a source of variations, but also as a direct influence in the transmutation of species. Thus Darwin contributed to the popular tendency to downplay natural selection in favor of environmental factors, a view that also appealed to the American faith in the power of environment and education over birth and in a universe both orderly and teleological. Again, strictly speaking, Lamarck was not a forerunner: Darwin posited the possibility of an objective view of nature, and ultimately, the idea that biological order resembled physical order (whatever it should be)—a view directly opposed to Lamarck's frank dualism between organic and inorganic. But by incorporating Lamarckian principles, Darwin contributed to the idea in the minds of many that his own theory was simply Lamarckianism with a twist.[17]

The concept of a struggle for existence was also familiar in scientific and philosophical circles long before Tennyson gave it literary expression in his image of nature "red in tooth and claw." In one of many early examples, Erasmus Darwin wrote that "'Eat or be eaten!'" was the "first law" of nature. In 1803, he expressed the idea more poetically in *The Temple of Nature; or, the Origin of Society:*

> —Air, earth, and ocean, to astonish'd day
> One scene of blood, one mighty tomb display!
> From Hunger's arm the shafts of Death are hurl'd
> And one great Slaughterhouse the warring world!

Tempering this image, however, was an equally pervasive assumption that struggle ultimately produced balance and harmony. In the same poem, Erasmus Darwin added:

> Shout round the globe, how Reproduction strives
> With vanquish'd Death,—and Happiness survives;
> How Life increasing peoples every clime
> And young renascent Nature conquers Time;
> —And high in golden characters record
> The immense munificence of Nature's Lord!

Struggle, that is, appeared within a context that tended to mitigate its baneful effects.[18]

The immediate source of Charles Darwin's concept of struggle in nature was the work of Charles Lyell. "In the universal struggle for existence, the right of the strongest eventually prevails," Lyell wrote in *The Principles of Geology* (1830); "and the strength and durability of a race depends on its prolificness." This view, as Barry Gale has pointed out, both resembled and profoundly differed from Darwin's. Like Darwin, Lyell pictured struggle within a broad ecological context in which conflict and extinction resulted from changes in the environment. But unlike Darwin he ruled out a creative role for struggle (a corollary of his antievolution stance); and he embraced a teleological concept of adaptation which rendered struggle superfluous. It was easy for Lyell "to admit in words" the truth of struggle, Darwin later commented. But it was another thing for him "constantly to bear this conclusion in mind."[19]

Malthus's *Essay on Population* confirmed this image of struggle in nature. Darwin acknowledged this debt in an often-quoted passage in his *Autobiography*:

> In October 1838, that is, fifteen months after I had begun my systematic inquiry, I happened to read for amusement "Malthus on Population," and being well prepared to appreciate the struggle for existence which everywhere goes on from long-continued observation of the habits of animals and plants, it at once struck me that under these circumstances favourable variations would tend to be preserved, and unfavourable ones to be destroyed. The result of this would be the formation of new species. Here then I had at last got a theory by which to work.

The reason for this influence is something of a mystery. Malthus saw no creative role for struggle, and an antievolution bias permeated his essay, consistently on the biological level and, in the early editions, on the social level as well. But there was equally good reason why Malthus's essay caught Darwin's attention, whether to suggest a theory or to confirm one already formulated. In sheer volume of illustration it outstripped all previous accounts of struggle, while at the same time placing struggle at the very center of a general theory.[20]

Malthus defined struggle as the battle of an individual or group against the environment. This struggle *in practice* might result in the further conflict of individuals; indeed in savage society it did so. But it need not *logically* do so, Malthus insisted. In his essay he, in fact, confined attention to the hardships of groups or societies faced with a dwindling food supply and not to intra- or intergroup conflict. More than squeamishness, this focus reflected basic assumptions concerning society. The poor, a single class, constituted the mass of mankind. Their poverty resulted not from exploitation by the rich, but an imbalance between society and nature. Hard work and competition, not artificial combination, constituted the sole means whereby a temporary equilibrium could be established.

Malthus thus undermined one part of the eighteenth-century concept of a natural harmony between all species and their environment. But, as Peter Bowler has argued, "he did not abandon the idea of natural harmony as far as the internal workings of society are concerned."[21] Although he challenged one tenet of laissez faire theory, he refused to identify individualism and competition with the struggle for existence against environment. Critics later turned a jaundiced eye to this view. Malthus *must* have seen that his view encouraged dog-eat-dog competition! But this judgment grew as the result of a collapse of faith in social and natural harmonies rather than from secret "tendencies" in Malthus's thinking.

Darwin's defenders later insisted he merely applied Malthus's views in the one area where they were valid. Writing soon after the appearance of the *Origin of Species*, the American scientist Asa Gray attempted to dissociate Darwin's biology from any possibly damaging connections. Gray admitted that Darwin's views were grounded in those of Malthus (and Thomas Hobbes). "However moralists and political economists may regard these doctrines [of struggle] in their original application to human society and the relation of population to subsistence, their thoroughgoing applicability to the great society of the organic world in general is now undeniable." No one, that is to say, could tar Darwinians by claiming that they underwrote Malthusianism! Somewhat later, the sociologist Lester Ward added: "Malthus framed a law which was applicable to animals below man and to plants, and it was reserved for Darwin to confine it to its legitimate field."[22]

But, these disclaimers aside, Darwin had extended Malthus's theory in one important aspect when he extended the concept of struggle to include intra- and interspecies conflict. The connection between the two forms of struggle (Malthusian and Darwinian) is subtle to be sure. But precisely because Darwin confined attention to the natural realm, he was able to take the step from which Malthus shrank. Moreover, Darwin's struggle for existence was a matter of ultimate survival, as evidenced in reproduction, not simply one of subsistence. He used the phrase "in a large and metaphorical sense," he wrote, "including dependence of one being on another, and including (which is more important) not only the life of the individual, but success in leaving progeny."[23] Plants producing seeds within a given area were not literally struggling for existence; rather their progeny were.

Like his accommodation to Lamarckian environmentalism, Darwin's reference to the metaphorical meaning of the struggle for existence, and his inclusion of mutual dependence as a factor, softened the implication that brute force was a critical factor in evolution, natural or human. In fact, theorists were left with several choices: retreat to the original Malthusian assumption that the struggle for existence pitted species against their environment and not against each other (a position William Graham Sumner adopted, for example); or insist that for religious or ethical reasons mankind suspended the struggle for existence; or attempt to describe the process of social association that produced the "dependence of one being on another" (the direction of later sociology and reform-Darwinists). There remained the possibility of course that some would welcome Darwin's extension of Malthus and call for unfettered social struggle and "the devil take the hindmost." But this possibility, as it turned out, existed largely in the minds of critics.

The concept of natural selection also had a lengthy history, of which Darwin was mostly unaware. In the early nineteenth century at least three naturalists described its operation in human history: William Charles Wells, whose *Two Essays* showed how different races originated; Patrick Matthew, whose *Naval Timber and Aboriginal Culture* (1831) Darwin acknowledged in the second edition of *Origin of Species;* and John H. Klippart, who in 1858 demonstrated how nature replaced one variety of wheat with another.[24] Darwin's conception, like most of these forerunners, proceeded directly from his notion of a struggle for existence and his familiarity with *artificial selection* as practiced by gardeners and stockbreeders.

The concept of natural selection gave Darwin the greatest difficulty. True to the principles of mechanistic determinism, which like others of his generation he thought to be the essence of science, Darwin rejected Lamarck's view of an inherently progressive tendency in nature, just as he shed William Paley's notion of static, designed adaptations. But the phrase *natural selection*—by analogy with *artificial selection*—reintroduced overtones of voluntarism since a *selector* seemed implicit. Although partly the result of his attempt to derive his principle by analogy, these overtones were also a vestige of Darwin's earlier ambivalence concerning mechanistic naturalism—an ambivalance that surfaced in frequent references to the Creator in his earlier writings.[25] This ambivalence was at the heart of Darwin's genius; he insisted both on the uniformity of law in nature *and* the operation of natural selection, even though he was unable to provide an adequate mechanical explanation for the appearance of those variations upon which natural selection worked.

Darwin's persistence on this point produced finally not simply reinforcement of the mechanistic philosophy, but a fundamentally altered conception of order in nature. "[The] so-called law of natural selection," the historian John Greene has explained, "was a law in a quite different sense from that in which the Darwinians conceived a law of nature." Although contemporaries viewed anything that was not a mechanical law as chance or chaos—"a law of higgledy-piggledy," as one observer protested—natural selection implied a statistical concept of order in place of a mechanical one. Among the first to recognize this fact was the American philosopher Charles S. Peirce:

> In biology, that tremendous upheaval caused in 1860 by Darwin's theory of fortuitous variations was but the consequence of a

theorem in probabilities, namely the theorem that if very many similar things are subject to many slight fortuitous variations, as much in one direction as in the opposite direction, which when they aggregate a sufficient effect upon any one of those things in one direction must eliminate it from nature, while there is no corresponding effect of an aggregate of variations in other directions, the result must, in the long run, be to produce a change of the average character of the class of things in the latter direction.

Evolution in this view was creative without being lawless or chaotic.[26]

Since Darwin did not see things this way—indeed could hardly have been expected to, given reigning assumptions—he faced serious difficulties in defending natural selection. A major problem concerned the source of "variations to be selected." Ignorant of mutation theory (Mendel's work was not to be discovered and extended by DeVries for several decades), Darwin relied on a variety of essentially conventional explanations of variation: (1) the direct effect of environment; (2) indirect effect through the inheritance of acquired characteristics; (3) habit, use, and disuse; (4) correlation of growth; and (5) compensation or balance. Here Darwin was again true to the spirit of mid-Victorian science. Variations were never spontaneous nor the result of chance—to admit as much would be to rest the theory on unscientific grounds.[27]

At the same time, Darwin and later his critics doubted whether such minor variations, however numerous, could produce so dramatic a result as a new species. This argument gained force from physicists who insisted that geological time was simply inadequate to have allowed the accumulation of changes necessary to create the myriad species in nature, a corollary not only of Biblical theory but also of their conception of the sun as a sort of coalpile destined to burn up in a relatively short time.[28]

Darwin's ignorance of the principles of modern heredity compounded his difficulties. In this area the most fundamental issues were only recently settled. *Epigenesis* (the modern notion that organisms develop by successive differentiation of the fertilized ovum) triumphed over *prefiguration* (the notion that the total individual exists in miniature in sperm and/or ovum) only a century before; and the theory was not widely known until the early nineteenth century. In the 1820s von Baer accurately described the mammalian egg, but it was two years after the *Origin of Species* first appeared that Gegenbaur identified the egg as a cell derived from the parent and carrying its protoplasm. Still in the future were the theories of August Weismann, the German biologist who described the germ cell in the late 1880s.[29]

Deprived of modern knowledge, Darwin proposed a theory of *panegenesis*, whereby traits of both parents blended to produce the traits of their offspring. Critics noted that such blending further diminished the probability that selected variations could produce a transmutation of species since minor changes would quickly be "swamped," that is, would cancel one another out.

Little wonder, in light of these difficulties, that natural selection remained in dispute even among professed Darwinians. "Despite some historians' statements to the contrary," the biologist Garland Allen has written, "the literature of the period indicates that the idea of natural selection had by no means gained wide currency or whole-hearted acceptance as late as 1915."[30]

If natural selection seemed to violate the canons of science, then an alternative was needed to eliminate any hint of a selector. Thus entered Herbert Spencer, whose phrase the survival of the fittest, at least in Spencer's view, described the impersonal operation of entirely natural forces. But Spencer's notion, as will appear in the next chapter, was far from neutral. In accepting the substitute, Darwin almost unwittingly wed his theory to a doctrine of progress, which from the modern perspective seems also metaphysical or nonscientific.

This union of Darwin and Spencer was part of a more general process whereby a theory of *transmutation through adaptation* (Darwin's main theme) became a theory of evolution. Again some etymology is useful. The term evolution, as Peter Bowler has pointed out, was in fact rarely used in the *Origin of Species*, and was totally absent in most early reviews. This omission reflected the fact that the most prominent uses of the term, before Spencer appropriated it in the fifties, were not in relation to the transmutation of species. Rather the term described the unfolding of pre-existing structures in embryology, and more generally, any sequence of events. During the early nineteenth century, the term came gradually to describe a progressive unfolding of life. But there was little association with *progressive transmutation*. Although Darwin occasionally used the term evolution in his early writings, the notion of *progression* was neither a central nor necessary element in the hypothesis. Popularization of the term during the 1860s and 1870s in connection with Darwin's work was a measure of the degree to which the theory was accepted within the framework of Spencer's cosmology.[31]

Given the complexity of Darwin's relation to Uniformitarianism, to Lamarckianism, to Malthusianism, and finally to Spencerianism, it is little wonder that the implications of the *Origin* remained problematical for some time. If one viewed the *Origin* simply as further proof of a law-bound cosmos, ignoring the troublesome concept of natural selection, then Darwin might support a number of attempts to render social thought equally scientific—the essence of the positivistic spirit Spencer represented. However, if one took seriously the role of struggle and selection, the result was the reintroduction of the arbitrariness of force and brutality of power that was anathema even to Malthus. Although Darwin was no philosopher, and Huxley and Wallace were primarily concerned with the scientific issues, these three scientists were among the first to wrestle with these problems once the initial furor over the *Origin* quieted down.

Four

Darwin avoided the issue of human development altogether in the *Origin of Species,* in part to skirt unnecessary controversy. However, in letters and notebooks during the 1860s, he ventured some speculation, cautious and inconclusive, concerning the social implications of his theory. When in 1860, Lyell asked him why the Athenians of Pericles's time had failed to advance despite their eminent superiority, Darwin was momentarily stymied. Only later did he speculate that his theory, in tying progression to conditions, better explained the decline than "the Lamarckian or Vestigian doctrine of necessary progression." Conditions of anarchy and barbarian invasion guaranteed that force rather than intellect would triumph, he noted (anticipating thereby a common view in the 1870s that survival of the fittest in a depraved environment was survival of the depraved). However, in addressing the same issue in *The Descent of Man* he dropped even this explanation, perhaps aware, as James Rogers has suggested, that so simplistic a version ignored the complexities of social change.[32]

In other comments Darwin punctured the speculations of those who sought to enlist him under their banner. The remark that the *Origin* proved "every cheating tradesmen . . . right" merely amused him. When two years later a correspondent suggested that natural selection validated aristocracy, Darwin also responded in a light vein:

> The "Origin" having made you in fact a jolly old Tory, made us all laugh heartily. I have sometimes speculated on this subject; primogeniture is dreadfully opposed to selection; suppose the first-born bull was necessarily made by each farmer the begetter of his stock! On the other hand, as you say, ablest men are continually raised to the peerage, and get crossed with the older Lord-breeds, and the Lords continually select the most beautiful and charming women out of the lower ranks; so that a good deal of indirect selection improves the Lords.

When some years later, the news reached Darwin that the German biologist Rudolf Virchow rooted socialism in Darwinism (to discredit the latter), he dismissed it as another "foolish idea."[33]

On several occasions Darwin apparently took seriously the idea that social policy might be judged by analogy with natural selection in nature. In particular, he repeated that natural selection was an argument against primogeniture several times.[34] The crucial question, however, concerned the poor laws and other humanitarian reforms. Should society attempt to preserve its weaker members? Could it do so without fatally weakening the social fabric? Here lay the nub of the charge that Darwin provided the basis for a new and harsher utilitarianism.

Darwin addressed these questions in print in *The Descent of Man* (1871, rev. ed. 1873) in a key chapter titled "On the Development of the Intellectual and Moral Faculties." The most often quoted passage reads as follows:

> With savages, the weak in body or mind are soon eliminated;
> and those that survive commonly exhibit a vigorous state of health.
> We civilized men, on the other hand, do our utmost to check the
> process of elimination; we build asylums for the imbecile, the
> maimed, and the sick; we institute poor-laws; and our medical
> men exert their utmost skill to save the life of everyone to the last
> moment. . . . Thus, the weak members of civilized societies propa-
> gate their kind. No one who has attended to the breeding of
> domestic animals will doubt that this must be highly injurious to
> the race of man. It is surprising how soon a want of care, or care
> wrongly directed, leads to the degeneration of a domestic race;
> but excepting in the case of man himself, hardly anyone is so ignor-
> ant as to allow his worst animals to breed.

Darwin added however that this ignorance was basic to man's humanity. "The aid we feel impelled to give to the helpless is mainly an incidental result of the instinct of sympathy, which was originally acquired as part of the social instincts, but subsequently rendered . . . more tender and widely diffused," he wrote. "Nor could we check our sympathy, even at the urging of hard reason, without deterioration in the noblest part of our nature."[35]

In discussing these social issues, Darwin drew the conventional distinction between "savage" and "civilized" societies, emphasizing that the struggle for existence diminished as man progressed. Had the earlier struggle for existence been less severe, man "would never have attained to his present rank," he observed. But even this statement he softened in the second edition of the *Descent* by adding that the "more efficient causes of progress" in modern society "seem to consist of a good education . . . and of a high standard of excellence, inculcated by the ablest and best men, embodied in the laws, customs and traditions of the nation, and enforced by public opinion."[36]

In effect, Darwin stated the issue without resolving it: natural selection had implications for human society but arrangements that seemed on the surface to impede these natural laws could not on that account be eliminated. Unlike religiously inclined contemporaries (such as Wallace), he did not ground these higher sentiments in some spiritual faculty. Unlike Spencer, he was unwilling to assume that an increase of *altruism*, the result of automatic natural laws, would neutralize *egoism* in advanced societies. Nor was he endorsing eugenics or racism, two possible extrapolations from this particular portion of *The Descent of Man*. Moderate in his social views, humanitarian by instinct, Darwin fell back on customs, traditions, and public opinion because he did not know what else to do.

Translating this quandary into a philosophy, Thomas Henry Huxley (1825-1895) attacked Spencer and laissez faire more explicitly. Like Darwin, he avoided social issues through most of the 1860s, and focused in *Man's Place in Nature* (1863) on scientific and religious issues. In "Administrative Nihilism" (1871), however, he began an ongoing battle with Spencerianism. Although the issue was not evolution but Spencer's organic analogy, Huxley's argument set the tone of later debates. Spencer insisted that the social organism must grow and develop without artificial interference, which he equated with governmental action of any sort. Huxley dissented. "If the analogy of the body politic with the body physiological counts for anything, it seems to me to be in favour of a much larger amount of governmental interference than exists at present, or than I, for one, at all desire to see." Huxley then implied that Darwinism supported the mean between the extremes of Spencerian individualism and the centralization of the organicists (he had St. Simon especially in mind). It was Kant, he continued, who anticipated "the application of the 'struggle for existence' to politics," and suggested "the manner in which the evolution of society had resulted from the constant attempt of individuals to strain its bonds." For Huxley this was again a lesson in political moderation. "If individuality has no play, society does not advance; if individuality breaks out of all bonds, society perishes." In terms of policy, this meant that government should work positively for Locke's "Good of Mankind"; maintain peace and security; foster commerce and the arts; and, in particular, establish the compulsory public education that Spencer opposed.[37]

In later years "Administrative Nihilism" won Huxley a reputation as a leading opponent of laissez faire, reinforcing the view that an accurate reading of Darwinism led to state activism. For his own part, Huxley remained ambivalent while recognizing the "logic" of this conclusion. "Have you considered that State Socialism (for which I have little enough love) may be product of Natural Selection," he wrote rather nervously in the late 1870s, when a leading German scientist suggested such a conclusion. "The societies of Bees and Ants exhibit socialism *in excelsis*."[38] Such ambivalence convinced him finally that social ethics and policy could in no way be derived from laws of nature, the frank if startling conclusion of his Romanes address at Oxford more than a decade later.

Of the three leading Darwinians, Alfred Russel Wallace (1823-1913) alone beat an apparent retreat into supernaturalism, but in the process offered even less comfort to individualism and laissez faire. Wallace's earliest essays on the implications of Darwinism for society appeared in the *Anthropological Review* in 1864, which with others was later collected in *Contributions to the Theory of Natural Selection* (1869). More frankly dualistic than either Darwin or Huxley, Wallace drew sharp distinctions between the animal and human realms, and between the savage and civilized stages of human development. Animals lived in a state of "self-dependence" and "individual isolation" while humans were "social and sympathetic," he wrote. "Mental" and "moral" qualities distinguished men from beasts and from his savage forebears. These qualities became important as physical characteristics became less so. Treating readers to a Cook's tour of man's ascent from "barbarism," Wallace pictured a final, comforting destination: "the wonderful intellect of the European races."[39]

As he described the "limits of natural selection" Wallace revealed a theological penchant that disappointed more naturalistically inclined Darwinians. At a certain stage of development, natural selection ceased operating entirely, he wrote. Thereafter, development was entirely, "mental" and "spiritual." No mere products of organic law, these qualities were due to the action of some unknown higher law. Although Wallace predicted that natural selection in the future would continue to act on man's "mental organization"—by replacing the "lower and more degraded races" with the "more moral and intellectual"—he saw no role for it among "civilized nations," for, as he wrote, "it is indisputably the mediocre, if not the low, both as regards morality and intelligence, who succeed in life and multiply the fastest." He was certain there was an advance, but as he could not "impute this in any way to 'survival of the fittest,'" he was "forced to conclude that it is due to the inherent progressive power of those glorious qualities which raise us so immeasurably above our fellow animals."[40]

Americans welcomed Wallace's version of the limits of natural selection. "We must congratulate the scientific world that the ablest advocate of Darwinism has had the philosophical acumen to perceive ... that there are features in the physical and mental structure of man which cannot have been produced by natural selection," wrote the *Nation*. It was "singular" that a thinker who had "gone furthest on the road which is generally believed to lead inevitably to atheism" had declared an "abiding faith that there is, beyond this range of physical events, an intellectual guiding force." Charles Loring Brace, a reformer active in charity work, likewise expressed pleasure that Wallace allowed "at least . . . one cataclysm in human history."[41]

In later years Wallace was other reformers' favorite Darwinian. After attacking evolutionism in *Progress and Poverty* (1879), Henry George was converted to the cause by Wallace in the early 1880s. In *Looking Backward* (1888) Edward Bellamy built on Wallace's view that evolution ceased at some point in the case of man's physiological development. Wallace in turn praised Bellamy's theory of the eugenic effects of social reform. By the turn of the century, Wallace's distinctions were the basis of a new conventional wisdom. In a course on the "Evolution of the Modern State" a Cornell undergraduate recorded in his notebook: "Natural Selection—Physical Power was the selecting force among savages. It is intellect among civilized people. See Alfred Russel Wallace, 'Man's Place in the Universe.'"[42]

Finally, of course, there is no way of determining conclusively the inherent social logic of Darwinism, if there was one. *The Descent of Man* later provided a text for eugenicists whatever Darwin's intent; and Wallace's remarks about higher and lower races would later reappear in less lofty contexts. At the same time, there seems little ground for assuming that Darwinism logically and immediately gave support to unbridled individualism, unregulated competition, and laissez faire or in other ways championed brutality and force in social affairs. Instead, the more one stressed natural selection through struggle in nature, the more it appeared that human society operated on different principles. In extending Malthus, Darwin removed the one prop that made society possible: Malthus's assumption that the struggle for existence was a collective one against nature. To reapply the extended version to society had implications Darwin and his contemporaries found unacceptable.

In opening the gap between society and nature, Darwinism implicitly undermined the intellectual strategy of most social theorists since Newton. Although Darwin, Wallace, and Huxley differed on the policies they endorsed, these specifics were less important than their common rejection of the proposition that sound social policy was the result of allowing free play to the automatic operation of natural law. In this way each anticipated the basic premise of the varieties of reform Darwinism that later flourished. Not everyone, including they themselves, accepted the full implications of this view. Herbert Spencer in particular built his career on opposing it.

2.   Hushing Up Death

[The] logical implication of the views of some thinkers would seem to be that government . . . is an interference with a kind of natural justice. Mr. Herbert Spencer is one whom I have in mind—not that he would say this, but that he has a general mode of thought from which this would not be an illegitimate inference. . . . In other words, Mr. Spencer believes that each individual should stand on his own legs and that the fittest should survive . . . .
    William M. Salter, Anarchy or Government? *(1895)*, *pp. 58-9.*

[The] struggle for existence plays an important part in [Spencer's] political system which cannot be found in the teaching of Bentham. Logically, the weak must go to the wall and the survival of the fittest take place.
    Edward Aveling, "The Philosophy of Herbert Spencer," Dublin Review, 134 *(1904), p. 258.*

One

Soon after the appearance of *The Descent of Man*, Herbert Spencer began to discover that public identification with Darwinism had some distinct disadvantages. In 1875 the economist John Elliott Cairnes charged that Spencer "transferred laws of physiology (including the 'survival of the fittest') to the domain of social science." James Martineau, a prominent Unitarian clergyman, alleged that the Spencerians failed to see that "fittest" in the absence of certain preconditions, equated "best" with "strongest." Thus they invested their "favorite lord and master, competition, with an imperial crown and universal sway." A decade later the Belgian sociologist, Emile de Laveleye, added that Spencer was "anxious to see the law of the survival of the fittest and of natural selection adopted in human society." By this time the charge was widespread. And in an Italian translation of Laveleye's attack, it assumed its modern name, Darwinisme social or social Darwinism.[1]

Spencer repeatedly denied the charge. Responding to Laveleye, he insisted that he would not "countenance violent methods of replacing the inferior by the superior." "Aggression of every kind is hateful to me," he added elsewhere. "Why, then, did E. Laveleye make it seem that I would, if I could, establish a regime of injustice in its most brutal form?" When the *Pall Mall Gazette* repeated a similar charge, Spencer wrote an American friend: It "will show you what amount of conscience exists among journalistic leaders of opinion over here." Later in his life he again insisted that his books overflowed with ideas "diametrically opposed to that brutal individualism which some persons attribute to me."[2]

A few of Spencer's contemporaries sprang to his defense. Enlisting Spencer behind socialism (!) one observer surmised that Spencer on the occasion of the Laveleye attack was "laughing in his sleeve at the British public, and enjoying the joke of being held up as Defender of the universal-scramble and Devil-take-the-hindmost Faith which not once only, but all his life, he has laboured to destroy." The American writer and reformer Hamlin Garland added later that "nothing is more mistaken than the attack upon Mr. Spencer as 'the advocate of war between man and man.'" Historians, however, sided with Spencer's opponents. "To Spencer belonged the credit of applying Darwinism most systematically if not always soundly to psychology, sociology, and ethics," wrote Carlton Hayes in *A Generation of Materialism* (1941). Others agreed that Spencerianism paralysed the will to reform.[3]

An interesting difference distinguished the historical from the contemporary indictment however. Contemporaries generally viewed Spencer's *Social Statics* (1850) and his early essays as an antidote to Malthusianism and the "dismal science" of Ricardo. His later work drew the charge of misapplied Darwinism. In *A Perplexed Philosopher* (1892) Henry George, the American Single Taxer, voiced a common complaint that the winds of modern science had chilled the warm humanitarianism of *Social Statics*. In *The Cooperative Commonwealth* (1883) the socialist Laurence Gronlund cited Spencer's early writings on the social organism to discredit his later defenses of individualism. In this view, the later installments of the Synthetic Philosophy were the villains of the piece. Historians on the other hand found the clearest evidences of social Darwinism in *Social Statics* and the early essays.[4]

These differences were in part the result of imprecise definitions of social Darwinism. But they also reflect a misunderstanding of the fundamental challenge that Darwinism posed to Spencer's grand scheme of *universal evolution* and the complex uses of the social Darwinism label in the debates that followed. In *Social Statics* Spencer attempted nothing less than a restatement of the assumptions and principles of Enlightenment liberalism in the face of the developments in science and society that seemed to threaten them. Gradually this scheme came unraveled, as Spencer first altered his arguments and eventually actually revised his earlier texts. He also discovered that Darwinism was a double-edged sword. As such, it played a complex role in his lapse into doubt and frustration in his final years: directly, in undermining the view of nature that sustained his neo-Enlightenment synthesis; indirectly, in providing his opponents a convenient slogan with which to attack him.

Two

Born in Derby, Yorkshire, in 1820, Herbert Spencer molded his early experiences into the guiding principles of *Social Statics* (1850), his first book. At the core of his thought was that peculiar combination of piety and practicality, religion and science, that flourished in the English provinces no less than in America. Descended from Methodists, schooled in Quakerism, Spencer was heir to the troublesome energies of the English dissenting tradition. But piety for young Spencer was no barrier to learning. His father, a private schoolmaster of impressive abilities, imbued his son with a passion for knowledge and a penchant for self-instruction. A clergyman uncle, with whom Spencer boarded in his teens, provided him the rudiments of formal learning, particularly in the sciences. At age seventeen Spencer joined the staff of the London and Birmingham railway. There he observed at first hand the force of technology, which was already transforming the Midlands.[5]

Spencer's uncle also introduced him to the heady principles of radical politics. During the 1840s, as Chartism and the issue of Corn Law repeal agitated British politics, Spencer launched a career as publicist. His first substantial effort was a series on "The Proper Sphere of Government," which appeared in the *Nonconformist* in 1842. When a crisis at the railway threw Spencer out of work four years later, he served briefly as an editor for the London *Economist*, where he continued his battle against governmental power and social privilege.

While remaining the partisan, Spencer in *Social Statics* attempted to set his arguments within a more comprehensive cosmology. Vindicating the radical position, the book was a restatement of the *moral sense doctrine* against the utilitarianism of Bentham and Paley. Spencer was a friendly critic. In the spirit of utilitarianism, he subtitled his work "The Conditions Essential to Human Happiness." But the "expediency doctrine," as he viewed it, had fatal drawbacks. At the extremes it bred either chaotic subjectivism or intolerable centralization. Although the utilitarians pretended to provide a principle, their position, in Spencer's opinion, rested finally on each individual's subjective conviction as to what constituted happiness. In the absence of agreement, the government inevitably stepped in with its own definition of the "greatest good of the greatest number." The "expe-

diency philosophy," Spencer wrote, "implies the eternity of government."
Social Statics proposed a single standard, a true principle, that ultimately
left individuals free to think and act as they chose.[6]

In restating the moral sense position against the utilitarians Spencer, as
J. D. Y. Peel has observed, adopted a strategy which since the time of Hobbes distinguished thinkers on the periphery from those closer to the court
and commercial centers of London—a clue to the Yorkshireman's great appeal in America.[7] However, Spencer saw a major defect in the earlier efforts, whether the moral sense of Shaftesbury and Hutcheson; the Common Sense of the Scottish moralists; or Samuel Clarke's "fitness of things."
None successfully explained why the same "sense," presumably common
to all men, yielded different conclusions at different times:

> "If," say the objectors, "this 'moral sense,' to which all these writers
> directly or indirectly appeal, possesses no fixity, gives no uniform
> response, says one thing in Europe, and another in Asia—originates
> different notions of duty in each age, each race, each individual,
> how can it afford a safe foundation for a systematic morality?
> What can be more absurd than to seek a definite rule of right,
> in the answers of so uncertain an authority?"

Despite this flaw, these thinkers "consulted a true oracle," Spencer added.
"Although they have failed to systematize its utterances, they have acted
wisely in trying to do this."[8]

Spencer looked to the moral sense school less for specific formulations
than to establish the *possibility* of certainty. Turning the tables on the
utilitarians, he argued that they themselves acknowledged this possibility
—even while denying it explicitly—since they assumed necessarily that
one person's happiness is as important as another's. This axiom could be
justified only on grounds other than those proposed within utilitarianism.
Spencer likened the concept of sense at once to perception and sentiment.
A sense impression included both the mechanical registering of a percept
(color, weight etc.) *and* a sentiment concerning the perception (its reality,
desirability, etc.). Applied to morals, the perception of the "good" carried
with it an impulse to behave accordingly. "Imperfect" man could not act
on complete knowledge since no finite being could totally comprehend a
universe in the process of becoming. The attempt to do so was the folly of
utopians and other doctrinaires. But individuals might yield to the
promptings of sentiment. "It is not for nothing that he has within him
these sympathies with some principles and repugnance to others," Spencer
assured his readers. "He (man), with all his capacities, and desires, and
beliefs is not an accident, but a product of time," he added. "The moral
sentiment developed in him was intended to be instrumental in producing

further progress; and to gag it, or to conceal the thoughts it generates, is to balk creative design."[9]

Armed with this possibility of certain knowledge, Spencer broke with the moral sense school in picturing human history as an ongoing evolution, rather than a static affair. Differences among men were real. The eighteenth century erred in assuming that man could be defined in terms of a universal reason or other unchanging quality. Custom and opinion in existing societies were bound to differ. Expanding this point, Spencer castigated human frailty with a passion that revealed his religious upbringing:

> When we say that mankind are sinful, weak, frail, we
> simply mean that they do not habitually fulfil the appointed law.
> Imperfection is merely another word for disobedience.

Nonetheless, this "imperfect" man could "sense" the ideal to which evolution tended with the same certainty that the moral sense school had promised. Since "sensing" combined perception and action, one was comforted by the apparent paradox that "imperfect" humanity might live by the "perfect" moral law.[10]

Recast in social terms, Spencer's philosophical argument had significant implications. Since each individual had an equal if imperfect intuition of truth, neither government nor church could claim higher authority. Such was the principle that since Locke had joined empiricist epistemology and liberalism. Spencer's "first principle" as formulated in Social Statics turned out to be the basic tenet of classical liberalism: "Everyman has freedom to do all that he wills, provided he infringes not the equal freedom of any other man." In Spencer's scheme this principle was no longer self-evident as this term was used by the moral sense school or, in America, by the framers of the Declaration of Independence. Rather it was a deduction based on knowledge of the absolute, uniform, and inevitable laws that governed evolution throughout all nature.[11]

Spencer thus broke with eighteenth-century social thought in two regards. Most immediately, he questioned the image of man as a wealth,power, or happiness maximizer—the common denominator of classical economics, political theory, and utilitarian ethics. "And, waiving all other objections," he wrote of the latter, "we are compelled to reject a system, which, at the same time it tacitly lays claim to perfection, takes imperfection for its basis." More generally, Spencer abandoned the psychological reductionism that united the moral sense philosophers and their utilitarian critics. Social development must henceforth be understood in terms of laws external to the individuals composing society, not as deductions from human psychology.[12]

Despite these departures, *Social Statics* was a halfway house in Spencer's development and in the transition from Enlightenment to post-Darwinian evolutionary social thought. Spencer proposed that individual intuitions would find empirical verification in the future through evolution. Thus he could validate an inherited faith in individualism, morality, and progress by appealing to the very science that seemed in the early nineteenth-century to be undermining these eighteenth-century values. As one of Spencer's American reviewers put it: "The sciences, which taken singly seem only good to expel the false, have been summoned together to declare the true."[13]

The result was a delicate balance: between intuitionism and empiricism; between idealism and materialism; and between a universe of transcendent ideals and one of ceaseless change. Inspired by Lamarckian biology and by philosophic idealism via Coleridge and Schelling, Spencer reconciled an evolutionary view of nature and society with inherited conviction. Commenting on the Spencer "vogue" several decades later, the American philosopher Borden Parker Bowne attributed Spencer's success precisely to this balancing act. Bowne, a popular lecturer who launched his career with a study of *The Philosophy of Herbert Spencer* (1874), now compared Kant and Spencer. "The Synthetic Philosophy conveyed an air of conciliation," he wrote. "It seemed to make a place for views which had hitherto been regarded as contradictory," and to unite opposites in "some higher insight."[14] Spencer thus mediated the conflict between rational intuition ism and empiricism by insisting that, while the individual does not get all knowledge from experience (intuitionism) the race does so collectively (empiricism). Philosophically, Spencer's spectres lay at the extremes. Empiricism, as David Hume had shown, led to scepticism and materialism. Intuitionism and idealism buttressed the established orders. Spencer would have it both ways at once.

Spencer's attack on the Poor Laws in *Social Statics*—an alleged example of his social Darwinism—must be read within this context. Urging that the treatment of poverty be put on a scientific basis, he agreed that

> the well-being of existing humanity, and the unfolding of it into this
> ultimate perfection, are both secured by that same beneficent,
> though severe discipline, to which the animate creation at large
> is subject: a discipline which is pitiless in the working out of good:
> a felicity-pursuing law which never swerves for the avoidance of
> partial and temporary suffering.

"The process *must* be undergone, and the sufferings must be endured," he continued. "No reforms that men ever did broach or ever will broach, can diminish them one jot." Denouncing "Sanitary Supervision," he likewise warned against aiding nature's "failures," a group that included the ill and those whose "stupidity, or vice, or idleness, entails loss of life"[15]

Spencer's remarks concerning the struggles among races of men were, on the surface, equally harsh:

> Whilst the continuance of the old predatory instinct after the fulfilment of its original purpose, has retarded civilization by giving rise to conditions at variance with those of social life, it has subserved civilization by clearing the earth of inferior races of men. The forces which are working out the great scheme of perfect happiness, taking no account of incidental suffering, exterminate such sections of mankind as stand in their way, with the same sternness that they exterminate beasts of prey and herds of useless ruminants. Be he human being, or be he brute, the hindrance must be got rid of.[16]

In context, however, Spencer blunted these harsh words in two ways. First, he insisted that the discipline which brought suffering also produced an attendant increase in social sympathy or benevolence. Drawing on Adam Smith's theory of *moral sentiments* he suggested that individualism and what he would later term altruism increased together. In attacking the Poor Laws, he wished in no way to limit the full exercise of natural sympathy as expressed in voluntary assistance. So also the development of fellow-feeling would diminish war among groups. Higher civilizations would not *by definition* (being more fully evolved) war on less developed ones, a principle Spencer "proved" through a survey of contemporary societies. Fellow-feeling or altruism, the product of evolution, provided an absolute standard of conduct. "Let not the reader be alarmed," he wrote, discussing slavery. "Let him not fear that these admissions will excuse new invasions and new oppressions. Nor let any one who fancies himself called upon to take Nature's part in this matter, by providing discipline for idle negroes or others, suppose that these dealings of the past will serve as precedents."[17]

Second, his distinction between past and present rested on an implicit dualism between everyday reality and an ideal order to which events tended. From the "higher point of view" suffering was "partial and temporary," Spencer wrote, sounding not unlike the American Emersonians at their most sanguine. Progress not only explained the ills of the past but made them somehow less real. True to empiricism, Spencer never explicitly posited a dualism between a *noumenal* and *phenomenal* world. Nor did he find the workaday world quite the shadowy place of some philosophic idealists and their disciples. But he consistently subordinated fact to ideal.

To those who knew where things were going, daily life was not a miscellany of unpleasant facts but a pale reflection of a greater plan.[18]

In an essay on "A Theory of Population" (1852), Spencer demonstrated how so seemingly harsh a law as Malthus's appeared when viewed in this light. Malthus's law of population was under attack, and Spencer admitted that circumstances in midcentury England apparently suspended its operation. Rather than abandon it, however, Spencer framed an explanation that allowed for the truth of the law and for its permanent cessation. Thanks to evolution, the law of population would eventually cancel itself out. Just as high development bred benevolence, so the demands of an increasingly complex civilization created a larger and more complex nervous system in man (proved by measurements of the crania of developed and underdeveloped peoples)—and hence greater intelligence and self-discipline. These traits diminished fertility. Excess of fertility, on the other hand, led to "increasing difficulty of getting a living." Prolific "families and races" were thus "on the high road to extinction; and must ultimately be supplanted by those whom the pressure does so stimulate." In a revised version of this argument a decade later, he made the process even less bloody, the guarantee more certain. The increasing complexity of the nervous system and declining fertility, he explained in the *Principles of Biology*, were physiological necessities. The demands of modern life, by enlarging the size of the brain, diminished sexual energies. No longer did self-discipline play a role. The process was now purely automatic as the "peaceful struggle for existence" resulted in a "diminished reserve of materials for race maintenance."[19]

Three

In *First Principles* (1861), Spencer spelled out the assumptions that underlay this revision. A law-bound universe no longer contained a Creator. Gone were references to "laws of Providence" and other "metaphysical" lapses, which he now believed had marred his earlier work. Spencer insisted that all laws be reduced to the "ultimate form" of the redistribution of matter and motion, themselves manifestations of "force." Although this terminology was derived from recent developments in thermodynamics, his model was a physical universe that underlay Anglo-American social theory since the time of Newton. At its heart was the conviction, as Talcott Parsons has observed, that "in the last analysis the categories of classical mechanics were alone adequate to the scientific understanding of reality, and that all other systems, if they were sound, were ultimately reducible to this one."[20]

The key was the uniformity of law in every sphere. "The changes everywhere going on, from those which are slowly altering the structure of our galaxy down to those which constitute a chemical decomposition, are changes in the relative positions of component parts," Spencer wrote; "and everywhere necessarily imply that along with a new arrangement of Matter there has arisen a new arrangement of Motion." This rearrangement resulted in the establishment of successive equilibria, wherein inner and outer forces achieved temporary balance, in biological terms the adaptation of organism to environment. Rendered in these terms, the classical economists' picture of the market mechanism, for example, appeared as follows:

> The production and distribution of a commodity imply a certain aggregate of forces causing special kinds and amounts of motion. The price of this commodity, is the measure of a certain other aggregate of forces expended in other kinds and amounts of motion by the labourer who purchases it. And the variations of price represent a rhythmical balancing of these forces. Every rise or fall in the value of a particular security, implies a conflict of forces in which some, becoming temporarily predominant, cause a movement that is temporarily arrested, or equilibrated by the increased opposing forces; and amid these daily and hourly oscillations lies a more slowly-varying medium, into which the value ever tends to settle, and would settle but for the constant addition of new influences.

Gone were buyers and sellers, rich and poor, and the personal hardships the market economy involved.[21]

Was equilibrium ever realized? Was adaptation ever perfect? Would industrialism, to put the question less abstractly, produce the ideal Utopia? In the original edition of *First Principles*, Spencer seemed to say that perfect (final) equilibrium was possible. Universal evolution, as he termed it, led finally to a perfect balance of inner and outer forces. In social terms this was the industrial Utopia he promised in *Social Statics*. "The changes which evolution presents cannot end until equilibrium is reached," Spencer concluded confidently, "and that equilibrium must at last be reached." Again in social terms this was the guarantee that "evolution can end only in the establishment of the greatest perfection and the most complete happiness."[22]

But critics quickly pointed out that complete equilibrium of this sort meant omnipresent death; and Spencer knew that life as life never achieved static repose. He thus sometimes spoke of a "moving equilibrium" in which there was no final or perfect state. Here Spencer took advantage of a fundamental ambiguity in contemporary use of the term equilibrium, making it, as Cynthia Russett has observed, "not only the mechanism of evolution but also the ultimate goal." In doing so, he smuggled in assumptions concerning an ideal state, now more thoroughly disguised in the apparently scientific language of thermodynamics.[23]

This ambiguity paralleled a very special sense in which Spencer defined *scientific laws*. The result was an extension of his earlier compromise between empiricism and intuitionism. The scientific laws of *First Principles* were presumably strict generalizations from fact, free from the intuitionist metaphysics of his earlier work. Thus they ostensibly satisfied the empiricist. Yet the intuitionist might take comfort in the fact that "ultimate Scientific Ideas" were "all representative of realities that cannot be comprehended"; they were "merely symbols of the actual." "By the Persistence of Force" (the conservation of energy), Spencer further observed, "we really mean the persistence of some cause which transcends our knowledge and conception." The transformation and equivalence of forces, also ostensibly inductive generalizations, were actually not verifiable empirically. Intuition paved the *a priori* high road to truth. Induction trudged behind, "disclosing the many particular implications which the general truth does not specify."[24]

Metaphysical confusion followed. The relation between the perfect law and the imperfect world of man, noumena and phenomena, was unclear by design. Spencer conceded as much in the conclusion of *First Principles*: "The connexion between the conditioned forms of being and the unconditioned form of being, [is] forever inscrutable. The interpretation of all phenomena in terms of Matter, Motion and Force, is nothing more than the reduction of our complex symbols of thought, to the simplest symbols." This reduction "afford[ed] no support to either of the antagonist hypotheses respecting the ultimate nature of things," the spiritualistic or the materialistic.[25]

From the conviction that scientific laws were but proximate representations of an uncomprehendable reality and that an identical process occurred in every sphere, Spencer legitimated reasoning "by analogy," a strategy he first developed in his essay on "Progress" (1857). Since von Baer and others "had established the truth that the series of changes gone through during the development of . . . an ovum into an animal constitute an advance from homogeneity of structure to heterogenity of structure" it was legitimate to assume that the same process operated in every sphere. The distinction between *knowing* and *sensing* was implicit. Regarding society, one could not know definitively that change would bring progress. But one could sense this outcome of social evolution and rest certain that "progress is not an accident, not a thing within human control; but a beneficent necessity."[26]

This same reasoning surfaced in Spencer's handling of biological evolution and ultimately shaped his entire reaction to Darwinism. In the *Principles of Biology* (1865-67) his framework remained almost entirely pre-Darwinian. He not only reiterated his belief in the sufficiency of the Lamarckian mechanism of direct adaptation and *use-inheritance*, but equivocated concerning the one Lamarckian principle that Darwin branded nonsense: the belief that organisms possessed *inner tendencies* to develop in certain fashion, and that desire shaped the adaptive process. Interpreting Lamarck, Spencer ostensibly shifted the burden of change to the external environment. He chided Lamarck for his faith in inner tendencies. But he could not deny the efficacy of effort. That is, he could not adopt the materialist position. Again Spencer had it both ways. Desire was important, for example in "leading to increased action of motor organs." But the critical question was "Whence do these desires originate?" The answer, he concluded, would be clear "only when the process of organisms is affiliated on the process of evolution in general," that is only when the inductions of biologists were reconciled "with the universal laws of the redistribution of matter and motion." Desire and environment would then be translated as inner and outer forces, manifestations of a single process. Readers might be left wondering if giraffes had literally "willed" longer necks. But in the transcendental language of physics the problem somehow dissolved.[27]

Although Darwin's theory of natural selection posed greater difficulties, Spencer adopted a similar strategy in reconciling it with his theory of universal evolution. The differences between Spencer and Darwin were potentially enormous. Spencer's theory was basically nonempirical, "a theoretical deduction," as Gavin De Beer has characterized it, "from the impossibility of accepting special creation." At its heart was the persistence of a "Power" (force) that was both "unknown" and "unknowable." Darwin's genius in large measure derived from assumptions he refused to make, concerning metaphysics or "final causes." Drawing on a wealth of factual observation, Darwin proposed a concrete mechanism for change rather than a theory of the universe.[28]

But metaphysics could not be barred. Spencer found the phrase natural selection troubling. Suggesting a selector (on the analogy of artificial selection), it seemed to return to the outmoded notion of special agencies. It contained, Spencer wrote, "a decidedly theological suggestion." For this reason Darwin seemed to violate the fundamental tenet of mid-Victorian science, as Spencer defined the term. The concept was "manifestly one not known to physical science." That is, the hint of volition seemed antithetical to the impersonal and orderly redistribution of matter and motion, the adjustment of inner and outer forces.[29]

Spencer wrestled with the problem for several years following the publication of the *Origin of Species*. In *First Principles* (1861) he relegated Darwin to a footnote, distinguished by lack of enthusiasm. He conceded that natural selection might facilitate differentiation, but could affect "comparably little" in the absence of direct adaptation to changed circumstances. He had anticipated the "general cause" (evolution); Darwin merely added a "special one." In short, the Lamarckian mechanism provided those variations that were the raw material for natural selection, a position Darwin himself accepted in the absence of knowledge of modern genetics. Spencer opined further that Darwin himself would accept these positions "if he did not indeed consider them as tacitly implied in his work." When Spencer began the *Principles of Biology* in the fall of 1862, however, he was obviously not satisfied with this formulation, for it was almost two years later before he wrote his father: " . . . yesterday I arrived at a point of view from which Darwin's doctrine of 'Natural Selection' is seen to be absorbed into the general theory of Evolution as I am interpreting it."[30]

Spencer announced this reconciliation in the *Principles of Biology*. There he distinguished between those forces that operated continuously on organisms and those that operated only occasionally—the first on individuals, the second on the "species as a whole." In the former case a "new incident force" will "immediately call forth some counteracting force, and its concomitant structural change" (direct equilibration). In the latter instance, "disturbing forces" overthrow existing equilibria entirely, thus acting "fatally" on the individual organism but producing a new equilibrium between changed conditions and surviving members of the now altered group (indirect equilibration). Common sense might suggest a significant difference between gradual and continuous adaptation *and* the operation of fatal forces, at least for the individuals concerned. But in Spencer's "ultimate form" both involved an identical operation—the redistribution of matter and motion, which according to the laws of physics, would result in new equilibrium.[31]

The phrase the survival of the fittest, which Spencer first coined in the *Principles of Biology*, was central to this reconciliation of Darwin and universal evolution. In the process of *indirect equilibration* (natural selection) every organism in a group experienced countless "disturbing forces." Given differences in constitution "some [are] . . . less liable than others to have their equilibria overthrown by a particular incident force." The swiftest animals, for example, could best flee a forest fire. Those organisms die whose equilibria are overthrown; and "those will survive whose functions happen to be most nearly in equilibrium with the modified aggregate of external forces." This process, Spencer concluded, was the survival of the fittest.[32]

Since Darwin himself accepted survival of the fittest as equivalent to natural selection, and since the phrase figured prominently in debates over social Darwinism, it is worth noting carefully what Spencer was doing. The term fittest had two meanings, depending upon the assumptions one made. It meant best (as critics quickly charged), if one assumed that temporary equilibria tended to the establishment of a permanent equilibria as some ideal state—that is, if equilibrium was the end as well as the means of universal evolution. In the first edition of the *Principles of Biology* Spencer made this goal explicit as applied to human life: "Changes numerical, social, organic, must by their mutual influences, work unceasingly towards a state of harmony . . . . And this highest conceivable result must by wrought out by that same universal prcess which the simplest inorganic action illustrates."[33] But if one abandoned this goal, picturing instead an endless succession of temporary and imperfect equilibria, fitness meant only adaptation to existing conditions no matter how debased from some moral perspective. In the ambiguity between these two positions, an ambiguity made possible as the impersonal language of physics masked metaphyscial assumptions, Spencer effected yet another compromise between instinctive conviction and scientific law.

Spencer's handling of natural selection resembled his other compromises in several respects. Although he enumerated the modifications produced by direct adaptation as opposed to natural selection (assigning the majority to the first cause), he finally cared little for facts. Because all change brought equilibrations one could be certain a priori "that all processes of modification which do not come within the class of direct equilibrations must come within the class of indirect equilibrations." The facts seemed to favor Lamarck. Spencer criticized Darwin for underestimating the effects of use and disuse. But future inductions (that is, evidence) would in no way alter the deductive truths of universal evolution. Nor need Spencer engage in protracted debates as to whether strength, cunning, or other qualities assured survival, or whether struggle was bloody or benign. Viewed in light of universal evolution, the death and extinction of individuals somehow did not matter. As one critic put it: "The philosophers of the ultra-evolutionary school put out of sight, in the scientific sweep of their social theories, two commonplace facts—individuality and death." The Enlightenment hoped death might be abolished: "those of the present appear to think that, if we will all be quiet and refrain from ill-omened words, it may be hushed up."[34]

Having construed natural selection as indirect equilibration, Spencer pursued a second strategy in denying that survival of the fittest operated in modern society. Describing an ascending scale, he explained that direct equilibration played by far the larger part among highly developed organisms. Among the "civilized human races" the process was "mainly direct." The *mainly* recognized the action of natural selection in "the destruction of those who are constitutionally too feeble to live, even [n.b.] with external aid." Since "social arrangements" preserved everyone else, "Survival of the fittest can scarcely at all act in such a way as to produce specialties of nature, either bodily or mental." Human progress in recent centuries "must be ascribed almost wholly to direct equilibration."[35]

This distinction reflected a general tendency of Spencer and his contemporaries to distinguish higher and lower stages in all development: barbarism and civilization, status and contract, militarism and industrialism. In this instance, he also joined the controversy that developed in the late sixties between Darwin and A. Russel Wallace as to whether natural selection altered bodily structure at all stages of evolution. Darwin believed it did. Wallace maintained that, with the attainment of a certain level of intelligence, mental changes superceded physical ones. Spencer preferred the thrust of Wallace's view. He himself had earlier identified the importance of cerebral development among the races of man. But he rejected Wallace's view that such cerebral development within societies resulted from the natural selection of spontaneous variations in the brain. Rather "functionally produced modifications" produced all changes. In sum, Spencer by the mid-1860s openly endorsed natural selection while at the same time denying its uniqueness (Darwin had merely described a "special" cause of evolution, Spencer the "general" one), and limiting its scope.[36]

Four

Between the publication of the *Biology* (1866) to *The Study of Sociology* (1873) developments in the world of affairs and in science conspired to alter Spencer's vision. The erosion of liberty seemed to him an increasing reality. Spencer's expanded catalogue of dangers included the "late catastrophes on the continent" (the Paris Commune), the corruption of post-Civil War America, and even the proto-welfare measures of the Gladstone ministry. The first revealed a spectre of socialism; the second a perversion of the antislavery crusade which Spencer applauded in *Social Statics*; and the third the fact that the Liberals could deprive England of her liberties no less than the Tories could. The subsequent growth of imperial fervor and labor militancy heightened this pessimism as the decade progressed. In England a "militant" society coexisted uneasily with an "industrial" one, he announced.[37]

Spencer conceived of this world more and more in biological rather than mechanical terms. This shift in perspective took several forms. Evolution became increasingly a *moving equilibrium* that ruled out the ultimate attainment of equilibrium in a static sense. *Dissolution,* which he had slighted in *First Principles,* balanced evolution in the revised edition (1875). An organic conception of society replaced the mechanistic and atomistic one of his earlier writings. Following Walter Bagehot and a growing school of biologically oriented anthropologists, Spencer stressed cohesion within social groups that fostered strength for struggle among them. Ethnographic evidence also eroded his confidence in the easy classification of barbarous and peaceful societies on an evolutionary scale. To Spencer the scientific vision of dissolution, struggle, and reversion was no more comforting than parallel trends in contemporary society.[38]

In separate exchanges with critics in the early 1870s Spencer suggested some implications of his altered vision. At issue was the definition of survival of the fittest. Depending on their persuasion, several critics charged that the phrase was tautological, untrue, and/or immoral. If it meant only that survivors survive, "it might have suggested itself even to a child." However, if translated to "Persistence of the Stronger" it was factually debatable and morally dubious. Accepting this construction, the clergyman James Martineau framed the charge that Spencerians underwrote cutthroat competition.[39]

Spencer mounted a two-pronged defense. Fittest meant neither best nor strongest, but merely accommodation to whatever conditions happened to exist. Affirming his new appreciation of dissolution, he noted that "retrograde metamorphoses" outnumber all others. "It is the survival of those who are constitutionally fittest to thrive under the conditions in which they are placed," he stated; "and very often that which, humanly speaking, is inferiority, causes the survival." Moreover, survival of the fittest described evolution in a somewhat peculiar, almost symbolic sense. Having reduced natural selection to indirect equilibration, he explained in a letter to *Nature,* he needed a term more appropriate to biology but lacking the teleological implications of a selector. Survival of the fittest was not a literal statement of everyday facts, but instead "the most convenient physiological equivalent for the purely physical statement (concerning equilibration)." In further cleansing the universe of metaphysics, Spencer subtly retreated from a belief in progress.[40]

The Study of Sociology (1873), a popular preview of Spencer's sociological system, mirrored his growing pessimism. Worried about the "unfit," Spencer urged "biological truths" as a basis for a "scientific policy." But he did not, as one critic charged, propose that natural selection be allowed to operate in present-day society. Rather he preached "biological lessons" in only the most general terms. He wished "simply to show that a rational policy must recognize certain general truths of Biology." Concerning natural selection he was notably evasive. "How far the mentally-superior may, with a balance of benefit to society, shield the mentally-inferior from the evil results of their inferiority, is a question too involved to be here discussed at length," he equivocated. "Most readers," he admitted in an enigmatic footnote, would conclude that he was "simply carrying out the views of Mr. Darwin in their application to the human race." But they were mistaken. He had anticipated Darwin in *Social Statics* and the "Theory of Population" (1852), and was merely restating his views. Thus Spencer, again asserting his primacy in the field of evolution, seemingly endorsed Darwin while muting the issue of natural selection.[41]

Concerning social policy, Spencer *had* trimmed his sails. "Rational criticisms," he confessed in conclusion, have "a depressing influence" on "visionary hopes." But he did not wish to paralyze activity. "The man of higher type must be content with greatly-moderated expectations, while he perseveres with undiminished effort," he wrote. "He has to see how comparatively little can be done, and yet find it worthwhile to do that little; so uniting philanthropic energy with philosophic calm."[42]

Spencer's critics however made "calm" increasingly difficult. With the publication of the first part of the *Principles of Ethics* (1879), he learned again that science was double-edged. Describing the evolution of the moral sentiments he traced the development of egoism and altruism. As societies advanced, social sympathy played an ever larger role in securing group security and hence the well being of each individual. Thus egoism and altruism, apparent opposites, were reconciled in the fully evolved, heterogeneous society. And, as Spencer made explicit in later installments of the *Ethics*, altruism or *beneficence* became a significant factor in survival.[43]

This scheme, essentially a recasting of utilitarianism, brought a predictable response. Since evolution implied a struggle for existence in which brute force triumphed, the very notion of an "evolutionary ethics" was contradictory, charged Henry Calderwood, a philosopher and long-time critic of Spencer's alleged agnosticism. More pointedly, Goldwin Smith, a noted British historian resident in Canada, wondered what answer Spencer would give to an organism "indisposed to altruism."

"Why," a Borgia or a Bonaparte will ask, "is the law (of survival of the fittest) to be confined to the case of the carnivores and herbivores? Do not I equally fulfill it by making a prey of the herbivores of humanity, or by destroying in any way I can other carnivores who stand in my way? If my acts are well adjusted to these ends, as Machiavelli says they are, why are they not good? The result will be that survival of the fittest which science proclaims to be the decree of Nature."

The answer, of course, was "the hope of a future state," a motive Smith thought merely a ruse whereby agnostics fill "the void left by the discarded hope of a future life." Should Spencer lose sight of the ideal, or come to share his critics view of nature—so Smith implied—morality would evaporate.[44]

Five

In *The Man vs. the State* (1884) Spencer appeared to fulfill Smith's prediction. In four articles, originally published in the *Contemporary Review,* sociology yielded to propaganda—and scholarship to near hysteria. Convinced that England was "on the highway to communism," Spencer described the dissolution of modern society. Liberals had betrayed their heritage. The result was a combination of imperialism and socialism that signalled reversion from the industrial to the military stage of society. The "new Toryism," as he labelled the Liberal apostasy, was coming, not receding. "The Coming Slavery" was an inevitable byproduct of "the current assumption . . . that there should be no suffering, and that society is to blame for that which exists."[45]

So persuaded, Spencer took a step that apparently contradicted his earlier position concerning natural selection and society. Quoting from *Social Statics,* he explained that Darwinism confirmed the earlier argument. "The beneficial results of the survival of the fittest" seemed to him "immeasurably greater" than they had earlier. Natural selection had been a major factor in yielding "present degrees of organization and adaptation," he continued. "And yet, strange to say, now that the truth is recognized by most cultivated people . . . now more than ever, in the history of the world, are they doing all they can to further the survival of the unfittest!"[46]

Natural laws should be left alone. Survival of the fittest was a natural law. Therefore survival of the fittest must go on unhindered. Spencer thus completed a syllogism he had studiously avoided, even denied. Critics, who claimed that laissez faire meant jungle law, welcomed the fact that Spencer made the equation explicit. Spencer himself was aware of the criticism that would follow. Nine out of ten readers, he predicted, would charge that he derived his principles "from the laws of brutes."[47]

Emile de Laveleye, the Belgian sociologist, quickly proved this prediction correct. Spencer was "anxious to see the law of the survival of the fittest and of natural selection adopted in human society." This position could be traced even in *Social Statics*. Spencer in reply denied he was simply applying Darwin to society, noting again that *Social Statics* antedated the *Origin of Species* and was in fact "an elaborate statement of the conditions under which, and limits within which, the natural process of elimination of the unfit should be allowed to operate." Restating the argument of the *Ethics* he noted that altruism fostered survival among the highly developed. "Aggression of every kind is hateful to me," Spencer added. Laveleye conceded that Spencer personally endòrsed no such conclusion. But, he added with more frankness than many critics, "it is important to ascertain whether the application of Spencerian or Darwinian laws is *likely to lead us.*" (emphasis mine)[48]

This exchange revealed that Spencer's marriage of Lamarck, Darwin, and universal evolution was coming unglued. In making natural selection a footnote to direct adaptation, Spencer found a place for Darwin in a universe of inexorable, mechanical law. In making adaptation and natural selection two aspects of the same law of force and then confining natural selection to early stages of development, Spencer in effect drew a distinction between the animal and human realms, while preserving the illusion that an identical law governed all nature, organic and inorganic. This distinction required the twin assumptions (a) that through all evolution direct adaptation plays a larger role than natural selection; and (b) that progress from barbarism to civilization makes this fact true *a fortiori* in modern society.

As the furor over *The Man vs. the State* died down, a final challenge to Spencer's position came from Thomas Henry Huxley, Spencer's long-standing critic. At issue again was the scope of natural selection, a question that assumed new urgency with the publication in the late 1880s of the theories of August Weismann, the German biologist who postulated the immutability of germ plasm. Weismann's followers, soon dubbed neo-Darwinians, insisted that acquired characteristics could not be inherited, a position with far reaching social implications.

Spencer quickly emerged as a leader of the *neo-Lamarckians*, as Weismann's opponents were termed. He particularly criticized Huxley, who seemed to him to emphasize natural selection to the point where it assumed "too much the character of a creed." But Spencer's position was itself equivocal, a measure of an acute dilemma. He admitted that he had over-emphasized use inheritance. He agreed that natural selection explained "the greater part of the facts." The inheritance of functionally produced modifications was merely a "minor part" of biological change, "very extensive though less."[49] Since he likewise qualified his earlier faith in progress from barbarism to civilization—indeed saw the two as coexisting in modern England—a series of awkward questions intruded. Why not assume that a primitive struggle for existence continued to occur? Why not admit that natural selection had work to do in modern England? But the logic of these questions led straight to policies Spencer abhorred: imperialism, militarism, industrial strife, and finally socialism.

His attempts to restate his previous position were agonizing. Survival of the fittest was a "convenient and indeed needful term." But it was merely symbolic of "actual agencies" that could not otherwise be expressed in "physiological terms." Direct adaptation, no matter how secondary or minor, was responsible for social development. Applied to pressing social issues, this meant that the perfection of peaceable industrialism, not imperialistic struggle, was the best guarantee of survival. Spencer conceded that real-world evidence for this generalization was thin. But he remained confident that "deductive interpretation" harmonized "with the several inferences reached by induction."[50] Huxley in another context asserted that Spencer's idea of a tragedy was a theory killed by a fact. Spencer in effect stated that such a thing was impossible.

In his Romanes lecture at Oxford in 1893, Huxley confronted Spencer head on. Viewing nature in neo-Darwinian terms, Huxley denied that nature offered a guide to individuals or society. In an obvious attack on Spencer, he charged that "evolutionary ethics" promoted the fallacy "that because . . . animals and plants have advanced in perfection of organization by means of struggle for existence and consequent 'survival of the fittest' [that] therefore men in society . . . must look to the same process to help them towards perfection." Huxley wished that struggle might be "rigorously suppressed." Ethics was a suspension of cosmic struggle, human values a legacy of past battle against the universe. Huxley concluded that men, guided by instinct and tradition, must henceforth "grope," faintly trusting "a larger hope of abatement of the essential evil of the world."[51] In essence, Huxley restated Hume against Locke, combining skepticism and traditionalism against the liberals' claim that social policy might be grounded in the laws of nature.

Although Spencer rejected Huxley's dualism, he was less certain than ever that nature contained an ideal, an *absolute* by which to judge the *relative* ethics of expediency and accommodation. He still insisted that awareness of an absolute must operate "if not consciously still unconsciously." Recognition of the ideal was essential, "vague as it may be, but still a recognition." But in his writing of the 1890s the recognition was vague indeed. The facts of struggle and change, no longer redeemed by a final goal, seemed inescapable. In a half-barbarous society, natural selection had a role to play. The result sometimes sounded like the social Darwinism that some critics termed the logic of his position. Yet its significance was different than that alleged, then or later. Far from buttressing the optimism of the fifties and sixties, his Darwinian diatribes, that today might be called liberal backlash, registered personal disillusionment and intellectual defeat.[52]

This new mood and altered vision surfaced most clearly in the revisions of earlier work Spencer undertook in his final years. In *Social Statics, Abridged and Revised* (1891) he eliminated reference to the overarching cosmic process that redeemed temporary pain and suffering. In other ways he made it clear that the ideal was neither forthcoming nor a blueprint to blueprint to which the real would eventually conform. Discussing the role of the predatory instinct in 1850, he carefully tempered its apparent harshness by stressing its ultimate benefits:

> Whilst the continuance of the old predatory instinct after the fulfilment of its original purpose, has retarded civilization by giving rise to conditions at variance with those of social life, it has subserved civilization by clearing the earth of inferior races of men. The forces which are working out the great scheme of perfect happiness, taking no account of incidental suffering, exterminate such sections of mankind as stand in their way, with the same sternness that they exterminate beasts of prey and herds of useless ruminants.

The revised version, however, was a blunt statement of fact:

> The forces at work exterminate such sections of mankind as stand in the way, with the same sternness that they exterminate beasts of prey and herds of useless animals.

Spencer omitted entirely the optimistic "Conclusion," in which he described how perfect law operated in an imperfect world.[53]

A "Theory of Population," in the version of the first edition of the *Principles of Biology*, underwent a similar fate. In the 1860s Spencer wrote:

> And after having caused, as it ultimately must, the due peopling of the globe and the raising of its habitable parts into the highest state of culture . . . the pressure of population, as it gradually finishes its work, must gradually bring itself to an end.

In the second edition of 1899 the same passage concluded: "the pressure of population must gradually approach to an end—an end, however, which for the reasons given it cannot absolutely reach."[54]

In this same revision of the *Biology* and in a sixth edition of *First Principles* (1900), Spencer pictured the universe of man and nature as a state of continual and endless flux. In the first edition of the *Biology*, equilibrium promised, "Changes numerical, social, organic, must . . . work unceasingly toward a state of harmony." In *First Principles* he equated this state with "the greatest perfection and the most complete happiness." In the revisions of both works he eliminated these guarantees entirely.[55]

In this world of flux, with the outcome of evolution unclear, the reconciliation of opposites was more difficult. In no case was this difficulty more apparent than in the discussions of beneficence (altruism) that occupied so much of Spencer's attention in the final installments of the *Ethics* and other works of the nineties. In "Justice" (1891), he restated the scheme of *Social Statics* whereby evolution guaranteed the harmonious growth of both efficiency *and* benevolence. Natural selection, in this restatement, produced an industrial and a social fitness, the latter including a charitable impulse. Yet Spencer now believed that the result was an insoluable dilemma. Public and private charities were doing much to "save the bad from the extreme results of their badness, . . . unmanageable multitudes of them," it seemed. Spencer confessed his inability to resolve the problem with which he had wrestled for three decades. "If left to operate in all its sternness the principle of the survival of the fittest . . . would quickly clear away the degraded." Popular sentiment made this course "impracticable." Spencer felt that "no serious evil would result from relaxing its operation if the degraded were to leave no progeny." However the numbers were too great. "The mass of effete humanity to be dealt with is so large as to make one despair: the problem seems insoluable," he concluded. "Certainly, if solvable, it is to be solved only through suffering."[56]

Suffering, pain, and struggle, redeemed only by an uncertain ideal, thereafter became a recurring motif. No longer a mere incidence in the lower stages of evolution, suffering seemed in the nineties a suitable punishment for the "unwise" policies that "brought into existence large numbers who are unadapted to the requirements of social life." "We cannot repress and gradually diminish this body of relatively worthless people without inflicting much pain." Revising the *Biology*, he made the same point in explicitly Darwinian terms by "advisedly" adding a warning that the Poor Laws were "hindrances to the survival of the fittest." In the later works, these social Darwinistic pronouncements joined visions of the cataclysm that would befall a people "emasculated by fostering their feebles." Perhaps, he decided toward the close of his life, catastrophe would be beneficial. Hard times "may open people's eyes and make them repent," he wrote. "However heavily the penalty they may have to bear, it cannot be too heavy to please me."[57]

Spencer's willingness to entertain, however crankily, a principle whose efficacy he initially doubted perhaps reflected a conscious desire to grant natural selection the larger role in society he accorded it in biology. But, more fundamentally, his jeremiads registered the breakdown of the assumptions that allowed him to find in nature an ideal scheme while pretending to look only at the "facts." The gap between fact and value, is and ought, change and progress could no longer be hushed up. Confronted by this realization, Spencer vascillated between celebrating a frankly intuitive ideal and recording the dreary contemporary scene. In 1886 he gladly accepted one critic's characterization, "Mr. Spencer against all England." A decade later, exhilarating martyrdom hardened into stern warnings and visions of the suffering that would follow the free play of survival of the fittest. In 1896 he abandoned a projected fourth volume of the *Principles of Sociology* on "Progress" because it was "impossible . . . for an invalid of seventy-six to deal adequately with topics so extensive and complex." Describing no ideal, his final book, aptly titled *Facts and Comments* (1902), cataloged the evils of imperialism, regimentation, "athleticism" and other tendencies that were leading to a "complete slavery . . . which [the world] will fully deserve." Unillumined by the ideal, even material progress seemed a sham. "The nineteenth century," he wrote in 1900, "bequeathed many remains of existing civilization, but it may well be doubted whether they will be as interesting as those which old times have bequeathed to us."[58]

The conventional portrait of Spencer's social Darwinism is both inaccurate and ironic. Rather than buttressing his initial position, the Darwinian revolution immensely complicated the strategy of basing social theory on laws of nature. Asserting that nature provided no guide, Huxley stripped the Creator of what metaphysical clothing the Enlightenment had left Him. He further suggested that henceforth social theorists must look to tradition, intuition, or perhaps human will for guidance. At the same time Darwin's rhetoric of struggle and survival provided the perfect vocabulary to caricature the alleged inhumanity and brutality of modern society, and to parody anyone who continued to ground policy in natural law or even science.

The label social Darwinism, as eventually applied to Spencer, made good propaganda for the same reasons it made bad history. Distorting Spencer's development from *Social Statics* to *Facts and Comments*, it ignored the forces in midcentury life and thought that sustained his original synthesis, and it obscured the crisis of faith that a number of midcentury liberals underwent in the 1890s, a disillusionment that anticipated the more celebrated cultural crisis following World War I. Spencer's lapse into pessimism, and his apparently cynical acceptance of suffering as punishment for abandoning older ideals echoed sentiments that were already producing a variety of "naturalisms" in literature and social thought.

Although Spencer's critics found it convenient to remember the dyspeptic Jeremiah, it was not this Spencer whom Americans welcomed to their shores in the early 1880s. By the time *The Man vs. the State* appeared, the original Spencer vogue was already past its peak. If during the 1880s and 1890s a few among the older generation of Spencerians echoed their mentor's gloom over the drift of events, more remembered the bright promise of the early work that first attracted them to this Victorian Aristotle.

3. Philanthropic Energy and Philosophic Calm

[If] we are not mistaken, it is [in America] that Mr. Spencer is to find his largest and fittest audience . . . . [His writings] betray a profound sympathy with the best spirit of our institutions, and that noble aspiration for the welfare and improvement of society which can hardly fail to commend them to the more liberal and enlightened portions of the American public.
    Edward L. Youmans, "Preface," First Principles
    by Herbert Spencer (1865), p. 10.

When Carlyle speaks of the universe as in very truth the star-domed city of God, and reminds us that through every crystal and through every grass-blade . . . the glory of a present God still shines, he means pretty much the same thing that Mr. Spencer means, save that he speaks with the language of poetry . . . and not the precise, formal language of science.
    John Fiske, Spencer on the Americans (1883)
    ed. E. L. Youmans, p. 55.

One

In August 1882, Herbert Spencer sailed for New York. During his three-months' stay in America, he toured Niagara Falls and as far west as Pittsburgh, where he visited Andrew Carnegie. The highlight of the trip was a public banquet at Delmonico's restaurant in New York in November, arranged hastily but successfully by Edward L. Youmans, Spencer's American literary agent and chief supporter. On the dock, awaiting his return to England, Spencer grasped the hands of Carnegie and Youmans. "Here," he proclaimed, "are my two best American friends."[1]

The visit triggered a flood of rumor. Denied an interview with the elusive Spencer, American reporters speculated on his alleged eccentricities, personal and intellectual. "He subsists entirely on dry toast and sardines," wrote one. Another reported that Spencer "is accustomed to carrying around with him a bag of hops, which when placed under his head has a soporific effect." A third imagined a conversation between Youmans and Spencer concerning the voyage:

> The Doctor: My dear Master, how did you enjoy that unceasing redistribution of matter and motion, which was brought about by the conveyance of your homogeneity across that condensation of the primordial nebulosity, which men have come to denominate the Atlantic ocean?
>
> Mr. Spencer: My dear disciple, not to occasion any disagreement between the objective order of phenomena and the subjective order of thought, I must say that upon the ultimate congeries of ultimate atoms the predominant disintegration of matter occasioned a dissipation of motion in my abdominal viscera which, though it was occasioned by the environment, was excessively disagreeable to the ganglionic interiority, and produced such an abdominable cephalagia that the coherent aggregate of sensations was far different from hedonic.[2]

In an actual conversation with Youmans, a widely reported interview on October 20, Spencer set these rumors to rest. His only discomfort on the voyage arose from insomnia, he noted. "Subsequent accounts of me in respect of disorders, diet, dress, habit, etc., have been equally wide of the mark." In the body of the interview, Spencer discussed America's republican institutions. While praising the nation's material progress and the energy of her citizens, he warned of dangers besetting her political institutions. "Bossism," a plague on democracy, was but one example of Americans' tendency to allow minor violations of their liberties. Responding to a suggestion from Youmans, he denied that education of the masses was the answer. "Not lack of information, but lack of moral sentiment, is the root of the evil," he continued. Evolution, as ever, held the key. "The American nation will be a long time in evolving its ultimate form," he predicted, "but . . . its ultimate form will be high."[3]

A convenient symbol, the Spencer visit became the focus of conflicting estimates of the nature and extent of his influence in the United States. The *New York Tribune* at the time judged the public interview with Youmans "one of the most profound estimates of the tendencies of republican institutions in the United States . . . ever . . . formed." In later years the Delmonico's banquet became visible proof of the romance between Spencer and American capitalism. Although the speakers of the evening showed an "imperfect" grasp of Spencer's thought, the farewell embraces by Youmans and Carnegie—like the entire visit—"symbolized the harmony of the new science and its interpreters with the outlook of a business civilization," wrote Richard Hofstadter. Yet it was this same imperfect grasp that convinced Irvin Wyllie that Spencer's admirers were a minority of intellectuals rather than businessmen.[4]

Who then were Spencer's disciples? What was the nature of his appeal in America during the Gilded Age? At the outset it should be noted that, if Spencer was not a folk hero, he was at least widely known among educated Americans from the 1860s to the turn of the century. A subscription list for installments of the Synthetic Philosophy included New England's leading intellectuals. The best periodicals, including the *Atlantic Monthly* and the *North American Review* received his work favorably. *Popular Science Monthly*, established as a platform for his views in 1872, attracted 11,000 readers during its first year. American sales of Spencer's books topped half-a-million, if one includes unauthorized editions. Those in a position to know attested to this influence. "Probably no other philosopher," wrote the publisher Henry Holt, "ever had such a vogue as Spencer had from about 1870 to 1890."[5]

At the same time, Spencer was consistently controversial—suspected by individuals who might "logically" have welcomed his message if they understood it—and for this reason often ignored. Although the New England intelligentsia gave him a hearing, some rejected the Synthetic Philosophy while more simply ignored it. "Mr. Spencer has what Tallyrand calls the weakness of omniscience," wrote Thomas Wentworth Higginson, denying that Spencer had made "any vast enlargement or further generalization of the modern scientific doctrine of evolution." Ralph Waldo Emerson, in a remark that infuriated E. L. Youmans, termed the Englishman a "stock writer."[6]

Theologians blasted Spencer's materialism and atheism. A reviewer for the *Methodist Quarterly* pronounced the universe of *First Principles* an "awful tenement," and the Unknowable an "almighty *Dead-Head.*" "An unintelligent absolute is an infinite Fool, and fools be they who accept its supremacy." In a similar vein, Charles Loring Brace, founder of the Children's Aid Society and a leading spokesman for industrial education, opposed Spencer less on social than religious grounds. "Would mankind not take chloroform if they had no future but Spencer's," he wrote a friend. "No individual continuance, no God, no superior powers, only evolution working towards a benevolent society here, and perfection on earth, with great doubts whether it could succeed, and, if it succeeded, whether it would pay."[7]

The doors of academia remained closed to Spencer. The Harvard faculty lined up squarely against him. Despite affinities between his own philosophy and Common Sense realism, Noah Porter, the president of Yale and a leading spokesman for the Scottish philosophy, attempted to ban Spencer's work from his institution. In *The Nation* (1870), a widely used text in politics, Elisha Mulford relegated Spencer to two brief footnotes. "It would scarcely be necessary to notice these statements of this theory [that the state is a necessary evil]," he commented, "but if they be received in the thought of a people, they must work inevitable disaster."[8]

Other individuals who might "logically" have welcomed Spencer's support were businessmen who also found his work tainted with an *odium theologicum*. An illuminating instance involved Chauncey Depew, railroad lawyer, prominent politician, and one of the most popular after dinner speakers of his generation. A liberal Republican in the 1870s, he moved steadily upward in his party's counsels and as U.S. Senator seemed by the turn of the century to have become the archtypical conservative— a fit target for the attack launched upon him in David Graham Phillips's *Treason of the Senate*. Depew also later joined the gallery of social Darwinists, when in his *Memoirs* he described the guests at one of the great banquets of the eighties as "the survival of the fittest of the various settlers of New York."[9]

But did this remark, forty years later, accurately represent Depew in the 1880s? During the 1920s when the *Memoirs* appeared, liberal Christians faced a fundamentalist reaction, unlike the earlier years when Darwin remained suspect even among educated Christians. Depew's speeches of the earlier years reflected a distinct uneasiness over what he termed "the shibboleth known in all the schools of America, that evolution is the great principle of modern science." In one speech he made a humorous play on the language of Darwinism, but grew serious in discussing the theory itself. "I am a practical man, overwhelmed with the cares of business," he observed, disputing John Fiske in a speech of 1886. "I believe in the Old Testament and the New Testament precisely as they are presented by Christianity." He disagreed equally with the Higher Criticism which "dismisses the Bible as entirely a mess of legend, and with Professor Fiske, who accepts it with an interpretation entirely his own." As to the theory of evolution itself: "They tell us of evolution from dust to monkey and then to man; but all the scientists have never found the missing link."[10]

Other businessmen also refused the help of evolutionism in making the case for classical economics. Writing in 1872, the Boston manufacturer Edward Atkinson attempted to rescue economics from its image as a dismal science, an image fostered by its popular identification with Malthusianism and, by extension, Darwinism. "That the creator of the universe can have placed men upon earth to be swept away by war, pestilence, and famine, for all time . . . is to my mind an utterly atheistic and abhorrent doctrine on simple *a priori* grounds," he wrote. He thus rejected the "fatalistic philosophy" which held that life must always be a "mere struggle for existence." Discussing the financial panic two years later, the editor of the *Commercial and Financial Chronicle* also sought to separate classical theory from evolution. "Some cynical observers may see in these commercial troubles a normal 'struggle for existence' ending in 'the survival of the fittest,' " he wrote. But he would leave this "fashionable philosophy . . . to spin its shining web and to apply its specious theories where it can." Agreeing that "temporary disaster to individuals" would in the long run be for the good of the country, the *Chronicle* preferred "the old adage: 'Experience keeps a dear school but she teaches well.' "[11]

American Spencerians should be judged against this background. Lacking a readymade base of institutional support, most of Spencer's disciples operated outside the colleges or the churches. John Fiske, a Harvard graduate, found himself, like Emerson a generation earlier, often at odds with his alma mater. No leading Spencerians were scientists. In fact, in an exchange in the *Nation* in the late 1860s, Fiske and Henry Holt, a young Yale graduate who also embraced Spencer, revealed a certain sensitivity to the charge that scientific experts held Spencer in low regard. Neither had the Spencerians any illusions concerning his popularity among the general public, aside perhaps from a reputation for being controversial. "As for the 'general public' having *any* opinion of its own about the merits of *First Principles* or the *Psychology*," Fiske wrote, "I imagine it is about as well qualified to have an opinion about Schraut's 'Physikalische Studien' or Schleicher's 'Vergleichende Grammatik.' "[12] What the Spencerians lacked in numbers or prestige, however, they made up in enthusiasm. A minority cause from the 1860s to the 1880s, Spencerianism provided an important link between midcentury American liberalism and the New Liberalism of the progressive era.

Two

Although *Social Statics* appeared in 1850, Spencer was virtually unknown in the United States before the end of the Civil War. An early supporter and later a close personal friend was a Salem businessman named Edward A. Silsbee, who apparently displayed sufficient enthusiasm to offend some Bostonians in the early fifties (among them the senior Oliver Wendell Holmes). Although Silsbee left no record of the nature of his enthusiasm, he was instrumental in bringing to Spencer's attention the work of Edward Livingston Youmans, then a popular lecturer on scientific topics. After journeying to Britain to meet Spencer in 1862, Youmans became his American literary agent and chief propagandist.

The background for this early interest in Spencer was the crusade against slavery and the warfare between religion and science, not business and wage rates. In *Social Statics* Spencer consigned slavery to the "savage stage" of social development. Its elimination was a measure of man's forward progress, he implied, as he warned anyone against using the past as justification for present policy. Youmans and Fiske welcomed this message. "The great slave system . . . had well nigh paralyzed the mind of the nation," Youmans wrote Spencer in 1864. "But the war has broken the spell. I have never known such boldness of inquiry and demand for first principles." Inspired by the Emancipation Proclamation, young John Fiske, still a student at Harvard, confessed that, while he was not an abolitionist, he found scientific reason for wanting a northern victory. "No one can start from 'Social Statics' and logically deduce conclusions which shall be other than unfavorable to the South at present," he wrote his fiancée. The reformer Carl Schurz, in his testimonial speech at the Spencer banquet at Delmonico's, remembered reading *Social Statics* by candlelight while bivouacking during the war. Had the South read it, he surmised, the North might have been spared the need to "hammer" home its lessons.[13]

The conflict between science and religion, well underway before the appearance of the *Origin of Species*, also conditioned reaction to Spencer. For more than a century, educated Americans escaped the potential skepticism of British empiricism by adopting the moral sense doctrines of the Scottish Common Sense school. Spencer restated this position within an evolutionary framework. "The moral sense is triumphantly rescued from the assaults of Paley and Bentham," wrote the *Atlantic Monthly*, reviewing the first American edition of *Social Statics*, "and is declared capable of generating a fundamental intuition which may be expanded into a scientific morality."[14]

Youmans expanded this point in the preface to the first American edition of Spencer's essays. Finite man could not "understand" the infinite, but he could "sense" it. Spencer "demonstrates that though we cannot grasp the Infinite in *thought*, we can realize it in *consciousness*," Youmans explained. "He shows that though by the laws of thinking we are rigorously prevented from forming a *conception* of the Incomprehensible, Omnipotent power by which we are acted upon in all phenomena, yet we are, by the laws of thought, equally prevented from ridding ourselves of the *consciousness* of this power." The doctrine of the Unknowable was thus a positive not a negative doctrine, a consciousness that permeated all thought and activity.[15]

To these early supporters Spencer promised a renewal of idealism. The earliest notices of *Social Statics* and the essays bristled with phrases such as Truth and Humanity, the service of science and society, progress of thought, and the enlightenment of the human mind. To those who feared that science had somehow fragmented the universe, Spencer provided a new unity. Youmans repeatedly stressed the comprehensive and universal character of the system. Spencer's philosophy, he noted, "combines the precision of science with the harmony and unity of universal truth."[16]

"The peculiar condition of American society has made your writings far more fruitful here than in Europe," the clergyman Henry Ward Beecher wrote Spencer in 1866. This "condition" he explained related to "the cause of emancipation and enlightenment of the human mind . . . so dear to us all." In its review of the first American edition of *Social Statics*, the *Atlantic Monthly* agreed that the work had "special application to the needs of great masses of our countrymen." This "need" it turned out was also to bolster traditional ideals. "The calm deductions of reason are brought to enforce the distinctive American doctrines in which the loyal citizen has sentimental belief." The enemy was "Giant Indifference," the offspring of Bentham, Comte, and others who put "all the tares and brambles of society [under their] . . . microscope." This new cynicism breathed "a ghastly whisper, that money, popular reputation, political power, and the sensual gratifications which these may command are alone worth getting off the sofa to realize." Against this mood, Spencer was "a very able combatant." Although less enamored of Spencer, the philosopher Chauncey Wright put it succinctly: "Moral idealism colors all Mr. Spencer's views, both in science and politics. This gains him a popular hearing, especially with the youth of democratic America."[17]

By the early 1870s, John Fiske (1842-1901), the popular historian and lecturer, was the leading spokeman for this ethico-philosophic strain of American Spencerianism. Feared in the orthodox Congregationalism of Middletown, Connecticut, Fiske journeyed through revivalism to positivism and finally Cosmic Theism (or Cosmism, as his system was known) based largely on Spencer's *First Principles.* Following a conversion experience at age fourteen, Fiske shared briefly the emotional fervor of antebellum revivalism. During the year 1858-59, however, he discovered a number of ideas that quickly weaned him from traditional Christianity: the liberal theology of Horace Bushnell; the radical Unitarianism of Theodore Parker; the positivism of Henry Thomas Buckle (a starting point for many later Spencerians); and among German authors, von Humboldt's *Cosmos*, and Goethe's *Faust*. "What's war," he remarked when battle began in 1861, "when a fellow has 'Kosmos' on his shelf, and 'Faust' on his table." During Fiske's entire career, society and its struggles took a backseat to philosophy.[18]

During his first year at Harvard (1860-61), Fiske discovered Spencer, who became his private tutor, as it were, in an otherwise dreary curriculum. Having rejected Yale orthodoxy for the promise of Harvard liberalism, Fiske found the faculty suffocating and their rules insufferable. Required to attend church, he received a public admonition his second year for reading Comte during Sunday services. Darwinism was also a hot issue. Botany professor Asa Gray proclaimed Cosmic Theism and the geologist Louis Agassiz mobilized almost everyone else against evolution. To Fiske, however, Darwin was but one of the great "English Positivists," an assumption that shaped his later accommodation of natural selection within the Spencerian framework. In the Cambridge of the sixties, positivism alone was enough to win one a reputation for religious radicalism. This suspicion clung to Fiske despite his later efforts to make Spencer more palatable to America's religious sensibilities.[19]

In the *Outlines of Cosmic Philosophy* (1874), his first major work, Fiske completed his intellectual migration. An expansion of earlier lectures, the massive study began in 1869 as a survey of positivism, synthesizing the work of Comte, Lewes, J. S. Mill, and Spencer. As the work developed, Fiske rejected Comte entirely, basing the work more squarely on Spencer. But it was Spencer with a difference. Aware of audience sensitivity to attacks on religion, anxious to quiet the fears of family and friends that he had become an infidel, Fiske made his system distinctly theistic. Writing to his mother on the eve of the publication of the *Cosmic Philosophy*, he underlined this point: "If I were to say that my chief comfort in affliction would be the recognition that there is a Supreme Power manifested in the totality of phenomena, the workings of which are not like the workings of intelligence but far beyond and above them, and which are obviously tending to some grand and worthy result, even though my individual happiness gets crushed in the process . . . you would probably reply, 'Why this is Christianity!' Well, so it is, I think."[20]

The title of the *Cosmic Philosophy* itself suggested further differences in emphasis between the Englishman and his American disciple. Spencer's initial concern was social change: his Synthetic Philosophy was an attempt to validate his vision of industrial utopia. Fiske's interest was religion. "Above all," his most recent biographer has written, "he wanted a universe that would be both emotionally and logically compelling.[21] Spencer recoiled at Fiske's use of *cosmic*, and ordered that *synthetic philosophy* be henceforth the running title of all his works. Warning Spencer that Fiske might nonetheless carry the day, Youmans again captured the spirit of New World Spencerianism. "Nothing short of the Cosmic," he confided, "will satisfy the American spread-eaglism."[22]

Fiske's philosophy was inherently conservative in that he stressed the slowness of change, which he neither wanted nor urged. However, the context was also usually religious. His system would bring no religious revolution, no attacks on existing churches, he assured readers in the conclusion of the *Cosmic Philosophy*. In the one section in which he discussed social evolution—published earlier in the *North American Review* under the title "From Brute to Man"—Fiske differed little from the speculations of A. R. Wallace, whose work he described as "one of the most brilliant contributions ever yet made to the Doctrine of Evolution." Like Wallace, he believed that natural selection ceased operating on bodily factors with the appearance of the human brain. "And hence in the future as in the recent past," he told readers of the *North American Review*, "the dominant fact in the career of humanity is not physical modification but civilization." Giving his theory a Spencerian twist he argued further that the prolongation of infancy gave rise to the family and through it to morality, the substitution of altruism for egoism, and ultimately to religion. He thus sanitized the overt spiritualism of Wallace's version, while preserving his central tenet concerning future mental development. Like Wallace he coupled these lofty ideals with a belief in the superiority of "higher" over "lower" races—a cultural ethnocentrism and incipient racism that later readers found offensive and which led to the indictment of Fiske as a proto-imperialist. On the whole, however, Fiske continued to ignore the current scene.[23]

In this same spirit, reviewers, many still hostile to the materialistic implications of Spencerianism, discussed the *Cosmic Philosophy* almost exclusively in its bearing on religion. Faulting Fiske for blurring the difference between idealism and materialism, the *Nation* felt that Cosmism, despite postulating the existence of God, was "ill-fitted to replace the martyr-zeal of Christianity." The *Atlantic Monthly* also found it a "faltering pause in the progress from anthropomorphic theism to the undisturbed indifference of science." "The Positivists will be as puzzled as ever," the reviewer wrote, "to understand how the Cosmists can swear so stoutly by their own law of relativity, and yet smuggle in the much-coveted but contraband belief in external reality."[24]

Although Fiske later published numerous essays on Spencer and evolutionism, he remained essentially uninterested in the social views of his mentor. During the 1880s, as his theism became more pronounced, representatives of various Protestant denominations hailed his religious essays.

At the same time, Cosmic Theism proved no less immune to Darwinism than Spencer's social optimism. "His acceptance of the laws of natural-selection and of the development of life upon the earth is full and unreserved," wrote a caustic reviewer of *The Destiny of Man* (1884); "but, having committed himself upon these points, he proceeds to construct sophistical distinctions between man and the lower animals, in order to provide a support for the optimistic conclusions he has in view."[25]

Here was the issue that Darwinism posed from the start. Was man distinct from nature or not? If the former, was not the positivistic quest for a universe of law fatally compromised? If the latter, was mankind not reduced to an unacceptable brutality? These same questions lived to haunt other Spencerians who in these same years were probing his sociology.

Three

By the mid-1860s the magic phrase was *social science*, a relatively new term that had gained respectability in the war years. Antebellum social science, inspired by Comte and often linked with communalism, was radical and utopian. During the 1860s the movement turned conservative, trading utopian vision for the more patient study of *social laws*. It was in this climate that Spencer first entered the mainstream of American social science.[26]

An early example of social Spencerianism was the *New York Social Science Review* (1865-66), the official organ of the Society for the Advancement of Social Science formed in New York in 1862. During its two-year existence this journal gained national attention. Aimed at "publicists, legislators, editors, teachers, bankers and merchants," it sought to bring social science directly to the halls of Congress, and at one point claimed success in reshaping the nation's internal revenue system.[27]

Its editors were avowed Spencerians and typical of the educated professionals who provided much of his early audience. Simon Sterne (1839-1901), twenty-six-years-old, was admitted to the Pennsylvania bar at twenty and was already a successful lecturer on current affairs. Alexander Del Mar (1836-1926), a twenty-nine-year-old mining engineer turned journalist, earlier worked for *DeBow's Review*, *Hunt's Merchant's Magazine*, and the *Commercial and Financial Chronicle*. Amateurs in social science, both men were professionals by training and instinct. Each had received the latest in advanced training in their respective fields: Sterne at the University of Pennsylvania and Heidelberg; Del Mar in England and at the Madrid School of Mines. Cosmopolitan in outlook, urban in interests, neither had links or sympathy with an older, rural America. The jack-of-all-trades was the sign of a "barbarous" America, Sterne wrote in a revealing passage. Specialization was the mark of "civilization." In later years each worked in light of this perspective to reshape America, championing reforms only a later generation would brand patrician or genteel.[28]

In their editorials these young men defended free trade, private property, and laissez faire. In their view, the Civil War gave these issues special urgency: with Lincoln's excessive centralization of the executive; skyrocketing taxes; the tariff; shipping subsidies; and—as a last straw—appropriation of public funds for a world's fair. These and related measures were ranked in orderly lists of "over-legislation," and "true legislation"—the phrases echoing Spencer.

Praise of Spencer was sometimes lavish. "We do not think that we are asserting too much when we say, that, [from *Social Statics*] will date modern social science," they wrote, hailing the first American edition. They particularly commended Spencer's essays on "Progress," "Railway Morals," "Railway Policy," and of course, "Over-Legislation." At the same time, they had few illusions concerning Spencer's popularity, but pictured him rather as appealing to an educated elite such as themselves:

> It is, perhaps, idle to hope that Spencer will ever become a popular author, but he is fast becoming a well-understood and appreciated thinker. His direct influence will, in all probability, be restricted to a circle composed of a few thinking men in the community, but that suffices; and from that circle will be reflected . . . upon the outside world, the light of his ideas . . . .

In this same spirit, Sterne reported enthusiastically on a personal meeting with Spencer during a trip to England.[29]

Spencer, although the latest oracle, served alongside earlier theorists. The *Social Science Review* in fact focused almost exclusively on the specifics of Spencer's essays, ignoring the conceptual framework that distinguished *First Principles* and his later work. "Natural laws control as well the actions of men as the rest of the domain of nature," Sterne wrote, in a characteristic statement; "and legislation as a general rule, is a mere hindrance and impediment to the full, free, and harmonious operation of these natural laws." Although Spencerian in tone, the source in this case was the work of the physiocrats.[30]

Nor did this quest for social laws breed indifference or a fatalistic acceptance of the status quo. During the 1870s Sterne worked actively for municipal reforms and a civil service. He urged the professionalization of social science and its inclusion in the law school curriculum. On occasion, he seemed almost to anticipate the *sociological jurisprudence* of two decades later. With social science as a part of law school training, he wrote, "every student . . . would understand the law not only as it is, but as it should be; and would, at all events, comprehend the direction that reformatory measures should take . . . so as to promote the object of all human efforts—human happiness." Although he remained generally true to the orthodoxies of classical economics, he took an active part in railway reform, and, apparently forgetting the lessons of Spencer's essays, eventually defended the Interstate Commerce Act. Although Sterne rarely mentioned Spencer in his later writings, he paid sentimental homage to his early enthusiasm in joining the celebrants at Delmonico's in 1882, perhaps aware that the Englishman had helped galvanize his reform energies.[31]

Del Mar broke more dramatically from the announced policies of the *Social Science Review*. In 1866 he became director of the National Bureau of Statistics, despite the fact that the creation of such an agency appeared in the *Social Science Review* as an instance of over-legislation. Active in municipal reform, he supported the Liberal Republicans in 1872, and later pursued a successful career within the federal bureaucracy. Opposing the gold standard in favor of bi-metallism, he once chided an opponent for parading the "great laws of Nature" in defense of "immutable principles of money."[32]

While one may debate the merits of patrician reform, these activities fail to sustain charges of "indifference" or "paralysis" of the reform spirit. Rather they confirm the energizing effects of Spencer's early work on social thought no less than on religion and philosophy. The *Social Science Review* anticipated the theoretical impulse from which later progressives would build their visions of *sociocracy* and the regulatory state. Working for more efficient government, Sterne and Del Mar also helped create the administrative basis upon which this later program would rest.

Four

During the 1870s Edward Livingston Youmans (1821-1887) became the chief spokesman of social Spencerianism in America. Born in Albany County, New York, of predominantly New England Puritan stock, Youmans enjoyed few of the educational advantages of others within the social science movement. Until age sixteen he attended the district school, when not helping his father on the family farm. From age eighteen to twenty-three, he suffered from eye troubles that rendered him temporarily blind. Denied a collegiate education, he anticipated, as he wrote his sister, "an eternity of tripled, yea quadrupled misery."[33]

Science and Spencer freed him from this slough of despond. Several elements in his background prepared the way. Like Spencer, Youmans encountered the wonders of technology firsthand when the industrial revolution remained bright with promise. From his father, a sometime wagonmaker, he absorbed the lore of Yankee ingenuity. At the Youmans's home, neighbors discussed the latest laborsaving devices and traded tales of steamboats plying the nearby Hudson and experimental locomotives then being developed. Like Spencer, he matured in an atmosphere of political and religious radicalism. An ardent abolitionist, the senior Youmans was viewed with suspicion and hostility by many townfolk. To young Edward, if his biographer is to be believed, abolition assumed a personal dimension when a young black, a close boyhood friend, was later sold into slavery. A freethinker in religion, the elder Youmans also provided inspiration for his son's later assault on religious orthodoxy.

Youmans discovered the latest in scientific theory in the library of close family friend Ransom Cook. Manufacturer, inventor and a freethinker of local note, Cook personally symbolized the union of science and liberality that became the bedrock of Youmans's mature thought. In Cook's library, he found Robert Chambers's *Vestiges of Creation* (1844), his first glimpse of evolution. Although he later heard Louis Agassiz condemn the work as "unworthy of notice by any serious scientific man" (as indeed it was, although not necessarily for the reasons Agassiz believed), the seed was planted. As happened with John Fiske somewhat later, Agassiz unwittingly made a convert to the development theory he opposed.

During the 1850s and 1860s, Youmans pursued a successful career as a popular lecturer and writer on scientific subjects. In 1851 he produced a *Class Book of Chemistry*, in which he outlined his faith in science on the eve of his discovery of Spencer. No mere catalog of facts, science in his view was an ongoing process whereby the developing mind achieved unity with the natural world. The fact that nature was bound by immutable laws was an aspect of its infinite beauty, he wrote in a passage almost Emersonian in tone:

> The superiority of natural sciences over all other objects of study . . .
> is conceded as a fact of experience by the ablest teachers. This
> cannot be otherwise; for the infinite wisdom of the Creator is
> nowhere so perfectly displayed as in the wonderful adaptation which
> exists between the young mind and the natural world with which
> it is encompassed. On the one hand, there is the realm of Nature,
> endless in the variety of its objects, indescribable in its beauty,
> immutable in its order, boundless in its beneficence, and ever

admirable in the simplicity and harmony of its laws; on the other hand there is the young intellect, whose earliest trait is curiosity, which asks numberless questions, pries into the reasons of things and seeks to find out their causes as if by the spontaneous promptings of instinct.

A similar spirit informed his other early works: *The Chemical Atlas* (1854) and the *Handbook of Household Science* (1857). Older ideas of knowledge, he wrote, "drew all things inward, engulfing them in a maelstrom of selfishness." "Science" was "radiant and outflowing like the sun."[34]

The appearance of *Popular Science Monthly* in 1872 capped a decade of efforts to bring Spencerianism to America. Although Youmans first discovered Spencer in the mid-1850s, his working relationship with him began with a personal visit to Britain in 1862. During the sixties he arranged American editions of Spencer's essays, and of *Social Statics*. The early issues of *Popular Science* served as a vehicle for *The Study of Sociology*, an attempt to popularize the sociological views Spencer later elaborated in successive installments of the *Principles of Sociology*. Youmans knew it was an uphill battle. Both the *Atlantic Monthly* and *Harper's* rejected the manuscript. Likewise Horace Greeley of the *New York Tribune* upon hearing Spencer's name responded that he was "dead and forever opposed to the whole laissez faire school, and if the articles contained any of that he didn't want them."[35] At this point, Youmans decided to start his own magazine.

A journal of science and current affairs, *Popular Science* contained more social Spencerianism than any previous publication. For one thing, Youmans simply understood Spencer better than any other American save Fiske. For another, the worsening political and social situation of the seventies gave issues of corruption and industrial conflict new prominence. The laws of nature, earlier evidence of the glory of Creation, seemed now to be reason why legislative "meddling" was dangerous. There were natural laws in trade, as "harmonious as the solar system," Youmans lectured supporters of the Civil War "greenbacks." Progress and "improvement of the social condition" were to be credited "not to politics but to the laws of nature and the spontaneous agencies of social life."[36]

Youmans's specific recommendations were the staples of Gilded Age liberalism: free trade, hard money, and good government. To these he added such special causes as the creation of an international copyright law and the reform of education, which in its present form seemed to him a "smattering of languages, the cramming for examinations . . . and the labeling of degrees." On labor issues he was notably moderate, avoiding the stridency that crept into such journals as the *Nation*. "So long as strikes are peaceful," he wrote in 1872, "they are legitimate means of advocating the interests of labor."

Nor was Youmans pro-business, in the sense of defending current practice. As with many good government reformers, anticommercialism rippled just below the surface of his prose—in references to the "speculators of the world," for example, or attacks on the "wealthy mining interests." Listing the causes of the corruption of the era, he lumped together the "swindle of speculators, and the frauds of petty traders" and "the quackeries of the platform, the bar, the state-house, and the pulpit."[37]

Science was an antidote to the evils of the age. The business of social science was the study of the bounds within which successful reform must operate: "the values and limits of those activities which belong to the natural constitution of society . . . . " As Youmans continued to invoke the blessing of *science* there was indeed a subtle shift in the meaning of the term. Although he had no explicit theory on the subject, he looked increasingly to science to provide the stability which in traditional societies, adhered in established customs and institutions, rather than being a weapon to liberate man from his history. "There is no salvation for this continent except in the acquirement of some proximately scientific conception of the nature of government," he wrote to Spencer. "We are without the stability that comes from long habit, and without any guidance in the shape of national theory." In this sense his faith in science turned conservative in the postbellum years.[38]

But like Spencer himself, Youmans did not embrace a Darwinian theory of change through struggle, the antithesis of the stability he desired. *Struggle for existence* and *survival of the fittest* were phrases he rarely used, and never to justify a competitive economic order. Rather, like his mentor, Youmans learned that Darwin made it increasingly difficult to rest social policy on any appeal to natural law.

His first lesson in this regard came during the Cairnes-Spencer dispute of the mid-1870s. Answering Cairnes's charge that Spencer simply transferred "laws from physiology and zoology to the domain of social science," Youmans exploded: "He goes back to an old essay on the 'social organism,' in which Mr. Spencer, nearly twenty years ago, pointed out some analogies between the structure and actions of the body politic and those of individual organisms, and says that Spencer's doctrine of social evolution is based on this analogy." Youmans thought this construction outrageous. "We cannot conceive a grosser misapprehension than this," he continued. "Mr. Spencer maintains that the law of evolution is universal because the evidence of it is found in each of the great divisions of natural phenomena." The key lay in a distinction between the natural and human spheres, each governed by laws that science could discover. "In the social sphere the principle rests upon observed effects, and is an induction from the facts belonging to that sphere," Youmans concluded. The search for laws was the glory of science at every level. Cairnes's obtuseness on this point was due to "his prejudices as a politician, as an Englishman, or some other perversity."[39]

The shadow of Darwin also clouded Youmans's relations with the *Nation*, whose chief critic of Spencer (as Youmans later learned) was the philosopher Chauncey Wright. The *Nation* supported most of Youmans's political views. E. L. Godkin its editor shared Youmans's faith in social science, defined simply as "knowledge of the laws that regulate the condition of men." But contributors to the *Nation* sedulously avoided Spencerian rhetoric; and in choosing Wright to review Spencer the editors selected one of America's most sophisticated critics of the Synthetic Philosophy. During the seventies Youmans thus carried on a running battle over what appeared to be an attempt to downgrade Spencer in favor of Darwin. When the *Nation* virtually ignored Spencer in an account of evolution, for example, Youmans reacted immediately. In not commending Spencer's views, the editors were "tacitly" warning readers against them, he charged. In formulating the theory of evolution, Spencer was more important than Darwin since the latter merely gave a partial instance of a universal law, which Spencer alone described in its fullest extent.[40]

In 1879 Youmans again confronted the issue of a Darwinian versus a Spencerian view of nature and its lessons in reviewing James Ram's *Philosophy of War* (1878), a treatise by a military tutor in Britain. Echoing a growing belief that Darwinism somehow legitimated international warfare (a view that was anathema to older liberals such as Spencer), Ram argued that nature was pitiless, and that war was "nature's way of operation." Although Youmans conceded that there was "much truth" in this view of nature, he denied that this fact provided excuse for private or group violence. Evolution as expounded by Spencer taught a different lesson:

> The essence of evolution is transformation—the substitution of higher agencies for lower in the unfolding economy of the world. War is certainly one of the things that must certainly be left behind.[41]

A third critic raised a similar issue in an attack on the *Principles of Ethics,* on the eve of Spencer's American tour. The critic was Goldwin Smith, the British historian, who had been waging war on Spencer in articles in *Macmillan's*, the *Atlantic Monthly*, and the *Contemporary Review*. Youmans republished the last of these articles in *Popular Science*, titling it "Has Science Yet Found a New Basis for Morality?" Although proclaiming himself an evolutionist, Smith insisted that modern science posed a clear threat to traditional morality, a danger obscured by the fact that "the intellectual world" dwelt still "in the twilight of religion" (a variation of the common charge that Spencer's thought was metaphysical, even theological, rather than strictly positivistic). Translating Spencer's *Ethics* into the narrowest utilitarianism ("His tests of right and wrong ... are pleasure and pain") Smith argued that Spencer failed to see the "logical conclusion" of his own position.[42]

To illustrate this logic, Smith adduced passages from a work on *Modern Thinkers* (1880) by Van Buren Denslow, an economist at the old University of Chicago, and (in Smith's version) an avowed disciple of Spencer. In these passages Denslow appeared to argue that nature gave no guide to morality. Laws, he wrote, "represent the view of the winning side, in the struggle for subsistence." In this passage, Smith found "the practical tendencies [n.b.] of a certain school of thought," namely a brutal Machiavellianism.[43]

Youmans, in response, denied that Denslow was a disciple of Spencer and reasserted his conviction that Spencer alone provided a solid basis for morality. In actuality, however, the case was more complicated. Smith was playing a game that was becoming increasingly popular among Spencer's opponents, namely, criticizing the logic of his position by reducing utilitarianism to its crudest extreme. At least one observer commented on this strategy. Smith was one of a growing number of critics who pretended sympathy for a "scientific morality," in order to undermine it, wrote a friend of "rationalism" in the *Fortnightly:*

> They generally begin by admitting, or implying, more or less dejectedly, that the voice of science has to be listened to, as on the whole the most credible voice within earshot of this century. Then, having made this admission, they commonly proceed to dilate on the prospective misery and degeneration such listening will bring upon our illfated race.

Goldwin Smith was precisely this type:

> While nothing that he says leads one to suppose that he considers the objective grounds of the evolution doctrine invalid, his thesis is that the code of ethics he conceives [n.b.] to be suggested and supported by it is certain to prove generally detrimental; and that it in particular negatives the legitimacy of the belief in "human brother-

hood," the spread of humane feeling, and the protection of the interests of weaker races against the selfishness of the stronger.[44]

The irony was that Van Buren Denslow (1834-1902) had adopted a similar strategy for his own ends. A rigorous positivist, Denslow praised Spencer in general terms, but faulted him for introducing a priori assumptions, which, like Goldwin Smith, Denslow attributed to a pervasive "religious atmosphere." A rabid protectionist in the tradition of Henry Carey, Denslow hoped to base economics on "facts," which for him meant statistics rather than elusive natural laws. His parody of utilitarian morality was designed, not to support Machiavelli, but to underline the point that economics and morality were entirely separate. Although Denslow left unstated what a *true* basis for morality should be, his background and career (the old University of Chicago was a narrowly Baptist institution) suggest that his frank dualism between science and morals was intended to allow an opening for divine inspiration.[45]

Youmans's final defense of Spencer turned on this same issue, as in 1885 the editor parried the blunt questions of Emile de Laveleye, the Belgian sociologist. Did Spencer urge survival of the fittest in society? And if so, did not this Darwinian principle necessitate the "abolition of all laws which punish theft and murder?" Like the earlier critics, Laveleye adopted the increasingly popular device of translating Spencer's words into Darwinese to discredit the entire scheme.

Youmans mobilized familiar arguments. "Survival of the fittest" was Spencer's phrase, not Darwin's, and could be understood only within the framework of Spencer's philosophy: "Nature, of which man is a part, is a mixed system, in which good comes out of evil, and suffering is made tributary to everincreasing beneficence." As in his review of Ram's *Philosophy of War* Youmans seemed ready to accept Laveleye's grim portrait of "Nature, full of violence and death." But this concession did not produce the settled despair of naturalism. Rather, salvaging his optimism, Youmans widened the gap between a brutal present and peaceful future:

[Nature's laws] have been in operation in [man's] development many thousands of years before he began to take a conscious and intentive part in the work of his own elevation; and they must continue in operation as long as the present order of natural things prevails, and the movement is upward and onward toward greater good.

"The sole question is," he continued, "whether these great laws are to be wisely recognized and made use of by man in furtherance of those ameliorations to which they have already so immensely contributed." As in answering Cairnes a decade earlier, he attributed Laveleye's charges to "gross inappreciation of the subject, or sheer intellectual perversity."[46]

More than perversity, however, had produced this decade of debate. In Spencer's world, the actual and the ideal, the present and the future, were bound together by threads of assumption that a younger generation branded metaphysical and, hence, illusory. For Youmans, as for the early Spencer, the promise of progress took the sting from unpleasant realities. Forced to emphasize the gap between present and future, postponing Utopia as it were, Youmans stood at an intellectual crossroads. In one direction lay a frankly naturalistic view of man and society; in the other lay an explicit dualism between man and nature—the latter being precisely what Spencerianism was designed to avoid. Edward Youmans's death in January 1887 spared him this choice.

Was Youmans a social Darwinist? A final perspective on this question may be gained by examining how he got this reputation among later historians. Much of the credit belongs to Henry George, author of *Progress and Poverty* (1879) and father of the Single Tax movement. Although George owed considerable debt to Spencer, and at first cited *Social Statics* in support of his land tax, he grew bitter when Spencer repudiated his scheme. In 1892 he poured his disillusionment into a small book titled *A Perplexed Philosopher* in which he attacked Spencer's materialism, determinism, and fatalism. To illustrate his point, George recalled a conversation a decade earlier between himself and Youmans concerning the state of American society. "What do you propose to do about it?" George had asked. To this Youmans responded "with something like a sigh": "Nothing! You and I can do nothing at all. Its all a matter of evolution. We can only wait for evolution. Perhaps in four or five thousand years evolution may have carried men beyond this state of affairs. But we can do nothing."[47]

Setting aside the issue of the accuracy of George's memory after ten years, the Single Taxer himself acknowledged that this remark scarcely characterized Youmans. Rather it illustrated, from George's somewhat embittered perspective, how the Synthetic Philosophy could chill an otherwise warm heart. It was an "illfitting coat" that Youmans had "accidentally picked up and put on." In fact, the main subject of the remembered conversation was an issue that absorbed the reform energies of Youmans and most liberals of the seventies: "the political corruption of New York, of the utter carelessness and selfishness of the rich, and of their readiness to submit to it, or to promote it wherever it served their money-getting purposes to do so."[48]

Moreover, George's memory contradicted more verifiable remarks Youmans made concerning reform about this same time in a lengthy editorial on *Progress and Poverty*. The book irritated Youmans less for its proposals than its cosmology. "It sounds like last century talk," he wrote, noting

George's ignorance and equivocation concerning evolution. (Here You-mans echoed George Bernard Shaw who ridiculed George's "quaint eighteenth-century superstitions.") Rather than inventing utopias, man must understand "nature's method" and "consciously [take] part in the progressive work," he wrote, embellishing a familiar theme. Although human understanding was itself the product of evolution—and hence "nature"—man's goal was "to take the work of human progress out of the hands of Nature, and carry it on in his own way." Then, as if anticipating George's later attack, Youmans concluded:

> Let it not be said that science thus becomes obstructive and para-lyzes exertion; on the contrary, it is promotive of real progress by checking futile effort, and disclosing the conditions and the way by which exertion may be made more effectual and substantial conquests achieved. And, in these times that are so prolific of social Utopias, no teaching is more valuable or more wholesome.[49]

Probably this paraphrase of Spencer's call for "philanthropic energy" and "philosophic calm" did not entirely please George. In a moment of de-spair the aging and ill editor of *Popular Science* may even have indulged the cosmic pessimism of his alleged comments on evolution. But his life and work testified to a faith that "science" did not "paralyze exertion." More likely, the notion that Spencerianism tended to produce social cal-lousness told more about the reform imagination than Youmans's social philosophy.

Five

Whatever the future held, the dinner at Delmonico's on 9 November 1882 was Spencer's finest hour. "The gathering . . . was large, cultivated, and brilliant," Youmans exulted. "The dinner was elaborate and elegant, and the decorations quiet but in admirable taste." The audi-ence was distinguished. The presence of half-a-dozen clergymen —including Lyman Abbott, Henry Ward Beecher, Minot J. Savage, and R. Heber Newton—attested to Spencer's appeal in liberal theological circles. The professions were amply represented and included New York's most distinguished lawyers, jurists, physicians. Among the businessmen and bankers who attended were those known particularly for public service: Abram Hewitt, the iron manufacturer and philanthropist; August Bel-mont, the banker; and Andrew Carnegie. For some of the guests— Edward A. Silsbee, John Fiske, and Simon Sterne—the evening capped a lifelong interest in Spencer. For the majority it was a chance to honor a man whose name was better known than his ideas.[50]

The honor of introducing Spencer fell to William M. Evarts, a Harvard-trained lawyer who had recently served as secretary of state under President Hayes. His brief remarks reflected the nature and limits of Spencer's appeal. Stock Spencerian phrases were turned to humorous advantage: the audience was chosen by "natural selection . . . out of the mass," a reference not to New York's teeming slums but the many celebrities who regrettably could not be invited. "By the process of differentiation and of multiplication of effects," Evarts continued, "we have come to a dinner of a dozen courses and wines of as many countries." While these quips brought laughter, his more serious remarks went to the heart of the matter. "You give us that knowledge of man which is practical and useful," he observed. Spencer's system was "benevolent," "serious," and "reverent." It "treats evil not as eternal, but as evanescent, and it expects to evolve at what is sought through faith in the millenium—that condition of affairs in which there is the highest morality and the greatest happiness."[51]

Most of the other speakers revealed an uncertain grasp of Spencer's "system." Underlying Evarts's praise was an acknowledgement that the system remained controversial. Carl Schurz testified to the importance of *Social Statics* in his own career as a reformer, but only in the most general terms. Although Henry Ward Beecher endorsed Spencer's views for the first time publicly, he only partially abandoned his earlier reservations. His views of evolution, Youmans later wrote Spencer, were "very crude, being of the same sort as his address at the dinner." Othniel C. Marsh, the lone scientist among the speakers, virtually ignored Spencer, while celebrating the spread of development theory. William Graham Sumner of Yale, despite his later reputation as one of America's leading Spencerians, confessed that, as to "sociology," he had "only got so far as to have an almost overpowering conviction of the necessity and value of the study of that science."[52]

References to the application of Spencer's views to contemporary social problems were few. In written comments he was unable to deliver, a New York lawyer, Eugene R. Leland, insisted that Spencer taught lessons "which even [n.b.] businessmen must need to learn." These lessons however turned out to be commonplace parallels between the laws of physics and society, for example, "that every manifestation of power must be preceded and followed by equivalent manifestations." In the most pointedly political remark of the evening, Leland added: "If the laws of matter, which prove that by no sort of manipulation can something be had for nothing, were more familiar, men would not be led away by the vagaries of fiat money, nor be deluded by the sophistries of protection."[53]

Spencer's speech was naturally the highlight of the evening. Preaching a "gospel of relaxation," he warned his audience that the American passion for "business" and "money getting" was soul destroying. This was the true lesson of evolution. Just as business replaced war among civilized men, so the creation of material abundance forecast a new age. "Among reasons for thinking this," he continued, "there is the reason that the process of evolution throughout the organic world at large, brings an increasing surplus of energies that are not absorbed in fulfilling material needs, and points to a still larger surplus for the humanity of the future."[54] Spencer's message, in brief, was that peace lay behind the battle, harmony above the daily discords, and as Evarts noted, there would come a future in which mankind would enter a permanent plateau of "the highest morality and the greatest happiness." If one assumes that Americans looked to Spencer and evolution to defend their competitive order, the audience must have found the speech disappointing. However, contemporary reaction and the many favorable references to it in later years, suggest that Spencer caught another side of the American spirit.[55] New in its mode of expression, the "gospel of relaxation" was consonant with the lofty idealism of Spencer's appeal during the previous three decades.

4.   Amending the Faith

*[The concentration of wealth] is an evolution from the
heterogeneous to the homogeneous, and it is clearly another
step in the upward path of development.*
  Andrew Carnegie, *"Popular Illusions About Trusts,"*
  Century, 60 *(May 1900), p. 144.*

*We are not much in the habit of attributing purpose to Nature;
but the language of teleology is sometimes convenient, and
shall perhaps not be misunderstood if we say that the
apparently enforced idleness of thousands of men, with all
the poverty and distress thus resulting, cannot be part of
Nature's plan.*
  William Jay Youmans, Popular Science Monthly, *44 (1894),
  842.*

One

During the final decades of the century, a dwindling band of
American Spencerians kept the faith against considerable odds. Although
the economic upswing and relative calm in the early 1880s gave temporary
relief from the troubles of the previous decade, the promise proved illusory. The rise of the trusts, renewed labor militancy, and persistant poverty defied the formulas of individualism and laissez faire. Meanwhile, a
remarkable flowering of books laid the basis for a New Liberalism, among
them Oliver Wendell Holmes's *Common Law* (1881); Lester Frank Ward's
Dynamic Sociology (1883); and Richard Ely's *Past and Present of Political
Economy* (1885). The first wave of the antiformalist revolt that ultimately
transformed American thought, these works placed Darwin and evolution
squarely at the service of government intervention and social welfare. To
add insult to injury, it was even suggested that Spencer deserved credit.
"May it not be in telling us what society is, and how it became such,"
wrote Ward in remarks prepared for the Delmonico's celebration, "he has
unconsciously pointed out the way in which it may be made better."[1]
Although most American Spencerians repeated familiar arguments in
Spencer's defense, some sounded variations on older themes. In the published discussions of the Brooklyn Ethical Association, the moral idealism
of the early Spencer continued to flourish, coupled with a running battle
against the rising tide of governmental legislation. Fashioning a new

Gospel of Wealth, the industrialist Andrew Carnegie wed Spencerian evolutionism and the Puritan concept of stewardship. A bastion of laissez faire and undiluted Spencerianism, *Popular Science* under the editorship of William Jay Youmans came finally, as did Spencer himself, to recognize the problems of following natural laws when society and nature seemed increasingly Darwinian. Wrestling with a similar problem, the publisher Henry Holt made one last attempt to restate Spencerianism for the new century.

Two

Organized in 1885, the Brooklyn Ethical Association was an outgrowth of classes in ethics held for several years before at Brooklyn's Second Unitarian Church. Meeting in twice-weekly discussions, members chose Spencer's *Study of Sociology* as the principal subject for its first season. The choice itself—since the work was more than a decade old—indicated how gradual was the dissemination of Spencer's work. Although not officially associated with Felix Adler's Ethical Culture movement, the association attracted a wide assortment of agnostics, freethinkers and liberal Christians. Within a few years the active membership included two to three hundred "ladies and gentlemen," two-thirds of them from the New York area. Among its driving spirits and prominent spokemen on public issues were Lewis G. Janes (1844-1901), a prolific author and popular lecturer; and Robert G. Eccles (1848-1934), a physician and chemist active in public health and the study of food preservatives.

For more than a decade the Brooklyn Ethical Association was virtually an official club for American Spencerians. Spencer himself reviewed the first program and gave his personal blessing to the enterprise, wishing only that the presentation would not be "limited to a few listeners in Brooklyn." Seeking a wider audience, members published papers in the leading journals of rationalism and free thought, including the Boston *Index, the Unitarian Review,* and the *Westminster Review.* Between 1889 and 1895 their proceedings appeared as separate pamphlets and in five sturdy volumes in an "Evolution" series.[2]

Although the association took no official position on public issues, its members, as Lewis Janes explained, looked "for the regeneration of society and the advancement of civilization by means of the voluntary action of individuals, rather than by multiplication of state agencies." Among efforts they approved were the Society for the Prevention of Crime; the Societies for the Prevention of Cruelty to Children and to Animals; the Prison Reform Association; and the Social Science Association. In the spirit of the social science movement, its members urged careful study of the facts as an antidote to all *a priori* schemes. Janes underlined the gradualist approach: "Evolutionists realize that 'Nature does not advance by leaps,' and they would carefully note the trend of past events before urging [man] to a definite forward step, in a direction contrary to that which he has been pursuing." Stressing the ethical factor in civilization, these Spencerians believed that human intellect was the finest flower of evolution. As Robert Eccles put it, discussing the labor troubles of the late seventies:

> In early stages of human development, the accumulation of bodily vigor and strength was the main object of life.... Strategy soon competed with strength, and, when victor, intellect was picked with it. From among all the strategic devices of intellect property was selected as the fittest, and society became a necessity for its protection.

The basis of a creed of *noblesse oblige,* this emphasis on ideals bred little sympathy for strikers or governmental action. "Self restraint is more important to the poor man than legislation," Eccles continued, with reference to the railway strikes of 1877. "This will give him a fitness for the battle of life, while that but unmans and effeminates him."[3]

But it was not a summons to brutal individualism or callous indifference. Defining survival of the fittest Janes was careful to explain that the fittest qualities were those that "best serve the race in its struggle toward a condition of social equilibrium." Thus the "law of conflict," so painful at lower stages, "blossoms at last with the noblest flowers of unselfish character." After more than a decade of social turmoil, Eccles also moved beyond a call for self-restraint. In a symposium with the Spencerian title "Man and the State" (1892) Eccles argued that selfishness was not among the qualities preserved among men. "Natural selection," he wrote, "is constantly tending to weed out both extremes [individualism and socialism] because they put themselves at a disadvantage in the struggle." Since nature held us "responsible not only for our own shortcomings, but for those of our neighbors as well," he wrote on another occasion, "Nature therefore decides that we are all our brothers' keepers, since their lives depend upon our deeds and *vice versa.*"[4]

Although these Spencerians continued to insist that social policy be grounded in the careful study of nature—and hence they opposed speculative and utopian schemes—Eccles himself came close to embracing two arguments which at the same time in the 1890s were joining the New Liberal arsenal: first, *social efficiency,* as Benjamin Kidd termed it, was the measure of fitness; and second, a *struggle for the life of others,* in

Henry Drummond's phrase, was as important as the struggle for existence.[5]

Committed to the "regeneration of society," contributors to B.E.A. symposia also resisted the pessimism that nagged Spencer during the nineties. When Sumner of Yale, otherwise "an able student of social and economic problems," was bold enough to suggest that "natural liberty" was of purely metaphysical origin, rather than a deduction from evolution, Janes lectured him sternly:

> He is but a poor student of natural science, indeed, who would simply content himself with learning facts, without endeavoring to trace their relations, to study their causal connections, and therefore to draw prophetic [n.b.] inferences to guide his future investigations, to interpret underlying laws, and thus enable him to push forward to new discoveries.

The "synthesizing and prophetic quality" was the "noblest and most fruitful characteristic" of science in perceiving the dim outlines of "an ideal perfection." "The method of Evolution, as the name indicates, is in its very nature progressive," he added, unaware of the tautology.[6] Finally Eccles joined a growing consensus that "psychic factors," as Lester Ward called them, played the major part in man's evolution. Commenting on an article by the biologist Edward D. Cope, a leader of the so-called neo-Lamarckians against the neo-Darwinism of Weismann and his followers, Eccles agreed "that there is a psychical aspect to the problem that has been grossly neglected. While others have dealt mainly with the survival of the fittest in the struggle for existence, [Cope] undertakes to show that the principle source of variation among animals, and therefore the source of fitness, is to be sought for in feeling or sensation." Eccles therefore concluded that the "directing force of the universe is not all mechanical." Thus Spencerian metaphysics continued to feed optimism in Brooklyn.[7]

Three

Andrew Carnegie (1835-1919) salvaged his optimism only by modifying Spencer significantly. Ostensibly, few Americans were more indebted to Spencer. During the Englishman's visit, Carnegie was his personal host and, in a moving dockside tribute, heard Spencer describe him as one of his two best American friends. In a much-quoted passage from the essay on "Wealth" (1889) Carnegie repaid the compliment in some Spencerian rhetoric. The "law of competition," he wrote, "while sometimes hard for the individual . . . is best for the race because it insures the survival of the fittest in every department." "Few men have wished to know another man more strongly than I to know Herbert Spencer," he wrote in his *Autobiography* (1920), "for seldom has one been more deeply indebted than I to him and to Darwin."[8]

In reality Carnegie's understanding of Spencer's philosophy was superficial at best, and his debt rather slight. Although he implied that he discovered Spencer's work while in Pittsburgh in the early sixties, he probably encountered it in the rather more elite setting of New York literary circles later in the decade. Faith not factories was the governing context. After moving to New York in 1867, Carnegie first joined the Murray Hill salons of Anne Lynch Botta, wife of a professor at New York University; and later the Nineteenth Century Club, founded in the 1860s by a group of enlightened thinkers with a special interest in positivism and the religion of humanity. At these meetings, Joseph Wall has written, "Carnegie waded bodily into the writings of Herbert Spencer, and with his feet barely wet . . . imagined himself to be swimming in the strong current of a new faith."[9]

Carnegie was ripe for conversion. Torn between the Calvinist Presbyterianism of his Scottish ancestors and the Swedenborgian mysticism of his father, he felt completely at sea theologically. Evolution assumed the character of a revelation. "I remember that light came as in a flood and all was clear," he wrote in his *Autobiography*. "Not only had I got rid of theology and the supernatural, but I had found the truth of evolution. 'All is well since all grows better' became my motto, my true source of comfort." Echoing the early Spencer he added; "Nor is there any conceivable end to this march to perfection."[10]

However, for almost two decades Carnegie's prose showed little evidence of his conversion. In *Around the World* (1879), a book-length account of a journey to the Far East, he noted in passing that the "suggestively human" traits of orangutans should alone convince anti-Darwinians of their errors—a sign that controversy over transmutation of species continued to provide a frame of reference quite apart from the subtleties of the theory. Likewise, he noted that the "Heathen Chinee" in Singapore were a sure bet to triumph in the survival of the fittest against other groups—a contest, he was quick to add, that "is being fought out under the protection of the British flag, which insures peace and order wherever it floats." One further hint of Spencerianism—a wish that a shipboard preacher would discuss "the unknown [not capitalized], the mighty deep, the universe [and the stars]," rather than dogma—again reflected that religious concerns first led Carnegie to the Synthetic Philosophy.[11]

When in 1882 Carnegie learned of Spencer's impending visit, he hastily arranged to sail from Scotland on the same ship and even managed to share a dining table with his mentor. From the start, Carnegie fought disillusionment. He imagined Spencer to be "a calm philosopher brooding Buddha-like, over all things unmoved." Instead he found a querulous, demanding traveler who could make a fuss when Cheshire rather than Cheddar cheese was served. In Pittsburgh, where Spencer was his house-guest, things went little better. "Six months here," Spencer confided to his host concerning the steel capital, "would justify suicide."[12]

Before the appearance of "Wealth," Carnegie discussed public issues as though Spencer never existed. Celebrating "Business Success" before a group of Pittsburgh students in 1885, for example, he reiterated conventional pieties, closing with a quotation from Emerson to the effect that "no one can cheat you out of success but yourselves." Elsewhere he remarked in regard to the industrial situation, the "permanent relations . . . of labor and capital have not yet evolved," but said nothing more about evolution. In *Triumphant Democracy* (1885), his hymn to American progress, he mentioned Spencer only five times in 519 pages. His only significant references were to the American tour, all to illustrate Spencer's point that "Americans may reasonably look forward to a time when they will have produced a civilization grander than any the world has known."[13]

If general idealism explains Carnegie's enthusiasm for Spencer, his superficial grasp of his philosophy suggests why he was so ready to abandon a fundamental Spencerian principle in the essay on "Wealth" which appeared in the *North American Review* in July 1889. New in substance and tone, the essay faced for the first time the source of a pervasive uneasiness that lay just below the surface in Carnegie's earlier celebrations of hard work and progress. One source of this uneasiness, as Robert Mc-Closkey has noted, was a fear that capitalism was ultimately incompatible with democracy, the latter a faith that Carnegie, like Spencer, first absorbed from British radicals in the 1840s. Another source was personal doubt concerning a system that required unrelenting pursuit of profit to the neglect of the higher self, a "role strain" common among late nineteenth century entrepreneurs. "To continue much longer overwhelmed by business cares, and with most of my thoughts wholly upon the way to make more money in the shortest time," Carnegie wrote in the sixties, "must degrade me beyond hope." The Gospel of Wealth provided at once a device for reconciling capitalism and democracy; and, as Carnegie later explained, a "refuge [for businessmen] from self-questioning, in the thought of much greater portion of their means which is being spent upon others."[14]

This uneasiness surfaced at the same time in Carnegie's other essays. Businessmen, he wrote in 1886, "are in the midst of an anxious and unceasing struggle to keep their head above water." This struggle was not ennobling: "We should not expect much from those who have to engage in the struggle for existence [during their business life] . . . except, perhaps, the absence of folly and the presence of negative virtues."[15] Carnegie's appeals to natural law, as Edward Kirkland has suggested, made particular sense not because they provided the businessman with a justification for things he wanted to do, but rather because they diminished his responsibility in a situation that combined apparent power with a minimum of ability to control the economic situation. Thus, in an essay which immediately preceded "Wealth," Carnegie wrote of the laws of supply and demand: "there is no more possibility of defeating the operation of these laws than there is of thwarting the laws of nature which determine the humidity of the atmosphere or the revolution of the earth upon its axis." Although opinion will differ as to the soothing effect of a million dollars on a troubled soul, this anxiety may also explain the frequency with which Carnegie praised Spencer's dignity and repose. "Spencer was always the calm philosopher," he later remembered.[16]

"Wealth" must be read against this background. Carnegie began with a frank recognition of the growing gap between rich and poor, not in the sense that Henry George proposed (a charge leveled by one critic), but rather in asserting that wealth was concentrated in relatively fewer hands. Although this development was "salutary" in providing cheaper goods, the social price was great:

> We assemble thousands of operatives in the factory, and in the mine, of whom the employer can know little or nothing, and to whom he is little better than a myth. . . . Under the law of competition, the employer of thousands is forced into the strictest economies . . . and there is often friction betwen the employer and the employed, between capital and labor, between rich and poor.

The sole reason for accepting this state of affairs was "our wonderful material development." The "survival of the fittest in every department" referred unequivocally to material efficiency alone.[17]

This grim vision of a law-bound universe prefaced Carnegie's proposal that the rich become "stewards" of the wealth of society, a doctrine with roots in his Calvinist past and a precedent in the growing number of public benefactions during the 1880s. Carnegie's models were fellow New Yorkers Samuel Tilden and Peter Cooper and Enoch Pratt of Baltimore, each of whom had recently endowed libraries and cultural facilities for the public. Such bequests in the future would be the norm, a duty of men of wealth. In the new era, Carnegie surmised in a much-quoted remark, "The man who dies thus rich dies disgraced."[18]

Opinion divided sharply over the merits of Carnegie's proposal. The idea that the rich die disgraced accompanied a call for stiff inheritance taxes, anathema to many Americans. Whatever the practical limitations of Carnegie's notion that a millionaire ought personally dispense his funds, his blueprint for philanthropy went far beyond current views of organized charity. In the future Age of the Foundation, the Gospel of Wealth contributed an important element to the developing relation among business, government, and society that has proved an important part of the American alternative to both laissez faire and to socialism.[19]

Only a few critics, however, noted how fundamentally Carnegie's assumptions and conclusions departed from Spencer's scheme. Quoting the *Study of Sociology* against Carnegie, a prominent Methodist minister gleefully cited Spencer's comparison of modern millionaires and medieval barons, the implication being that the former represented not a natural development but were "the unnatural product of artificial social regulation." Also questioning the "inevitability" of concentrated wealth, a critic in the *Andover Review* observed that Carnegie's necessitarian premise was central to the argument: "If [Mr. Carnegie] is to preach the gospel of wealth to the rich, he must above all things make them feel the inevitableness of their lot." Necessity and patronage were inextricably bound together.[20]

What none quite stated was that Carnegie thus faced a dilemma similar to the one with which other Spencerians grappled. Stripped of its metaphysical basis, fitness meant simply wealth and power. Unlike the early Spencer, Carnegie was unable to view the harsh realities of present inequality through lenses tinted by the hope of the future. In reaching behind modern science to the Christian doctrine of stewardship, Carnegie provided a transcendent basis for moral behavior and reintroduced into the universe precisely that element of arbitrariness that Spencer intended to banish.

In later years Carnegie also differed from most Spencerians on the issue of state power. Perhaps predictably, he defended the protective tariff against the charge it violated natural law. "What is there of a man's triumphs in any branch of his activity that is not artificial?" he asked readers of the *North American Review* in 1890. Likewise he called for a Pennsylvania railroad commission to regulate rates on the model of the Interstate Commerce Commission. Although his defense of the trusts was naive in assuming that market forces would prevent excessive pricing, Carnegie contributed to a mounting consensus that evolution meant that bigger is better. On one occasion he urged wage and hour legislation. "I differ from my great master Herbert Spencer in regard to the duties of the state," he told a stunned reporter. "No hard and fast rules can be drawn in the matter." When somewhat later Carnegie defended trusts as an evolution from the heterogeneous to the homogeneous—exactly the reverse of Spencer's formula—readers may also have been puzzled. But again this error was probably evidence of his uncertain grasp of "first principles."[21]

Whatever they thought of Spencer, many Americans by the turn of the century shared Carnegie's view at least on the trust issue. Beginning with the railroad consolidations of the early 1880s, and continuing with the formation of the industrial trusts, the argument developed that, since competition was jungle law, combination was another instance of human intelligence applied in the interests of order and stability. Arguing for a proposed railroad federation, Charles Francis Adams, Jr., defended price discrimination as follows:

> This system in railroads, as in everything else, leads to one thing—
> a thing much discussed of late years and known as the survival
> of the fittest. . . . This may not be republican; it certainly is not
> democratic. Nevertheless it is a fact, and like most facts, has,
> sooner or later, got to be recognized. In the savage struggle for
> supremacy, and just so long as that struggle lasts, railroads must
> and will be forced to measures of practical discrimination.

The proposed federation, he added, was an attempt "to find some mode of escape from the survival of the fittest." The problem of "ruinous rates," explained another railroad man before a Senate hearing on the proposed Interstate Commerce Commission in 1886, "is not to be remedied by awaiting on 'the survival of the fittest.' This misapplied phrase of the scientist cannot furnish appropriate data in any recognition and adjustment of difficulties which may attend the commercial affairs of a people."[22]

During the 1890s, this logic confirmed a growing consensus that in industry big was not only better but also in accord with a "correct" reading of evolution—an assumption, as William Letwin and Gabriel Kolko have shown, that helped undermine support for totally prohibitive antitrust legislation.[23] Samuel C. T. Dodd, a prominent lawyer and architect of the Standard Oil trust, noted that competition carried to an extreme "would be a fit mode for savages, not for civilized men." "The rule in business is emphatically the survival of the fittest," he added. "Only thus can the public receive benefit from superior skill and economics in business." In a collection of essays called *The Trust: Its Book* (1902) a variety of contributors, including Spencer's former secretary, James H. Bridge, and left-wing Social Gospeler George Herron, sounded variations of this theme. Evolution, wrote Herron, was a "wholly divine and resistless force making for cooperation and association."[24]

As the 1912 presidential campaign approached, Darwinian caricatures of competition joined together with praise of *association* to become part of the defense of *regulated monopoly*, a catchphrase of Theodore Roosevelt's New Nationalism. Reasonable bigness would create stability. "Competition carried to its logical conclusion is destructive, and would mean concentration and monopoly," warned one businessman in a speech before the American Paper and Pulp Association in 1908. "It is as relentless as that brute law of creation, the survival of the fittest." Consolidation eliminated this "destructive competition," he continued. "It makes the strong help the weak." In *The New Competition* (1912), Arthur J. Eddy, an Illinois lawyer and earlier author of *The Law of Combinations* (1901), likened competition to the inhuman doctrine of the survival of the fittest. Several years later, George W. Perkins, a Morgan partner and one of TR's principal backers in 1912, stated more simply, "Competition has always enriched the strong and impoverished the weak."[25]

This reasoning posed problems for those favoring *regulated competition*, the announced position of Woodrow Wilson and the Democrats. On social issues, many Wilsonians accepted reform Darwinist assumptions concerning the merits of cooperation and were themselves quick to caricature "selfish individualism" in Darwinian terms. How could one then defend competition? Louis D. Brandeis, the Boston lawyer Wilson credited with being the chief theorist of the New Freedom, met the problem head on. "The purpose of combining," he wrote in *Collier's*—in a statement the *Nation* applauded—"has often been to curb efficiency, thus frustrating the natural law of the survival of the fittest." Coming from a prominent reformer only three years after the death of William Graham Sumner, this statement was one of the final ironies in the saga of social Darwinism.[26]

As with Carnegie's reinterpretations of Spencer, the double-edged use of Darwinism to condemn competition while defending combination, supported an emerging status quo in American industry—no less than pre-Darwinian defenses of laissez faire and competition as laws of nature had in the post-Civil-War years. In this sense Darwinian arguments, like earlier appeals to natural law, were conservative, if one uses the term as many historians seem to insist, to describe anyone who supported industrial capitalism or even private property. But this similarity obscures the fact that Darwinian arguments, in the industrial sphere as well as in the social, fed fears of disorder while promising stability through organization and conscious control. If the result in industry as well as in social policy was conservative, it was the conservatism of self-proclaimed reformers.

Four

Upon the death of E. L. Youmans in January 1887, his younger brother William Jay Youmans (1838-1901) assumed the editorship of *Popular Science*. A product of the Yale Scientific School and the medical course at New York University, he brought to the task the formal scientific credentials his older brother lacked. During 1865 he completed his education in London, where he studied under Huxley. After practicing medicine for three years in Minnesota, he joined his brother in establishing *Popular Science* in 1872. True to tradition, the new editor stubbornly restated Spencerian principles for more than a decade in the face of the same forces, social and scientific, that led Spencer to the bitter recriminations of his final years. More learned than Carnegie, less sanguine than the Spencerians at the Brooklyn Ethical Association, the younger Youmans came finally to admit, as the other did not, that Spencer's image of nature rested on teleological assumptions which in the strict sense could not be proved. This realization, like the final purchase of *Popular Science* by the McClure-Phillips company in 1900, symbolized the end of an era.[27]

More thoroughly grounded in Darwinism than his older brother, William Jay Youmans returned repeatedly to the knotty problems of applying survival of the fittest and natural selection to society. Discussing the causes of poverty in one of his earliest editorials, he announced that it was "all a question of fitness." Qualifying this statement he then added:

> In the social sphere, as elsewhere, the fit will survive and flourish; the pre-eminently fit will flourish pre-eminently. It may be that pre-eminent fitness for present social conditions may not imply ideal excellence of character; no doubt it does not; still the fact remains that success is a question of adaptation, and that want of success or poverty means non-adaptation.

The answer was not the sentimentalism of the recently established Anti Poverty Society, but "to bring such influences to bear on the unfit as shall render them fit; to make war against idleness, inefficiency, stupidity, extravagance, weak self-indulgence." While this catalog of sins, and the personalizing of guilt, were unexceptional, the concession that fittest was not best once again raised the oldest ghost in the Spencerian closet.[28]

As national concern over poverty mounted, Youmans's tone grew more urgent. Attacking sentimentalists and American society, he seemed by the end of 1889 almost willing to allow natural selection to have its ruthless way:

> It is common for sentimentalists to speak of natural selection as the very type of a "merciless law." But who will dare to say with confidence that natural selection is not more merciful, on the whole, than man's vaguely altruistic interferences with the natural source of things? Nature makes incompetence and misery short-lived, and reduces them in every way to a minimum. Man steps in and accuses Nature of cruelty; he tries his own hand, and,

lo! thousands and hundreds of thousands are leading a languishing physical and a depraved intellectual and moral existence.

"The result," he concluded, "is not one to be proud of."[29]

In this same spirit Youmans urged extreme measures for dealing with the situation. Countering the suggestion of A. Russel Wallace and Edward Bellamy that society practice *human selection* by adopting eugenically beneficial reforms, Youmans offered his own version of selectionism through the incarceration of defectives, criminals, and paupers to prevent their reproduction; and even the removal of civil rights from "those who do not merit them through an active cooperation in the industrial life of the community"—the sort of draconian measure then being endorsed by younger charity and social workers, including the prominent pediatrician and child welfare reformer Henry Dwight Chapin, who had recently published a series of such proposals in *Popular Science*.[30]

Although Youmans never quite urged that natural selection be allowed literal reign in society, he soon had second thoughts concerning this entire line of reasoning. The more one stressed natural selection, as Darwin himself realized in *The Descent of Man*, the more one saw how at odds were the laws of nature and the morals of society. That incarceration of the unfit was not a natural but an artificial selection was the conclusion to which such reasoning always seemed to lead. Why not go further, as Wallace and Bellamy suggested, and practice human selection? Why not admit that social standards of fitness were not nature's—the concession implicit in saying that the fittest were not the best?

During the nineties, Youmans wrestled with these issues. Discussing "Science and Civilization" in November 1891, he argued that natural selection was one example of "countless useful analogies to be drawn between the laws of matter and those of mind and society." But it was easily misunderstood:

> If life is a struggle, it is a struggle not so much against living competitors—that is a view of which quite too much is made [n.b.]— as against antagonist influences chiefly in the way of ill-regulated desires; and the law of natural selection rightly expounded will teach us that, if we wish to survive, we must cultivate all the qualities that make for fitness, and repress those that tend to produce unfitness.

Two years later, as the Spencer-Weismann controversy pushed natural selection to the fore, he stated the dilemma in almost the terms Darwin used in the *Descent*: "There is perhaps no greater or more serious problem confronting society today than this: how to pay just heed to the above law without injury to our own moral sensibilities and particularly to our sense of the sacredness of life."[31]

The depression of 1893 and mass unemployment brought Youmans finally to realize that natural laws had in effect two dimensions, one descriptive, the other prescriptive:

> We are not much in the habit of attributing purpose to Nature; but the language of teleology is sometimes convenient, and we shall perhaps not be misunderstood if we say that the apparently enforced idleness of thousands of men, with all the poverty and distress thence resulting, cannot be part of Nature's plan, or at least cannot illustrate the normal working of natural law. Nature, we know is severe in her methods, and recks little of human life when she sets her forces of fire and flood, of storm and earthquake in motion. There is nothing analogous to these catastrophes in the social phenomena before us to-day.

Nature as harmonious law: nature as avenging and capricious,—of the two, one Spencerian and the other Darwinian, Youmans accepted the first, confident in his knowledge of "Nature's plan".[32]

The "language of teleology" was also the focus of his later attack on the Duke of Argyll, the English statesman and philosopher who was a powerful voice in the antiscientific reaction of the 1890s. Arguing that Darwinians had no monopoly on evolution, Argyll presented his own theological version in *The Philosophy of Belief* (1896)—in Youmans's words, "evolution . . . with little touches of special creation thrown in here and there." Argyll's particular target was natural selection through which Darwinians "resorted to the old, old Lucretian expedient of personifying Nature and lending the glamour of that personification to the agency of bare mechanical necessity and to the coincidences of mere fortuity." In essence, Argyll was arguing that Darwinians *really* believed in either a mechanical fatalism or mere chance but hid this fact, a variation of the charge against social Darwinists.[33]

Youmans responded that "human language" was so freighted with "teleology" that Darwin could not avoid it. But unlike Spencer, who coined survival of the fittest to avoid just this implication, Youmans could not entirely regret the fact: "From our point of view, we must frankly confess, the idea of purpose is simply a drag on the interpretation of Nature." But he added: "It does not follow . . . that because the idea of purpose is a drag on the scientific interpretation of Nature, it has no place in a rational scheme of thought. It is possible to believe, and with deep conviction, in purposes that cannot be traced; and this, in our opinion, implies a more truly religious spirit than the attempt to read the petty thoughts of man into the everlasting statutes of the universe."[34]

Measured against "purposes that cannot be traced," the situation in the late 1890s was dismal indeed. Much like Spencer himself, Youmans at the close of his career hovered uneasily between the ideal and the real, uncertain of the connection between them. His final editorials were bitter, sustained criticisms of domestic and international events, with such revealing titles as "The Conflict of Modern Society"; "Social Decadence"; "External and Internal Aggression"; and "The War Spirit." Echoing other cataclysmists of these years, these neo-Calvinist sermons chronicled the dire consequences of abandoning traditional ideals. Commercialism and prosperity, in this view, gnawed at the vitals of the American soul. In this Darwinian world, men were alike, not in their higher instincts, but their animal passions. "It is not a difference of kind but only one of degree that separated the slaughter of Spaniards in Cuba and Tagals in Luzon from the slaughter of negroes in the South and the explosion of dynamite under street cars in the North," he concluded one of his very last editorials. "The inhuman instincts that impel to the one impel to the other."[35]

Five

The task of amending Spencerianism in the new century fell finally to Henry Holt (1840-1926), the distinguished editor and publisher. Holt's interest in Spencer followed the usual pattern. Educated at Yale (class of 1861), young Holt, as he later told it, "left college a rebel against such theory and scraps of metaphysics as had been taught there." *First Principles*, which he discovered in 1865, opened his eyes to "a new heaven and a new earth." Within a few years he was a member of a Spencer circle that included Fiske and Youmans ("a big fellow with a big voice, and so full of enthusiasms that those who didn't understand him were in danger of considering him a bore"). Although he knew William Graham Sumner (class of 1862) only slightly as an undergraduate, in later years Holt became his chief publisher.[36]

Yale gave Holt little interest in social issues. The text he was assigned in a course on politics and society was, he later recalled, "the very worst book I ever saw." But he soon became a staunch defender of liberal principles of the *Nation* variety, including laissez faire. E. L. Godkin became his "infallible pope." Nor did his brief clash with the *Nation* concerning Spencer's reputation keep Holt from wedding this political faith to a simple if crude evolutionism. Spencer, he later wrote, "taught me that, roughly speaking, what is, is the best possible at the moment, and can be made better only by Evolution, which can be promoted by gradual and experimental supercession, but not by blind destruction. Social questions are very complicated, and can be wisely settled only by the slow methods of trial and error."[37]

Holt like other Spencerians found the events of the 1890s a severe test of this faith. Discussing "Social Discontent" in the *Forum*, he restated the case for altruism against extremes of radical utopianism and callous pessimism. Evolution ruled out all panaceas, he insisted:

> It has taken some millions of years for Nature to evolve man as he is and society as it is, and, regret it as we may, there is no more reason to believe that now, all of a sudden, all men are going to become capable or enjoy the results of capability, than that they are all at once to become strong and beautiful.

Poverty could be cured "by regular processes of evolution." But these processes might "be promoted, of course, by intelligence and morality." Although there was "not the slightest indication that the cure can be continued in any quicker way, . . . all the indications are that its rate can be accelerated."[38]

But what were the "regular processes of evolution"? With Weismannism and neo-Darwinism the burning issues of the day, Holt in the 1890s sensed that this question was the critical one. Evolution taught *two* truths. Both must be the basis of a sound education:

> . . . the simpler of these truths is the inevitable, even if cruel, necessity of Natural Selection. I do not say it's justice. Nature knows nothing of justice . . . . True, she has evolved in us intelligences to slightly direct her course and it is in using them that the function of justice comes up. But we can direct her only in channels fitted to her own currents: otherwise we are overwhelmed.

But a second and more important truth concerned the "universal reign of law," which manifested itself in every sphere. In biology this law:

> would include that most important general conception . . . of the survival of the fittest. From this, the transition to the survival of the psychically fit is easy, and thus the standpoint is reached for a view of Law in non-material things.[39]

Faced with these two truths, Holt qualified his belief in laissez faire. Elaboration of the first law would show "that no human law can make the unfit survive, except at somebody else's expense; and that the only way to enable them to survive on their own is to make them fit." Aware that this sentiment echoed Benjamin Kidd, whose *Social Evolution* (1895) was then the rage, Holt added that effort directed to fitting the unfit was not "irrational or ultra rational." More concretely, he suggested that once the public was educated in these principles, "the whole community [might]... secure the benefit of such natural monopolies as could then be reasonably handled by the Government, and vastly more of the recreative and intellectual resources too immense for private creation." To underline the point that his was not a blind defense of old-fashioned competition, he added that his reference to the dangers of eliminating competition in an earlier article had meant to include the qualifier "suddenly," since this was the danger.[40]

Although Holt was critical of many proposals for change during the Roosevelt-Wilson years, he fashioned what might be termed the enlightened capitalist version of reform Darwinism, calling for increased morality and responsibility in business and advertising. Wary of the trusts, he sought to distinguish "good" from "bad" competition, much as TR attempted to do for the industrial giants. Although the rhetoric was often Spencerian, the upshot was new emphasis on "sympathy, mercy [and] justice." These qualities, he told the senior class at Yale's Sheffield School in 1908, "have begun to restrain and narrow competition, to shape popular opinion, and even to express themselves in law."[41]

In 1914 Holt launched the *Unpopular Review*, a quarterly dedicated to exposing the "fallacies" he believed were blighting political discourse. One sort of fallacy affected the arrogant rich: such as the assumption that "the tax-paying class ... can afford to be indifferent to the other class." But a greater number influenced "too many of both classes": for example, the belief "that something can be had for nothing ... that the march of progress should be timed to the pace of the slowest ... and that wisdom can be attained by the counting of noses." In this spirit, the *Unpopular Review* defended Hughes against Wilson, leaders against the led, and private property against anyone who proposed to take it away.[42]

Among unpopular causes, the defense of competition by this time ranked high. During the Wilson years, one contributor noted, most Americans had come to accept either the antitrust or regulated monopoly approach to the industrial problem. Even temporary anonymity (the *Review* identified authors only in later issues), failed to induce contributors to defend unregulated competition or private monopoly. Perhaps for this very reason, Holt took up the challenge, at least against "socialists" who, he alleged, would eliminate competition altogether. The result was a final restatement of the old Spencerian distinction between a brutal (Darwinian) past and a present in which cooperation, altruism, and similar qualities provided new standards of fitness.[43]

Although it was not Holt's intent, his efforts also showed how thoroughly the Darwinian case against the natural order permeated all discussion of the issue. Bad competition (or "the Nietzsche-Treitschke theory of competition," as he termed it in these war years) was one of "Nature red in tooth and claw," and "of the struggle for existence, the destruction of the least fit, and the survival of the fittest." Holt repeated that "nature's ways" included "cooperation as well as competition." But without Spencer's metaphysical passion, whereby cosmic outcomes made past brutality somehow unreal, Holt's tortured distinctions revealed only, as he himself said, "the old struggle between facts and ideals"—the very dualism Spencer's system was designed to overcome. Given reigning assumptions concerning the struggle for existence, his appeal was bound to remain unpopular. Perhaps for this reason, Holt dropped this rhetoric, after a single attempt, in favor of more general appeals to nature and evolution.[44]

Writing somewhat earlier on civic relations, Holt revealed another dimension to the problem of amending Spencer. Although his views were doubtless conservative by progressive standards, he believed he had altered his position significantly since his youth. "I confess," he wrote,

that, having started with a faith that progress can be hoped for only through the struggle for existence and the survival of the fittest, this appearing to be the only course supported by natural law, I have come to realize that with the evolution of intelligence and sympathy, standards of fitness to survive have materially changed. . . . Now the struggle of brute force has become a struggle of intelligence, and even a competition in honesty and amiability.[45]

In one sense his memory was probably accurate: Holt and certainly the *Nation* under Godkin were once less compromising in their defense of competition and laissez faire. But had he defended these policies in Darwinian terms, or did he thus describe his earlier views only after abandoning them? From the written record, it would appear that Holt unwittingly applied to himself the stereotype under which so many Spencerians had labored for several decades. In a small way, he was now his own straw man.

These instances of American Spencerianism in its final phase are by no means the only examples of Spencer's influence in the United States. By the turn of the century, wrote the philosopher John Dewey, Spencer "so thoroughly impressed his ideas [upon Americans] that even non-Spencerians must talk in his terms and adapt their problems to his statements."[46] By that time, his impact was perhaps even greater on his critics—younger sociologists, pragmatists, and psychologists—than upon the Spencerians, such as Carnegie, who gathered at Delmonico's two decades earlier. However the problems these Spencerians faced were an important index to a general crisis in American thought, which is too often eclipsed by attention only to Spencer's "anti-formalist" critics—the "winners" as it were. As faith in the future waned, and with it the belief in automatic progress, Spencerians found themselves caught between relativism and expediency, on the one hand, and an unacceptable *a priorism* on the other. In this plight William Jay Youmans was not alone. In particular, his career provides the background for the work of the one figure who gave these questions their most sustained and sophisticated formulations—William Graham Sumner of Yale, a sometime Spencerian and the Gilded Age's best-known social Darwinist.

5.   William Graham Sumner

"Dost thou not know, deluded one
  That Adam Smith has clearly proved
That 'tis self-interest alone
  By which the wheels are moved?

"That competition is the law
  By which we either live or die;
I've no demand thy labor for,
  Why, then, should I thy wants supply?

"And Herbert Spencer's active brain
  Shows how the social struggle ends;
The weak die out, the strong remain;
  Tis this that Nature's plan intends.

"Now really 'tis absurd of you
  To think I'd interfere at all;
Just grasp the scientific view,
  The weakest must go to the wall."

My words impressed his dormant thought;
  "How wise," he said, "is Nature's plan;
Henceforth I'll practice what you've taught
  And be a scientific man.

"We are alone—no others hear
  Or even within hailing distance.
I've a good club, and now right here
  We'll have a struggle for existence.

"The weak must die—the strong survive,
  Let's see who'll prove the harder hittest,
So if you wish to keep alive
  Prepare to prove yourself the fittest.

"If you decline the test to make
  and doubt your chances of survival
Your watch and pocket-book I'll take
  As competition strips a rival."

What could I do but yield the point
  Though conscious of no logic blunder;
And as I quaked in every joint,
  The tramp departed with the plunder.

From Phillips Thompson, "The Political Economist and
the Tramp," Daily Evening Traveller, 28 September 1878.
"Dedicated to Prof. W. G. Sumner of Yale."

One

William Graham Sumner (1840-1910) made enemies easily. An
Episcopalian minister in the late 1860s, he accepted the chair of Political
Economy at Yale in 1872 and was soon embroiled in hassles over curriculum reform. In 1880 his battle with Yale President Noah Porter over the
use of Herbert Spencer's Study of Sociology, one of the earliest academic
freedom cases in the modern American university, made national head-
lines. During the eighties, in dozens of articles in popular magazines, he
championed laissez faire and free trade, the former anathema to a growing body of younger economists, the latter unacceptable to many indus-
trialists. Although his Folkways (1906) was a classic in the literature of
early American sociology, many remembered best his spirited defenses of
capitalism and free enterprise.

The basis of Sumner's reputation as a social Darwinist, a fitting monu-
ment to this lifetime of controversy, was laid quite early. Reviewing some
essays in the 1880s, the Nation, otherwise sympathetic to Sumner's views,
regretted his "method of exposition," specifically his vision of "Nature,
red in tooth and claw." Shortly after his death he was included among the
social Darwinists in several books that popularized the term. In his Social
Adaptation (1915) the sociologist L. M. Bristol described Folkways as "the
neo-Darwinian formula applied to the development of folkways and social
institutions." Another sociologist, Arthur J. Todd, singled out Sumner a
few years later as "the American echo to English and German selectionism." In The Goose Step (1923) Upton Sinclair commented concerning
Sumner, "Never that I know of has stark brutal selfishness been so deified,
and covered by the mantle of science." Incorporating this view, historians
made Sumner the unofficial dean of American social Darwinists.[1]

Most observers recognized the complexity of Sumner's thought. Maturing in the age of Spencer and Darwin, he drew primarily on the Protestant
ethic and classical economics. A defender of property, he was not a
"business hireling" but a spokesman of an older middle class threatened
by a variety of developments in American life. Accepting relativism and
naturalism, he never relinquished an inherited faith in individualism and
democracy. By the end of his life, there were in effect two Sumners: the
one a defender of an orthodoxy that most of his own middle class had

deserted for progressive reform, and the other a pioneering sociologist whose *Folkways* never seemed quite reconciled with the rest of his thought.[2]

But what of Sumner's social Darwinism? Did he endorse an unabashedly Darwinian struggle within society? And if so, what of the labored distinctions he drew throughout his career between the struggle for existence against nature *and* the competition of life among men in society—a distinction harkening back to Malthus and one that appeared to mute, if not deny entirely, the suggestion that individuals within society engage in an animal-like struggle?[3]

Sumner insisted upon this distinction because it was crucial to his position. Failure to take him seriously on this point has been at the root of a number of problems in the popular image of his social Darwinism—and even of his reputation as one of Spencer's chief American disciples. In political economy, Sumner began with Malthus, whose man-land ratio remained the bedrock of his thought. Distinguishing between the struggle for existence and the competition of life, Sumner attempted to clarify Malthus's own distinction between the collective struggle against nature and the social laws that governed that struggle—the latter a final vestige of an eighteenth-century faith in natural harmonies. The success of this strategy depended on holding the line against Darwin's notion that intra-species conflict was an inevitable concomitant of the struggle against nature.

Nor was Sumner a Spencerian in any important sense, other than sharing a common faith in individualism and laissez faire, and an animus against social "meddlers." Introduced to positivism in the work of Buckle and Martineau, Sumner developed a passion for facts over theory, and a bias against metaphysics that put even Spencer beyond the pale. Despite his brief salute at Delmonico's in 1882 (when in effect he confessed he barely understood Spencer's theory), and a biographical sketch in *Popular Science* in which he or the editors exaggerated the debt, Sumner had no fondness for Spencerian rhetoric and implicitly attacked the fundamental premises of his cosmic evolutionism. For this reason, Sumner was personally attacked by Spencerians almost as much as by their opponents.[4]

This reassessment of Sumner's intellectual framework broadens earlier challenges to the social Darwinist thesis in his case. In a study of Sumner's ministerial career, Merwin Sheketoff ignored social Darwinism to argue that the young clergyman fashioned a doctrine of Christian social responsibility, which, although not a program of state intervention, anticipated ideas that would later flower in the Social Gospel movement. Sumner's desire to improve the world, Sheketoff argued, was transformed but not diminished when he left the ministry. In a study of Sumner's later thought, Bruce Curtis also stressed elements in his vision that may be termed protoprogressive. Challenging Sheketoff, Curtis insisted that naturalism blighted Sumner's reform impulse. Finally, however, Sumner "became a progressive in spite of his naturalism," accepting at the close of his life the need for government intervention to preserve competition. A sociologist, denying that *Folkways* barred change through law, has suggested that Sumner anticipated later analyses of the constructive use of law in reform, thus challenging a further item in the social Darwinist interpretation.[5]

More important than the reformer who might-have-been was the appearance of *Folkways* as the final product of Sumner's lifelong attempt to provide a scientific basis for social policy at a time when science and Darwinism were increasingly intertwined. Sumner's response to Darwinism is revealing, not because he adopted slogans of struggle and survival willy-nilly (he did not) nor because he finally became a progressive, but because his piecemeal accommodation to the new science reflected a changing assessment of man and society that a number of his contemporaries shared. Science attracted Sumner, first as he battled in the war of science and religion in the late 1860s, and then as he sought the certainty of social law during the troubled seventies. In mood and assumption this Sumner resembled many champions of social science and others, such as the literary realists, who celebrated "fact" as antidote to change. Deeply affected by the corruption and violence of the age, Sumner preached a return to individualism and laissez faire. But no less than the reform Darwinists, he came gradually to see (however much he regretted it) that history (in fact) and Darwinism (in theory) pointed toward solidarity and social control. A tension between inherited belief and the lessons taught by society and Darwin finally produced an accommodation to Darwinism that is poorly described by culling scattered references to the survival of the fittest. Sumner, increasingly disillusioned, resisted the alleged reform lessons of Darwinism. But his later thought owed much of its originality to this very resistance.

Two

Like many educated young Americans maturing in the 1860s, Sumner could not easily resist the siren call of science. Studying theology at Gottingen, he absorbed the Higher Criticism of the German theologians, marveling especially at the "scientific accuracy of their methods." In England he discovered in the positivism of Henry Thomas Buckle, even in Spencer's *Social Statics* (the metaphysical caste of which offended him), that science clarified social as well as religious questions. Returning to America, where the warfare of science with theology was especially severe, he attempted to instruct his parishioners in Morristown, New Jersey, concerning the proper limits of tradition and rationalism, orthodoxy and the Higher Criticism.[6]

His theology, unsystematic as it was in his weekly sermons, was a compromise. He repeatedly stressed the importance of science, using the term indiscriminately to refer to rationalism of a freethinking variety and to the more systematic inductions of the historical school. "Caesarism and popery," he wrote his fiancée in 1870, are "going down before civilization and science." On several occasions he stressed the dangers of carrying science too far. Several times he censured rationalists who denied "the claims of any church, any creed, any God." "Modern speculation and science," he observed in his farewell sermon, held the possibility that "all religion may be lost." A balance must be achieved between "tradition" and "progress."[7]

To sustain this compromise, Sumner distinguished science as a method from the "speculations," as he imagined them, of individual scientists. Thus, in one of his earliest references to the champions of the new biology, he asserted that he found "no great fault" with Darwin, Huxley, and Spencer in "their original works. . . . They may be right or wrong in their speculations and theories," but they were "honest, sincere, and industrious" in method. But he had no use for "professional scribblers" who hawked speculation under their presumed authority. Defending Bishop Colenso, the rationalist biblical critic, Sumner made this distinction even clearer. To understand Colenso, it was necessary "to call attention to the true meaning of the sadly abused word science":

> In our language a mischievous ambiguity has arisen between science and natural science, and it has greatly obscured the true meaning of the former word. Science is the source of rules by which the human mind is guided in investigating truth. These rules are given in the structure and methods of the action of the human mind. They are universal. It is obedience to them and in no other way that the human reason can apprehend any ideas. Hence science is a trained method of using the human reason.

This ambiguity in the word *science* and Sumner's ambivalence toward the theories of natural science, also explain an interesting early appearance of Darwinian rhetoric in his sermons. In these sermons he preached, not unbridled individualism and competition, but the "solidarity of the human race." Excessive rationalism (science), in the blunt equations of which Sumner was fond, underlay irresponsible individualism, "'ill-gotten-wealth," and the entire "get-rich-quick" mentality he deplored in post Civil War America. Speculations drawn from natural science to justify such behavior were invariably superficial, for example, "the widespread idea that the law of life is to struggle out of one situation into another in the pursuit of happiness." "Nature," he wrote toward the close of his pastorate in one of several attacks on Darwinism, "indeed" taught "a sad lesson of violence, of right which depends on might only." But this only if one "stops . . . with the first and superficial view."[8] When in 1872 Sumner abandoned his pulpit for the chair of Political Economy at Yale he was not prepared to state the deeper implications of Darwinism for social theory. But he was convinced that Darwinism, if crudely applied to human affairs, yielded a picture of society quite unacceptable to him.

Three

Leaving the ministry, Sumner neither rejected religion nor lost his moral fervor. Concerning religion, as he later quipped, he merely put his beliefs in a drawer for safekeeping. In some way he might still profess belief in realms of experience science could not comprehend. But his concern henceforth was primarily to be those areas in which it could. Adopting what amounted to a naive materialism, he separated the ideal from the real, as it were, for tactical purposes. Only then might the dispassionate scientist measure cause and effect, the physician prescribe for an ailing society.

This tactic, and Sumner's worship of scientific method in the 1870s and after, reflected a deep-seated need he shared with many of his generation. It is especially instructive to compare Sumner in this regard with the literary realists whose sense of disinheritance Roger Salomon has recently analyzed. Like the realists, Sumner in the early seventies felt cut off from the past. "All traditions of government and society," he wrote, "have been called in question and put on trial." The Civil War was but one episode in a destruction of old beliefs and institutions that had been going on for several centuries. But, he explained to a Memorial Day audience in 1872, the movement also had "its positive and constructive side." Scientific methods, allowing one to trace cause and effect in a clearly defined real world, provided the certainty that tradition no longer could. "We turn away from tradition and prescription," he told his class at Yale, "to reexamine the data from which we may learn what principles of the social order are true."[9] With the inclusion of data and the careful tracing of cause and effect, Sumner undoubtedly smuggled cherished convictions disguised as natural laws into this antiseptic new order. But, as with the realists, the basic impulse was otherwise. For Sumner, as for the realists, science offered a device for atomizing experience into manageable proportions—data—the relations between which could be definitely and conclusively fixed.

In Sumner's case the upheavals following the crash of 1873, underlining the uncertainties of the times, transformed this positive and constructive program into a defensive and critical one. The financial situation, and the battles over greenbacks and specie resumption, provided proof of the folly of ignoring natural laws. Politics underscored this lesson. The harshness of Reconstruction, as he saw it, marked a failure to apply science in the passing of legislation. "Untrained in the difficult art of legislation, incompetent to judge of the forces which their projects would arouse," he wrote of the radicals, "they set out by arbitrary legislation to control a social revolution a thousand miles away."[10] The Hayes-Tilden election, for which he served on the Electoral Commission to investigate conflicting returns, increased his disgust at popular government. Labor agitation and the strikes in 1877 fueled his conviction that protectionism and socialism, similar evils, were violations of natural law.

Science yielded two lessons in this situation, the one negative, the other positive. Huxley, Sumner observed, "has called our attention to the fact that nature's discipline does not consist of a word and a blow . . . but of a blow without a word." This, as he earlier expressed it, was the "sad lesson of violence, of right which depends on might only." But the interest of the lesson was Huxley's (and Spencer's) further insistence that scientific method could "save us from this rude discipline by warning us what are the laws of nature."[11]

So persuaded, Sumner was also troubled by dissent within the social science academy. His plea for science was of course elitist to some degree. "Scientific truth," as one of his colleagues at the Social Science Association remarked, was the province of "educated men."[12] Quarreling among gentlemen, always distasteful, doubly bothered Sumner. If natural laws were immutable, why could educated men not agree upon their formulation? And if they could not, how could the masses be persuaded to accept the truth of social science? Sumner, raised on the strict precepts of classical economics as expounded by Malthus and Ricardo and in Harriet Martineau's *Illustrations of Political Economy*, discovered in the seventies that agreement on these principles was scarcely universal. The social sciences, he regretted to say, were "as yet, the stronghold" of many "pernicious dogmatisms." Worse, leaders of the German historical school—Roscher, Brentano—were seducing a younger generation of American graduate students from the true gospel. "We have seen the economists," Sumner lamented in 1879, "instead of holding together and sustaining, at this time when it was most needed, both the scientific authority and the positive truth of their doctrines, break up and run hither and thither."[13]

Four

But what precisely were the laws of nature as they pertained to man's life in society? Sumner, against this background of concern over national affairs and over divisions within the social sciences, turned to this question in a series of papers that resulted in his widely read *What Social Classes Owe to Each Other* (1883). In these essays he formulated a distinction between the struggle for existence and the *competition of life*, the battle of man against nature and the social forces to which it gave rise. During these years he also stated baldly on several occasions that the alternative to the survival of the fittest was the *survival of the unfittest*, a bit of phrasemaking that provided proof to his opponents then and since that his social views involved at heart a harsh misapplication of Darwinism. For this reason, these statements, which Sumner made only in the period 1879 to 1884, demand especially close attention.[14]

The first of these essays, "Socialism," Sumner's most systematic statement of his views on the social question to that date, was an attack on socialism that appeared in *Scribner's* in 1878. Sumner began with a forthright statement of his Malthusianism, a doctrine he knew was under attack from several quarters. "Human beings tend to multiply beyond the power of a limited area of land to support life, *under a given stage of the arts*, and a given standard of living" (emphasis mine). Emigration and technology had temporarily suspended the immediate pressure of population, but the struggle for existence remained an inescapable fact of life. In this struggle, man was pitted against nature, Sumner's model here of economic life being man against the wilderness—an English colonist, for example, as Harriet Martineau used as one of her *Illustrations of Political Economy*. Paralleling this struggle was the competition of life, a social struggle which Sumner left undefined both as to its nature and its relation to the struggle for existence. But the distinction, he insisted, was important. Socialists erred in confusing the two. Thus they blamed the competition of life for hardships properly laid to the struggle for existence.[15]

In attempting to relate the natural and social spheres, Sumner grappled with a problem that likewise concerned Herbert Spencer and his followers. Like Spencer, Sumner insisted that fitness in the purely natural realm implied no social or ethical judgment. Like Spencer he believed that the rules governing the social sphere (the competition of life) tempered the natural process. But with characteristic bluntness, and in line with the tactical materialism he adopted in the interest of scientific precision, Sumner allowed a greater dualism between the natural and social than most Spencerians would admit. Hence Sumner refused to view evolution as the source and guarantee of altruism (whereas Spencer did so view it), just as he rejected the reform Darwinist argument, as propounded by the sociologist Lester Ward, that evolution produced social intelligence and a regulative sociocracy. Eventually this refusal, spurring Sumner's own sociological inquiry, forced him to define the relation between the material struggle and the rules which governed the social sphere. But in the eighties it plunged him into bitter controversy.

The appearance of Henry George's *Progress and Poverty* (1879), with its extended attack on Malthus, fired Sumner's determination to defend his thesis. George had "wasted his effort" because "the 'Malthusian doctrine' is swallowed up in a great biological law." Darwin, that is, had generalized Malthus's notion of the continued pressure of population against limited resources to all of nature, making it a starting point for his further hypothesis concerning natural selection. Sumner, avoiding entirely the issue of this still controversial doctrine, merely wished to assert that Darwin gave support to the idea of a struggle for existence as a starting point for all speculation concerning beings. But why then not carry Darwinism further? Sumner, indulging his flair for epigram, appeared to do precisely this. At a speech before the Free Trade Club in 1879, and on several subsequent occasions, he noted that in the struggle for existence there were but two alternatives. "The law of the survival of the fittest was not made by man" went the argument. "We can only, by interfering with it, produce the survival of the unfittest."[16]

This phrasemaking, as critics were quick to point out, raised at least two difficulties. If social laws boiled down to the survival of the fittest, a phrase widely understood to apply to the natural realm, was Sumner not in effect denying any difference between the struggle for existence and the competition of life? By implying that individuals fought individuals for the means of life, was he not applying a brute standard to human affairs? Sumner, insisting that he had been misunderstood, defended his distinctions. The problem for the scientific study of society was one of proper definitions. "Strong" and "weak," as used in popular reform jargon, had no meaning unless reduced to the materialist terms of man's struggle with nature. "Idiots, insane persons, cripples, etc. are weak and society has to support them," he wrote. But if in addition society, from its stockpile of "capital" won in past battles with nature, attempted to treat equally those who were succeeding and those who were failing in the battle against nature, the stockpile manifestly would be reduced. His epigram implied no moral judgment. "Rattlesnakes survive where horses perish," he wrote, "or a highly cultivated white man may die where Hottentots flourish." Such narrow logic, Sumner admitted, might not get one very far in prescribing what ought to be done. But he insisted it was the only means of bringing precision to current discussion of the social issue.[17]

The criticism these few brief passages drew suggested that, whatever Sumner's faults, he had not voiced a position that was very popular. Although there is no record of comment when he first coined the epigram, a member of the Nineteenth Century Club, where he repeated it on one occasion, was especially outraged. "Of all the bald truisms" in the world, the "survival of the fittest" was the baldest, this critic noted tartly. The "real duty" of sociology was "to see that only the best survive, the men who believe that there is something to live for beside grasping and accumulating wealth." Others took up the attack. The *New York Times*, editorializing on "The Selfish Sciences," condemned the "lame analogy of the survival of the fittest." "In such a society," wrote another critic, "the strong would prey upon the weak, the poor would grow poorer and the rich richer, and the law of such a society would be that which prevails in the wilderness and jungles inhabited by beasts of prey. . . . That might suit Professor Sumner. He is welcome to it."[18]

Two other critics suggested that Sumner had in fact misconstrued his sources and even contradicted his own basic position. An avowed Spencerian, a reform-minded lawyer, wrote to the *New York Times* that Spencer himself would not accept the implication that fitness was fitness in any social sense. "Indeed," added the editor of the *Index*, the journal of the Free Religious Association, "several passages of [Sumner's] essay led us to suppose that, like Darwin, Spencer, and the leading evolutionists, Mr. Sumner believed that the law of the survival of the fittest was, in man, either in great measure annulled or its character greatly changed by moral and rational considerations. . . . Therefore the epigram with which he closed seemed to be opposed by much of his own argument."[19]

Sumner did not easily escape the reputation thus earned. Although in *Social Classes* he made no reference to the survival of the fittest, a reviewer in the *Index* claimed that Sumner urged that the "laws of competition, of the struggle for existence, and of the survival of the fittest" be allowed "to work out their legitimate results." The sociologist Lester Ward, who also reviewed *Social Classes*, had Sumner in mind in later charges that the advocates of laissez faire deduced their position from the doctrines of the survival of the fittest and natural selection.[20]

The *Nation*, in a review of Sumner's *Collected Essays* (1885), was closer to the truth. This guardian of traditional liberalism was sympathetic to Sumner's conclusions. But it regarded his way of expressing himself as "occasionally unfortunate." Sumner, for example, stated that there could be no "definition of a man's deserts, . . . except what he actually gets in return for his efforts under the free play of natural forces." His aim again was to obtain precision by isolating a real world of things, introducing the ought later. Yet, as the *Nation* observed, if natural forces included the institutions of civilized society, one had "the absurd proposition that every man actually gets justice." If not, justice was possible "only among the lower animals," a proposition which, in connection with other statements, seemed none other than:

> . . . the good old rule,
> . . . the simple plan,
> That they should take who have the power,
> And they should keep who can.

"The stern law of natural selection is modified by the institution of government," the *Nation* lectured, "in response to the craving for an ideal justice that is never realized in Nature."[21] Sumner in other words imperiled his principles by laying himself open to a charge of social Darwinism.

In retrospect it is clear that the portrait built on this charge not only exaggerates and distorts Sumner's use of Darwinism in the 1880s but seriously misrepresents the problem he faced. Having reduced experience to manageable data, in the spirit of positivism, how could one reintroduce social and personal values? How get mind from matter? ought from is? How deduce a "correct" ideological and institutional superstructure from the struggle for existence? Sumner's hard-headed realism, the obverse of the Genteel Tradition, was the hallmark of a generation for whom, as Lewis Mumford has written, the imaginative fusion of ideal and real seemed no longer a genuine possibility. Sumner's error, if it may be so termed, lay not in making crude appeals to Darwinism, certainly not to natural selection, but in adopting an intellectual strategy historian Edward Kirkland has termed "divide and ruin"—the illusion that one could "operate under the aegis of a 'distinct perception of things themselves distinct.'" A frequent tactic in the works of the classical economists of whom Sumner was one, this was also a favorite of businessmen accustomed to dividing life into business, social, and religious spheres. Likewise Sumner, maintaining that the basic struggle between man and nature could be isolated as a single variable, tried to divide economics from politics and morals. Opposing *plutocracy*, the illicit union of economic and political power, Sumner sought a solution in the strict separation of the two spheres. So also a final chapter in *Social Classes*, awkwardly appended like a visit to church at the close of a busy week, carried the full burden of explaining why Sumner's analysis did not rule out humanitarianism. This tactic was not suggested by Darwinism, but rather was deeply rooted in older traditions, for example, in J. S. Mill's *Essays on Some Unsettled Questions of Political Economy* (1844) or the empiricist psychology of the Common Sense philosophers who taught midcentury Americans to divide mind into will, affections, and reason. This approach, as Kirkland notes, especially appealed to troubled souls who, in time of rapid change, sought exact answers to bewildering and unmanageable problems. This, and not a harsh social Darwinism, linked Sumner to the business mood of his generation.[22]

Characteristically stubborn, Sumner never formally renounced his troublesome epigram. But there are several indications he was sensitive to the criticism, some of which he carefully pasted in a scrapbook. One indication was the unaccustomed humility he displayed in describing his grasp of sociology. Despite several tortured attempts to explain how biology and sociology were related, he confessed that all one could "affirm with certainty" is that social phenomena are subject to laws that "are in their entire character like the laws of physics." Further clues to his change of heart were the absence of the offending epigram in *Social Classes* and his addition of the chapter—"Wherefore We Should Love One Another"— in which he explained that the sociologist qua scientist merely provided "one element necessary to an intelligent decision" by allowing an observer to trace one sort of impact of any given action.[23] Following a public exchange on the survival of the fittest issue, Sumner after 1884 apparently decided to drop the phrase entirely.[24] In his later work and for his classes at Yale, he etched more deeply the distinction between the struggle for existence and the competition of life. Turning from political economy to sociology in the late eighties, he gave increasing attention to the laws governing the latter.

Five

The decade of the nineties, a difficult time for Sumner, marked a turning point in his career no less than the early seventies. In 1890 he suffered an emotional collapse that forced him to take his first academic leave. The growth of imperial sentiment, culminating in the Spanish American War, deeply disturbed him, as did the apparent increase of the twin evils of socialism and plutocracy. Mirroring his domestic concerns, his celebrated denunciation of "The Absurd Effort to Make the World Over" (1894) constituted his last extended discussion of the issues that had absorbed him for more than a decade. His popular writing increasingly focused on the international situation. At the same time he began with new seriousness his long planned *Science of Society*, of which *Folkways* was to be a first installment.

His sociology reflected the changing social situation and his assessment of it in the light of a more serious reading of the literature of the social sciences than he had previously undertaken. Three aspects of this later work relate it to his earlier concerns. Firstly, he clarified the cooperative element in the competition of life, making it a major emphasis of his social theory. He had of course never entirely ignored it. Expressing the conclusions of current anthropology, he described as early as 1878 the process whereby struggle engendered solidarity within primitive groups and communities. Civilized men, he wrote several years later, fought the struggle for existence "side by side." By the late nineties he termed this group effort *antagonistic cooperation*, a phrase intended to honor both his belief in competition and a growing body of opinion that cooperation was an undeniable factor in society and even in nature. "The struggle to maintain existence," he wrote, explaining the origin of folkways, "was carried on, not individually but in groups." Folkways, generalized into custom, became finally "a philosophy of right living and a life policy for welfare," which Sumner termed the *mores*.[25]

Several factors propelled Sumner toward this greater emphasis on cooperation within what he now termed the *in-group*. The growth of trusts and labor unions, especially in the late 1880s, became at that time a major concern in his essays. Imperialist struggles and war in the nineties, which Sumner vigorously opposed, made vivid the anthropologists' description of group solidarity for external combat. This theme, which Sumner early found in such works as Bagehot's *Physics and Politics*, he now found elaborated by Gumplowicz, Ratzenhofer, and other sociologists of the *struggle school*. Because the competition of life arises between groups, not between individuals, Sumner concluded, "it is the competition of life that makes war, and that is why war always has existed and always will."[26]

Secondly, Sumner faced squarely the essential irrationality of human behavior. Again there were hints of this view in his earlier thought. "Tradition, prejudice, fashion, habit, and other similar obstacles continually warp and deflect the social forces," he wrote in 1881.[27] Yet he could not then accept these obstacles as facts, let alone study them dispassionately. Facts were hard and certain: these obstacles were errors to be condemned, impermanent phenomena that would disappear when the positivist stage was attained. Gradually Sumner's certainty on this point faded. "Time," as his biographer stated, "disillusioned him."[28] The complexity of the industrial organization, the tangle of human interests involved in its operation, and his gradual realization that men are not controlled by cold logic pushed him steadily to sociology. American jingoism, which reached fever pitch in the late nineties, confirmed this new view of human nature. Man, as he now saw him, was driven to social activity by four principal motives: "hunger, love, vanity, and fear of superior powers." In *Folkways* he concluded, "Fashions, fads, affectations, poses, ideals, manias, popular delusions, follies, and vices must be included in the mores." Disguised as mores, codes, or taboos, human folly became amenable to scientific study.[29]

Finally, Sumner also accepted a more thoroughgoing relativism than before. Again, roots can be found in his earlier work. The rules governing the competition of life were, he insisted, relative to population, resources, and the "stage of the arts." Humanitarianism and even democracy were the products of a relatively painless competition of life in the modern period. By 1900 however, industrial and imperial warfare gave this conclusion new urgency. Simply one of the mores, democracy would inevitably be replaced when conditions changed. In his more pessimistic moments he believed its days were numbered.[30]

By this time, Sumner the realist, to revert to a literary parallel, more closely resembled such literary naturalists as the later Twain, Dreiser, Norris, and London, however different his politics. He, as they did, saw the world in biological, even Darwinian, terms: giant combinations of labor and capital, lapsing periodically into warfare; nations adopting a similar course to the peril of Western civilization; individuals driven by primal instincts. Sumner was not happy with this situation. Unions, although he accepted strikes as a legitimate test of the market when they succeeded in raising wages, clearly disturbed him.[31] Although he defended trusts, his writings on the subject betrayed a worried ambivalence even before his eleventh-hour conversion to the view that government must intervene to preserve competition.[32] He opposed imperialism in a series of brilliant essays.[33] His list of mores was essentially a catalog of American folly, as he saw it, in the progressive period. *Folkways*, like *The Education of Henry Adams*, written at the same time, was testament that genius sometimes flourishes best in a hostile intellectual and political climate.

With some naturalists Sumner shared what Frederic Jaher has termed a "cataclysmic vision"[34] that predicted total destruction if present tendencies continued. Summing up the "Bequests of the 19th Century to the 20th," Sumner foresaw disaster if social science did not match man's industrial accomplishments. The twentieth century, he noted, would be "as full of war" as the eighteenth. This warning he intensified in the final decade of his life. War was perennial, he wrote in *Folkways*. The present period of relative ease was "exceptional," he repeated in his final published

essay in 1909. Eventually "groups and parties will form and war will occur between them. Great slogans will be put forth at all stages of these
movements," he wrote resignedly, "and appropriate watchwords will
never be wanting."[35]

This naturalist vision—superficially resembling one form of militarist
social Darwinism—was a measure, not of Sumner's success in fashioning a
Darwinian rationale for things in which he believed, but of the disillusionment and despair that turned others of his generation to naturalism. For
Spencer and the Youmans brothers, cosmic evolutionism provided an un-
acknowledged guarantee for inherited conviction: its collapse left them
wandering uneasily between this theory and uncomfortable facts. Unen-
cumbered by theory, but not immune to similar convictions, Sumner settled deeper than most of his generation into the mood and assumptions of
naturalism. Naturalism provided the perfect vehicle for expressing regret
and disgust, a language for disillusionment. Sumner further illustrates
what Charles Walcutt has called the "divided stream" of American
naturalism: the projection of a universe without pity or purpose, coupled
with an irrepressible desire to redeem it. Ultimately, as Walcutt suggests,
this dual vision rested on "a profound uncertainty as to whether science
liberates the human spirit or destroys it."[36] Sumner displayed this ambivalence from the time he first distinguished the methods of science from
its speculations.

In *Folkways* this dual vision surfaced as Sumner wrestled with the
status of traditional values in the modern world. Science on the one hand
postulated a universe in which men were imprisoned by mores which
alone made things right. Since those mores survived that commanded the
support of the most powerful groups, "nothing but might has ever made
right." Yet science also provided escape from this dreary logic, especially
anathema to a middle class threatened by a socialism and a plutocracy
bent on imposing their mores on modern America. The key was the difference between a *posterior* and an *anterior* view. On the former "Nothing
but might has ever made right, and . . . nothing but might makes right
now." But on the anterior view the case was different. "If we are about to
take some action and are debating the right of it, the might that can be
brought to support the view of it has nothing to do with the right of it."[37]

Scientific method, applied to the study of history (the sociologists'
laboratory), could provide this anterior view by predicting the probable
outcome of following particular mores. In this fashion Sumner defended
"the ethical policy taught in the books and the school," the old private and
public virtues, by arguing that, despite short-run appearances, they yielded
maximum success in the struggle against nature. Using history, he

demonstrated that middle-class virtue yielded maximum group power. At the same time, the rightness of these virtues was not a function of the group's ability to impose them by force.[38]

Sumner turned this approach on the mores of plutocracy and socialists. The first preached a "cult of success" that brought a "deep depreciation of all social interests by the elevation of success to a motive which justified itself." This cult was a legacy of the Renaissance, as Sumner read Burckhardt, an individualism that said "any man might do anything which would win success for his purpose." In the Renaissance such individualism led to the total corruption of private life. The decay of Renaissance Italy resulted from ignoring the few who preached an alternative, the virtue policy, the forerunners of Sumner's "forgotten man." The history of that period showed that "although moral traditions may be narrow and mistaken, any morality is better than moral anarchy."[39]

Similarly, history since the Renaissance revealed the decay that came from following the sentimental preaching of socialists and reformers. The opening of the lands of the New World began an "exceptional period" in which the competition of life and the struggle for existence were not severe. But gradually, harmful myths had pervaded the mores—among them "ambition" and "equality"—which were only "relatively true in the exceptional period." Purveyors of these myths coined slogans to support their causes, the result being the quackery of which the modern world was full. Like Frederick Jackson Turner, but on a worldwide scale, Sumner warned that the end of the frontier meant the end of democracy. Unlike Turner (who clung to a naive environmentalism) Sumner believed that renewed struggle between groups and nations would be the instrument of its destruction.

The accomplishment of *Folkways* does not refute many valid criticisms of Sumner's social and economic views. While one may agree with him that the Single Tax and Bellamyite Nationalism were no panaceas, the scientific philanthropy to which his theories reduced in practice often meant a tightening of relief when suffering was greatest. His dogmatic insistence that virtually any humanitarianism or government intervention was liable to weaken the joint struggle for existence proceeded on the assumption of full employment and an ignorance of the importance of consumer demand in advanced industrial society. Static and short-run, his analysis showed little understanding of the workings of impure or imperfect competition that allows less than optimum allocation of resources under laissez faire.[40] Ironically, not only did Sumner's hard-headed realism seem finally to subordinate all values to the acquisition of property, but his program, from the point of view of modern economists, failed even to achieve his stated goals of efficiency and maximum productivity.

But Sumner was not guilty of celebrating a struggle for existence, nor did he believe that Darwinism justified the dog-eat-dog practices he observed about him. Nor did he really, as some critics have charged, equate might and right, reducing everything finally to social power.[41] This implication was always the ghost in the Spencerian closet. The good society was the strong society, the argument went, because the nation which made its unfit "fit," materially and socially, maximized production and group cohesion. Yet was not the nation which triumphed in war ipso facto the best? Were not material and moral power identical? Sumner's distinction between the anterior and posterior view in *Folkways* was meant to forestall just these conclusions.

Instructed by Darwin, Sumner came to believe that monumental struggles lay in the future. The creative tension that inspired *Folkways* was born of this realization and his deep abhorrence of it. The social Darwinism of his late thought, the naturalism of *Folkways*, expressed a growing pessimism over man's willingness (although not his ability) to use social science to escape this plight. To sneer at his social Darwinism or to confuse it with his early defenses of laissez faire is to ignore the important insights that resulted as Sumner moved from realism to naturalism. After three-quarters of a century of near-constant struggle, during which watchwords have indeed never been wanting, Sumner deserves a better fate.

6. The Survival of the Fittest Is Our Doctrine

"How to Succeed," "Self Help." "The Way to Win"
"How to Make Money." "Men Who Have Made Their Way"
etc., are on the Darwinian side of life.
Henry Demarest Lloyd, Notebook *(1886)*.

On tend, depuis vingt ou vingt-cing ans, à appliquer aux
sciences sociales et economiques les résultats obtenus
par les sciences naturelles, grace a Darwin: cette
tendance, ce darwinisme social, comme on l'appelle, a
pris un développment considérable et mérite toute notre
attention.
Achille Loria, *"Darwinisme Social,"* Revue Internationale
de Sociologie, 4 *(1896)*, 440.

One

American reformers of the late nineteenth century were un-
derstandably less interested in their opponents' intellectual difficulties
than in capitalizing on apparent gaps in logic. New Liberals and socialists
asserted in almost a single voice that opponents of state activity wedded
Darwinism to classical economics and thus traded illicitly on the prestige
of the new biology. In *Progress and Poverty* (1879), Henry George charged
that Malthusianism was now "buttressed" by the new science, and be-
moaned "a sort of hopeful fatalism, of which current literature is full."
"The final plea for any form of brutality in these days," wrote the Nationalist Edward Bellamy, "is that it tends to the survival of the fittest."
"The survival of the fittest is our doctrine," echoed the reformer Henry
Demarest Lloyd. "The representatives of science," noted the sociologist
Lester Ward more soberly, "stand boldly in the track of current events."
Ward acknowledged that appeals to natural law antedated the Darwinian
doctrines of survival of the fittest and natural selection. But, he added, "it
cannot be denied that these doctrines . . . have greatly strengthened this
habit of thought."[1] This charge usually prefaced a "correct" reading of
evolution, the so-called reform Darwinism that sustained proposals for the

regulation of industry and an attack on poverty and other ills of industrial society.

This apparently unanimous testimony assumes special interest in light of the foregoing interpretation of the social views of the early Darwinians and Spencerians. Which conservatives were specifically under indictment? How reliable were such contemporary statements? Did reformers themselves believe that their opponents literally demanded a social struggle for survival, or was this construction rather the logic of their position? Since this contemporary testimony was a major source for historical portraits of social Darwinism, these questions concern not only the ideas of the critics but the accuracy of our view of Gilded Age thought.

Two

Although elements of the charge of misapplied Darwinism surfaced in early religious opposition to the *Origin of Species*, the indictment took more definite shape in America during the mid-seventies, echoing similar attacks on Spencer in England. In the *Religion of Evolution* (1876), Minot J. Savage, a Unitarian clergyman and champion of natural theology, expressed concern that a popular view of the cruelty of nature "has been fostered somewhat by inconsiderate writing on the part of some scientists, or by popular misconception of scientific writings." The same year, a German theologian Rudolf von Schmid outlined a similar danger in *The Theories of Darwin*, a work published in Chicago in translation a few years later:

> That Darwinistic ethical naturalism also comes into conflict with concrete moral life, becomes evident from the joy with which the advocates of subversion and negation greet the new principle of the "struggle for existence," and make it the principle of their own actions and social theories.[2]

When religion, philosophy, and politics fused, the indictment took more complete shape, notably in the work of Henry Carey (1793-1879) a prominent Philadelphia journalist and econonomist; John Lord Peck, a professor of political economy at the University of Pennsylvania; and Francis Bowen (1811-1890), professor of philosophy at Harvard. United in their opposition to free trade, Malthusianism, and atheism, each made a subtle if tentative case against the pitfalls of misapplied Darwinism.

Son of Mathew Carey, who helped shape Henry Clay's American System, Henry C. Carey fused Adam Smith's faith in natural law with the elder Carey's devotion to the American dream of economic opportunity for all. Like his father, Henry rejected the ideas of Malthus and Ricardo but he amended Smith's theories to adopt protectionism in the 1840s. Nature, Carey urged in opposition to Malthus, worked toward a universal harmony of interests, the theme of his many books of the pre-Civil War period. The perfect social science would provide men "the highest individualism and the greatest power of association with his fellow men," an "association" which the twentieth century would term national planning.[3] In *The Unity of Law* (1872), his final work, Carey restated this creed for the postwar generation. Rooting social science more firmly than ever in natural philosophy, he drew heavily on E. L. Youmans's *Correlation and Conservation of Forces* (1865), which translated the latest findings of physics into a celebration of the ultimate unity of matter and spirit. So sustained, Carey insisted again that the laws of society and of nature were one, thus further guaranteeing absolute certainty to principles he secretly feared had not brought perfection or unity to society.[4]

In the original text of *The Unity of Law*, Carey ignored Darwinism, perhaps because he suspected the *Origin* threatened his purpose, or perhaps because Darwin's views concerning human society were being published in *The Descent of Man* just as Carey prepared his work for press. With the appearance of the *Descent*, however, Carey answered Darwin in hastily added footnotes and textual insertions. The result was an early instance of the spectre of conservative Darwinism. Carey conceded that most men faced a life of poverty, pestilence, and war. For this state of affairs the followers of Adam Smith offered no cure: material wealth and its transfer were their sole concern, not the mental and moral aspect of economic life. "Need we now wonder," Carey asked, "that a system so thoroughly materialistic should have given rise to a school from which we learn, that 'survival of the fittest,' and crushing out of the less 'fitted,' constitute the basis of all natural arrangements for promoting advance in civilization?"[5]

Had Darwin himself actually taught such a lesson? A careful reading of *The Unity of Law* suggests that Carey compounded several quite different elements in his charge. He specifically criticized the passage in the *Descent* in which Darwin wondered briefly what effect vaccination and similar measures would have upon the future well-being of the human race. Darwin—in passages that Carey ignored—made it clear that his concern was fleeting: men had no choice but to go ahead with such measures. Carey ignored this conclusion because, more than with vaccination, his concern was with the general neglect of social problems that had "from the days of Malthus," been "the tendency of the teachings of the British school." Religion and economics merged. How could one continue to believe in a God, Carey asked, "whose laws, as now generally exhibited, tend toward reducing the millions to a condition of mere hewers of wood and drawers of water for those few who are encouraged to eat, drink, and make merry, while providing measures for securing at the earliest moment, the 'elimination' of those who, being poor and uninstructed, are incapable of self-protection." Darwinism and Malthusianism shared a common spirit. Each was materialistic, a symptom of the worst tendencies of the new age. Together they provided "for the use of science a politico-economic man, a monster, on the one hand influenced solely by the thirst for wealth, and on the other so entirely under the control of sexual passion as to be at all times ready to indulge it." That such a philosophy appeared further to justify international warfare, Carey added, made it only the more reprehensible. Thus were routed atheistic Darwinism, callous laissez faire, and for good measure, the militarist spirit.[6]

Like Carey, the economist-philosopher John Lord Peck joined concern for man's soul with interest in his social condition. In his first book, *The Ultimate Generalization* (1876), philosophical and spiritual concerns sparked a vigorous attack on Spencer's Synthetic Philosophy. Peck for the moment avoided the social implications of evolution, but in *The Political Economy of Democracy* (1879), he spoke directly to social issues. His specific program included a graduated tax; compulsory education; the appropriation of railroad land for settlers; a steady money supply (neither hard nor soft); and moderate protection in the interests of labor. But more generally he focused on a comparison of the classical English school and the views of Carey, whom he (somewhat inaccurately) made a supporter of his proposals. After describing the views of both schools, and in particular Carey's attacks on Malthusianism, Peck then echoed a charge of conservative Darwinism much like that which appeared in *The Unity of Law*. "It is assumed that the best man will win in the struggle for existence (that is, wealth)," he wrote, summarizing the English school, "and thus the survival of the fittest, in agreement with the law of Natural Selection will be secured." Peck even more than Carey did not suppose that men could "escape the law of the survival of the fittest." "The Superior will live and thrive at the expense of the inferior, in trade and industry as truly as in the conflicts of savages, or in the chase of wild beasts for their prey," he conceded. "But the superiority should be superiority of intelligence and character, not one of wealth and good fortune merely." Government, by enacting his proposals, would guarantee such superiority.[7]

Like Carey, Francis Bowen of Harvard absorbed Darwinism in the latter part of a distinguished career devoted to Christianity and the protective tariff. Like Peck and Carey he was also a staunch opponent of Malthusianism. But Bowen was also a philosopher whose devotion to idealism gave his crusade an added dimension. In the early 1860s, he joined battle with both positivism and evolutionism, whether manifested in the *Origin of Species* or in Henry Thomas Buckle's "gospel of fatalism and unbelief." In the mid-1870s he added other philosophers to his list, in particular the Germans Schopenhauer and von Hartmann whose work he criticized in *Modern Philosophy* (1877).[8]

In an attack on "Malthusianism, Darwinism, and Pessimism," which appeared in the *North American Review* in 1879, Bowen wed these several concerns into a call for an increased birth rate among the native New England population; the strengthening of family life; and colonial (or western) settlement. Taking his three foes in turn, Bowen first attacked Malthus and his followers for callousness in the face of human misery, an attitude which in Bowen's view was the more unjustified since decline in population during the century had entirely disproved Malthus's theory. The Harvard professor was especially appalled that people of "wealth, culture, and refinement" had apparently taken Malthus to heart in limiting their own numbers. He then noted that Darwinism as an extension of Malthusian theory was refuted by these same demographic facts: in the struggle for existence among men the lower orders, not the upper classes, survive; "And this victory is a survival not of the fittest, but of the unfittest." Anyway, he added, Darwinism had triumphed not because it was proved, but because it served the cause of irreligion. The "sole innovation" of Darwinism upon general evolutionism was a mechanical materialism, and it was this that provided "the pepper which made the dish palatable to . . . those English and German naturalists who had a previous bias in favor of materialism. . . ." Finally came pessimism, which in German philosophy was but an extension of this same spirit, depriving men of all hope of future happiness, and hence of the will either to reform the world or to multiply and "fill the vacant places on the earth's surface." Unless the spell were broken, Bowen concluded, sounding a familiar variation on New England's fears of decline, America would go the way of the Roman Empire.[9]

Although Bowen implied as much, he was less direct than Carey and Peck in charging that Darwinists literally called for a survival of the fittest in society.[10] Instead he merely assumed Darwinists so argued in order to demonstrate that demography refuted their entire position. Like Carey and Peck he reasoned that Malthusianism (which he disliked) issued in Darwinism (which he also disliked). The two might thus be interchanged and attacked accordingly. Neither Carey, Peck, nor Bowen identified specific contemporaries who buttressed laissez faire with Darwinism, an omission all the more surprising in Peck's case given his animus toward Spencer.[11] In fact Carey's cautious mention of the "tendency" of British thought, Peck's obvious paraphrase, and Bowen's circumlocutions make one wonder if any meant literally to identify conservative Darwinists, or if rather they had forged their various fears and uncertainties into a highly inaccurate description of modern thought.

Three

A fuller case against conservative Darwinism appeared in the writings of reformers who during the 1880s laid the basis for much later activity during the progressive era, among them Social Gospelers, Single Taxers, Nationalist followers of Edward Bellamy and other socialists. In a book titled *Working People and Their Employers* (1876) the Social Gospeler Washington Gladden set the pace. "Political economy" could not secure social peace, he wrote, "its maxims breed more strife than they allay".

> Political economy only deals with natural forces; and the natural forces even those which manifest themselves in society, often seem to be heartless and cruel. The law of nature would appear to be the survival of the strongest; and it is the workings of this law with which political economy has to do.[12]

Within two decades, similar charges were the common currency of the reform community.

Although Henry George (1838-1897) opposed protectionism and singled out Henry Carey for special attack, his indictment of buttressed Malthusianism in *Progress and Poverty* (1879), another early instance of the stereotype, echoed the protectionist critique.[13] Malthusian doctrines had always obstructed reform, George wrote, and "of late years" the theory had "received new support in the rapid change of ideas as to the origin of man and the genesis of species." Poverty, a noted economist had written, provided a powerful stimulus to industry and progress. "What is this," George demanded, "but the recognition in regard to human society of the developing effects of the 'struggle for existence' and 'survival of the fittest?' " The evolution philosophy bred materialism and fatalism. A philosophy that denied God, allied itself naturally with an economics that believed "that nature wastes men by constantly bringing them into being where there is no room for them."[14]

Sustaining these charges was George's instinctive devotion to Christianity and his faith in a universe in which natural and moral law were ultimately one—"eighteenth century superstitions," as Bernard Shaw described them when he heard George speak in London. George was not ignorant of the latest thought: *Progress and Poverty* bristled with the names of Buckle, Bagehot, Maine, and Spencer. But George's sympathies and assumptions were those of the Enlightenment—of Benjamin Franklin or Joseph Priestly, through whose eyes he invited readers to survey nineteenth-century progress. The best efforts of social science and economics could not improve the moral law: this was the message of *Progress and Poverty*. Purged of impurities, Bagehot, Maine, and others demonstrated that "association in equality is the law of progress," which in turn was naught "but the moral law." "The economic law and the moral law" were also "essentially one." "The truth which the intellect grasps after toilsome effort is but that which the moral sense reaches by a quick intuition."[15]

Darwinism upset such happy assumptions. Throughout his career George harbored suspicion of the theory, a suspicion that colored his thought no less than Carey's and Bowen's. In *Progress and Poverty* he attempted to evade the issue. How men had originated was not his concern: "all we know of him is as man." But his hostility was plain. During the 1880s he mellowed somewhat, comforted by the views of the British biologist A. R. Wallace (who early preached the "limits of evolution as applied to man," and who also befriended George during his English crusade), and of St. George Mivart, a leading Christian evolutionist who, more firmly than Wallace, denied that natural selection has shaped human faculties. By the 1890s George could manage grudging acceptance. "In a sense" all men believed in evolution, and indeed *always had*, he wrote. But, he confessed, he remained "unable to see the weight of the evidence of man's descent from other animals."[16]

The absence of Darwinian rhetoric in George's writings mirrored these doubts. At a time when reformers increasingly turned to Darwinism for their arguments (reform Darwinism), George chose his analogies from physics, astronomy, or pre-Darwinian anatomy. Evolution, insofar as it figures in his work, boiled down to Spencer's formula that progress was a movement from an "indefinite, incoherent homogeneity to a definite, coherent heterogeneity." The laws of society were as unchangeable as the "laws of gravitation." The "evolution of society" and the "development of the species" revealed a "close analogy" only in the sense that the "bodies," physiological and political, resembled one another.[17] Whom did George consider the buttressed Malthusians and evolutionary fatalists? The answer is interesting because George did name names, at least four of which have figured in later accounts of conservative Darwinism.[18]

The first Darwinist was the British author Winwood Reade, whom George cited as an evolutionary fatalist, and who later appeared in at least two accounts of social Darwinism.[19] The work in question was Reade's *The Martyrdom of Man* (1872). The author had intended to make his subject "The Origin of Mind" until *The Descent of Man* seemed to leave little to add. Reade instead contented himself with illustrating Darwin with the aid of his own observations of savage life in Africa. Reade's central point, in keeping with the conventional wisdom of mid-Victorian England, was that civilized man transcended the struggles that marked his emergence from barbarism. Reade's contrasts of savagery and civilization forecast Darwinian blueprints of colonialism that would emerge in later decades, while his descriptions of the origin of mind and of man's ability to control nature were of the sort that later inspired many reform Darwinist formulations. Reade was also a Comtean and it was his final aim to picture the triumph of positivism over orthodox religion, which he did in his closing chapters.[20]

George chose the example of Reade because "in a semi-scientific or popularized form this modern fatalism may perhaps be seen . . . best." To illustrate his point, he provided a brief quotation in which Reade observed that "our own progress is founded on the agonies of the past." Reade wondered, "Is it therefore unjust that we also should suffer for the benefit of those who are to come." George here saw the spectre of Malthusianism. "In this view progress is the result of forces which work slowly, steadily, and remorselessly, for the elevation of man," he noted. "War, slavery, tyranny, superstitution, famine and pestilence are the impelling causes which drive men on, by eliminating poorer types and extending the higher." He then attacked Reade's materialism.[21]

In his haste to illustrate his argument, however, Geroge overlooked the remainder of the same passage in *The Martyrdom of Man,* an oversight perpetuated in later histories. Reade indeed believed that past suffering had yielded civilization. But he was equally certain that such physical suffering had no present or future role. The complete passage continues:

> Famine, pestilence, and war are no longer essential for the
> advancement of the human race. But a season of mental anguish
> is at hand, and through this we must pass in order that our pos-
> terity may rise. The soul must be sacrificed; the hope in
> immortality must die. A sweet and charming illusion must be taken
> from the human race, as youth and beauty vanish never to return.[22]

The argument, that is, concerned positivism. The new agonies would be spiritual, the "disturbance and distress," as Reade termed it, that resulted from moving from the religious through the metaphysical to the positivist stage. Irreverent Reade was, and perhaps condescending toward "inferior" peoples. For these reasons he stirred George's sensibilities. But he was not, as George suggested, urging poverty and social inaction in the name of Darwin and progress.

During the 1880s George added a second name to support his conviction that science somehow fostered inaction. William Graham Sumner of Yale, the "reverend professor" of Political Economy as George called him, offended the Californian's deepest convictions no less than did Reade, and was a considerably greater threat to the Single Tax program.[23] Progress, said Sumner, was the result of man's victory in a struggle for existence against nature—capital being both the instrument and effect of such triumph. Among men there obtained a competition of life, the rules of which were relative to the character of the struggle with nature, and which thus altered only gradually. A confirmed Malthusian, Sumner argued for strict laissez faire, and, as discussed above, on two or three occasions (of which George was apparently unaware) did indeed attempt to buttress his position by saying that the alternative to the survival of the fittest was the survival of the unfittest. But this tactic drew criticism and he avoided it in *What Social Classes Owe To Each Other*. However conservative he may have been, Sumner was firm on two points: the struggle for existence was not necessarily fierce (in fact was relatively easy in the modern period) and was not a battle among men as Darwinian-oriented critics often interpreted it; and free access to nature would benefit everyone (not just an elite), in particular the forgotten men of the middle classes.[24]

In attacking the "reverend professor," George blurred precisely these points. The result was a number of subtle distortions. Engaged in polemics, George was little concerned with the finer points of Sumner's position. But more important than the distortions (that need not be detailed here) was the fact that George's hostility to Darwinism clearly figured in his attack. His charge that Sumner accepted a "fierce struggle for existence" and slow "race evolution" required little further argument, because to George the phrases instinctively suggested an undesirable state of affairs.

In *A Perplexed Philosopher* (1892) George added Herbert Spencer to his list. Although he insisted that Spencer was his target all along, his earlier work owed a great deal to the Englishman, both in the idea of a land tax and in the general contours of his argument. He continued to praise *Social Statics*, judging it "a noble book, and in the deepest sense a religious minded book." It not only refuted the expediency philosophy, but contained the germ of his entire theory that private property in land violated the law of equity and was at the root of the social problem. Like Spencer, George desired minimal government. Despite its call for abolition of private property in land, sections of *Progress and Poverty* read like Spencer on overlegislation. More generally, he shared with the Englishman a desire to ground matter and spirit, expediency and morality, in an overarching cosmic law. If in 1879 George had doubts concerning the direction of Spencer's thought, he muted them, and invoked both the name and rhetoric of the philosopher in support of his cause.[25]

A Perplexed Philosopher, in contrast, was the work of a jilted suitor and read like breach of promise proceedings. George learned as early as 1882 that Spencer would not endorse the Single Tax. The loss was a distinct blow to his pride and his crusade. Spencer was "horribly conceited," George confided to a friend following their first meeting. Spencer had not merely changed his mind, George added later: he was "going the way of Comte . . . going insane from vanity." When Spencer formally revised *Social Statics* in 1892 and removed the sections concerning land tenure, George published his bitterness. Spencer had been "dishonest . . . in a way that makes flat falsehood seem manly." He had "betrayed" the cause. His motives had been sordid throughout.[26]

In this spirit George again considered the evolutionary philosophy. Forgetting Winwood Reade, he moved Spencer to center stage. The foe remained materialism. But George now leveled the charge against the Unknowable, which was not God whatever Spencer's defenders claimed. *Social Statics* (which he continued to praise) had been "a protest against materialism," a call to reformers to regard, not simple expediency, but "a divinely appointed order to which, if it would prosper, society must conform." The Synthetic Philosophy, however, was materialistic and fatalistic.[27]

Yet did fatalism necessarily mean conservatism? Answering this question, George surveyed some of the same philosophical issues with which Bowen had earlier wrestled. Fatalism, George noted, was very much like its opposite—the emphasis on total will and the "renunciation of the will to live," such as Schopenhauer preached. This doctrine, in turn, was the European equivalent of a philosophy which in India, as everyone knew, led to a "hopelessness of reform." "It seems to me that the essential fatalism of the philosophy of Mr. Spencer would have a similar result," George speculated. He then plunged to his conclusion: "as the pessimistic philosophy of the one [Schopenhauer and/or Indians] seems to flow from the abandonment of action for mere speculation . . . so the evolutionary philosophy of the other seems to be such as might result from the abandonment of a noble purpose . . . to embrace the pleasant ways of acquiescence in things as they are." "It is not for me to say what is cause and what is effect."[28] At this point he introduced his fourth conservative evolutionist, Edward Livingston Youmans, who as already noted, was a dubious proof at best.[29]

Although one may judge the merits of the Single Tax superior to those of civil service reform, hard money, or laissez faire (and on this opinion will surely differ), it is another matter to fashion George's subjective characterizations of Reade and others into an objective description of Spencerianism. George's rhetoric, like that of Carey and Bowen, was punctuated with circumlocutions and qualifications: "What is this but . . . ."; "seems to me"; "would have had a similar result." Was not George thus acknowledging, as did Bowen and Carey, that he found a meaning in the words of his opponents that they themselves did not intend?

The writings of two other Gilded Age reformers shed further light on this question. Henry Demarest Lloyd, critic of Standard Oil, and Edward Bellamy, author of *Looking Backward* (1888), agreed with George that appeals to survival of the fittest and natural selection had strengthened the conservative defense. Reform, in turn, demanded a rereading of Darwin, which they provided.

As each made his case, a threefold pattern could be discerned. First, Darwinism accurately described the nature of contemporary American society. "In cannibalistic times, the best mankillers and maneaters survive," Lloyd noted in the mid-1800s, "in a selfish civilization the Vanderbilts and Rockefellers." As he put it in *Wealth against Commonwealth* (1894) "some inner circle of 'fittest' " had sought and obtained control of América.[30] Bellamy agreed. The utopians in *Looking Backward* saw nineteenth-century civilization as a struggle for existence. "The principle of competition," intoned the Bellamyite Nationalist platform, "is simply the application of the brutal law of the survival of the strongest and most cunning."[31] Secondly, each alleged that an increasing number of Americans invoked Darwinian terminology to justify this situation. Seizing upon a statement in a trust hearing in which a witness confessed the "weakest must go first," Lloyd gave it a Darwinist twist and charged that the creed was that "practically professed" in business.[32] "Charity," wrote one Bellamyite, "preaches that some must go to the wall in order that others may ascend to the top round of the material ladder: which is complacently declared to be the law of the survival of the fittest."[33] Finally, each insisted that, if properly understood, Darwinism really supported reform. "Darwinian principles," argued Lloyd, "are enough to give a scientific basis to the doctrine that no class can be allowed . . . to hold an exclusive proprietary interest in anything."[34] In *Looking Backward*, Bellamy likewise saw both general evolution and the more specifically Darwinian doctrine of *sexual selection* as chief agencies producing the new utopia.[35]

Like George, Lloyd and Bellamy provided few particulars in their indictments. Lloyd at one point in the 1880s jotted in his notebook an isolated Darwinian remark by the Englishman Henry Maine (the often quoted comparison of competition to a "beneficent private war" issuing in "the survival of the fittest"). In 1896, he seized upon Benjamin Kidd's *Social Evolution* (1894) as yet another example of what had been going on for some time. But even his analysis of this volume suggests that he read what he expected and that he missed the unique twist that Kidd had given the Darwinian argument. More significantly, in noting in *Wealth against Commonwealth* that survival of the fittest was the creed "practically professed" in business, Lloyd tacitly acknowledged that the practice was as he himself, not the businessmen, saw it.[36]

Bellamy and his followers were equally offhand in their choice of conservative Darwinists, discrediting the opposition by finding Darwinian meanings where they were not intended. The Hegelian William Torrey Harris was a Darwinist, suggested one writer in the *Nationalist*, because the conservative commissioner of education defended competition by going back "as he must . . . to 'natural law.'" What was this law but the survival of the fittest, the Nationalist asked, "the acme of individualism, and a colossal selfishness?" "But this seems [n.b.]," he concluded, "to be Professor Harris's ideal." On at least one occasion a defender of modified laissez faire, goaded by references to the brutal laws of nature, offered protest in order to counter the reformers' advantage, when the economist Francis A. Walker in a review of *Looking Backward* attacked such a reference in the Nationalist platform. "There is an old proverb that says, Speak well of the bridge that has carried you safely over," he cautioned, lecturing the Bellamyites on the past role of struggle. Walker added that he would deem anyone who ignored this debt "utterly lacking in the biological sense," and urged more, not less, competition. And, for this brief excursion, he became to readers of the *Nationalist* another representative of dominant Darwinian reactionism.[37]

Had these charges of conservative Darwinism been confined to openly partisan appeals they might well have been dismissed by historians. But from the start the allegation had support of a more weighty sort from social scientists who were disturbed, as the president of the Social Science Association put it, by "our friends of the pessimistic school [who] dwell with grim satisfaction on the doctrine that teaches the 'survival of the fittest.'" During the 1880s others within the social science movement reiterated the charge. As with the reformers, the term natural selection characterized an unacceptable situation. Mankind was still "darkly striving" for perfection, wrote a contributor to the *American Anthropologist*,

because it has not yet caught the teleologic principles which should be the guides of its rational selections in political science, and so it suffers in wide fields of political and economic activity, to fall an easy prey to the brute forces of that "natural selection" which perpetually expresses itself in the vegetable and animal kingdom.

"The term natural selection," he explained further, "is here used in deference to its conventional meaning, though I deny the exclusive applicability of the term to the selection of plants and animals, because the more rational selections of man are just as natural to him as the unconscious selections of plants and animals are natural to them."[38]

Academic economists and sociologists, then developing their own specialties within social science, added their authority to the developing stereotype. "I have said to you that the railway industry was peculiar in that it was subject to the law of increasing returns," lectured the economist Henry Carter Adams to his students in Michigan, "and that the competition was of a peculiar sort, a struggle for existence and not normal." Liberal in their politics, most also regretted growing evidences of social conflict in American society. "Nothing could be wilder or fiercer than an unrestricted struggle of millions of men to gain," wrote the economist John Bates Clark, one of the founders of the American Economic Association, "and nothing more irrational than to present such a struggle as a scientific ideal."[39]

This indictment was ironic since many younger social scientists, raised on Darwinism and from the mid-1890s on neo-Darwinism, took it for granted that struggle was a permanent fact of all life, an assumption that older Spencerians acknowledged reluctantly and with regret. Many also insisted struggle among humans was a group rather than an individual affair, and further, struggle in its higher forms was a conflict of ideals rather than of brute force. Together these assumptions formed the bedrock of reform Darwinism, and underlay the moral strenuousity of much progressive thought.

But how could one blast Darwinized-social theory while simultaneously grounding one's own position in a Darwinian vision of struggle? No one better illustrates this dilemma than Lester Frank Ward (1841-1913), the author of *Dynamic Sociology* and America's leading sociologist during the 1880s. Born in Joliet, Illinois, Ward translated his own struggles against economic hardship into a lifelong faith in the common man. At the same time, his work in government service in various scientific agencies convinced him of the value of expertise. During the eighties he welded these convictions into a blueprint of sociocracy, for which he was later best known. In *Dynamic Sociology*, essentially an attempt to synthesize Comte and Spencer, and in *The Psychic Factors of Civilization* (1892), Ward also helped shift sociology from a biological to a psychological orientation. Attracted by the theories of Ludwig Gumplowicz and Gustav Ratzenhofer, he became in the late 1890s a leading American spokesman for the so-called struggle school of continental sociology, a position he incorporated into his *Pure Sociology* (1905).[40]

Throughout his career, it also happens, Ward persistently warned contemporaries of the dangers of conservative Darwinism, or as he himself finally called it by its modern name, social Darwinism. Although he first used this term late in his career, Ward began to fashion the image of a conservative Darwinist opposition in the mid-1870s. As with Lloyd, Bellamy, and other reformers, a first step was the definition of nature as a perpetual battleground. Nature, wrote Ward in an early critique of Spencer, was not the orderly integration of matter postulated in the Synthetic Philosophy, but a wasteful push and pull in which massive positive *(integrative)* forces were necessary merely to hold negative *(disintegrative)* forces at bay. Ward noted further that this struggle and waste had parallels in society: "[The] wars of men with their surroundings, with wild beasts, and with one another, are the strict analogues of those of the lower forms . . . Even the silent battle for subsistence has its counterpart in the competitive struggles of industry." Waste was everywhere: "in wanton destruction of forests, slaughter of wild animals, and the pestilence and filth of urban civilization."[41]

During the 1880s Ward came to the further conclusion that defenders of the existing order were interpreting natural law in Darwinian terms. At first he was merely suspicious: of "representatives of science" who stood "boldly in the track of current events" or of the social "tenor and tendency" of recent scientific theory. In *Dynamic Sociology* (1883) he voiced some of this suspicion. But despite his criticism of Spencer in this book he continued to insist that the Englishman was one of several pioneers who, in Emerson's phrase, had "builded better than he knew." He thus stopped short of charging Spencer with misusing Darwinian terminology.[42]

However, William Graham Sumner's *What Social Classes Owe to Each Other* (1884), a book that outraged Ward, provided the proof he needed for his earlier suspicions. Ward's attack had a familiar ring. Translating Sumner's Malthusianism into Darwinism, Ward charged that Sumner "degraded" human activity "to a complete level with those of animals." Refutation followed. "Those who have survived simply prove their fitness to survive." The "fact that fitness to survive is something wholly distinct from real superiority, is, of course, ignored by the author because he is not a biologist, as all sociologists should be." At the same time, Ward recognized parallels between human and animal struggle that Sumner would have denied, using such parallels as reasons why art must replace nature. In subsequent articles Ward suggested that Sumner was not alone in his errors. The Yale professor was but the most extreme of Spencer's "disciples, particularly in America, [who] delight in going even further than their master," he wrote in 1884.[43]

Between the mid-1880s and the time when Ward attempted to define social Darwinism in 1905, at least one additional factor shaped his thoughts concerning the conservative Darwinist opposition.The assault of the so-called neo-Darwinians (led by August Weismann) in the early 1890s pushed Ward squarely into the neo-Lamarckian camp, and in doing so further identified Darwinism, in his thinking, with animality and generally ignoble activity. In response to Weismann's suggestion that no acquired characteristics could be inherited, he proposed what amounted to a division of labor between neo-Darwinians and neo-Lamarckians. Natural selection explained man's animal characteristics, up to and including the intellect manifested in commercial cunning. Lamarckianism explained the higher faculties, the "intense exercise" of which impressed them "profoundly upon the plastic brain substance and reacting upon the germs of posterity, . . . transmitted [them] to descendents through centuries of developing civilization."[44]

Not coincidentally, this division accompanied fresh allegations that unnamed conservatives were misusing biology. In several articles of the early 1890s Ward repeated his earlier censure of "nature-worship" by "a certain type of mind . . . strengthened since Darwin." Upon examining the "practical applications" of neo-Darwinism he found it "to be strikingly in line with the last described." In methodological terms neo-Lamarckianism stressed the importance of the "Psychologic Basis of Social Economics." In practical terms it repudiated "biological sociologists" urging survival of the fittest. "Every one is now familiar with the general nature of animal economics," Ward wrote. "It is the survival of the fittest in the struggle for existence."[45] George and Lloyd certainly were. And Bellamy, in an article describing the "Psychologic Basis of Nationalism," told his followers that Ward's arguement "will bear study as furnishing the best of ammunition for replying to the 'survival of the fittest' argument against nationalism."[46]

The blend of methodological and political concerns in this charge of "animal economics" seemed to Ward only natural. Had not Herbert Spencer in his "Justice" (1891) and in revising and reissuing Social Statics with Man vs. The State (1892) hardened his conservative position? Had he not violated crucial distinctions upon which he had insisted in his earlier writings, in particular his statement that survival of the fittest had no role to play in modern civilization?[47] Moreover, was not this same Spencer under attack by a growing number of sociologists who stressed imitation and psychological factors in social development, an attack that might conveniently, if somewhat imprecisely, be termed a criticism of biological analogies? Was not this same emphasis on mental factors reinforced by the resurgence of idealism in philosophy, and in particular by Schopenhauer's concept of will, to which Ward himself was especially attracted?[48] In sum, if the charge of animal economics had roots in Ward's social concerns in the 1880s, it was revitalized by scientific, sociological, and philosophical currents in the 1890s.

In 1905 and 1906, Ward learned that others had their own version of the same charge—social Darwinism—directed not only against laissez faire, but also against certain eugenic arguments and against the view that international struggle and warfare produced progress. The irony, and the cause of Ward's concern, lay in the fact that he had argued each of these latter positions himself. Since the early 1890s he had been mildly interested in *negative eugenics,* as the movement to improve the race via marriage laws and other precautionary measures was termed.[49] In these years he also emerged as a major American champion of the *struggle sociology* of Ratzenhofer and Gumplowicz, a view that stressed the role of racial conflict in the formation of societies.[50]

Not surprisingly, opponents of these views quickly found in the rhetoric of Darwinism a convenient weapon for discrediting them. "There is no actual struggle among such spheres, any more than there are mortal wounds or rivers of blood," lectured the Spencerian John Collier in an attack on "The Struggle for Existence in Sociology" that appeared in *Current Literature* in 1903. "The world is not a battlefield," he added after outlining the views of Gumplowicz and others. Spencer's survival of the fittest was meant to convey this fact, he noted, "but the laws of adaptation remain to be generalized." What was needed was some "new great thinker" to "supply us with a new nomenclature, or . . . strip our present terminology of misleading associations."[51]

Two years later the sociologist Iaknv Aleksandrovich Novikov, or as he was later known in France, Jacques Novicow (1849-1912), singled out Ward, Ratzenhofer, and Gumplowicz as leading exponents of *le Darwinisme social.* Born in Russia, Novikov grew up in an intellectual milieu similar to that which also inspired Peter Kropotkin's *Mutual Aid* (1902), another major contribution to reform Darwinism.[52]During the 1890s he became a leading advocate of international peace and arbitration, and a leading foe of struggle sociology. His attack on Ward echoed the general charges of misapplied Darwinism he expressed more than a decade earlier in *Les Luttes entres Sociétiés Humaines* (Paris, 1893). In later years, this same charge, as embroidered by a disciple,the American Quaker George Nasmyth, became a major source for historical accounts of social Darwinism.[53]

Responding to this turn of events, Ward was in a quandary. He felt that in a certain sense the charge against some eugenicists and militarists was not unjust: extremists in both camps often spiced their appeals with Darwinian slogans.[54] How could Ward maintain his positions—which called for neither positive steps like sterilization on the one hand, nor for militarist—imperialism on the other—and at the same time escape the social Darwinist charge? How in domestic affairs could he urge a sociocracy (that would accept permanent struggle but channel and transform the cosmic conflict), against socialist utopias or a laissez faire jungle in which brute law was totally accepted?

Attacking these problems, Ward decided that the term social Darwinism must be eliminated. The tactic of Novicow and the others infuriated him. "The sociologists . . . confound the so-called 'struggle for existence' with Darwinism, and very few of them have any adequate idea of what Darwin's phrase 'natural selection' means," he wrote. "With this vague notion in their minds certain of them have invented the phrase 'social Darwinism,' and have set it up as a sort of 'man of straw' in order to show their agility in knocking it down." He protested "in the strongest possible terms against the application of the term Darwinism to the race struggle." Malthusianism was wrongly called Darwinism since "it falls far short of embodying even the principle of natural selection." When he heard eugenics also being called social Darwinism, Ward simply ducked the terminological question and focused instead on its inherent elitism.[55]

But what of his own charges against animal economics? Had Ward also created a straw man? Did not allegations of social Darwinism merely state explicitly what he and others had been saying for some time? Ward answered in effect that the difference lay in the fact that he understood Darwin, and others did not. He insisted that his suspicions were valid: classical economists were misusing Darwinian phrases to buttress their position. Ward illustrated this misuse by citing a paraphrase of the laissez faire argument by the Italian sociologist Achille Loria, also a critic of the classical position. ("Men . . . they say, have carried on a terrible struggle for life . . . It is therefore wrong to deplore the bloody battles between men and the fierce competition which makes them trample upon one another.") "He does not say who defended this doctrine," Ward continued, "but it cannot be denied that something near akin to it is held by many biologists . . . and that it is practically the attitude of most scientific men and evolutionists in so far as they have expressed themselves on the subject." Like Loria, Ward simply denied their claim to such rhetoric. He had "never yet seen any distinctly Darwinian principle appealed to in the discussions of 'social Darwinism'. " He then went on to explain as he had so often before, how his own teachings harmonized with Darwin's.[56] Yet, Ward's "something near akin" and "practically the attitude," like similar qualifiers in the writings of the others considered, strongly suggest that he too was fashioning from his own concerns a portrait of the opposition that was more effective than it was accurate.

Four

As one moved leftward on the political spectrum, the uses and complexities of the social Darwinist stereotype multiplied. Since the publication of the *Origin of Species*, the relation of Marxists and other socialists to Darwinism had been a complicated one.[57] After some hesitation, Marx and Engels praised Darwin's biology but rejected the social extrapolations made by some of his followers. Engels called Darwin's doctrine a "bitter satire on mankind and especially on his countrymen, when he showed that free competition, the struggle for existence, which the economists claim is the highest historical achievement, is the normal state of the *animal kingdom*."[58] In 1870, Marx denounced all attempts to interpret social struggles in light of the struggle for life.[59]

Although Marx feared that the identification of socialism with Darwinism would discredit the former, an exchange between two prominent German scientists in the late 1870s revealed what a bottomless pit biological theorizing could become. Speaking before a scientific congress in Munich in 1878, the pathologist and anthropologist, Rudolf Virchow (1821-1902), warned that Darwinism led directly to socialism:

> Now, picture to yourself the theory of descent as it already exists in the brain of a socialist. Ay, gentlemen, it may seem laughable to many, but it is in truth very serious, and I only hope that the theory of descent may not entail on us all the horrors which similar theories have actually brought upon neighboring countries. At all times this theory, if it is logically carried out to the end, has an uncommonly suspicious aspect, and the fact that it has gained the sympathy of socialism has not, it is to be hoped, escaped your notice.

A staunch liberal in politics, active in the moderate Progress party, Virchow, as his words made clear, was no friend of socialism. Rather his argument was intended, in the climate of Bismarckian Germany, to be the final blow against the teaching of Darwinism, at least in the more extreme forms advocated by the biologist Ernst Haeckel.[60]

Haeckel (1834-1919), a professor of biology at Jena, responded in kind. The doctrine of descent, if it proved any political theory, showed "that the equality of individuals which socialism strives after is an impossibility." If the theory of natural selection were "to be compared to any definite political tendency—as is, no doubt, possible—that tendency can only be aristocratic, certainly not democratic, and least of all socialist." To prove his point, Haeckel outlined at length what a conservative reading of Darwinism would look like. "If, therefore, Darwinism logically carried out, has . . . 'an uncommonly suspicious aspect' ", he concluded, "this can only be found in the idea that it offers a helping hand to the efforts of the aristocrats." Although some observers later made Haeckel a conservative Darwinist, he, no more than Virchow, wanted the result that logic dictated. He was "nothing less than a politician," and he thought such direct application of scientific theories at once dangerous and foolish.[61]

To Darwinists, Virchow's attack seemed slanderous. In a preface to Haeckel's rebuttal, Thomas Huxley denounced "the introduction of unscrupulous political warfare into scientific controversy, manifested in the attempt to connect the doctrine's advocates with those of a political party which is, at present, the object of hatred and persecution in his native land."[62] For socialists it stood as a warning of the infinite ingenuity of the opponents of Darwinism, socialism, or both, in using their alleged similarities for polemical purposes.

Anti-Marxists across the political spectrum attempted to turn the alleged link to advantage. "Who, for instance, has affected the thought of the age more powerfully than Darwin," asked the British conservative, W.H. Mallock in 1888. "Our modern socialists, among others, confessedly owe half their theory of life to him." At the other extreme, Richard Ely of the University of Wisconsin wrote that some Marxists claimed "that [Marx] has found a law of evolution working in society like that which Darwin found in the natural world." Ely, an economist whose pro-labor sympathies were just then causing a major row at the university, made clear his opposition to this brand of socialism. "The ethical element plays almost, if not wholly, as subordinate a part in this socialism as in the Darwinian natural science."[63]

In a study of Socialism and Modern Thought (1895) the Reverend Moritz Kaufmann, a British Christian Socialist, alerted socialists to the dangers of this line of argument. A moderate in the tradition of Lester Ward's Dynamic Sociology (which he endorsed), Kaufmann opposed both "the militancy of commercial competition and the correlative attitude of militant socialism"—each of which were the result of an uncritical acceptance of Darwinism. For socialists the Darwinian viewpoint was particularly perilous:

> . . . as Darwinists and others have not been slow to recognize, the more shrewd among the socialists do not fail to see that the doctrine of natural selection is not in favor of Democracy; that, on the contrary, its tendency is aristocratic; and that, like the theological doctrine of Election, it speaks of "an elect fragment of the human race," a favoured minority, a remnant saved in the survival of the fittest.

Kaufmann emphasized that he personally did not accept this construction. But, citing Haeckel's reply to Virchow two decades earlier, he was convinced that others seriously believed it.[64]

By the 1890s a few socialists were nonetheless ready to proclaim their allegiance to what they termed *socialist Darwinism*. Describing himself as a "convinced Darwinian and Spencerian," the Italian criminologist Enrico Ferri argued against those who "contend that socialism is in conflict with the fundamental facts and inductions of the physical, biological, and social sciences."[65] Other European revisionists and their American followers likewise proclaimed the marriage of evolution and socialism in a series of books that appeared during the first decade of the century: Arthur M. Lewis's *Evolution Positive and Negative* (1902); Michael A. Lane's *The Level of Social Motion* (1902); Walter T. Mill's *The Struggle for Existence* (1904); Ernest Untermann's *Science and Revolution* (1905); Karl Kautsky's *Ethics* (1907); Anton Pannekoek's *Marxism and Darwinism* (1912); and Henry Jager's *Social Evolution, or Socialism Made Easy* (1916).

Most of these authors based their case on the common "scientific" character of socialism and evolution, an affinity that somehow proved the two could not be in conflict. However, a few directly confronted the issue of struggle, given new force by the neo-Darwinism of August Weismann and his disciples. Since environment could not affect genetic make-up, the neo-Darwinians argued, struggle was the sole engine of change in biological evolution, a view many feared held reactionary social implications. "The tangle in the details of Darwinism and Spencerianism will not be straightened out," wrote the Chicago socialist Ernest Untermann, expressing concern over Weismannism, "until a socialist Darwinian will bring order out of this chaos."[66]

A few accepted the challenge, arguing that *class struggle* was a special case of biological struggle, precisely the comparison Marx had earlier repudiated. "For Marx . . . the class struggle was but a particular instance of the universal law of evolution," wrote Karl Kautsky, distorting the historical record, adding that its "essential qualities are in no case peaceful."[67] Another socialist argued that if Weismann were correct, then bourgeois control of the environment would not poison future generations. Turning Spencer on his head, this critic observed that the "old theory" of heredity (Lamarckianism) postulated that habits developed in a degraded environment "become fixed and enter the heredity of the animal. . . . If this were true the habits of man formed by harsh conditions in the slums would be transmitted to his children." Weismann in contrast held "out more hope for the present generation," he concluded, in an argument more ingenious than it was convincing.[68]

The discovery of mutation by Hugo DeVries at the turn of the century seemed to some to offer another sort of biological support. "Long before DeVries and Burbank came to our aid with the proof of mutations in the physical world, we knew out of history that social evolution has other movements than those of gradual and uniformitarian stages," wrote W.J. Ghent. "Nature multiplies her effects by infinitesimal gradations, but when this multiplication reaches one alloted sum she overturns . . . states and systems, as she explodes mountains and valleys." Gaylord Wilshire, California's "millionaire socialist," likewise argued that mutation theory supported socialism.[69]

As with some New Liberals, the fact that socialists appealed to Darwinism proved no bar to the charge that reactionaries were misusing evolutionism. "It is certain that the opponents of socialism have made a wrong use of the Darwinian law or rather of its 'brutal' interpretation in order to justify modern individualist competition which is too often only a disguised form of cannibalism," Ferri wrote in Socialism and Modern Science (1895). In Our Benevolent Feudalism (1902) Ghent quoted John D. Rockefeller, Jr., on the benefits of pruning the "American beauty rose," a statement wrongly attributed to the senior Rockefeller, which became a staple in later accounts of conservative Darwinism.[70] From the 1890s onward, the portrait of Darwinian individualism was a commonplace in socialist no less than in New Liberal writings.

While caricaturing their opponents, socialists continued to be reminded that their own cause was vulnerable to attack for alleged affinities with materialistic and atheistic Darwinism, an echo of the Virchow-Haeckel exchange two decades earlier. In an almost incomprehensible polemic titled Socialism: The Nation of Fatherless Children (1903), an embittered ex-socialist flayed his former associates for grasping at the straws of evolution to "prop up" their "atheistical beliefs." "What Darwin put forth as a theory the socialists proclaim as a science," he wrote:

> The Darwinian doctrine is accepted as proof that through social
> evolution (through the action of the "class struggle") man will

attain unto the ideal socialist society. The "class struggle" in the sociological world is declared to be the complement of the "struggle for existence" in the biological world . . . It is well, however, to note that socialist belief in the complementary relationship of these two schools is so fixed that the fall of one would involve the fall of the other.

In a masterpiece of guilt by association, the author then argued that true science supported religion not "economic determinism."[71]

From a more secular perspective came a similar charge. Describing the bankruptcy of "scientific socialism", Vladimir Simkhovitch, a professor at Columbia, described as a "mouthful of big words" all attempts to make the class struggle "an extension of the Darwinian principle of the struggle for life." Lester Ward, in his comments on social Darwinism in 1907, noted that "continental sociologists" confined the term to two doctrines (neither of which he approved)—one being the socialist idea of the "economic struggle". "The socialists", he wrote in the *American Journal of Sociology* the following year, "for the most part, regard the social struggle as a practical extension of the biological struggle into the human field." "For a long time the modern doctrines relating to life were regarded as highly favorable to socialism, and they are still so regarded by many," he continued. "Nevertheless, it is a fact that they are looked upon . . . by biological philosophers in general, as completely opposed to socialism, and as sustaining the old 'let-alone' political economy." Playing the middle against both extremes, as it were, Ward proceeded to explain the "true" meaning of evolutionary science.[72]

Five

The many Americans who in the late nineteenth century still championed competition, individualism, or the success ethic were not without intellectual resources. Classical economics, Lockean liberalism, a Franklinesque success mythology: each could be bent, quite without Darwin, to serve the needs of the emerging capitalist order—by abridging the *Wealth of Nations* to omit Adam Smith's concern for the public good; by debasing the "liberty" of the Declaration of Independence to an uncompromising defense of property; or by forgetting everything Franklin said about character. Alternately, a new invasion of Germanic idealism also served conservative purposes, and was especially attractive to those who disliked materialism. During the 1890s idealism joined the success myth in New Thought. All these defenses contained a significant leaven of

Christian sentiment, and in one way or another posited natural laws that promised ultimate harmony.[73]

As the case of Spencer and his American followers revealed, evolutionism and organic analogies also contributed to a defense of the status quo, without violating Enlightenment fundamentals—by suggesting that change comes slowly, that society is a complex organism, and that nature provides reliable guidelines. But Darwinism—with its slogans of struggle for existence, natural selection, and survival of the fittest—was another matter. Darwinian nature presented society a mirror, not of its possibilities, but of its failures. Dedicated to natural law, defenders of laissez faire took little comfort from this development. The intellectual difficulties of Spencer and Sumner were one measure of this discomfort: the social Darwinian stereotype popular in reform circles was another.

The paucity of bona fide examples of conservative Darwinism—both in Gilded Age reform literature and in later histories—was not due simply to the ignorance of conservatives to whom the new ideas had not yet filtered. Rather their silence and the tentativeness of the few who attempted to incorporate Darwinian slogans, reflected the not remarkable fact that individuals who desire stability, consensus, homogeneity, and peaceful change under a capitalist regime—as did businessmen and many of their middle-class defenders—found little comfort in a cosmology that posited permanent struggle as the engine of progress. Darwinism, far from buttressing these older virtues, sounded their death knell in a double sense: first in providing an emotionally charged rhetoric to describe the existing order, and second by restating the older values in a form that discredited their proponents. The sincerity and persistence of the stereotype of conservative social Darwinism suggest that its recurrence in reform literature was no cynical tactic. Industrial America seemed a jungle in which human purpose and effort played increasingly less role. Some rugged individuals appeared to defend the situation in the name of science, and therefore the science in question must be the jungle law of Darwinism. This reasoning had special appeal for a generation whose warm embrace of science masked a covert fear of its logical implications. So viewed, the conservative social Darwinism stereotype represented an anti-utopian blueprint of a world guided solely by scientific considerations, a recurring motif in the Anglo-American reaction against scientism.

7. Neo-Darwinism and the Crisis of the 1890s

> *"Whatever is, is right," is the only motto of the consistent evolutionist. This is embodied in the phrase "survival of the fittest," which is used—illegitimately, as we shall see—to effect the transition from the merely natural to the ethical world. . . . Such, I must insist, is the only logical position of a naturalistic ethics. But an important outcome of the recent discussion has been to show that the most prominent upholders of the theory do not hold it in its logical form.*
>
> Andrew Seth, "Prof. Huxley on Nature and Man," Blackwood's, *154 (1893), 824, 831.*

> *From the failure to get at the heart of the first principles of Evolution, the old call to "follow Nature" has all but become a heresy. Nature as a moral teacher, thanks to the Darwinian interpretation, was never more discredited than at this hour; and friend and foe alike agree in warning us against her.*
>
> Henry Drummond, The Ascent of Man *(1895), p.43.*

One

During the 1890s labor violence, agrarian protest, and disturbing new evidence of urban poverty convinced many Americans that "the wolfish struggle for existence," as one contributor to the *Arena* called it, was growing worse. At Andrew Carnegie's Homestead steel mill near Pittsburgh seven men died in a single clash in 1892. Two years later strikers and police again battled during a bloody strike at the Pullman Palace Car Company in Chicago. As farmers joined laborers in their fight against the trusts, a Chicago poet turned instinctively to the rhetoric of Darwinism to describe the new barbarism:

Ne'er before has time recorded
Such increase of millions hoarded,
Such a fierce and bitter struggle
Of the weak against the strong;

> Men with itching palms unheeding
> Freedom's right or poor man's pleading
> As their stocks and shares they juggle,
> In a carnival of wrong.

With the publication of Jacob Riis's *How the Other Half Lives* (1890) urban poverty also assumed new urgency. "The struggle for existence," reported a New Jersey labor commission, striking a common note, "is daily becoming keener."[1]

Among middle-class professionals, the pressures of urban life took their own toll. A weary urbanite, reflecting on his theatrical career in one of the stories in Hamlin Garland's *Main Travelled Roads* (1891), commented bitterly:

> What was it worth anyhow—success? Struggle, strife, trampling on someone else. His play crowding out some other poor fellow's hope. The hawk eats the partridge, the partridge eats the flies and bugs, and bugs eat each other and the hawk, when he in his turn is shot by man.

Noting the proliferation of law schools, the *Scientific American* observed that "the consequence is a steadily increasing annual deluge of underdone lawyers cast upon the barren shore of a congested profession to struggle for existence in 'ways that are dark' and tricks that are in reverse of elevating to American manhood." The "rat race," as a later generation would call it, was on.[2]

Reinforcing this vision of a world grown Darwinian, the theories of the German biologist, August Weismann (1834-1914), gave Darwinism new and ominous overtones. Postulating a *germ plasm* wherein determinants of heredity were forever sealed from the effects of experience, Weismann in one stroke undermined the hopeful environmentalism of Lamarck's theories of the acquisition and transmission of biological characteristics. In biology as in life, struggle and selection moved to center stage.

Published in German in the eighties, Weismann's work reached the English-speaking world in translations of his *Essays Upon Heredity* (I: 1889; II: 1892) and *The Germ Plasm* (1893). Coinciding with the arrival of the first wave of the European *fin de siècle*, Weismannism joined the pessimism of von Hartmann and Schopenhauer; the naturalism of Zola and Nietzsche; and the brooding *weltschmerz* of Wagner.[3]

On both sides of the Atlantic, Weismann's work triggered a spirited debate between neo-Darwinians, as his followers were called, and neo–Lamarckians. Although a significant number of British scientists embraced the new hereditarianism, most American biologists, already wedded to environmentalism, rushed to the neo-Lamarckian banner. Led by Herbert Spencer, many social theorists restated his compromise between direct and indirect equilibration, effectively splitting the difference between use-inheritance and natural selection. Others took advantage of any modesty on Weismann's part. For example, Samuel Garman, a former student of Agassiz, argued in the *Nation* that external factors such as climate could in the long run "work changes in the germ" and hence "originate predispositions" that would be preserved by natural selection. "After all," he noted, without saying precisely what constituted a predisposition, "Weismann does not make it clear that the predisposition itself is not an acquired character, a consequence of the action of external causes."[4]

As important as the scientific issue, however, was the question of the social implications of neo-Darwinism. Leading neo-Lamarckians claimed that Weismannism blasted all hope of human betterment. "If Weismann [is] . . . right, if natural selection be indeed the only factor used by nature in organic evolution and therefore available for use by Reason in human evolution," wrote Joseph LeConte in 1891, "then, alas for all our hopes of race improvement, whether physical, mental, or moral!" "In this century of pessimism," added another critic, "I know of no theory more pessimistic than the Weismann theory of heredity." (It mattered little that Weismann's mechanistic determinism denied the element of "sporting" that more sophisticated observers such as Charles S. Peirce saw as the critical element in Darwinism, and thus judged the German an "opponent of Darwinism"). Resisting this pessimism, the distinguished English naturalist C. Lloyd Morgan wrote Alfred Russel Wallace that there was "no cause to despair. Human progress is still possible."[5]

Neo-Darwinism also predictably multiplied suspicions concerning the *real* import of the *Origin of Species*. In the eyes of Darwin's critics, biology and social theory became more than ever a two-way street. The most obvious strategy was to discredit all evolution theory by citing its alleged social consequences. Conversely, at least one critic attacked the scientific validity of the struggle for existence and natural selection by demonstrating the shortcomings of Malthusian population theory and the general absence of struggle in society.[6]

Distrust of the new biology and the *fin de siècle* congealed in Edward A. Ross's "Turning Toward Nirvana," a critical dissection of the new mood that appeared in the *Arena* in 1891. Fresh from study abroad, on the eve of his own career as one of America's leading sociologists, Ross was deeply disturbed by the irrationalism and subjectivism of recent continental thought. "The rank corn and cotton optimism of the west," he wrote, "quickly feels the deep sadness that lurks behind the French balls, Prussian parades, and Italian festivals." Citing Ibsen and Tolstoy, Schopenhauer and von Hartmann, Ross, like the critics of Weismann, found a common denominator in despair. "Naturalism in fiction, 'decadence' in poetry, realism in art, tragedy in music, scepticism in religion, cynicism in politics, and pessimism in philosophy, all spring from the same root." Science, he continued, must shoulder part of the blame for "disturbing men's minds." Lifting the "veil of mystery" from institutions and personality alike, science produced a new fatalism. "The doctrines of transmission and inheritance have attacked the independence of the individual," he charged in oblique reference to Weismannism. "Heredity rules our lives like that supreme primeval necessity that stood above the Olympian Gods."[7]

In Britain, this same ambivalence toward science produced outright reactionism. Several prominent public figures restated the case for traditional Christianity—notably Arthur Balfour in *Foundations of Belief* (1895) and Lord Salisbury in a vigorous attack on Darwinism before the British Association of Science in 1895. In different ways each discredited science by turning it upon itself. Reducing science to the rankest materialism, Balfour argued that it had no firmer foundation than religious conviction. Given the choice between two unprovable positions men ought follow their "deepest needs" and accept religion. Lord Salisbury, citing Weismann as his authority, argued that design was the sole alternative to natural selection and hence was valid since the latter was unproved.

Despite the evidence of despair and reactionism, the spectre of neo-Darwinism, for the very reason that it seemed to undermine traditional values, also quickened the reform impulse and in the long run widened the gap between biological inheritance (instinct) and social inheritance (culture) in Anglo-American sociology. Stressing the importance of ideals, Joseph LeConte looked to man's apparently autonomous consciousness as the engine of human direction. "Man contrary to all else in nature is transformed, not in *shape* by external environment," he wrote, conceding the central point in the arguments of both Weismann and A. R. Wallace, "but in *character by his own ideals.*" The capacity of forming ideals and pursuing them "when analyzed and reduced to its simplest terms," he concluded, "is naught else than the consciousness in man of his relation to the infinite and the attempt to realize the divine ideal in human character." Edward S. Morse, a zoologist who also studied with Agassiz, found in Weismannism "the principle with which to fight crime and pauperism," the one through harsher penalties, the other through the application of the "selective method" whereby the dilligent and industrious would be provided "wholesome tenement houses" complete with amusement halls, gardens, and reading rooms.[8]

Much of the reaction to neo-Darwinism also revealed a curious combination of antiscientism and scientific fervor such as first surfaced in reform
thought in the previous decade. No single observer saw this more clearly
than Karl Pearson, the English philosopher of science, who attacked the
"new bigotry" of Balfour and Salisbury in two lengthy articles in the
Westminster Review. Balfour's portrait of science was a "caricature,"
Pearson charged, and Salisbury's acceptance of Weismann's dichotomy
was totally capricious. Moreover, this new bigotry, in attacking scientific
inquiry, threatened the future of liberalism. Here Pearson noted a significant paradox:

> So little has [the] need for consistent principle been recognized by
> the radical newspapers, that we find columns of praise for the
> new bigotry in juxtaposition with a rationalistic programme of
> social reform. On the one hand, science is branded as the basest
> materialism, the reason is proclaimed as an anti-social force, and
> Christian belief asserted to be the sole basis of ethics; while, on
> the other hand, the new economics are hailed as the only rational
> theory of social reform, without the least regard to the fact that
> their creators and supporters have been almost entirely guided
> by rational and non-religious views of life.[9]

A similar paradox of reason and emotion, science and faith, appeared in
American social thought. Comforted by neo-Lamarckianism and an
abiding faith in reason, Americans avoided the extremes of traditionalism
and irrationalism found in British thought. Neo-Lamarckianism, as
George Stocking has shown, remained the bedrock of American social
thought for two decades. But the neo-Darwinian challenge, emphasizing
the specifically Darwinian aspects of Darwin's theory, dramatized concerns that had lain just below the surface for some time. Herbert Spencer
and his followers, despite their protests, sustained a fatal blow in Weismannism. For others, it underlined the need for a new basis for ethics and
social policy now that the "old call to 'follow nature'" was discredited.[10]

In this quest American reformers tended to one of two possibilities. On
the one hand, one might abandon nature and reason (in the sense of short-
run utilitarian calculation) for the less definite benefits of the long-
run—an ideal the Englishman Benjamin Kidd, labeled *projected efficiency*.
On the other hand, one might reexamine nature for evidence of what Peter
Kropotkin called *mutual aid*, an updating of Spencer's altruism.

During the progressive era, these approaches fed distinct, if overlapping,
streams within American reform—the one, a harsher utilitarianism that
stressed social control and group welfare; the other, an older humanitarianism that emphasized individual well-being. During the nineties, four

books from abroad helped crystallize these positions: Thomas Henry Huxley's *Evolution and Ethics* (1894); Benjamin Kidd's *Social Evolution* (1894); Henry Drummond's *The Ascent of Man* (1894); and Peter Kropotkin's *Mutual Aid*, a series of articles that appeared in book form in 1902.

Two

In May 1893 Thomas Henry Huxley presented "Evolution and Ethics" as the annual Romanes lecture at Oxford, before a packed audience in the Sheldonian theater. Although a throat infection muted his delivery, his message was widely reported in the press. Afraid he had been misunderstood, Huxley added a lengthy "Prolegomena" to the published version which appeared early the next year. While not mentioning Weismann, these essays dramatized some startling implications of neo-Darwinism. In an hour's talk, and some extraordinarily fine prose, he brought into the open a number of fears that had nagged his generation for decades.[11]

Huxley's central theme was disturbingly clear: ethics and evolution were forever at odds. "Let us understand once for all," he told his Oxford audience, "that the ethical progress of society depends, not on imitating the cosmic process, still less in running away from it, but in combating it." Cosmic nature was "no school of virtue, but the headquarters of the enemy of ethical nature." Explaining this dichotomy, he defined the ethical process as the development of a primitive fellow-feeling "into the organized and personified sympathy we call conscience"—his source being Adam Smith's "Theory of the Moral Sentiments." In restraining self-assertion, conscience "tends to the suppression of the qualities best fitted for success in [the natural cosmic] struggle," he added. But in thus strengthening society in its collective "struggle for existence with the state of nature," it also weakened individuals and, after a point, society also. The result was a permanent quandary:

> Just as the self-assertion, necessary to the maintenance of society against the state of nature, will destroy that society if it is allowed free operation within; so the self-restraint, the essence of the ethical process, which is no less an essential condition of the existence of every polity, may, by excess, become permanently ruinous to it.[12]

In the "Prolegomena," Huxley developed this position by analogy with horticulture. The gardener was perenially at war with the cosmos. "The characteristic feature of the latter is the intense and unceasing competition of the struggle for existence," he wrote. "The characteristic of the former is the elimination of that struggle, by the removal of the conditions which give rise to it." But the analogy had limits. Barring drastic changes in conditions, the gardener could maintain something approaching his ideal almost indefinitely. In society however, such a policy would require a draconian selection that would itself destroy the bonds that held society together.[13]

In seeming to declare an area of human activity off-limits to rational inquiry, did Huxley not abandon science just as his fellow-Darwinian A. R. Wallace had appeared to do in discussing the limits of natural selection? On this issue, Huxley equivocated at best. Of course the " 'horticultural process' is, strictly speaking, part and parcel of the cosmic process." No one had labored harder than he "to insist upon the doctrine . . . that man, physical, intellectual, and moral, is as much a part of nature, as purely a product of the cosmic process, as the humblest weed." But common sense also revealed a sense in which human value and nature were in opposition. To those who argued that such a position was "logically absurd," Huxley answered that he was "sorry for logic, because . . . the fact is so."[14]

As a corollary, Huxley reassessed the so-called struggle for existence in society, a phrase he admitted he had used "too loosely myself." Strictly speaking, a struggle for existence that literally eliminated progeny through hunger and disease affected at most 5 percent of the population, leaving another 95 percent upon whom the quest for subsistence "can have no appreciable selective influence." For this majority, social struggle was rather one for the "means of enjoyment"—a process that bore "no real resemblance" either to adaptation in nature, or to "the artificial selection of the horticulturist." Although Huxley left the point undeveloped, he thus echoed the move in late nineteenth-century social thought from economic explanations to those framed in terms of the quest for status or power.[15]

To the frustration of many readers, Huxley offered no clear resolution of the dilemma he posed. After reviewing Indian philosophy, Buddhism, and the Stoics, he concluded that man was destined to combat evolution with ethics, even while knowing the impossibility of a permanent victory. As possible consolation, he confessed that he saw "no limit to the extent to which intelligence and will, quickened by sound principles of investigation, and organized in common effort, may modify the conditions of existence, for a period longer than that now covered by history." Indeed humanity might entertain a "larger hope" on this score than ever before. But its realization demanded that man "cast aside the notion that the escape from pain and sorrow is the proper object of life." Like other passionate Victorians, Huxley found the good fight its own reward.[16]

Despite his attempt to depoliticize nature, Huxley's worries about British society were not far from the surface. The background of many of his later writings, as Michael Helfand has suggested, was the steady erosion of British prosperity through two decades of so-called Great Depression; mounting agitation over Ireland and land reform; and the industrial violence that produced Bloody Sunday in 1887 and the London dock strikes two years later. Although Huxley sided with the Liberal Unionists against Gladstone and Irish land reform, he drifted reluctantly into public debate. By 1890 however, he was warming to the role—writing a friend that he was now inclined to "set up as a political prophet."[17]

Ironically, Huxley's first opponents were also popularly identified with evolution: A. R. Wallace, whose sympathies for non-Western peoples and land-socialism brought him increasingly into both the public arena, and potential conflict with Huxley; and Henry George, who continued to cite *Social Statics* in support of the Single Tax until his public break with Spencer and who, thanks to Wallace, had softened his earlier opposition to evolution. Appalled by socialism and already on record against the extremes of Spencerianism, Huxley gradually developed a strategy that was both simple and obvious: he denied that nature yielded any guide for man. "The course of nature," he wrote in an essay "The Struggle for Existence" (1888), was "neither moral nor immoral, but non-moral." In a footnote, he later observed that this statement anticipated "the argument of the Romanes lecture."[18]

In this and several other essays of 1890, Huxley countered Wallace's plea for land-socialism with a call for philanthropy and moderate reform, in a sense restating the case for the sort of humanitarian paternalism earlier associated with Lord Shaftesbury. Huxley also noted that such reforms were vital to the strength and stability of Britain in her international dealings—an echo of the position historian Bernard Semmel has termed *social imperialism*. Since the final test of policy was success in international struggle, Huxley in effect violated the central tenet of his Romanes address. Considered logically (as Huxley did not) evolution remained the standard of social value. In another essay of 1890 he even appeared briefly to suggest that the fact of struggle in nature somehow sanctioned land ownership and the political inequality that resulted from it.[19]

Despite Huxley's disagreements with Wallace and his occasional lapses in logic as he developed his position, his principal target in the Romanes speech was Herbert Spencer and individualism of the extreme sort. "There are many signs that Mr. Huxley had Mr. Spencer in mind in many of his contentions," wrote John Dewey, voicing a common assumption. Any doubt was removed when Spencer himself submitted a highly personal rebuttal in the *Athenaeum* in August. The impact of the address depended in large measure on Huxley's well-known opposition to Spencer. Unlike Spencer he had never viewed evolution as an inevitable movement upward.[20] His criticism of the social organism in the essay "Administrative, Nihilism" had been a beacon for Spencer's critics for several decades.[21] His essay on "The Struggle for Existence in Human Society" (1888) sparked a vigorous exchange between the two men, further underlining their fundamental differences over ethics.[22]

In "Evolution and Ethics" Huxley gave new authority to familiar charges against the Spencerian position. Since natural selection chose moral and immoral qualities alike, it provided no standard for good and bad. "The thief and the murderer followed nature just as much as the philanthropists," Huxley wrote, virtually paraphrasing Laveleye's earlier attack. The basic fallacy of "evolutionary ethics" stemmed from an "unfortunate ambiguity" in the phrase "survival of the fittest" since a "moral flavour" inevitably attached to the term "fittest." In cosmic nature, however, what is "fittest" depended upon conditions, he lectured, making a point most Spencerians conceded, but never fully appreciated.[23]

Despite his criticism of Spencer's ethics, and what Huxley termed "fanatic individualism," the scientist shied from urging any significant expansion of state power. He could imagine some omniscient "administrative authority," he wrote, which might manage human society as "the gardener selects his own plants." This authority might theoretically limit self-assertion so as to eliminate struggle and selection, while providing a panopoly of welfare measures. But this "logical idea of evolutionary regimentation" was a danger and a delusion. No evidence suggested that human society was competent to foster such an administrator "from its own resources." Moreover, the very attempt to suppress struggle might seriously weaken society. The dream was just that—an "unattainable" prescription for a "pigeon-fanciers' polity."[24]

The absence of specific proposals was not entirely accidental. The terms of the Romanes lecture forbade specific reference to religion or politics. For Huxley this condition presented a special challenge. "I hope you will appreciate my dexterity," he wrote a friend shortly before presenting his talk. "The lecture is a regular egg dance." He assured George Romanes in advance that the talk contained "no allusion to politics." "If people apply anything I say about these matters to modern philosophies . . . and religions, that is not my affair." But candor also demanded a slight confession. "To be honest, however, unless I thought they would, I should never have taken all the pains I have bestowed on these 36 pages."[25]

It is not surprising that the political implications of this so-called egg dance, and the question as to whether Huxley was really advocating reform through state action or subtly supporting social reactionism, remain in dispute. For present purposes however, Huxley's very ambivalence toward individualism and socialism was the most important feature of the Oxford address. As with others of his generation in both Britain and America, this ambivalence resulted in a Calvinist portrait of nature as a bloody arena in which natural order was at once in need of control (from the perspective of ethics) and beyond control (as seen by evolution).

This dual image of nature, the final legacy of the address, was also rooted in Huxley's earlier thought. His conception, as Oma Stanley has shown, vacillated between the romantic and the scientific, between nature active *and* impersonal, moral *and* nonmoral, unfathomable *and* lawbound. Usually conceived of as feminine, nature was as mysterious as woman. Translating Goethe for the journal *Nature* in 1866, Huxley captured this spirit in his prose: "with all men she plays a game for love, and rejoices the more they win. With many her moves are so hidden that the game is over before they win." Or, again: "She broods over an all-comprehending idea, which no searching can find out." In Huxley's scientific work, romantic nature often surfaced, as in *Crayfish* (1879): "in relation to the human mind, Nature is boundless, and, though nowhere inaccessible, she is everywhere unfathomable."[26]

From the mid-1870s onward, possibly after reading Mill's "Three Hypotheses Respecting the History of Nature," Huxley reverted to a more scientific conception of nature as "a system of things of immense diversity and complexity," referring also to "the constancy of the order of Nature." In the early 1890s he stated this conception clearly:

> Experience speedily taught [thinking men] that the shifting scenes
> of the world's stage have a permanent background; that there is
> order amidst the seeming confusion, and that many events take
> place according to unchanging rules. To this region of familiar
> steadiness and customary regularity they gave the name Nature.[27]

In "Evolution and Ethics" the two senses coexisted uneasily, as if the scientist regretted the very knowledge his science gave him. Nature remained the mysterious woman: the "present state" was "but a fleeting phase of her infinite variety." But science also provided a basis for the conviction that "eternal order" underlay this ceaseless change.[28]

Huxley expressed his ambivalence in presenting an image of evolution— the realm of law which science disclosed—as animality and selfishness. Admiring science in one breath ("intelligence and will, quickened by sound principles of investigation" were the basis of man's "larger hope"), he feared its power in another. Sustaining this fear was a lifelong suspicion that natural knowledge was no more than "a fairy god-mother" providing "omnipotent Aladdin's lamps" of technology. "If this talk were true," he wrote in the mid-1860s, "I would just as soon be quietly chipping my own flint axe after the manner of my forefathers."[29]

In "Evolution and Ethics" the implied link between science and materialism again underlay his description of evolution. In picturing man's ascent to the "headship of the sentient world," intellect indicted its own failure-in-success:

> The conditions having been of a certain order, man's organization has adjusted itself to them better than that of his competitors in the cosmic strife. In the case of mankind, the self-assertion, the unscrupulous seizing upon all that can be grasped, the tenacious holding of all that can be kept, which constitute the essence of the struggle for existence, have answered.

This catalog of traits was a mirror of the worst in nineteenth-century industrial society: cunning, imitativeness, ruthless and ferocious destructiveness—all these qualities man shared with the ape and tiger. Like "Jack and the Beanstalk," Man had ascended to a heavenly realm but could not escape the world of the past "where ugly competitors were much commoner than beautiful princesses." Reverting to jungle imagery, Huxley observed that mankind "would be only too pleased to see 'the ape and tiger die,' but they decline to suit his convenience; and the unwelcome intrusion of these boon companions of his hot youth into the ranged existence of civil life adds pains and griefs, innumerable and immeasurably great, to those which the cosmic process necessarily brings on the mere animal."[30]

One measure of Huxley's ambivalence was the variety of conclusions reviewers extracted from his prose. St. George Mivart, a biologist and former student of Huxley, sparked a flurry of speculation that his mentor might convert to Roman Catholicism. Herbert Spencer, after criticizing contradictions in Huxley's dualism between ethics and evolution, insisted that Huxley added nothing to points he himself had already made. The New York *Nation* linked Huxley with Spencer and Zola to illustrate the growing recognition that ethics did not rest finally in nature, and science and morality were *not* incompatible. While some reformers enlisted Huxley behind their call for increased social activism, others denounced his "nihilism" and "reactionism." Offering no public clarification, Huxley apparently enjoyed this spectacle. "Don't you know," he wrote a friend, "that I am become a reactionary and secret friend of the clerics? My lecture is really an effort to put the Christian doctrine that Satan is the Prince of this world upon a scientific foundation."[31]

As the debate over social Darwinism developed however, Huxley's real message became less important than the pattern of response it evoked. A minority, predictably on the left, charged that he in fact advocated the reactionary Darwinism he appeared to condemn. Huxley's talk was "inconclusive," charged Edmond Kelly, a New York reformer sympathetic to socialism. "[He] made no effort to reconcile the lessons to be drawn from evolution with the task of justice. He contented himself with proving his case; then shook his head sadly and bade us, notwithstanding, hope, for we had nothing else to do." Kelly's study of *Evolution and Effort* (1895) was an answer to the determinism of Huxley no less than of Spencer.[32] Reading the Romanes speech in light of Nietzsche's philosophy, a later critic alleged that if Huxley had the courage of his convictions he should, like Nietzsche, have concluded: "The weak and ill-constituted shall perish. . . . Sympathy thwarts on the whole the law of development which is the law of selection . . . nothing in our unsound modernism is unsounder than Christian sympathy."[33] A Chicago socialist noted that reactionary arguments had been "so strong" in the 1890s that even Huxley was "swept" into the "swirl"—although he admitted that Huxley repudiated "the social atrocities which capitalist apologists such as Spencer sought to deduce from it."[34]

A majority however took Huxley's message at face value, as the starting point for conscious, ethical, social policies. "Loose popular argument . . . is accustomed to suppose that if the principle of struggle for existence and the survival of the fittest were rigorously carried out, it would result in the destruction of the weak, the sickly, the defective, and the insane," wrote the philosopher John Dewey. But, he added, "Mr. Huxley himself hardly falls into the pit." A municipal reformer cited Huxley in the course of delivering a now conventional reform lecture:

> While in the animal world, the adaptation to purely natural conditions and the unrestricted struggle for existence may be necessary . . . the moment we enter the field of human society, we have the struggle modified at many points. . . . And it is well that this is so, for as Professor Huxley has shown, evolution does not necessarily mean progress, nor is the cosmic process necessarily identical with the ethical purpose.

Quoting Huxley's injunction that ethics demanded "the fitting of as many as possible to survive," the author of *Socialism and the Ethics of Jesus* (1912) concluded: "No better exposition of the element common to the teachings of Jesus and the aims of Socialism has ever been made than this, by one who was neither Christian nor Socialist."[35]

Spencerians, confirming in their own way the image of Huxley's socialist tendencies, insisted that altruism and humanitarian sentiment were also products of nature. Lewis Janes of the Brooklyn Ethical Association was outraged by Huxley's presumption. "By what authority as an evolutionist," he asked, "does Prof. Huxley revert to the old theological conception which places Nature and man in radical antithesis?" Once ideals were detached from the "cosmic process" the way was open for socialism and other attempts to "force" the natural process. In urging this position, Huxley—no less than William Graham Sumner and Benjamin Kidd—"render a questionable service to sociological discussions."[36]

Others pictured Huxley, the would-be-reformer, as the exception among evolutionists. "What is Competition?" asked Arthur J. Eddy, a reform-minded lawyer and author of *The New Competition* (1912): " 'It is the fierce struggle for life and means, the elimination of the weak, the survival of the strong,' the biologist says, and dismisses the subject." But if this is so, he continued, traditional competition "like the familiar doctrine of the 'survival of the fittest' . . . is more than non-human, *it is inhuman.*" Citing the Romanes lecture as his authority, he then attacked a defense of competition in John Bates Clark's *The Control of Trusts* (1912). One of the founders of the reformist American Economic Association in the eighties, Clark now joined those progressives who wanted to control competition rather than to limit the trusts. Paraphrasing Clark's argument, Eddy first translated it into Huxleyish rhetoric not in the original, then dismissed it as "the theory of the thoroughgoing evolutionist," a special irony given Clark's earlier use of the same stereotype.[37]

Although in referring to a "pigeon fanciers' polity" Huxley criticized all biological engineering, eugenicists—like other reformers—tried to enlist the great biologist in their cause. Introducing a speech by Huxley's son Leonard in the 1920s, Sir Arthur Keith quoted the senior Huxley concerning the folly of "extirpating the unfit" through deliberate social selection. But, he continued:

> Much has happened since Huxley expressed himself thus, and it is possible that in light of later-day experiences his opinions might have been modified. Indeed, it is probable that in separating these extracts from their context, I may have made him to appear as a champion of the free working of evolution in human societies to an extent he himself would have deprecated.

Keith went on to recall that Galton, a contemporary of Huxley, "advocated the belief that man, by taking thought and adapting rational eugenic measures, could expedite his evolutionary progress and reach a still higher estate in mind and body." Underlining the point, Leonard Huxley then deplored the fact that, despite the popularity of environmental reform, "we do not select the human raw material that goes into the distilling vat of society."[38]

These contradictory appraisals reflected the fact that Huxley left critical questions unanswered, combining, as one critic noted, his usual agnosticism with a touch of stoicism.[39] On the one hand, he appeared to invite subjectivism, irrationalism, or blind devotion to tradition. If ethics were not rooted in the cosmic order was not the door open to revealed religion, as Mivart suggested? or to other "new fables of value," as another critic wrote, referring to Nietzscheanism?[40] Was social science possible if society were distinct from nature, or was emotional humanitarianism the sole guide to policy? If on the other hand the larger hope lay in "sound principles of investigation," if morality demanded making fit as many men as possible, ought one not develop precise measures of social and physical efficiency? Ought social policy not be more strictly biological? Ought society not seek the social engineer that Huxley imagined but rejected, whether in eugenics, "scientific charity," or racial policy?

However these questions were answered, the Romanes lecture marked a turning point in debate over social evolution and was a final blow to the Spencerian world-view. Gone was the Enlightenment's easy familiarity with the laws of nature, the self-evident truths upon which the American experiment was based. Meanwhile, others suggested alternate routes out of the dilemma Huxley had identified without resolving.

Three

In *Social Evolution*, published in February 1894, Benjamin Kidd offered a direct response to the alleged nihilism of Huxley's speech at Oxford. As obscure as Huxley was famous, Kidd was the son of a sometime member of the Royal Irish Constabulary, and had worked half of his thirty-five years in the Inland Revenue Service. The product of wide reading albeit meagre formal education, *Social Evolution* strode boldly through contemporary social scientific literature. An early example of "pop sociology," it won its author the sort of instant recognition that confounds and embarrasses later generations.[41]

Kidd's thesis was appallingly uncomplicated. Human history was a saga of unmitigated competition, selection, and survival. "Progress," he wrote, citing Weismann, "is the result of selection and rejection. . . . Where there is progress there must inevitably be selection, and selection in turn involves competition of some kind." This fact was no less true for societies than individuals: " . . . societies like the individuals comprising them, are to be regarded as the product of the circumstances in which they exist— the survival of the fittest in the rivalry which is constantly in progress."

Reason, rather than tempering this process, threatened to "have the effect of ultimately staying all further progress," since it could provide no "sanction for progress" for the "large masses of the people" living in suffering and poverty in advanced societies. "A future in which they could have no possible interest, must undoubtedly have been left to take care of itself," he observed, "even though it might involve the suspension of the conditions of progress."[42]

Only religion could provide the needed sanction, he continued. This sanction he termed *ultrarational*. Describing this "central feature of human history," he marveled at the "extraordinary spectacle of man, moved by a profound social instinct, continually endeavouring in the interest of his social progress to check and control the tendency of his own reason to suspend and reverse the conditions which are producing this progress."[43]

Kidd's target was utilitarianism, a tradition which in his view stretched from Hobbes and Locke to Herbert Spencer. Despite their differences, these thinkers shared the common assumption that society was created through a multiplicity of decisions that were both individual and rational. Kidd challenged this assumption. He attacked Spencer on two grounds. Spencer's view of religion (which Kidd found "hard to follow") imperfectly appreciated its "immense utilitarian function" and hence denigrated it. Kidd reminded readers that one of Spencer's leading disciples termed religion a "grotesque fungoid growth," a characterization that particularly rankled. Kidd also faulted Spencer for an ambiguity that allowed his writings to become a gospel for both individualists and socialists. Indeed, the heart of Kidd's thesis was that *reason* (which he defined as selfish and individualistic) led either to a destructive individualism or debilitating socialism, both of which he condemned.[44]

Kidd characterized Huxley as "almost as outspoken as a Nihilist in his dissatisfaction with the existing state of things," lumping him with those who were "convinced that their duty to society was to take away its religious beliefs," while offering no new faith. Holding little hope for the improvement of humanity, Huxley was living proof that reason found no sanction for progress. His pessimism attested to the failure of intellect to quiet the vast battle that raged constantly at its borders. Religion provided men the understanding that science could not.[45]

A ninety-day wonder, *Social Evolution* was a book almost everyone disliked on second-thought. Widely reviewed, it went through numerous printings and was translated into several foreign languages. For a season, it commanded the attention of churchmen and philosophers, social scientists, and the general public. The most critical reviewers conceded that it

was "suggestive," "interesting," even "ingenius." An enthusiastic
Theodore Roosevelt wrote in the *North American Review*: "Mr. Kidd's
Social Evolution is distinctly one of the books of the year."[46]

Its meaning was less clear. A lengthy review in *Popular Science* summarized a general consensus that the work was impossibly vague if not
deliberately obscure:

> It gives one the impression of a system with a shifting center of
> gravity. The author at once champions science and disparages it,
> exalts religion and denies it any footing in common sense; makes
> progress depend upon the unchecked action of natural selection,
> and again declares that its most important factor is the "ultra-
> rational" sanction which religion supplies for right action; condemns
> socialism as unscientific . . . and again presents as his ideal of the
> social state . . . something which it is difficult to distinguish
> from socialism; commiserates mankind for being involved in a per-
> petual struggle for existence, and yet looks forward joyfully to a con-
> dition of struggle which he says will be more "intense" than
> anything the past has witnessed.[47]

Three questions dominated this and other reviews: was *Social Evolution*
"scientific" or "religious"? "individualistic" or "socialistic"? "sociological"
or simply obscurantist? Its significance lay in the fact that Kidd never
quite answered these questions but rather expressed a vague dissatisfaction with the ways they were answered in the past.

Social Evolution reopened the warfare between science and religion,
which many Americans supposed long settled. Besieged defenders of the
faith welcomed his apparent support of religion. A reviewer in the New
York *Critic* recommended the book "to the earnest attention of our
religious teachers of the people" as "wise and inspiring." Richard Ely of
the University of Wisconsin recalled later that "scientific evolutionists"
and "religious teachers" had received it with "great enthusiasm." Some
theists doubtless resented the picture of religion as a chief obstacle to
progress. W. D. P. Bliss, a prominent Social Gospeler, described the work
as a "trap for clergyman." Henry Drummond, the popular evangelist, complained that "theological minds" gave Kidd "premature approval—as a
vindication of their supreme position." But in the atmosphere of the 1890s
these were probably a minority. As the Englishman Harold Laski commented at the time of Kidd's death in 1916: " . . . if Mr. Kidd did not base
the truth of religion, like Mr. Gladstone, upon the impregnable rock of
Holy Scripture, still he was a friend at a time when theology stood sadly in
need of defenders."[48]

Defenders of science attacked Kidd's dualism. Writing in *Popular Science*, William LeSueur, a Canadian civil servant and longtime Spencerian, denied that scientific writers ignored the role of religion, citing such authors as Maudsley, Tyndall, Clifford, and Spencer. "Mr. Spencer fully recognizes religion as an indispensable source of moral control in early stages of society," he insisted "and as one that can ill be discarded even in our own day." "It was not Darwin or Spencer who said that religion could not withstand the shock of evolutionary theory," he added; "it was . . . the party that spoke in the name of religion."[49]

At issue in this exchange was the meaning of science itself. To LeSueur science was a method, even an attitude, rather than a result or particular body of theory. "To understand the function of science in the world we have simply to remind ourselves that man possesses a faculty of comparison and judgment by which he is compelled to recognize . . . likeness or unlikeness, equality or inequality, agreement or disagreement, in the things which occupy his attention," LeSueur noted. "The exercise of this faculty leads to classification, which, in the higher form of generalization, is the source and vital principle of all knowledge." Religion, in contrast, was an expression of man's myth-making imagination, a pressing desire "to worship a Power that cannot be known, and to frame higher sanctions for life than those of the market place and the law courts." When religion incorporated assumptions within the domain of science, the latter was obliged to challenge error. But in doing so, true science recognized "that religion is something more than a misrepresentation of the world and history." Although often in competition, science and religion were thus ultimately compatible.[50]

Developing this theme, *Popular Science* noted a curious contradiction in Kidd's argument:

> If Mr. Kidd, . . . claims above all things to be pursuing rigorously scientific methods, why should he deny science any share in his work? It seems to us if Mr. Kidd, as a scientific man, can forecast the future of society, it would be only using words in their usual acceptation to say that "science" has, in a certain measure, solved the problem. Of course, if Mr. Kidd claimed to have a revelation from heaven, that would be a different thing; he claims on the contrary, to be an out-and-out evolutionist, a Darwinian of the Darwinians and a Weismannian to boot.

Kidd, that is, seemed to be turning science against itself. *Popular Science* agreed that science would one day discover the laws of human evolution no less than those that governed development at lower stages. But this would occur when "she gathered and sifted a sufficiency of fact," not by giving up.[51]

Kidd's attitude toward science was indeed ambivalent. Viewing science positively, he implicitly assigned it a crucial role in shaping a new order. However paradoxically, the discovery of the ultrarational santion was the product of the reason of the social critic. The sociologist must be "unbiased" (a favorite word of Kidd), and must rid himself of "pre-conceived ideas." Science, in the person of Huxley, abdicated this role. It left "human history as a bewildering exception to the reign of universal law—a kind of solitary and mysterious island in the midst of the cosmos given over to strife of forces without clue or meaning." The alternative was not irrationalism however. Kidd demanded a "more radical method" for the social sciences, not the abandonment of science but a more thoroughgoing application of scientific method—thus anticipating a growing recognition of the roles of emotion and imagination in science. Furthermore, the ultrarational sanction was really a deeper form of reason. Its importance showed "simply that the deep-seated instincts of society have a truer scientific basis than our current science."[52]

Underlying this affirmation and redefinition of science was a deep-seated suspicion of its present role. Science was corrosive of traditional community and society, Kidd charged. Rationalists (his example was a recent contributor to the *Contemporary Review*) went so far as to deny the material self-sacrifice that lay at the heart of the family! Describing Huxley and other evolutionists Kidd took his script from the social Darwinist stereotype with which, ironically, others would attempt to brand *Social Evolution*. "Science was callous": it was "content to sit still and wait for the arrival of the avenging comet"—a reference again to Huxley's Romanes speech. So also:

> The evolutionist may be convinced that what is called the exploitation of the masses, is but the present-day form of the rivalry of life which he has watched from the beginning, and that the sacrifice of some in the cause of the future interests of the whole social organism is a necessary feature of our progress. But this is no real argument addressed to those who most naturally object to be exploited and sacrificed, and who in our modern societies are entrusted with power to give political effect to their objections.[53]

George or Bellamy could not have said it better.

A similar ambivalence clouded Kidd's social message, producing spirited debate over his individualism and socialism. As often happens, opaque arguments became mirrors of reviewers' hopes and fears.

Defenders of individualism and laissez faire charged Kidd with socialism. The New York *Nation* found the "general trend of his thought, at least in all but the earlier chapters, [to be] unmistakably that of the so-called Christian socialist." Although *Popular Science* concluded from certain portions of the work that Kidd had "no faith in socialism," it regretted that in others "he seems to anticipate great and beneficial results from a vast extension of socialistic legislation." LeSueur, as already noted, wondered why Kidd condemned socialism as unscientific but then proceeded to recommend "something which it is difficult to distinguish from socialism."[54]

From the left came charges of conservatism. The socialist Henry Demarest Lloyd claimed that the book's popularity came from the fact that Kidd "put into a new vocabulary the old ideas which our civilization of selfishness does not want to give up. . . . He promised the business system a new lease of life and authority by his philosophy of struggle, and the ecclesiastical system renewed infallibility." The culprit was evolution, wrote Lloyd, pressing a popular stereotype to new use. Kidd's arguments were "mere individualism clothed in the skin of biological pretense." With clear reference to Kidd, a Harvard sociologist condemned the alliance of religion and natural selection. "Know, therefore, ministers of philanthropy and religion," he wrote, tongue-in-cheek, "that you are co-workers together with Nature, with a big N, in the grewsome [sic] task of eliminating the unfit." Some years later, William Jennings Bryan, further contributing to Kidd's reputation as a conservative Darwinist, observed that the Englishman completed the work of the evolutionists in showing "that Darwinism robs the reformer of hope."[55]

In reality, Kidd was neither an individualist nor a socialist, as these terms were used through the eighties, but rather a link between the earlier liberalism of a William Graham Sumner and the mood which in America produced progressivism. Rather than speaking for business, as Lloyd alleged, Kidd spoke for the British equivalent of Sumner's "forgotten man"—the middle-class citizen who by the midnineties was willing to accept some change as inevitable, but as Kidd described him had "no indication as to the direction in which the right path lies." As with American progressives, this middle class stood between powerful forces it could not control:

> Society is being organized by classes into huge battalions, the avowed object of which is the making war on each other. We have syndicates, corporations, and federations of capital on one side, and societies, trades-unions, and federations of labour on the other.[56]

This audience found socialism anathema. But in reading *Social Evolution* one is also struck as were contemporary critics, with Kidd's interest in the work of a variety of reformers, including the Americans Henry George and Edward Bellamy. Although critical of Marx's "thoroughly materialistic" philosophy, Kidd defended the notion of the exploitation of labor against counterattacks from Alfred Marshall and the "younger school of economists," who instead stressed the role of the entrepreneur. The Marxists, were not his "principle enemy" as one historian has claimed. Rather in "concluding remarks," he focused again on the utilitarians, the "hitherto predominate school of thought."[57]

Although Kidd argued that future progress depended on the "same cosmic process which has been in operation from the beginning," he insisted that fundamental changes were necessary to insure that competition resulted in maximum *efficiency*, a term that became a watchword for Kidd no less than it did for a generation of American reformers. Reduced to essentials, his program was a restatement of the *equality of opportunity*, a fundamental principle of traditional liberalism. But in his post-Darwinian version, opportunity required more than equality before the law. "It may be noticed that the characteristic feature of this [new] legislation is the increasing tendency to raise the position of the lower classes *at the expense of the* wealthier classes," he observed, in the sort of statement *Popular Science* regretted. "All future progressive legislation must apparently have this tendency. It is almost a *conditio sine qua non* of any measure that carries us a step forward in our social development." Anticipating the regulatory state that would develop in Britain and America in the next two decades, he added that "the general tendency must be expected to be towards state interference and state control on a greatly extended scale rather than towards state management." Regulation was the means; social efficiency the end; and humanitarianism the guiding spirit. Such were the contours of a New Liberalism that was neither individualistic nor socialistic.[58]

Kidd himself was aware of his anomalous position. Invited to give the Herbert Spencer lecture at Oxford in 1908, he chose as his theme "Individualism and After." Tracing the history of the doctrine, he observed that the "doctrine of evolution" had initially "appeared to give the last sanction" to individualism. But these extrapolations were invalid since Darwin dealt "almost exclusively with the struggle for existence as between individuals and among forms of life below human society." Kidd then described the development of "the more organic social type" (a position he traced to Spencer!) and outlined his plea for social efficiency, or what he now termed *the struggle for the life of the future*. He also endorsed the increase of state enterprises, at a time when Britain was on the eve of its first venture in the welfare state. "I do not know," he told his audience in conclusion, "whether you will call me a reactionary or a revolutionary."[59]

Kidd also made a sociological breakthrough of sorts. Although most academic sociologists felt that *Social Evolution* subtracted from the sum of knowledge in the field, his call for a "more radical method" in the social sciences was nonetheless significant. The goal of sociology, whether practiced by Spencer or Ward, was the discovery of laws that somehow linked society to human physiology or psychology. Although critical of classical economics and utilitarianism, sociology remained doggedly reductionist, since society ultimately reduced to man's animal or psychic needs. In stressing the ultrarational sanction, Kidd insisted that society was more than a congerie of individual wills, something different even from Spencer's social organism. In a sense the ultrarational sanction was a crude formulation of the *Protestant ethic*, which Max Weber would soon delineate more skillfully.

Kidd did not break completely with utilitarianism. His book, as one reviewer commented, might have been subtitled "An Attempt to Base the Truths of Revealed Religion on the Doctrines of Bentham, of Malthus, and of Darwin, by showing what advantages they have given to believers in their struggle for existence." Although Kidd rejected prevailing conceptions of reason (which he equated with narrow selfishness) he was unable to conceive a radical alternative—perhaps because he lacked contact with a tradition of philosophical idealism, certainly because he lacked Weber's genius. His strategy, as one commentor has noted, was a perennial one of nineteenth-century positivism: "Being unable to define the objective mind expressing itself in many and various ways in the relationship of individuals, he tried, like Comte, to sum up as religion what could not be defined by positivism." But Kidd's ultrarational sanction was more than Comte's Religion of Humanity, a doctrine he explicitly attacked. Kidd not only insisted on the importance of the ultrarational but argued that this realm was governed by universal law, a critical assumption of the modern sociological perspective.[60]

The aim here, however, is not to defend Kidd's definition of science, his social views, or his contribution to sociology. Rather it is to underscore the ambivalence towards both social change and science that made *Social Evolution* at once challenging and infuriating. Kidd's Darwinism served a dual function: negatively, as an image of a natural order for which reason found no sanction; positively, as inspiration toward a more radical scientific method. Liberals of the *Nation* school found Kidd anathema, not simply because he used Darwinian rhetoric in a different way than they, but rather because he insisted that Darwinism made untenable any defense of competition and laissez faire based on natural law—a conclusion Spencerians had tried to avoid for more than a decade. The difference between Kidd and his critics was not a contrast between conservative and reform Darwinism, but between a generation who minimized Darwin's significance and one who translated the new biology into a call for positive social action. In this sense all social Darwinism *was* reform Darwinism.

Four

Although Huxley and Kidd caused an intellectual flurry, most Americans found the work of two other European popularizers more acceptable: Peter Kropotkin, a Russian born geographer and revolutionary, whose series on "Mutual Aid" appeared in seven installments in the *Nineteenth Century* between 1890 and 1896 and in book form in 1902; and Henry Drummond, professor of natural science at the University of Glasgow, whose *The Ascent of Man* (1895) transformed Kropotkin's central theme into balm for the religious and scientific alike. While differing in emphasis they shared the common conviction that nature, ethics, and social policy, if properly understood, were governed by a single universal law.

For Kropotkin (1842-1921), *Mutual Aid* was a labor of love at the close of an active career. Born in Moscow, schooled in St. Petersburg, he settled permanently in London in 1886, after more than two decades of fomenting nihilism and anarchist doctrines in his native land, in Switzerland, and in France. By the time the first installments of *Mutual Aid* appeared, he was already gaining a reputation as one of Britain's more distinguished emigrés.[61]

Kropotkin derived the initial inspiration for *Mutual Aid* in 1880 from a lecture by Professor Kessler, a celebrated Russian naturalist and then dean of St. Petersburg University. "Kessler's idea," as he later summarized it, "was that besides *the law of Mutual Struggle* there is in Nature *the law of Mutual Aid*, which, for the success of the struggle of life, and especially for the progressive evolution of the species, is far more important than the law of mutual contest." The fact that individuals within species assist one another was of less importance than the claim that such assistance was *the* critical element in evolution at all levels. Unlike Spencer, who acknowledged such aid among animals only to deny it for primitive man until reinstated as the emotion of altruism, Kropotkin pictured an unbroken continuum. Although several critics felt that Kropotkin failed to prove precisely the point that such aid promoted evolution, particularly as regards subhuman species, many admired the wealth of detail that gave his work an air of scientific authority, at least among laymen.[62]

In addition to Kessler, Kropotkin later claimed other sources, notably several works dealing with the mental life of animals and the prehuman origin of instincts: Alfred Espinas's *Des Sociétiés animales* (1877); Jean Marie de Lanessan's *La Lutte pour l'existence et l'association pour la lutte* (a lecture given in April 1881); and Ludwig Büchner's *Liebe und Liebes-Leben* (1879). He also documented his thesis with numerous examples drawn from his own explorations in the wilds of Siberia and wide reading about primitive and medieval man.

But from its inception, *Mutual Aid* was also shaped by the developing conflict among evolutionists over the true meaning of Darwinism and the growing suspicion that science was somehow growing immoral. Kropotkin first crossed swords with Huxley in 1887 and a year later asked the editors of *Nineteenth Century* for space to rebut the biologist's "Struggle for Existence," which appeared in the magazine in February 1888. Their discussion made it clear that the stakes were nothing less than Darwin's tattered mantle. "Yes certainly, *that* is true Darwinism," the editor replied after hearing Kropotkin's proposal. "It is horrible what 'they' have made of Darwin." In the published articles Kropotkin wove this suspicion into a familiar stereotype. Spencer's followers (unnamed)

> came to conceive the animal world as a world of perpetual struggle among half-starved individuals, thirsting for one another's blood. They made modern literature resound with the war cry of *woe to the vanquished*, as if it were the last word of modern biology. They raised the "pitiless" struggle for personal advantages to the height of a biological principle which man must submit to as well, under the menace of otherwise succumbing in a world based upon mutual extermination.

While he could dismiss such views from "economists who know of natural science but a few words borrowed from second-hand vulgarizers," Kropotkin was distressed that Darwin's "most authorized exponents," including Huxley, "did their best to maintain these false ideas."[63]

Since *Mutual Aid* appeared in book form more than a decade after Kropotkin's first article, his argument never had the dramatic impact of Kidd's ultrarational sanction. The *Political Science Quarterly*, while granting the value of the work, observed that its "fundamental ideas . . . are perhaps not altogether new." Although the *Nation* faulted the book for its failure to meet "the demands of a scientific presentation of evolutionary theory," even this journal was ready to admit that the central idea "deserves the recognition which it here receives, as contrasting agreeably with the harsher aspects of competition." In reality, as the *Political Science Quarterly* also noted, Kropotkin's group effort seemed sometimes like "the *belli auxilia* in the Hobbesian sense," a "mutual struggle for existence" more than "mutual aid." Struggle, that is, seemed a permanent feature of the human experience.[64]

Whatever its shortcomings, *Mutual Aid* answered Huxley not simply with theory, but an apparent wealth of biological and anthropological fact that suggested that nature, if properly understood, could be trusted after all. Kropotkin's "serene and kindly outlook upon the universe," as a British reviewer characterized it, was a welcome antidote to the picture of "human life as an ever more tenacious combat . . . with a nightmare vision of a kind of universal Chicago as the consumation of man's activity."[65]

Born near Glasgow, Scotland, Henry Drummond (1851-1897) believed that the warfare between religion and science was based on a huge misunderstanding. At age ten, he had his first religious experience when, as he later told students at Amherst College, "he began to love the Saviour, and became a happy Christian." From 1866 to 1873 he studied at the University of Edinburgh and briefly at Tübingen. Training for the ministry in the Free Church of Scotland, he imbibed the tradition of Common Sense realism that was likewise the staple of the nineteenth-century American college. "I see him standing in that sombre quadrangle," a friend later reminisced, "laden with Hodge's *Systematic Theology*," a tome which kept young Scots "in the paths of peace."[66]

But orthodoxy did not satisfy Drummond. Early addicted to the Romantics, he turned eagerly to Ruskin (who "taught me to see"); to Emerson (who taught him "to see with the mind"); and finally to George Eliot (who "opened my eyes to the meaning of life"). Among theologians, he preferred the proto-transcendentalism of William Ellery Channing, and the popular liberalism of Horace Bushnell, two Americans who paved the way for his participation during 1873-1874 in the great revival tour of Dwight L. Moody and Ira D. Sankey. At the same time Drummond plunged into scientific work, for which Edinburgh was renowned: first natural science under the physicist Peter Guthrie Tait, author of work on thermodynamics and the Newtonian laws of motion; and later botany and geology. In 1877 his religious and scientific interests happily coalesced with his appointment to the Chair of Natural Science at the Free Church

College in Glasgow, where he gave five months a year to science and the rest to preaching.[67]

The product of this experience, *Natural Law in the Spiritual World* (1883), Drummond's first major work, won him international fame. Originally popular lectures, his argument was appropriately simple. The same laws operated in the natural and spiritual realms, not symbolically or by analogy but literally. "Analogous Phenomena are not the fruit of parallel Laws, but of the same laws," he wrote, although he continued to refer to "analogy" for convenience. For example, just as life could not develop from nonlife (Drummond cited recent attacks on spontaneous generation) so an absolute barrier separated material and spiritual. Just as life arose quickly and mysteriously, so spiritual birth or conversion occurred in a flash. So also, just as degeneration or reversion to type threatened all organic life, so backsliding imperiled salvation.[68]

Despite a frustrating imprecision that drew a shower of criticism, Drummond seemed to offer the general public everything it wanted to know about God but was afraid to believe. His thesis, he argued, was actually an extension to religion of the strategy Spencer adopted in applying "Natural Law to the Social World." In fact, Drummond based much of his argument on undeveloped metaphysical assumptions in the work of Spencer and other evolutionists, precisely those coming under fire in positivist circles in the eighties. "Eternal life," for example, was but the "perfect correspondence between organism and environment of which Spencer spoke."[69]

Philosophically, Drummond's reasoning was a crude amalgm of moral sense doctrine and a sort of Emersonian intuitionism. "We have Truth in Nature as it came from God," he asserted. "And it has to be read with the same unbiased mind, the same open eye, the same faith, and the same reverence as all other Revelation." "It is altogether unlikely that man spiritual should be violently separated in all conditions of growth, development, and life from man physical," he continued. The alternative was "difficult to conceive. . . . Evolution being found in so many different sciences, the likelihood is that it is a universal principle." Nature, after all, was wellbred. "Man as a rational and moral being demands a pledge that if he depends on Nature for any given result, his intellect shall not be insulted, nor his confidence in her abused." Above all, after these tests were applied: "There is a sense of solidity about a Law of Nature which belongs to nothing else in the world."[70]

Stung by criticism, Drummond by the time of Huxley's Oxford address wondered if his attempt to bind science to religion was not after all "immoral and unscientific." But Huxley's stark dichotomy between nature and ethics revitalized his interest in universal law. The result was *The Ascent of Man* (1895), initially a series of lectures in Boston, Chicago, and on the Chautuaqua circuit. Again his overriding theme was the unity of all being. "The sense of the whole comes first," he wrote, quoting from a study of Browning. Again, too, his strategy was the radical extension of arguments others allegedly left half-developed. Those who misread nature, thus rejecting her model, should not "discharge the teacher but beg her mutinous pupils to try another term at school," he wrote with obvious reference to Huxley.[71]

But he tacitly conceded that the text had changed in the age of neo-Darwinism: to the laws of "biogenesis, degeneration and growth" Weismann and Huxley added "struggle and survival." Fortunately, this image of the "Struggle for Life" was only half true. A second factor was "equally prominent", namely "Struggle for the Life of Others." Characterizing the two, he reiterated the conventional wisdom: "One begets competition, self-assertion, war; the other unselfishness, self-effacement, peace. One is Individualism, the other Altruism." Although this latter term revealed his continuing debt to Spencer, he insisted that the "Other-regarding instinct" operated "even in the early stages of development—much earlier," in fact, "than is usually supposed"—and was a critical factor in biological evolution.[72]

Although he sidestepped debates over Weismannism, Drummond's criticisms of Huxley and Kidd were predictable. Given Huxley's view of nature, he "hit upon the right solution." But his method violated the basic premise of his earlier work which emphasized "continuity" throughout the "world order." Huxley's partial view of nature resulted in a "biological error" that corrupted "a whole philosophy." Although Drummond felt that no sociologist saw the problem as clearly as Kidd, he charged that *Social Evolution* was but another evidence of this corruption, a tragic irony since "all that Mr. Kidd desires is really to be found in Nature."[73]

Drummond's claim that he had more fully developed Spencer's philosophy invited the inevitable reply. Although Spencer personally found *Natural Law in the Spiritual World* to be fuzzy-minded and hopelessly theological, he welcomed Drummond's support—albeit uneasily, even cynically. But *The Ascent of Man* was too much for Spencer. Asking a friend to reply in print, Spencer complained that Drummond "[with] the airs of a discoverer and with the tone of authority sets out to instruct me and other evolutionists respecting the factor of social evolution which we have ignored—altruism." Even worse, he added later, was the "public taste which swallows with greediness these semi-scientific sentimentalities." Heeding Spencer's request, the reviewer responded assailing Drummond's pseudo-science. "His is the sin of plagiarism," she wrote, "with the additional offense of distortion in the lifting." Moreover she added, Drummond's "sickly . . . eulogium on . . . Love" ignored the facts of struggle in human society: "the war going on between capital and labour; between the Haves and the Have-nots; between classes in England, races and religious in Ireland, anarchy and organization everywhere." Much better she concluded, was Spencer's account in the *Principles of Ethics* of "the soul of justice in things evil."[74]

Drummond's struggle for the life of others nonetheless joined altruism, particularly in the arsenal of those who wanted moderate change but feared extremes. Inspired by Drummond, Henry Wood, an American businessman who turned to New Thought after a nervous breakdown, combined classical economics and Emersonian mysticism in such works as *Natural Law in the Business World* (1887); *The Political Economy of Natural Law* (1894); and *Arbitrary Price-making through the Forces of Law* (1905).[75] Discussing *The Evolution of Industry* (1895), Henry Dyer, an Ethical Culturist and sympathetic critic of Spencer, cited *Natural Law in the Spiritual World* to support his own thesis that the solution of current problems would come neither through legislation "nor the storm and confusion of a revolution, but the agencies already at work." A decade later, with pressures for reform much greater, Lyman Abbott, the editor of the *Outlook*, again invoked Drummond—but this time to attack laissez faire: "the industrial application of the principle of the struggle for existence, the survival of the fittest."[76]

This debate over neo-Darwinism during the 1890s left no clear legacy. Confronted with nature as pictured by the neo-Darwinians, most commentators accepted neither Huxley's stoicism nor Kidd's apparent irrationalism. More acceptable were the solutions of Kropotkin and Drummond, although the first seemed to involve permanent struggle (albeit of groups) and the second a naive faith that love conquers all.

But the decade did shift the center of debate, as a split opened between two varieties of reform Darwinism. Perhaps comforted by Kropotkin, Drummond, or other similar arguments, a majority of reformers continued to urge regulation of industry and social welfare measures in much the same language as had the earlier critics of laissez faire and competition. A significant minority, however, now believed that a new situation demanded new controls if society were to escape from what a supporter of Drummond called "the shadow of Darwinism."

8.   A Pigeon Fanciers' Polity

Granting . . . the general position of the author [that the environment does not play the part in heredity formerly supposed], we find that when we carry his principle to its logical conclusion, the results are quite revolutionary. . . . We should, in short, cease all attempts to repress vice and disease and let them take their own course. . . . It is probable that the author would never accept these logical results of his attitude. . . . Nevertheless, just these conditions have represented the law of nature. If this is the law of nature, should it not be also the law for man?
Herbert W. Conn, "The Individual and the Race," Independent, 60 (1906), 385.

[Eugenics] too often accepts the present competitive, capitalist, exploitative regime as fundamentally right—so much so that success under it becomes the evidence . . . of a superior ability. . . . No doubt eugenicists will vigorously repudiate this as an interpretation, but their works need only to be carefully read to substantiate this indictment. . . . [It] must be sought between the lines in many places, in the form of assumption, implication, and inference. This subtlety, hiding itself even from its authors, perhaps, renders it nonetheless retroactive and socially injurious.
Clarence M. Case, "Eugenics," Journal of Applied Sociology, 7 (1922), 11-12.

One

In 1901 the sociologist Edward A. Ross published *Social Control*, a study of the foundations of order in modern society. Although he never defined the term precisely, Ross traced formal and informal means of *social control* through history and predicted the gradual substitution of the force of enlightened public opinion for the mystical and authoritarian agencies of the past. Although he made only brief reference to evolution, at the heart of the theory was a perception of neo-Darwinian chaos that had haunted Ross for more than a decade. The question, as he saw it, was frighteningly simple: given the fact that society was composed of "natural" men for whom the only law of nature was Darwinian self-assertion, what forces checked this impulse and made society possible?[1]

Sociologists and laymen applauded the work. Within a decade social control was the common currency of progressive reform. But inevitably, Ross's already imprecise definition blurred still further. For Theodore Roosevelt, who praised Ross extravagantly, *Social Control* taught "that public opinion, if only sufficiently enlightened and aroused, is equal to the necessary regenerative tasks and can yet dominate the future." Others used the term to describe government regulation of industry, as the opposite of laissez faire. A minority, taking the term more literally, proposed a variety of measures to contain forces that appeared to threaten the social fabric.[2] Behind these proposals lay the common assumption that, since society was a jungle, more systematic controls were demanded. Supplementing an older humanitarianism, there developed an ideal of rule by experts in the interests of efficiency.

During the progressive era this impulse bred a variety of proposed controls, from immigration restriction to new sanctions against nonwhite Americans. However, none was more controversial than the movement to improve the human stock through eugenics legislation, a reform that attracted a vigorous minority including Ross. Although the movement grew less quickly in the United States than in Great Britain, the American Breeders Association, founded in 1903, soon established a strong eugenics subsection: somewhat later the organization was renamed the American Genetics Association. By the middle of the decade, eugenics was a hot subject in sociological circles, drawing fire from such notables as Lester Ward. In 1910 a Eugenics Record Office was established at Cold Spring Harbor, New York, and soon became a center of propaganda for the movement. Between 1907 and 1915 a dozen states passed sterilization laws, while more revised their marriage codes.[3]

Partisans saw in eugenics the answer to Huxley's dilemma. "Knowledge has grown, no doubt, since *Evolution and Ethics* was written," noted a University of Chicago professor in 1911, "and new discoveries have gone far to discredit Huxley's belittlement of the potency of human selective agencies. . . . Possibly the social consciousness of a people is an abler guide than he recognized." Opponents, on the other hand, continued to look with suspicion at the "administrative authority" that in Huxley's view was an "unattainable" blueprint for a "pigeon-fanciers' polity."[4]

Historians since have viewed eugenics as the most enduring form of social Darwinism, indeed perhaps the only true form. At the same time they have tended to picture it as a perverse afterglow of earlier conservative uses of Darwinism. Thus the eugenics movement becomes the final proof of the reactionary effects of the Darwinian revolution. But, as with other varieties of reform Darwinism, this approach distorts Darwin's contribution to eugenic theory and the place of the social Darwinian slogan in eugenic debates.[5]

The idea of pruning humanity like so many roses was indeed a logical deduction from the *Origin of Species*, *if* one could stifle the moral sensibilities that troubled Darwin himself. This movement was also Darwinian, *at least* to the extent that Francis Galton, Darwin's cousin and the author of *Hereditary Genius* (1869), was a prime mover and later patron saint of the movement. But in its assumptions and intellectual strategies, eugenics was primarily Darwinian in the same way that other varieties of reform Darwinism were. Eugenicists found the neo-Darwinian world of Huxley no less disturbing than Kidd and others who responded to Weismannism in the 1890s. Like other reform Darwinists they assumed nature could no longer be left alone, and they were vigorous critics of laissez faire. But they differed from those who preferred environmental or sociological reforms in that they preferred to work directly on man's physical constitution. Weismannism, in forcing a sharper distinction between social and physical inheritance—nurture and nature—offered two paths to reformers, where before there had seemed only one. While some social scientists turned avidly to the study of culture, eugenicists attempted literally to weed the human garden.

In the resulting debates, the image of social Darwinism figured more prominently than ever before. Eugenicists charged that their opponents would leave things to the workings of a brutal natural law. Their enemies in contrast saw in eugenics the final proof that Darwinism was fatal to human sympathy. Whatever one's position, the conviction grew that social Darwinism was the villain of the piece.

Two

Interest in *stirpiculture*, as eugenics was originally known, grew from sources very similar to those that inspired the *Origin of Species*. Experience with plant and animal breeding inevitably suggested possibilities for human development. "Every race horse, every straight-backed bull, every premium pig tells us what we can do and what we must do for man," proclaimed John Humphrey Noyes, whose experiments with "complex marriage" in the Oneida community made him one of America's first eugenicists. Later eugenics literature bristled with references to stockbreeding. "The legislator must . . . conform to the principles of the stockbreeder, whose object is to rear the finest horses, cattle, and sheep," wrote a prominent British eugenicist. "Man is an organism—an animal," the American eugenicist Charles B. Davenport agreed, "and the laws of the improvement of corn and of race horses hold true for him also." When Davenport sought aid for his eugenics record office, he turned to Mrs. E. H. Harriman, who gave money because "the fact that she was brought up among well-bred race horses helped her to appreciate the importance of . . . heredity and good breeding in man."[6]

Malthus's *Essay on Population* also contributed indirectly. From midcentury onward a growing band of neo-Malthusians advocated birth control, thus challenging taboos against public discussion of reproduction. For some individuals neo-Malthusianism provided a natural transition to genetic planning. Prominent British birth controller Charles V. Drysdale later claimed that population quality as well as quantity was an important part of the program of the Neo-Malthusian League founded in London in 1877. In the mid-1880s, there appeared one of the first articles to combine birth control and eugenics. This alliance was unstable, however, since many eugenicists believed that birth control caused a disastrous decline in birth rates among the "better" classes.[7]

Work in criminal anthropology also stimulated interest in heredity and its control. By the early 1880s, as Mark Haller has shown, some Americans were familiar with Bénédict Morel's studies of hereditary degeneration and other work on the criminal brain. These studies helped undermine the Spencerian belief in automatic progress, already sorely strained, and planted the seeds of conviction that man must control his own biological development. "With the struggle for existence, and (let us hope) with the 'survival of the fittest' we are all familiar," a New York physician told the Social Science Association, explaining the new criminology; "but there is also another struggle going on in our midst, with far different results, the chief of which is the Survival of the Unfittest."[8] Toward the end of the decade, this conviction grew as the work of Cesare Lombroso and the Italian school of criminology became widely known. *Atavism* and *degeneration* became the new catchwords, surfacing even in such popular fiction as Frank Norris's *McTeague* (1899) and *Vandover and the Brute* (1914). By the close of the century some observers felt that only the most extreme measures could reverse the decay of civilization.

Given these similar sources, however, it is remarkable how small a role Darwinism per se played in discussion of eugenics before the 1880s. An apparent exception was Francis Galton (1822-1911), Darwin's cousin on his mother's side, who later claimed that *Origin of Species* marked an "epoch" in his mental development. But even his debt was a limited one. Darwin aroused "a spirit of rebellion against all ancient authorities," he remembered. In particular Darwin's theory of pangenesis was an attempt to bring order to the study of *heredity*, the term itself still under suspicion as a French import. Significantly, Darwin's chief contribution in this regard was to stimulate experiments that convinced Galton that Darwin was wrong. Galton also confessed that the initial inspiration for *Hereditary Genius* was not Darwin but his own observations of contemporaries while an undergraduate at Cambridge, where the same surnames appeared perennially on honors lists.[9] A more personal inspiration, a recent biographer has suggested, may have been Galton's realization that his own marriage was likely to prove infertile.[10]

In *Hereditary Genius* Galton mentioned his cousin's work, but his focus was heredity, not evolution or natural selection. His approach was that of the taxonomist and statistician, classifying and arranging human accomplishment in relation to ancestry. His view of social evolution, insofar as he expressed any interest in evolution, was the rough amalgam of Spencer and Darwin that by the 1870s was the common property of many Victorian intellectuals. Natural selection operating in the past evolved "intelligence in connection with sociability." Among intelligent animals, "the most social race is sure to prevail, other qualities being equal," he added. Galton's main concern was the *race*, since men cooperated in groups in the struggle for existence against nature and other groups.[11]

While emphasizing heredity, Galton assumed that intelligence and fellow-feeling profoundly modified the conditions of life. Accepting this inference, he urged in the 1860s that nations avoid social policies that patently diminished the reproduction of the "vigorous classes"—the celibacy of Oxford dons, for example, or favoring the oldest sons in marriage through primogeniture, both anathema to liberals. In his *Inquiries into Human Faculty* (1883), he argued that men had a "religious duty" to further evolution "deliberately and systematically." But on this and later occasions Galton's hopes for genetic planning were considerably more modest than those of many later disciples. Selection of the "best on an individual basis" was "like the labor of Sisyphus in rolling the stone uphill," he observed, and would never alter the race.[12]

Galton's work was immensely important. His early investigations laid the basis for the modern study of statistics and of genetics. Almost two decades before Weismann he announced his opposition to the inheritance of acquired characteristics, a position he substantiated experimentally in the early seventies. He convinced even Darwin that heredity was extremely important (although the naturalist preferred to think that "zeal and hard work" were more important among men).[13] But, when in *Inquiries* Galton first used the term *eugenics*, he did not propose to replace natural selection with artificial selection, nor did he see eugenics as a possible alternative to other reform.

When Darwinism appeared in early arguments over eugenics it functioned to characterize the bad side of modern life. In *Enigmas of Life* (1872) the popular British writer William Rathbone Greg took a hard look at the disease, destitution, and crime that seemed to threaten the old ideal of inevitable progress. Identifying three inhibiting agencies, he described each in Darwinian terms: the struggle for mere existence; the multiplication of the race from its least desirable elements, which he termed *non-survival of the fittest*; and increasing power in the hands of the ignorant. Philanthropic in his sympathies, Greg denied that man must forever accept this natural order:

A republic is *conceivable* in which paupers should be forbidden to propagate; in which all candidates for the proud and solemn privilege of continuing an untainted and perfecting race should be subjected to a pass or a competitive examination and those only be suffered to transmit their names and families to future generations who had a pure, vigorous, and well-developed constitution to transmit.

But even more than Galton, Greg doubted the practicality of genetic control: " . . . no nation—in modern times at least—has ever yet approached this ideal; no such wisdom or virtue has ever been found except in isolated individual instances." The only hope was internal restraint, he concluded. "We can only watch and be careful that any other influence we do set in motion shall be such as, when they work at all, may work in the right direction." Moreover, despite his fear of popular government, Greg further assumed that the benefits of eugenic self-control would accrue to everyone "till the human race, both in its manhood and womanhood, became one glorious fellowship of saints, sages and athletes."[14]

In a lengthy review of Greg's book, the British jurist A. V. Dicey implicitly seconded his indictment of a Darwinian world, although criticizing the theological cast of the work in general. "Mr. Greg's success is obviously not owing to any novelty in his subject," Dicey wrote. Even the apparent paradox in "The non-Survival of the Fittest" could "hardly appear paradoxical to any person who has reflected upon the nature of civilization and the true meaning of the theory of natural selection." Fitness, that is to say, was a moral quality, not to be defined simply as survival in any given environment. Implicit also was the notion that nature was no guide to social policy. As an English neo-Malthusian put it several years later in a debate over "Evolution and Small Families": " . . . the natural selection of Darwin [is] not of service to humanity."[15]

Three

In America the new hereditarianism was even less explicitly Darwinian, either in stressing selectionism or discussing the issue within the context of a struggle for existence. In his celebrated study of *The Jukes* (1877), Richard L. Dugdale virtually ignored development theory in presenting a catalog of facts and figures concerning criminality and pauperism through six generations of a single family. Without mentioning either Galton or Darwin, he embraced a Lamarckian view of environment and use-inheritance that his own evidence seemed implicitly to challenge. Although heredity provided dispositions, these developed only in certain environments. These in turn affected heredity. "Where the environment changes in youth the characteristics of heredity may be measurably altered," he wrote. "Hence the importance of education." Dugdale's specific recommendations were those then commanding the attention of America's most enlightened educators—notably his advocacy of industrial training and of infant training on the model of Froebel's kindergarten school.[16]

Discussing "Heredity" for *Popular Science* in 1879, the author George Iles summarized the American consensus after a decade of discussion of Galton's work. "Inheritance is not only physical, but intellectual as well," he wrote citing a celebrated study of the Bach family. So also there was "abundant testimony to prove that heredity can be moral as well as physical and intellectual." His explanation was directly from Lamarck via Darwin:

> The development of intelligence among mankind is accounted for
> in the same manner [as the advance of skills among honey bees]:
> efforts at first painfully made by our ancestors in new paths were
> at last rewarded by the facility that comes with repetition; their
> immediate descendents were born with new aptitudes and
> an organization with a wider range of powers; the acquisitions
> thus gained and transmitted have grown into the varied faculties
> of the men and women of today.

Just as struggle and selection played no part in his argument, so Iles's conclusions were moderate by the standards of turn-of-the-century eugenics, ranging as they did from permanent incarceration of certain incorrigible criminals to common sense in the choice of marriage partners.[17]

Although in his famous study of deaf-mutes in 1883 Alexander Graham Bell explicitly considered the impact of sexual selection, he also adhered to a Lamarckian framework and refused to endorse coercive controls. Bell observed that normally there was little prospect of individuals with similar congenital illnesses choosing one another for marriage partners. But the segregation of the deaf made their case an exception, posing the threat of a new race of deaf-mutes. But beyond this observation, Bell would not trespass. "We cannot control the marriages of men as we can the breeding of animals, and at first sight there seems to be no way of ascertaining how far human beings are susceptible of variation by selection," he wrote, with characteristic caution. Moreover, he stressed that he was interested only in the special case of deafness, known to be inheritable, not a broader spectrum of physiological and psychological traits.[18] If Darwin's work contained the seeds of the later eugenics movement, conditions were not ready for its flowering for several decades.

Four

During the 1880s, however, eugenics began to attract limited interest on both sides of the Atlantic, as part of the general upheaval of reform. Prohibitionists were especially active, warning of the dangers of alcohol to the unborn. An Institute of Heredity under temperance auspices flourished briefly in Boston; and in 1885 the Chicago chapter of the W.C.T.U. launched a *Journal of Heredity.* In this literature, as in that of the New Liberalism generally, prohibitionists coupled demands for state action with a Darwinian caricature of inaction. "The moral sense needs reinforcing," wrote the director of the Boston Institute of Heredity in 1882,

> so that a cold clear-cut intellect, backed up by force, may not condemn our humanity to the level of that brute law,—the "survival of the fittest"—which in the battle of life and the struggle for existence gives victory to the strongly armed,—the shrewd, the artful, and the cunning,—in which struggle the weakest in craft— the honest, truthful, the sincere and the unselfish—go to the wall, or are trodden under foot, and thus results in the "survival" of the unfittest.[19]

Eugenics gained further support in reform circles when, in *Looking Backward* (1888), Edward Bellamy pictured the happy consequences of sexual selection in utopian Boston of the year 2000. Liberated from economic dependence upon men, women chose mates for "pure love." This fact, explained Dr. Leete, Bellamy's spokesman for the future,

means that for the first time in human history the principle of sexual selection, with its tendency to preserve and transmit the better types of the race, and let the inferior types drop out, has unhindered operation. The necessities of poverty, the need of having a home, no longer tempt women to accept as the fathers of their children men whom they neither can love nor respect. . . . The gifts of person, mind, and disposition; beauty, wit, eloquence, kindness, generosity, geniality, courage, are sure of transmission to posterity. Every generation is sifted through a little finer mesh than the last.

Indeed, Leete suggested, this "untrammeled sexual selection" was "perhaps more important" than any other cause "tending to race purification." Julian West, Bellamy's representative of nineteenth-century man, found this new wisdom enshrined in reverent rhetoric in a best-seller then captivating Boston: " 'Over the unborn our power is that of God, and our responsibility like His toward us.' "[20]

At this point neo-Darwinism transformed the eugenics debate. Demands for rigorous control accompanied predictions of doom if something were not done. Writing in the Arena, Hiram M. Stanley, a frequent contributor on scientific subjects, took the lead. "Nurture is infinitely weaker than nature," he announced, citing Lombroso's Criminalité. In nature, sexual selection and natural selection secured "the perfection of kind." But in society this was not so. "Since natural selection fails so largely in the human species," he continued, noting the harmful effects of many reforms, "resort must be had to artificial selection, and that very speedily." The experience of stockbreeders, for example in developing the trotting horse, held hope for the future. "By a like selection of the fittest . . . man would quickly attain wonderful results in his own development." Attacking the "reckless individualism" that inhibited legislative control, Stanley also criticized the "false fastidiousness and vicious delicacy" that prevented open discussion of the issue.[21]

Although few Americans were ready for this extreme, the barrier of silence was broken. If Weismann were correct, wrote Amos Warner in his popular American Charities (1894), "our only hope for permanent improvement of the human stock would then seem to be through exercising an influence upon the selective processes." Although most commentators split the difference between heredity and environment, a new tone crept into the arguments of some writers sympathetic to eugenics. A contributor to the *Arena* seemed almost to suggest that something like natural selection be allowed a role in human evolution:

It will be by a judicious use of our functions—mental, moral, and physical—aided by a wise selection of environment, and the exercise of "the law of natural selection," that the problem of "the survival of the fittest" must be solved, the inertia of the evolution of the species continued, and humanity raised nearer and nearer toward a perfect ideal.

Attempting to circumvent the antireformist implications of Weismann-ism, a physicist from McGill University proposed that strong traits were more inheritable than weak ones: hence mediocre people would most bene-fit from education and other environmental reforms, which would remain as efficacious as before. A British physician, answering Pearson's sugges-tion that in a eugenic regime the state would gradually assume the func-tions of the family, argued that the family represented self-sacrifice and cooperation such as characterized social evolution at higher stages. Its development had helped mankind "to struggle out of the dismal swamp of the 'struggle for existence,'" which he deprecated no less than did the eugenicists.[22]

In response to Stanley's article, A. Russel Wallace also counseled moderation. Rejecting proposals to encourage early marriage among a genetic elite (such as Galton proposed) or to allow free divorce as a kind of sexual laissez faire (as the English Spencerian, Grant Allen suggested), Wallace endorsed Bellamy's "clear and forcible picture of the society of the future." Once elevated economically, women would impose their naturally higher moral standards in their choice of husbands. Men left at the gate in this marriage derby would "consist very largely, if not almost wholly, of those who are the least perfectly developed either mentally or physically. . . . The survival of the fittest is really the extinction of the un-fit." Rather than bemoaning checks on natural selection among modern man (where Wallace insisted it never had worked), men should rejoice that the increase in "humanity," in the person of the "Woman of the Future," would work its own selective magic.[23]

Five

The rediscovery of Mendel's work on mutations at the turn of the century ushered in the mature phase of eugenics. Armed with the belief (wrong, as it turned out) that separate traits were ties to individual genes, eugenicists set out to improve society permanently. While geneti-

cists remained a minority within the movement as a whole, one observer
has estimated that as many as half of America's geneticists loaned their
support at one time or another. Although many were only token members
of eugenics organizations, this support was an important source of
prestige. Calling for a scientific approach to social problems, eugenics for a
time also caught the imagination of American progressives. Leading eugenicists supported the conservation crusade and participated in such
characteristically progressive activities as municipal reform. Combining
science and moralism, eugenics tracts rang with references to "the religion
of evolution" and "the moral implications in the doctrine of evolution."[24]

Adopting the strategy of other reform Darwinists, eugenicists from the
start vied with each other in condemning laissez faire, a term they applied
to anyone who opposed *them.* "Let them know that *laisser aller* in marriage is no wiser than in other parts of life," wrote Annie Besant, the
British Fabian and prominent neo-Malthusian, in defense of birth control.
In the work of a conservative eugenicist several decades later this same
charge appeared as a warning that "the prevention of the multiplication of
the defective classes . . . is so obvious a duty and so feasible a project that
the continuation of our present *laissez faire* policy is nothing short of a
crime to society." Herbert Spencer wished to abandon charity, observed
the American eugenicist Roswell Johnson, "in order that sustentative
selection be again allowed full scope."[25]

Given nature as the neo-Darwinists pictured it, sexual laissez faire was
ipso facto brutal. "The disciples of Darwin, many of them, have held that
natural and sexual selection have been the chief factors employed by
nature to being about race improvement," wrote M. L. Holbrook, a physician and the author of *Stirpiculture* (1897), as preface to his support of
the eugenic ideas of Wallace and Bellamy. "Modern evolutionary science,"
added a British neo-Malthusianism, "assumes that if the fittest survive,
the unfit must be eliminated, and that this elimination must be a more or
less cruel process." He then went on to explain how absurd such a view
was since man certainly could do something about the situation.[26]

In his best-selling book, *The New Decalogue of Science* (1923), the American eugenicist Albert Wiggam passed on this legacy to the interwar
generation. Only through eugenics could mankind avoid nature's "three
swords of organic destiny, Famine, Pestilence, and War," he argued. Then,
parodying the opposition, he continued:

> "But," exclaims the *laissez faire* selectionist, "this gives natural
> selection her happy chance to produce strength and genius!"

"True enough," added Wiggam. "But what is the use of strength and
genius in a world not fit to live in?" The war itself fostered a similar con-

clusion. "It is not to eugenics that we shall look for peace on earth and goodwill to men," wrote an American sociologist in 1921. "Indeed, one might . . . point out the fact that the entire Nietzschean conception of life and morals, with its black oppression of the weak by the strong—'its splendid blond beasts lustfully roving in search of prey' after the manner of Belgium in 1914—is entirely consistent with the eugenic program."[27]

The charge of brutality was not without irony. Precisely because eugenicists proposed dramatic intervention in the process of nature, modeled after natural selection, they were neo-Darwinians with a vengeance in describing nature itself. "We must learn from nature's method for the preservation and elevation of races,—the selection of the fittest and the rejection of the unfit," wrote W. Duncan McKim in possibly the most extreme of prewar eugenics tracts. So horrible was this natural process in McKim's view that at this point he suggested the really weak be treated to "*a gentle, painless, death*" through carbonic-acid gas.[28]

Such extremes masked complex emotions that by the end of the decade began to eclipse whatever humanitarian goals the movement originally possessed. The result, as Kenneth Ludmerer has noted, was less a change of program than "changes in tone," more exaggerated claims, and the ascendency of racist and nativist elements. After World War I, as Ludmerer has also shown, eugenicists threw their political energies behind the blatantly biased Immigration Act of 1924 and state sterilization laws, many of which were later judged unconstitutional.[29]

In Britain, perhaps because the restraints of egalitarian ideology were less, some eugenicists appeared willing to consider both the sacrifice of the unfit, and the creation of a new elite. "Our race, viewed from a physiological standpoint, is not on the way to race improvement," wrote J. B. Haycraft in *Darwinism and Race Progress* (1895). Developing an earlier idea of Galton's, he proposed that selected individuals serve as "race producers." More dramatically inhumane was a suggestion from G. Archdall Reid, another British eugenicist, that the unfit be allowed to drink themselves into extinction. Since the very act of drinking was proof of unfitness, he reasoned, temperance legislation would have a harmful eugenic effect:

> . . . it is surely clear that if the world is to become more temperate it must be by the elimination not of drink but of the excessive drinker. If Artificial Selection be found impracticable in the future, as, owing to the state of public opinion, it undoubtedly is at present, then the only alternative is Natural Selection, in which case the world will never be thoroughly sober until it has first been thoroughly drunk.[30]

Although Reid intended in this statement to caricature natural selection, British journals by 1910 rang with predictions only slightly less extreme. Urging parental responsibility in the production of children (birth control), a British clergyman lectured the Victoria Institute of London on the real connection between Malthus and Darwinism:

> The phrases "survival of the fittest," and "elimination of the unfit" were not invented by Malthus; but they follow directly from his principles of population. Modern legislation, and indeed modern sentiment, without which legislation is powerless, have sought, and are still seeking to preserve the unfit and to encourage their multiplication. But the laws of nature will prove themselves too strong even for the strongest radical government, or the most plausible socialistic theory. The laws of nature will assert themselves in the end, even if it be by the end of our entire civilization. It is useless to complain of their harshness and severity. But we may do much, if we recognize them as facts, we may do very much to mitigate the harshness and severity of their application.

"National progress can only take place when means are taken to increase the fit and decrease the unfit," added a physician, who proposed to isolate the defective.[31]

In the interwar years, if not before, some American eugenicists shared this gloom and doom. Writing in 1921, the journalist E. E. Slosson commented on the prevailing pessimism at a recent conference of eugenicists. An outpouring of new eugenics literature contributed to the antidemocratic mood of the decade. But it was in Britain that this mood again produced extremes of which Americans were seemingly incapable. "All through nature we see a free production of young life with an equally free elimination of the greater number of those that are born," wrote the author of *Biological Politics* (1935). He continued:

> Human beings produce but few offspring and they threaten to produce fewer still. In despair at this tendency we attempt to prevent the loss of even a few; this must be dangerous; there must be some method of getting rid of the mass of poor, weak, and unfitted-for-survival children. These, too, are more liable to be the first born, so that when you have small families it is more urgent than ever to kill a large proportion of them.

In conclusion, he commended the ancient custom of sacrificing the first born.[32]

Some eugenicists, although proposing their own brand of state action, were outspoken critics of other reform—particularly socialism, which they viewed as a violation of fundamental Darwinian laws. It was "very difficult for a follower of Darwin and Weismann to be a socialist," one British eugenicist told the Fabian society in 1903. "The new socialism," he continued,

> aims at putting a stop to the struggle for existence altogether. There is to be, if not a luxurious, yet a soft, environment for all. The large elimination of the unfit, which still goes on in spite of our science and our wealth, is to be stopped. When a socialist takes any notice of Darwinian principles, he admits, apparently, that the human race has gained its present character, physical, moral and intellectual, through natural selection. But the time for such inhuman methods, he imagines, is over.

Then followed, in this and similar pieces, a gloom-and-doom portrait of the virtues of competition, and the struggle for existence. Upon closer inspection, however, such portraits were a plea, not for laissez faire or inaction, but for eugenics legislation.[33]

As the reactionary interpretations of eugenics became more pronounced, a mounting concern grew among those who viewed control of heredity *and* reform of the environment as necessary complements. In Britain, a disciple of Galton later recalled with regret how in the years before 1914 "social class was sometimes put forward as a criterion of eugenic value; and terms were sometimes used such as 'lower classes,' 'riff raff,' 'dregs,' which seemed to imply a contempt for certain sections of the poor." "Such language," he continued, with characteristic understatement, "gave offense to many social reformers." In a lengthy historical survey of the movement written in 1911, James A. Field, a social scientist at the University of Chicago, recalled the humanitarian ideals of Greg, while cautioning against attempts to impose purely biological (that is antihumanitarian) solutions on complex social problems. "The principle of the survival of the fittest normally involves wholesale sacrifice of the unfit," he wrote, "but such unmitigated rigor of selection does not commend itself as a humane method of social amelioration. Nor is the temper of the times favorable to aristocracies of any sort. It calls for the general betterment of mankind." Within a few years, leading American geneticists were openly deserting the movement, withdrawing both the prestige and whatever restraint their participation entailed.[34]

The emergence of reactionary tendencies within eugenics seemed to its opponents the final proof that the logic of Darwinism was inhumane. Ironically, a Scottish critic anticipated this strategy years earlier in reviewing Greg's *Enigmas of Life*, the work Field had cited for its humane sentiment. "Mr. Greg looks at civilization as something which interferes with the operation of the law of 'Natural Selection,' while I look on it as the outcome of an interference with that law." In response to Archdall Reid's tongue-in-cheek program of elimination via alcohol, the sociologist Franklin Giddings wondered: "Instead of wasting time and money on schools and sanitation, should we not rather turn our attention to a scientific breeding from selected human stocks, and, in our dealings with the unfit that must perish, follow Nietzsche's advice to give them not a helping hand, but a merciful little push over the cliffs of perdition?" The question, of course, answered itself. At the Victoria Institute a member of the audience challenged the implication that the "ideal non-radical government" would somehow ignore "the weak and sickly and underfed children of the nation." The Victoria Institute, he added, was "not the place" for a program of "sheer brutality."[35]

During the progressive era American reformers were easily persuaded of the truth of this charge. The social worker Edward Devine criticized biologists who stated that philanthropy interfered "with natural or a sound artificial selection, keeping alive the unfit, perpetuating a race of weaklings." Samuel Batten, a liberal clergyman from Lincoln, Nebraska, found Sumner, Spencer, and the eugenicist Archdall Reid guilty of the same error despite their apparent differences: none would "meddle with Nature's methods" or "seek to keep the unfit alive." In this same spirit, the editors of the *Independent* read the British eugenicist William Ridgeway a lecture on mutual aid to challenge the view that "helping the poor necessarily prevents natural selection."[36]

Since eugenicists sometimes opposed socialism, and even charity, the negative implications of the charge of social Darwinism, were doubtless warranted in some instances. Perhaps significantly, at least one observer sympathetic to eugenics actually accepted the label, possibly the only instance in the entire annals of debate over social evolution that this scarlet letter was claimed with honor.[37] But the further suggestion that eugenics was simply an extension of some previous misapplications of Darwinism, specifically the industrial laissez faire most eugenicists despised, further blurred the fact that the import of Darwinism from the start was the abandonment of natural for artificial sources of social policy.

Eugenics finally fell victim to a good deal more than its image as social Darwinism. By 1914, developments within genetics had undermined the one-gene-one-trait assumption. And the Army Intelligence Tests a few years later, although ostensibly a boon to all Cassandras of American "degeneracy," helped in the long run to show the absurdity of the concept of "feeble mindedness"—a mainstay of eugenics arguments. During the 1930s the popular association of eugenics with the Nazi ideology sealed its doom in respectable circles, perhaps regrettably also carrying genetics research to its lowest ebb in this century. But, whether for good or ill, the social Darwinist label shrouded eugenics in a cloud of suspicion that the most optimistic faith in science could never entirely dispel. As with the I.Q. controversy of later years, champions of a scientific approach to social problems found that some things are easier to study than others.

At the height of the prewar debate concerning misrepresentations of evolution, however, at least two critics acknowledged that something more was at issue than the actual proposals of eugenicists. One was Herbert W. Conn, a biologist at Wesleyan University, who spelled out the logic of Archdall Reid's program. The other was Leonard T. Hobhouse, the British sociologist and leading theorist of the New Liberalism. In a lecture to the Faculty of Political Science at Columbia University, Hobhouse attacked an article that appeared in the *Eugenic Review* by W. C. D. Whetham, a prominent English representative of the movement. Whetham, in Hobhouse's version, opposed all attempts to equalize social opportunity since this was " 'so clearly contrary to the order of the universe which progresses by natural selection.' " After tracing this view back to Malthus and Darwin and bedecking Whetham in the full regalia of the social Darwinist stereotype, Hobhouse noted that his retelling might seem a bit harsh since most of the "scientifically minded hesitate to draw out our arguments to their logical conclusion." But, he added:

> It is the more necessary that the legitimate inferences to be drawn from these hints and half-statements should be quite nakedly set forth, so that we may see precisely wither we are being led. And I think the view which I have stated is clearly implied, if only half expressed, in much of the biological criticism of society from the time of Mr. Herbert Spencer to the present day.

Although Hobhouse mentioned no other theorist except Whetham in his lecture, he explained further in his introduction to the published version how Spencer had made natural selection the "basis of an uncompromising economic individualism."[38] Regrettably, no record was made as to whether the Columbia audience included the historian Carlton Hayes, then beginning a celebrated career at that institution and soon to be one of the first American historians to identify a similar tradition of social Darwinism in Anglo-American social thought.

9. The Scaffolding of Progress

[If] you remove the thin veneering of so-called Christian and civilized nations, you will find under it a horde of savages glorying in the wholesale assassination of human beings by armies and navies. . . . Hence such nations are absolutely incapable of solving the problem of the antagonism of races . . . except by the utter extermination of the weaker by the stronger bestial race. . . . This is the dark cloud of pessimism.
James T. Holly, "Origin of the Race Antagonism," Arena, 21 (1899), 42.

As for the Jim Crow laws in the South, many of them, at least, are at present necessary to avoid the danger of clashes between the ignorant of both race. They are the inevitable scaffolding of progress.
Ray Stannard Baker, Following the Color Line (1908), p. 305.

One

Although ideas of racial inferiority antedated the *Origin of Species*, modern racism like eugenics appeared on the surface to be a direct legacy of Darwin's work. Darwin, after all, subtitled his masterpiece "The Preservation of Favoured Races in the Struggle for Life." In *The Descent of Man* he predicted, "At some future period, not very distant as measured by centuries, the civilized races of man will almost certainly exterminate and replace the savage races throughout the world."[1] His co-evolutionists Huxley, Wallace, and Spencer repeatedly contrasted the "lower" and "higher" races to the advantage of the latter. By the 1890s images of racial struggle spawned speculation concerning the ultimate demise of all blacks in the New World and, at the other extreme, a program of rigid segregation of the races through Jim Crow legislation.

Historians continue to discuss the nature and extent of this influence, although most have recognized that Darwinism was at most only one of several sources of racism, itself a protean concept that changed meaning throughout the nineteenth century. Tracing these twists and turns,

George Fredrickson has recently distinguished the *racial Darwinism* of the 1890s from the New South *paternalism* that preceded it and the *accommodationist racism* that finally dominated in the progressive era. These studies agree, however, that the *Origin of Species* was the source of later extremism, and somehow buttressed racism.[2]

As with eugenics, these accounts tend to ignore altogether or softpedal important developments in the meaning of Darwinism between 1860 and 1900, and to obscure the final contribution of neo-Darwinism to Jim Crow in the 1890s and after. Although talk of higher and lower races may make moderns cringe, the *Origin of Species* temporarily retarded that long march from Enlightenment egalitarianism that characterized European thought on race during the nineteenth century. In practice as in theory, Darwin, Huxley, and Wallace personally opposed programs premised on the permanent inferiority of nonwhites. From the seventies to the nineties Herbert Spencer and his American disciples and evolutionists generally provided an intellectual rationale for paternalistic programs of philanthropy and education that—again however objectionable by modern standards—were moderate, humane, and constructive by comparison with the theories and practices of the Jim Crow era.

The neo-Darwinism of the 1890s undermined this rationale, not in providing a blueprint for racial struggle, but in dramatizing the results of natural evolution that was the basis of the paternalist position. Although a tiny minority welcomed the prospect of black extinction (an indication that, where race was concerned, Christian and democratic traditions proved no barrier to outright social Darwinism), white progressives, North and South, became convinced that stricter controls alone could prevent social disorder. As in the case of eugenics neo-Darwinism tipped the balance from social justice to social control.

Racial Darwinism was a variety of reform Darwinism, just as white progressives, however paradoxically, viewed disfranchisement and Jim Crow as consistent with other progressive reforms. For white southerners the disfranchisement of blacks seemed the *sine qua non* of good government, just as did the attack on bossism for northerners. Racial segregation, it was alleged, would eliminate conflict and in the long run foster the cooperation which progressives desired. However, racial Darwinists differed from other reform Darwinists in one significant regard. Although the links that bound them to the *Origin of Species*, however imperfect, were at least as strong as those that tied Darwin to laissez faire or socialism, almost none of their contemporaries called them social Darwinists. In the complex history of myth-making, this silence was an exception to prove the rule.

Two

When race became a scientific concern in the late eighteenth century, racism assumed a perceptively modern form. America's founders, torn between egalitarianism and slavery, brought new wisdom to the old issue of the origins of man. Pricked by an attack on the unity of mankind in Lord Kames's *Sketches of the History of Man* (1774) Samuel Stanhope Smith, a clergyman and professor at Princeton, defended the Scriptural view of Creation in an *Essay on the Causes of the Variety of Complexion and Figure in The Human Species* (1787). A work in the tradition of Buffon and Montesquieu, Smith's treatise unknowingly paralleled Johann Blumenbach's more famous study *On the Nature and Variety of Mankind* (1781). During 1788, the *Columbian Magazine* aired a lengthy exchange on the same issue, including excerpts from Thomas Jefferson's *Notes on Virginia* (1785), an unequivocal statement of Negro inferiority, which nonetheless left open the issue as to whether humanity was one or several species. During the 1790s Benjamin Rush (1746-1813), a distinguished Philadelphia physician and prominent Jeffersonian, joined the debate. Meanwhile, a steady flow of similar works made their way from Britain, notably Charles White's *An Account of the Regular Gradation in Man* (1799); James Cowles Prichard's *Researches into the Physical History of Man* (1813); and William Charles Wells's "Account of a Female of the White Race" (1818), the latter of which anticipated Darwin in suggesting that sporting variations in conjunction with struggle and survival produced stable varieties.[3]

Although scientific by the canons of the day, this debate differed in several respects from that of a century later. Despite some tendency to look to anthropology as a defense of slavery, the extrascientific context, as John Greene has noted, was the truth of revealed religion. Conversely, much scientific evidence, however outrageous to modern sensibilities, was adduced in defense of human equality rather than against it. Benjamin Rush, after proposing that Negro color and other characteristics might result from a hereditary disease like leprosy, concluded therefore that "all the claims of superiority of the whites over the blacks, on account of their color, are founded in ignorance and inhumanity." Moreover, monogenists and polygenists, as the two sides in the origin of man debate were known, shared a common faith in stability and design in the universe, and hence, in the immutability of species—assumptions that proved a major obstacle to later development theory.[4]

At the same time, the Revolutionary generation radically altered the terms of the debate. Even when defending Scripture, these authors made race a problem in natural history, not theology. Explanations in terms of environmental differences replaced the "curse of Ham." This environmentalism, as Winthrop Jordan has argued persuasively, marked the culmination of several strains of eighteenth-century thought: secularism; the search for universal, even mechanical, principles of human behavior; the celebration of reason; and interest in the natural environment. A way of thinking rather than a set of conclusions, this approach raised questions better than it answered them. Typical in this regard was a young Virginian who, after cataloging in detail the many brutish traits of the African, left open the question of whether these traits were innate or modifiable through education. Nonetheless, this generation gave the issue of nature vs. nurture its modern formulation.[5]

During the nineteenth century, discussions of race followed three paths already marked in the earlier debate: (1) anthrometry, or the classification of mankind, in the tradition of Blumenbach and Samuel Smith; (2) medical testimony, increasingly statistical in form, such as Benjamin Rush offered; and (3) controversy over the origin of man, now joined by a polygenist American school of anthropologists, whose theory of multiple Creation became a new source of racism. Each of these strains continued to support racist arguments well into the twentieth century, as white Americans sought to rationalize new forms of discrimination. With or without the *Origin of Species* racism would have gained strength by the turn of the century. The question, however, is whether Darwinism inhibited or quickened this impulse.[6]

What then was Darwin's contribution? Aside from the subtitle of the *Origin* the case against his racism rests largely on guilt by association and scattered quotations. Darwin was familiar with the latest racist anthrometry and medical testimony (including the American Civil War studies). Moreover he seemed to resolve the origin of man controversy in a fashion that pleased the polygenists, many of whom were leading proponents of black inferiority. At least Josiah Nott, leader of the American school of polygenists, was able to claim that Darwin in no way substantially altered the notion of separate races since his theory "requires millions of years." Darwin himself predicted the triumph of "civilized" over "savage" peoples, and in a letter to a friend shortly before his death noted that the Turks failed to overrun Europe because "more civilized so-called Caucasian races have beaten the Turkish hollow in the struggle for existence." But in context these brief references attested only to his belief in the social power that results from increased adaptation, hardly a debatable point, and had no bearing on biology or skin color.[7]

Otherwise the indictment of Darwin rests mostly on sins of omission. Acknowledging that races in the subtitle of the *Origin* meant only varieties of plants and animals, one historian focused on the things he did not say:

> Although Darwin derived all races, like all species, from a single historic ancestor, he by no means denied the reality of separate races and species in the present. He did not dissolve all species into an undistinguished mass of individuals; he did not even suggest, as anti-racist theorists often do, that individuals constitute a spectrum, in which each differs from his neighbor so slightly that only artificially, statistically, can varieties, races or species be distinguished. . . . Nor did he deny that under certain conditions it was desirable to maintain, as far as possible, the purity of races.

On this basis Gertrude Himmelfarb concluded that his theory "easily [gave] comfort to the proponents of slavery and racism"; and that the subtitle of the *Origin* made a "convenient motto" for a more virulent racism.[8]

Upon closer inspection, however, the case against Darwin himself quickly unravels. An ardent opponent of slavery, he consistently opposed the repression of nonwhites, and thus had special reason to avoid crude applications of his theory—greater in this case perhaps, than for human society generally.[9] Although by modern standards *The Descent of Man* is frustratingly inconclusive on critical issues of human equality, it was a model of moderation and scientific caution in the context of midcentury racism. Darwin granted the "reality" of separate races at the present, for example, but insisted that evolutionists "will feel no doubt that all the races of man are descended from a single primitive stock." It mattered little whether one chose to express differences by terming the races "distinct species," he added, since the term species was so essentially arbitrary. The argument against using the term species derived from the obvious fertility among crosses of all the races of man, a point upon which Darwin insisted against continuing speculation to the contrary. So also, the overwhelming resemblance of all races in "bodily structure and mental faculties"—too "numerous and important" to have been separately acquired—argued for a single parent-stock. "So again it is almost a matter of indifference whether the so-called races of man are thus designated, or are ranked as species or subspecies," he concluded; "but the latter term appears the more appropriate." In sum, despite the attempt of polygenists like Nott to ride Darwin's coattails, the *Origin* and *The Descent of Man* effectively undermined the polygenist position.[10]

It is true that *The Descent of Man* reinforced a hierarchial view of human development and the assumption that history was a progression from barbarism to civilization, assuming these commonplaces needed strengthening. In this context, Darwin's predictions concerning the extermination of lower races were not prescriptions for racial imperialism but a summary of recent anthropology and the apparently undeniable results of European expansion since the Renaissance. But Darwin also insisted that this process was not to be confused with biological evolution or the process whereby racial differences originally appeared. On this issue he admitted he was frankly baffled: neither Lamarckian factors nor natural selection explained the differences, forcing him to fall back on the possibility that sexual selection might provide clues, a point neither he nor his contemporaries elaborated at any length.[11]

Wallace and Huxley also distinguished between the process of biological evolution and racial development. In an essay on "The Development of Human Races" (1864) Wallace attempted to show how the monogenist and polygenist views "can be combined . . . by means of Mr. Darwin's celebrated theory of 'Natural Selection.'" His argument turned on the fact that man, at a crucial stage in his development, was no longer affected by natural selection. At his point "mental and moral qualities will have increasing influence on the well-being of the race." Men were "once a homogeneous race," and remained so in a physical sense despite superficial differences in skin color and the like. But mankind was also distinguished by differential development of the "higher faculties," the result not of natural selection but (like mind itself) of "some unknown cause." The final result was "the wonderful intellect of the European races."[12]

Like Darwin (who drew on Wallace for *The Descent of Man*), Wallace underscored the hierarchial ranking of races and seemed even to hint at a sense in which those lower in the scale were not really "men":

> If . . . we are of the opinion that he was not really man till these higher faculties were fully developed, we may fairly assert that there were many originally distinct races of men; while, if we think that a being closely resembling us in form and structure, but with mental faculties scarcely raised above the brute, must still be considered to have been human, we are fully entitled to maintain the common origin of all mankind.

His view of "mental and moral progress" (which sociologists would later call *cultural evolution*) also led to the conclusion "that the higher—the more intellectual and moral—must displace the lower and degraded races." But his process was again not analogous to struggle and selection in nature. Certain that improvement would come, Wallace would not attribute it to survival of the fittest. Following a popular usage of the day, he equated such survival with the success of "the mediocre, if not the low, both as regards morality and intelligence." Rather, as with mind itself, mysterious forces were at work. The "glorious qualities" of men were the "surest proof" of "higher existences than ourselves." The goal was not racial imperialism but the brotherhood of man: "a single nearly homogeneous race, no individual of which will be inferior to the noblest specimens of existing humanity."[13]

Although Thomas Henry Huxley was also heir to a century of racist classification of mankind, he likewise refused to consign the lower races to permanent inferiority. In *Man's Place in Nature* (1863) he gave a lengthy account of cranial capacities, the start of a lifelong interest in racial geography. In "The Methods and Results of Ethnology" (1865) he presented his own modification of Blumenbach's classification. But at the same time Huxley consistently opposed midcentury racism. In 1867 he shocked the Birmingham town fathers by announcing that primitive peoples were not incapable of cultural development. More than two decades later he attacked the rising tide of *Aryanism* in an essay on "The Aryan Question and Prehistoric Man" (1890).[14]

Huxley explained the basis of his reasoning in a brief essay "Emancipation—Black and White" (1865), a defense of abolitionism and female emancipation. There he argued for a distinction between nature and social ethics, anticipating the strategy of his Romanes address three decades later. Nature dealt blacks and women a thin hand in the game of life, he argued. No "rational man" could believe in the innate equality of blacks and whites: "it is simply incredible that, when all [the black's] disabilities are removed . . . he will be able to compete successfully with his bigger-brained and smaller-jawed rival, in a context which is to be carried out by thoughts and not by bites"—an attempt at humor, offensive by modern standards, but summarizing half-a-century of anthrometry. Free of restraint, the Negro would reach whatever "stable equilibrium" the "laws of gravitation" dictated, he added, in a distinctly pre-Darwinian reference to nature. But the operation of nature did not alter the moral law that no human being can arbitrarily dominate over another without grievous damage to his own nature. "The duty of man is to see that not a grain is piled upon the load beyond what Nature imposes; that injustice is not added to inequality."[15]

If the leading Darwinians questioned the prevailing racism, why was Darwin alleged to have buttressed racist thinking? As with other charges of misapplied Darwinism, this one reflected the sometimes complex psychologies of individuals who were ambivalent toward Darwinism, black equality, or both. Darwinism was a convenient brush with which to tar racists, and vice versa.

An early instance occurred in London. A month after the publication of the *Origin of Species*, the London *Times* warned that abolitionists would make the southern population a "mixed race," a result "that tends not to the elevation of the black, but to the degradation of the white man." Although the remark made no reference to Darwin, Benjamin Moran (1820-1886), an official at the American consulate, confided to his journal: "This is bold doctrine for an English journal and is one of the results of reflection on mixed races, aided by light from Mr. Darwin's book, and his theory of 'Natural Selection.'" A Buchanan Democrat, who fervently believed "no full blown African is a man of talents," Moran also became an ardent defender of the Union cause and was consistently critical of the London press. His remark, hardly an endorsement of Darwinian racism, was rather a jibe at an increasingly prosouthern press—the reference to natural selection, a cynical sermon on what happens when one dines with the devil.[16]

An equally complicated case was that of novelist John William DeForest, whom George Fredrickson has called "one of the first Americans to discuss the freedman's prospect for survival in explicitly Darwinian language."[17] An official in the Freedmen's Bureau, DeForest described his experiences in the South for the *Atlantic Monthly*, in May 1868. An acute observer, DeForest in this and other articles analysed the complex social structure of the postbellum South, from the elite of "chivalrous Southrons" to the "low down peoples," white and black. Initially hopeful concerning the prospect of black progress, DeForest became disillusioned by the freedman's shiftlessness, irresponsibility, and apparent immorality. "I am convinced that the Negro as he is, no matter how educated, is not the mental equal of the European," he wrote. But facts not theory concerned him: the speculations of polygenists and other ethnologists were of "little practical importance." Blacks were there by the millions and had to be "educated mentally and morally."[18]

The real blame, DeForest continued, lay not with the blacks but on the circumstances that brought the race into the American struggle for existence without due preparation. "Will the freedman acquire property and assume position among the managers of our national industry?" he asked:

> The low-down Negro will of course follow the low-down white into sure and deserved oblivion. His more virtuous and vital brother will struggle longer with the law of natural selection; and he may eventually hold a portion of this continent against the vigorous and terrible Caucasian race; that portion being probably those lowlands where the white race cannot or will not labor.

Natural selection described a struggle that DeForest deeply regretted of blacks pitted against a "vigorous and terrible Caucasian race." He also regretted the outcome, which he had hoped would be otherwise. A deep human sympathy suffused DeForest's portraits of the "low down people," whether freed slaves or white crackers. But this compassion ran continually into a wall of concrete realities. Darwinism provided the rhetoric, not of settled conviction but of disillusionment that clung to hope. When the facts refused to fit preconceptions concerning progress and civilization, DeForest lapsed into a cynical sigh. "I cheerfully leave him to the operation of the great law of natural selection," he concluded in a discussion of the lowest level of poor white. "In other words, 'The devil take the hindmost.'" In light of his overarching humanitarianism, however, this remark was only half-serious.[19]

Three

During the 1870s and 1880s, Herbert Spencer and other leading evolutionists provided Americans with a rationale for a philanthropic policy Fredrickson again has termed New South paternalism.[20] By present-day standards this program was outrageously conservative: in reiterating the current if temporary "inferiority" of blacks; in assuming that acculturation and equality were the work of generations; in insisting that social and sexual segregation of the races was desirable; perhaps even in supposing that education rather than confrontation was the way to equality. But blacks had learned the hard way that there was no situation that could not be worse and, in racial theory at least, New South paternalism provided a temperate interlude between slavery and Jim Crow, between the racism of George Fitzhugh and of Thomas Dixon, Jr. In however attenuated a form, Civil War idealism lingered for several decades in the assumption that, save for differences in environment, all men were equal.

Herbert Spencer, like many of his contemporaries, instinctively placed blacks at the primitive end of the evolutionary scale. But he did not consign the race there permanently. Racial differences like other human characteristics were the product of environment. Race was cultural not biological. However at this point he equivocated, and with Lamarck's help effected an uneasy compromise between environment and heredity. Habits such as monogamy were initially acquired, he wrote. But the influence of environment in the past eventually became organized as a character of the race possessing it, innate in the form of a disposition. While primitive peoples were in theory capable of evolving to civilization, in practice they would require an indefinite future to do so. Thus again, utopia was transformed from a past golden age into a future promise.[21]

Spencer likewise endorsed intermarriage in theory but in practice drew the line between whites and nonwhites. The mingling of races, he often noted, was a positive benefit because of the increased number of traits available for adapting to the environment. Heterogeneity was the key to progress, a point American Spencerians made frequently in support of the "melting pot" and free immigration. But there were limits when the races were non-European. "If you mix the constitutions of two widely divergent varieties which have severally become adapted to widely divergent modes of life," Spencer wrote, degeneration would result. Intermarriage between whites and orientals, for example, should be "positively forbidden."[22]

John Fiske also believed that race was cultural rather than biological and that talk of separate creations was nonsense. But like Spencer he subtly qualified the environmentalist argument, further pulling the rug from beneath Civil War idealism. In his essay "From Brute to Man" Fiske ignored the freedmen except to remark that the sacrifices of the Civil War for "inferior men" revealed the high morality of "civilized" whites. He also turned an attack on the polygenists against the more radical policies of Reconstruction. In the evolutionary scale, the "all important contrast" was not between man and the brute (the starting point for all religious debate), but "between civilized and primitive man." The lower races were not brutes: the cubic inches of brain separating the aboriginal from the chimpanzee were an evolutionary "Rubicon." But among men, brain size did vary enormously: by Fiske's calculations from 114 cubic inches in the "refined and intellectual Teuton" to 70 cubic inches for the Australian aborigine. The development of the larger cerebrum in the higher races had been a lengthy process that began with the creation of family units that extended protection during a prolonged infancy. Fiske remained essentially a Lamarckian: changes in social environment induced alterations in mental ability, which were then passed to offspring. But even more than Spencer he emphasized that alterations could not occur overnight.[23]

From the 1870s to the early 1890s prominent American scientists and educators presented assorted variations of these Spencerian arguments. Joseph LeConte, the southern-born biologist who became one of America's leading neo-Lamarckians, argued in *Popular Science* in 1879 that, while crossbreeding was generally salutory, "the crossing of varieties so divergent as those called primary races is probably bad—these approaching too nearly the nature of different species"—an argument that in effect neutralized the liberal implications of the Darwin notion of crossbreeding by reintroducing the discredited concept of different species. Writing in the *Atlantic Monthly* in 1890, Nathaniel Shaler of Harvard conceded that blacks had made great strides. But "the negro is not as yet so far up in the scale of development as he appears to be," he cautioned; "in him the great virtues of the superior race, though implanted, have not yet taken firm root, and are in need of constant tillage, lest the old savage weeds overcome the tender shoots of the new and unnatural culture." Science, Shaler concluded, required paternalistic philanthropy, and a "perfect civil union without a perfect civil accord."[24]

These evolutionist arguments, as George Fredrickson has written of New South paternalism generally, appealed to an emergent white middle class who looked to industrialism as the salvation of their region. By contributing to the development of a dependable black working force, northern philanthropists were equally assured of orderly progress, although it remains to be proved whether many were conscious of its direct impact on their southern investments. However one judges this program, by the 1890s it was under new attack from extremists who found quite different lessons in Darwinism.

Four

In theory, neo-Darwinism totally undermined the leading assumptions of New South paternalism. If germ cells totally determined character, then it was fruitless to hope for the elevation of blacks through education. If struggle and selection were the rule in nature, racial conflict was also natural and inevitable. In race relations, as elsewhere in society, events seemed to confirm this neo-Darwinian logic. Beginning in the late 1880s there was a frightful rise in lynching. Within a decade racial tension exploded in riots in New York, Atlanta, and other cities. Meanwhile sociologists, led by the struggle school of Ratzenhofer and Gumplowicz and the racial selectionism of Vasher de Lapouge and Otto Ammon, found racial conflict throughout history.

Although a majority of Americans, immune to this logic, clung to the view that race traits were the result of long-run difference in environment, new "permissions to hate," as C. Vann Woodward has called them,[25] came from various directions. A small but vociferous group of southern Negrophobes gleefully predicted the extinction of all blacks. Others acknowledged regretfully that blacks could advance only through a tortuous process of struggle and selection, a view that translated into proposals for the narrowest sort of practical training as the only way to improve the efficiency of the race. But the major result of neo-Darwinism here as in other areas, was not a new creed of racial struggle but rather redoubled efforts to avoid it. Positive state action in this area as in others seemed the only antidote to the chaos of laissez faire. Social control demanded disfranchisement and the forced legal separation of the races.

The leading edge of the neo-Darwinist extremism was Frederick L. Hoffman's *Race Traits and Tendencies of the American Negro* (1896), possibly the most talked about work on race to appear in America in several decades. The German-born Hoffman (1865-1946), a statistician for the Prudential Insurance Company, marshaled the latest techniques of statistical science in defense of his thesis that American blacks, declining in fertility and social efficiency, were doomed to extinction unless somehow made to face the struggle for existence unaided by paternalism. Published by the American Economic Association, his 300-page analysis was essentially a summary of pre-Darwinian anthrometry and medical testimony, from which Hoffman concluded that blacks and whites, after thirty years of freedom, were "further apart than ever in their political and social relations." Evidence of Negro degeneration abounded: in decline of physical capacity; increase in mortality rates; even infrequency of suicide, an act which distinguished the "more cultured and more advanced races."[26]

In conclusion, Hoffman set his findings within a neo-Darwinian framework:

> The lower races, even under the same conditions of life must necessarily fail because the vast number of incapables which a hard struggle for life has eliminated from the ranks of the white races, are still forming the large body of the lower races. Easy conditions of life and a liberal charity are among the most destructive influences affecting the lower races; since by such methods the weak and incapable are permitted to increase and multiply, while the struggle of the more able is increased in severity.

Hoffman's target was the entire program of philanthropy, inadequate education, and social permissiveness (as he viewed it) since the Civil War.[27]

The solution was racial laissez faire. In a letter to the secretary of the American Economic Association, Hoffman made this point bluntly. "If man will ignore the dictates of nature and common sense and help a weaker race (and this is vital) at the expense of the stronger race, it is equally clear that the latter will suffer while the former will only temporarely [sic] be benefitted," he wrote. "To aid the least fit in the struggle for life is only an impediment to the progress of the stronger race who is burdened with a load out of proportion to its strength." In the book, he also stressed the special need for black self-help and strict insistence on "race purity . . . in marriage as well as outside it." When the "colored race" mastered its own "conditions of life," he concluded, it will have gained "a place among civilized mankind and will increase and multiply instead of dying out with loathesome diseases."[28]

Hoffman then pictured the consequences of ignoring this warning. "The last thing our civilization is likely to permanently tolerate," he wrote, quoting Benjamin Kidd, "is the wasting of the resources of the richest regions of the earth through the lack of the elementary qualities of social efficiency in the races possessing them." When the white race reached a stage where "new conquests are necessary, it will not hesitate to make war upon those races who prove themselves useless factors in the progress of mankind," he concluded.[29]

Did Hoffman thus urge racial conflict and the extermination of blacks? If not, what was the meaning of this warning and the final message of *Race Traits?* Various reviewers, unwilling to jettison paternalism for racial laissez faire, gave it a predictably mixed or hostile comment. The book took "too blue a view of the negro," wrote H. B. Frissell, principal of Hampton Institute. Despite a convincing attack on Hoffman's statistics by W. E. B. DuBois, several insurance companies refused henceforth to write life insurance policies for blacks. Blacks were naturally uneasy at reading their own epitaph. Booker T. Washington felt like one who had "just finished reading his own funeral sermon," he wrote the secretary of the American Economic Association. But the book's message lay only partly in its ostensible conclusions. Washington himself rightly acknowledged that, in its specific recommendations, *Race Traits* really presented only a variation of his own philosophy of economic self-help. He and Hoffman, he wrote, "agreed pretty fully" in regard "to the kind of education that has been given our people and [in] regard to what is needed in the future."[30]

The book's tone, to which Washington objected, was significant, not as a call to racial warfare, but as a confused plea for a program of hard work coupled with doubts that virtue alone could avoid an impending cataclysm. *Race Traits* in this sense was actually two things at once: a call for the ancient virtues of chastity and self-reliance and a neo-Darwinian jeremiad, by a writer who doubted the possibility of such a revival. Like the later William Graham Sumner and the muckrakers who would soon preach a return to "honesty" and "individual initiative," Hoffman combined moral indignation and a neo-Calvinist fascination with punishment.

At the root of this ambivalence was Hoffman's racism. He personally believed that blacks as a race were unsuited for urban, industrial life and would succeed only as agricultural laborers. An editorial referee in fact warned him to "recast all of that portion dealing with the moral inferiority of the negro." Like the muckrakers, Hoffman thus clothed his indignation in the rhetoric of objectivity, a quality at special premium within the economics profession in its early years. If he would downplay "moral inferiority" the referee continued, then "the scientific facts can be brought out in a more dispassionate form." As an outsider, Hoffman wanted especially to be scientific. He would turn the book into an object lesson on the "relation between economics and public health," he wrote the secretary of the Economic Association. "I have only to point out the facts

and the conclusion will be inevitable," he added. For this dual purpose—prophetic warning and scientific objectivity—the rhetoric of neo-
Darwinism served admirably.[31]

The reviewers who most liked Hoffman's book shared this spirit. An anthropologist at the University of Chicago took special comfort in
Hoffman's vision of punishment and redemption:

> What can be done? Not much. But faith in school book education
> as a means of grace must die. The negro must be taught that
> honesty and purity are necessary; that continued industry is
> the price of life. Less petting and more disciplining is needed; fewer
> academies and more work benches.

William Graham Sumner, who congratulated Hoffman on "a fine and
useful piece of work" likewise endorsed his neo-Calvinist warning to "our
politicians & philanthropists." As such, Hoffman's neo-Darwinism expressed a mood more than a new or settled policy. But departures in policy
soon followed.[32]

Within a decade a small group of Negrophobes carried the neo-
Darwinist argument to new extremes. In *The Negro in Africa and
America* (1902), Joseph A. Tillinghast, the son of a slaveholder, seconded
Hoffman's call for an end to paternalism. The "efficiency" of the white
race, he argued,

> was reached only through the struggle and sacrifice prescribed by
> evolutionary law. There are many who believe that a shorter path
> to greatness exists, since the science of education has been developed.
> But so long as the powerful conservatism of heredity persists,
> scarcely admitting of change save through selection of variations,
> it is to be doubted whether education has the efficiency claimed for
> it. Time, struggle, and sacrifice have always hitherto been required
> to create a great race.

"Under such circumstances," he added in a masterpiece of academic cir-
cumlocution, "[the Negro's] position can with difficulty be regarded as
other than precarious to the last degree."[33]

Three years later, as Thomas Dixon's *The Clansman* was making melo-
drama of racial strife, William Smith in *The Color Line* (1905) pushed neo-
Darwinism still further. "If accepted science teaches anything at all",
wrote Smith, a professor of mathematics at Tulane, "it teaches that the
heights of being in civilized man have been reached along one path and one
only—the path of *Selection*, of the preservation of favored individuals and
favored races." The rest of Smith's argument, as DuBois accurately

characterized it in a review, was "a naked, unashamed shriek for the survival of the white race by means of the annihilation of all other races." Precisely because of its nakedness, Smith's argument invited easy refutation by the conventional wisdom of reform Darwinism. Again in DuBois's terms, this counterargument held "that this arrogant manifesto . . . is an outbreak of old-world pharisaism and brute self-assertion;" and "that nations live for Mercy, Justice, and Truth, and not simply for breeding." But with Smith, as DuBois also acknowledged, the cat was out of the bag. Despite an apparent consensus among educated men on the merits of mercy and justice, Smith stated "flatly" and "with unnecessary barbarism a thesis that is the active belief of millions of our fellow countrymen."[34]

Similar statements from other southerners in these years seemed to confirm DuBois's charge. A southern woman concluded an account of Reconstruction with the prediction that evolutionary processes would eliminate the Negro. Benjamin Tillman, the extremist senator from South Carolina, likewise explained why blacks were losing out in industrial competition: "The old struggle of survival of the fittest is beginning in dead earnest, and it is not saying too much to predict that the negro must do better or 'move on.'" Senator John Sharp Williams of Mississippi, although more sympathetic to progressive reforms, foresaw a whitening of the South, as a result of "God's law of evolution, the survival of the fittest, and the extinction of the unfit." Daniel A. Tompkins, a New South champion who studied evolution under James Woodrow at the University of South Carolina in the eighties, was equally blunt: "Platitudes about equality and natural rights do not alter race prejudices and laws of nature. . . . [If] the negro stands in the way of progress, he will have to get off the earth."[35]

The most dramatic instance of neo-Darwinist racism, however, came not from whites but a deeply bitter black of mixed ancestry, William Hannibal Thomas (1843-?), author of The American Negro (1901). Born in freedom in Ohio, Thomas learned of the horrors of slavery from refugees whom his father assisted on the Underground Railroad. In the course of an active life as seminarian, lawyer, politician, and journalist, Thomas developed an Algeresque sympathy for all blacks who wished to better themselves, or as he put it, who sought "a clew and thread to Godhood and manhood." But he also confessed that he had "a deep-seated aversion to and unfeigned disgust for a distinctive phase of negro stolidity characteristic of those bereft of all uplifting desire, because I know that they deliberately and of set purpose pander to every phase of racial viciousness and resist every attempt for social betterment."[36]

As remarkable evidence of black self-hate, the bitterest fruit of white racism, The American Negro outdid the most virulent white writing in its denunciation of the mass of the race. Accepting the most extreme predictions of Negro decline, Thomas welcomed the unhindered operation of natural selection. "The adjustment and elimination of racial differences will finally come through sorting and sifting," he wrote in a passage another reviewer thought especially revealing; "The unfit will be pushed aside, but better so, that a nation may live." In conclusion, Thomas proposed total amalgamation of those elements within the black race ready to join the white, a practice to be facilitated by enfranchisement "based solely on character, intelligence, and a capable identification with public affairs."[37]

Allowing for hyperbole and even the fact that Thomas was urging only cultural and biological assimilation and not mass murder, his motives tantalized reviewers. The *Independent* wondered "why a negro should write such a book" since it would "justify the brutes who used just his language to defend oppression and lynchings." "Is he a crank of the sort that seeks notoriety by contradicting everybody?" the reviewer asked. "Has he any reason to pander to a white Southern demand?" Compounding the problem, DuBois noted blatant contradictions between the present work and a pamphlet Thomas wrote a decade earlier. In 1890, for example, Thomas found among blacks a "scrupulous regard for truth and virginal honor, and as much of the practice of Christian integrity" as among whites. Now he charged, "Soberly speaking, Negro nature is so craven and sensuous in every fibre of its being that a Negro manhood with decent respect for chaste womanhood does not exist."[38]

DuBois also suggested an explanation, not only of Thomas's neo-Darwinism but also, by extension, of the appearance at this time of the black as "devil" in other southern polemics. Thomas was "peculiarly the type of the Negro cynic," DuBois wrote. Although he spoke of "virtue, goodness, and hope," his book "at bottom" was "without faith or ideal." Thomas, who was elected to the South Carolina legislature in 1876, was one of the "embodied disappointments of Reconstruction." His indictment of his race illustrated the hopelessness that results when the gap between ideal and reality becomes insuperable. The failure of his earlier pamphlet, a personal disappointment as well as an intellectual one, gave the matter a special twist. Censuring the race that failed him, Thomas perversely vindicated hopes and ideals that seemed increasingly unreal, insisting now that punishment, at the least, must precede redemption.[39]

The competitive racism of the white Negrophobes of course admitted another explanation. In arguing that natural selection ought be allowed free reign, William Smith carried the logic of evolution to an extreme that was unacceptable in the case of industrial workers, for example, or the white urban poor. His extremism, by contrast with the views of others, highlighted the degree to which traditional Christian and democratic principles had shaped social applications of Darwinian biology for three decades. Where human society was concerned, the Darwinian view of nature had from the start argued for the substitution of human artifice for natural laws. To embrace nature in its Darwinian form, as Smith appeared to do, was quite simply to assert that, where nonwhites were concerned, one was not discussing human society.

Five

The competitive racial Darwinism of the Smith variety was in any case quickly eclipsed by what George Fredrickson has termed accommodationist racism, which arose in part as "a reaction against the brutality of the extremists."[40] The accommodationists pushed, on the one hand, for more severely practical education, a minimalist version of the Tuskegee program; and on the other, for removal of blacks from politics and the legal separation of the races. A racial variant of reform Darwinism, accommodationist racism called for government action in place of private effort; for social control in the interests of order; and for a clash of values and ideals rather than brute struggle.

Academic sociologists, familiar with the latest in social theory, provided the most explicit statement of this position. In their studies of Negro life these academics began with the key phrases of the new selectionism. In his doctoral dissertation on *The Negro Farmer* (1903) Carl Kelsey of the University of Pennsylvania put the case bluntly:

> The transition from slavery to freedom set in operation the forces of natural selection, which are surely and steadily working among the people and are weeding out those who for any reason can not adapt themselves to the new environment. . . . How many of the race will fall by the way is, in one sense, a matter of indifference. In the long run, for the whites as well as the blacks, they will survive who adapt their social theories and consequently, their modes of life to their environment.

"Theirs is a child race," added William Elwang, a student of Charles Ellwood at the University of Missouri, "left behind in the struggle for existence because of original unfavorable environment and consequent inheritance of physical and mental conditions that foredoom to failure their competition on equal terms with other races." Jerome Dowd, a sometime sociology student at the University of Chicago, turned selectionism against the older view of innate Nordic supremacy: "Other races are equally well adapted to their environments. . . . Each has gone through a long process of natural selection and has acquired physical and mental traits suited to its environment."[41]

From this analysis flowed calls for stoicism, training for efficiency, and racial separation. Kelsey urged industrial training, primarily to meet the needs of modern farming. Elwang called for total separation: a legal system for blacks only; black churches under white rule; and rigorous training to fit blacks for the keen competition in the struggle for existence. As a result, he predicted, "the unfit are thereby weeded out and the fit alone, however few in number, will survive." On a worldwide scale, Dowd demanded an end to missionary effort ("cramming the Negro brain with the highly abstract doctrines and philosophy of Christianity"), and in its place economic development and the cultivation of each race's special talents.[42]

In *Sociology and Modern Social Problems* (1910), the sociologist Charles A. Ellwood (1873-1946) popularized this line of reasoning. Born in upstate New York, trained at Cornell and the University of Chicago (Ph.D. 1899), Ellwood combined social psychology with an active interest in charity and social work. Egalitarian by instinct, he absorbed the prevailing race prejudice of the era while teaching for three years at the University of Missouri, where he became convinced that the negro was "totally out of adjustment" with American life. His discussion of the "Negro Problem," lengthy by the standards of textbooks of the day, and enlightened according to the conventional wisdom, presented the now-standard reform Darwinist analysis. Admitting that Weismann's theories could not be wished away, he drew a sharp distinction between modification of individuals (through education) and of the race as a whole (through selection). Viewed in this light, slavery had a mixed effect on Africans brought to the New World: negative, in securing "a better type of negro physically [but] . . . more docile mentally"; positive, in teaching individuals "to work, at least to some extent." Moreover, natural selection continued to bring the "elimination of the unfit," the proof being relatively high mortality rates. "The misery and vice which we see are simply in large degree the expression of the working of a process of natural selection among them."[43]

But Ellwood insisted this natural process was unacceptable: "It would be preferable . . . if the white race could by education and other means substitute to some degree at least artificial selection for the miseries and brutality of the natural process of eliminating the unfit." Despite tantalizing references to "other means," "artificial selection," and even "more radical methods," Ellwood pushed this argument no further. Rather, in conclusion he endorsed industrial training on the Tuskegee model, preferably underwritten by the federal government. He also supported disfranchisement insofar as it eliminated "the negro from politics," while questioning its possible bad effect on black education. Underlying these proposals was the spirit of his selectionist analysis. No longer was education primarily a humanitarian duty, the aim of which was to raise a "child-like race" to a higher moral and spiritual level. Rather the primary goal was the making of "industrially inefficient nature man . . . into the industrially efficient civilized man."[44]

A benign statement, more suited for popular consumption, was Ray Stannard Baker's Following the Color Line (1908). Initially a series of articles in McClure's and the American Magazine this study was the work of one of America's leading reporters. Studying lynching and observing the frightening facts of the Atlanta Riot of 1906, Baker had firsthand knowledge of the racial strife of which the neo-Darwinists spoke. In the spirit of his muckraking, he initially blamed racial violence on the "unpunished subversion of law in this country," and presented as "the only remedy" a "strict enforcement of the law, all along the line, all the time." After studying race relations in the North and South more extensively, however, he endeavored to set the issue in broader perspective. "It is a tremendous struggle that is going on," he wrote, "the struggle of a backward race for survival within the swift-moving civilization of an advanced race." At its center was the Negro's economic "struggle for survival," especially in northern cities, which was accompanied "by the severest suffering."[45]

Although Baker accepted these laws as inevitable, he insisted that the real struggle was spiritual and ethical, a commonplace strategy among reform Darwinists. The most enlightened leadership, recognizing this ethical dimension, eschewed struggle and violence, he argued:

> If the test has to come in the long run between white men and coloured men, as it will have to come and is coming all the time, they want it to be an honest test of efficiency. The fittest here, too, will survive (there is no escaping the great law!), but these new thinkers wish the test of fitness to be, not mere physical force, not mere brute power, whether expressed in lynching or politics, but the higher test of real capacity.

Thus transformed, the disturbing realities of everyday violence became a source of inspiration. "And what a struggle it is!" Baker exulted. "Whether the Negro can survive the conflict, how it will come out, no man knows, for this is the making of life itself."[46]

Within this framework Baker justified disfranchisement and Jim Crow despite the fact he had evidence that the new restrictions exacerbated struggle rather than mitigating it. His conclusions—delicately balanced to appease all sides in the current debate—rested finally on the assumption that physical struggle must be contained so that time and education could allow the ethical struggle to work its magic. "As for the Jim Crow laws in the South," Baker wrote, "many of them, at least, are at present necessary to avoid the danger of clashes between the ignorant of both race. They are the inevitable scaffolding of progress."[47]

Viewed from the higher perspective of progress, daily struggle for Baker, as for Spencer decades earlier, somehow lost its sting. In the end, all struggle would yield a utopia of perfect adjustment in which, as Baker saw it, individuals were but "functions" of a Higher Being. "That is the meaning the teaching 'Lose your life and save it,' " he wrote in his journal at the time he was preparing *Following the Color Line* for press. This teaching also shed light on the racial issue:

> There is, after all, a profound significance in the effort of the South to make the Negro 'keep his place.' That is what nature is trying to make us all do. Only the *idea* of the place of the Negro is wrong, as the conception of the white man concerning *his* place is equally wrong. It is as much the duty of the white man to serve the Negro as it is the duty of the Negro to serve the white man. Both are one body: the foot and the hand do not quarrel over inferiority.

This same reasoning underlay Baker's preference for the Washingtonian philosophy over that of DuBois and the radicals. "Booker Washington never remembers himself at all," Baker wrote "Dr. DuBois never forgets himself."[48]

In conclusion, it is worth noting that this racial debate differed from others in one important particular. Despite the fact that the link between the *Origin of Species* and the emerging racism was plausible if tenuous, and despite the fact that William Smith carried the logic of Darwinism beyond the bounds of respectability, few if any critics charged racial theorists—from paternalists to accommodationists—with perpetrating a monstrous social Darwinism or the equivalent. Ultimately, Smith's extremism and this silence were two sides of the same coin. Where race was not the issue, Christian tradition, democratic values, and faith in the harmonies of nature set limits on scientific defenses of power and privilege, at the same time suggesting a strategy (the label social Darwinism) for discrediting all such tendencies. Where race was concerned, logic was more appealing. Ironically, the result was a genuine social Darwinism upon which no one was apparently willing to blow the whistle.

Or almost no one. As an antiracist counterattack took shape, elements of the social Darwinist charge appeared. Writing in 1901, W. E. B. DuBois noted that "it did not altogether satisfy the conscience of the modern world to be told complacently that all this [attack on the black race] has been right and proper, the fated triumph of strength over weakness, of righteousness over evil, of superiors over inferiors." In *Sociology and Modern Social Problems* (1910), Charles Ellwood included "extinction by means of natural selection" among solutions to the race problem that were "either impossible or fatuous." "The doctrine of racial Darwinism no longer implies a struggle in which the defeated type is exterminated," another sociologist lectured. "Under conditions prevailing in modern civilized association, it implies rather an application of the selective principle through a combination of competition and cooperation, by which the superior qualities [n.b.] of each race are sifted out and brought to efficiency."[49]

The attack on racial Darwinism gained currency in reform circles with the rise of new militancy toward the end of the first decade of the century. Discussing "Science and Human Brotherhood," William English Walling, a leading socialist and charter member of the NAACP, attacked the "new theory of the dominance of the 'fittest' races." "Thanks to the new doctrines of the survival of the fittest," he alleged, southern aristocratic ideals of stockbreeding were "to be applied to the whole human race." Reminding Americans of their democratic heritage, Walling also laid the blame on European theorists: British eugenicists; Rudyard Kipling; the selectionist anthropology of Ammon and Lapouge; and the philosophy of Nietzsche. This "science of human inequality" had gradually replaced the discredited art of skull and body measurement, he charged. Its "inhuman caste spirit" was daily visible in the North as well as the South: in the exclusion of blacks from white colleges, in wholesale disfranchisement, and in anti-Negro riots such as the one that had recently occurred in Springfield, Ohio.[50]

A decade of international warfare confirmed this opinion. "A crude Darwinian philosophy seems to have percolated down into the mass of the people and taken possession of the common mind," Charles Ellwood wrote in 1923, "so that we not infrequently hear all the antagonism and antipathy of races, nations, classes, and individuals."[51] Thus, these voices in the wilderness put the stereotype of social Darwinism in position for a later generation of social critics.

10. The Nietzsche Vogue

The philosophical legacy left by Friedrich Nietzsche to the ruling classes of the world is a sword which, if they dare to draw it publically in their own defense, will turn upon and slay them . . . . Mr. Mencken has but pushed to their logical conclusions views which in embryo are held by many bourgeois opponents of Socialism, but which, lacking his courage, they dare not develop.
　　Wilshire's Magazine, ca. 1910 quoted in
　　Current Literature, 49 (1910), 67.

Nietzsche himself said that he was but carrying out the social implications of the doctrines of Charles Darwin. . . . Nietzsche was probably mistaken in this, but we cannot deny that a crude sort of social Darwinism was in the air at the time that Nietzsche wrote.
　　Charles Ellwood, The Story of Social Philosophy *(1938), pp. 294-5.*

"Nietzsche carried the Darwinian theory to its logical conclusion. . . ."
　　William Jennings Bryan, "Brother or Brute,"
　　The Commoner, *November, 1920, p. 12.*

One

　　While most Americans in the 1890s sought escape from the chilling logic of neo-Darwinism, a scattered few seemed deliberately to dramatize their contemporaries' worst nightmares. A decadent and sterile America required "the kind of courage that aids by active cooperation the survival of the fittest," wrote the author of *Might is Right*, a paperback shocker that appeared in Chicago in 1896. "Death to the weaklings, wealth to the strong." A decade later Henry Louis Mencken trumpeted an equally brash Darwinism. The "will to live," he wrote in *Men vs. the Man* (1910) inevitably entailed a fight to gain domination over others. "Such is the law of the survival of the fittest, and it stands immutable."[1] The common element in these statements was the philosophy of Friedrich Nietzsche, whose works were being translated into English from the mid-1890s onward.[2] With Nietzsche's help, at least a few apparently accepted a logic an earlier generation resisted.

Were Nietzsche's American disciples the social Darwinists of which the reformers complained? This question goes to the heart of Nietzsche's philosophy, which from the start bred a sharp division between two schools of interpreters, who have recently been termed the "tough" and "tender" Nietzscheans.[3] For the former, Nietzsche was a proponent of barbarism and *machtpolitik,* the source of Count von Bernhardi's *Germany and the Next War* (1911), for example, and the philosophy of Prussian militarism in general. For the latter, he was an existentialist prophet of spiritual and artistic rebirth, in America a moving force behind the prewar renaissance in arts and letters the historian Henry May has called the "innocent rebellion." Although the issue of the tough vs. the tender Nietzsche involves more than his relation to Darwinism, this connection constitutes yet another chapter in the complex history of the social Darwinian stereotype.

Two

"One might expect," wrote the journalist-philosopher Paul Carus, "that Nietzsche, who glories in the triumph of the strong over the weak in the struggle for life, red in tooth and claw, would look up to Darwin as his master." But, Carus continued, the odd fact was that he did not.[4] Although one may quarrel with this rendition of Nietzsche's philosophy, Nietzsche's own words on the subject of Darwin appeared unequivocal, despite the fact that some of the earliest English translations left just enough room for misinterpretation on this point. During the 1870s and 1880s, Nietzsche often attacked Darwin, heaping ridicule on his theory. "To the Disciples of Darwin" he wrote:

> You accept the mediocre
> Reasons of this English joker,
> For "philosophy"? And thus
> Set him next to Goethe! Lese-
> Majesty such purpose is—
> *Majesty of genius!*

He likewise made clear his opposition to prevailing concepts of progress as the result of a materialistic struggle for existence:

> In so far it appears to me that the famous Struggle for Existence
> is not the only point of view from which an explanation can be
> given of the progress or strengthening of an individual or a race.
> Rather must two different things converge: firstly, the multiplying
> of stable strength through mental binding in faith and common

feeling; secondly, the possibility of attaining to higher aims, through the fact that there are deviating natures and, in consequence, partial weakening and wounding of the stable strength; it is precisely the weaker nature, as the more delicate and free, that makes all progress at all possible.

In *The Twilight of the Idols* (1888) he returned to this same issue:

Anti-Darwin— As regards the celebrated "struggle for life," it seems to me, in the meantime, to be more asserted than proved. It occurs, but only as an exception; the general aspect of life is *not* a state of want and hunger; it is rather a state of opulence, luxuriance, and even absurd prodigality,—where there is a struggle, it is a struggle for *power*.

Nietzsche thus scorned the "learned cattle" who attempted to translate his philosophy into Darwinese.[5]

Herbert Spencer was Nietzsche's special target, his "decadent" philosophy the final proof of the limitations of middle-class British thought. The Englishman's attempted reconciliation of altruism and egoism "almost causes nausea to people like us," Nietzsche wrote in *The Joyful Wisdom* (1882): " . . . a humanity with such perspectives would seem to us deserving of contempt, of extermination!"[6]

Nonetheless, in the very act of condemning Darwinism, Nietzsche could, as this last sentence suggests, encourage a Darwinian construction of his words. "Life is a result of war," he wrote in *The Will to Power* (1888), a work later favored particularly by the tough Nietzscheans. "Mr. Herbert Spencer was a decadent in biology as also in morality (he regarded the triumph of altruism as a desideratum!)." As the first English editions of Nietzsche's work made their way across the Atlantic, it remained to be seen whether such statements would be the opening wedge for a union of Nietzsche and Darwin.[7]

In the preface to the first (and ultimately abortive) English edition of Nietzsche's complete works, Alexander Tille, a German expatriate living in London, tentatively explored the possibility of such a reconciliation. Tille urged Nietzscheans to make peace with Darwin, reap the prestige of the new evolutionary biology (interpreted in neo-Darwinian terms) and with it fashion a new moral and social standard. The entire "drift of [Herbert Spencer's] thought almost appears to be inspired by the question: How to evade and veil the logical [n.b.] consequences of Darwin's evolutionism for human existence?," Tille wrote in a preface to *The Case of Wagner* (1896). English philosophy, insofar as it noticed evolution, "endeavored to show that sexual and natural selection and elimination cannot possibly account for 'human progress.'" Huxley's Romanes speech was on the right track. But the new morality required a clearer standard than the "larger hope." If struggle were universal, and man nonetheless persisted in "forcing his own moral standard upon nature," must not the results of that effort—art, civilization, religion—be measured "by these effects upon his species, by the standard of his physiology"? Still tentative, Tille admitted it was difficult to see where such "transvaluation" of the "intellectual currency" would lead. But in another preface the following year, he made it clear that altruism and reform would be its victims. "Are these ideals actually worthier of human striving," he asked, "than the wish to get the upper hand in the same struggle for existence?" In a full-length study, *Von Darwin Bis Nietzsche* (1899), Tille again attacked the pusillanimity of English Darwinism.[8]

Three

Which Nietzsche attracted Americans? An early answer came in "Ragnar Redbeard's" *Might is Right or the Struggle for Existence* (1896), undoubtedly the most bizarre product of the American Nietzsche vogue. Chanting proto-fascist sermons in a barbaric yawp that reduced Whitman to a whisper, "Ragnar Redbeard" distilled "the world wide experience of an active life" into a virulent creed of anti-Semitism, nativism, racism, and male chauvinism ("A woman is two-thirds womb. The other third is a network of nerves and sentimentality"). "As long as the struggle for existence is 'moralized' or limited by Government and Gods," proclaimed the publisher's blurb, "the unfit and base, instead of being trampled down (as nature intended) are stupidly permitted to set up Imperial Injunction Seats and deal out death, bondage and ruin to Highest Types." Brute force in domestic and international dealings was "The Logic of Today," he concluded, in a poem dedicated to Darwin and Bismarck.[9]

Bluntness is not always clarity however, and *Might is Right*, the most forthright statement of social Darwinism in the annals of American literature, remains something of a mystery. "Ragnar Redbeard, LL.D University of Chicago" was in fact the pseudonym of a Chicago journalist whose only other literary effort was a potboiler titled *Rival Caesars* which he coauthored in 1903.[10] From the opening introduction by "Douglas K. Handyside, M.D., PhD," *Might is Right* was, if not outright parody, at least a tongue-in-cheek attempt to turn a dollar by outraging sensibilities, or as Handyside put it, upsetting "pet popular illusions." "Nothing like it has ever been permitted to see the light since A.D. 300," he added with characteristic bombast. "Undoubtedly it is bound to meet with the antagonism of University Monkeries, and the hatred of Idolators." He apologized that the author was unable to read German, but insisted he got the drift of Nietzsche from Tille and others. He also apologized for many typographical and other errors. "Meantime," he concluded, perhaps with a wink, "intelligent critics (there are a few) cannot possibly misunderstand the meaning."[11]

Since critics ignored the work, one is left guessing what author and readers had in mind. If Ragnar Redbeard intended his sermon seriously, it was indeed a message virtually unparalleled since the rise of Christianity. More probably he intended to parody the very views he presented. In any case, his unabashed social Darwinism, in warning where Huxley's New Reformation was heading, underlined the public unacceptability of this logic.

In any event, most Americans declined to follow the lead of *Might is Right*.[12] One or two Spencerians, in their pessimism, may have been sorely tempted. The new editors of *Popular Science* concluded a critical note on Nietzsche's philosophy with the following hope:

> Still Nietzsche deserves mention here, as his ethical views,
> based on the Darwinian theory of the survival of the fit, are not
> unlikely to be argued hereafter by saner men, and to become
> an integral part of ethics when ethics becomes a science.

But those sympathetic to Nietzsche's views declined the alliance. Without pretending that he left conventional values undisturbed, most found in his work the inspiration for new ideals or a revival of old, either ignoring or denying the Darwinian connection. Nietzsche's ideal of "naturalness," wrote a lawyer from Chicago, was "certainly not . . . the one to which Darwin refers, to become cannibals or beasts of prey." Religious and social reformers agreed. Nietzsche "accepted Darwinism, and did not accept it," wrote an Ethical Culturist in a masterpiece of equivocation: the issue was moot. A Baptist clergyman translated Nietzsche into Darwinese to indicate the portion he could *not* accept (his allegedly reactionary views), and then yoked the remainder of the philosophy to liberal Christianity. A socialist, after also purifying Nietzsche, observed that Nietzsche was "far from having been captured by the prevailing evolution worship, and is especially critical of the struggle for existence hypothesis."[13]

In his study of *Nietzsche* (1908) and the less well-known *Men vs. the Man* (1910) Henry Louis Mencken, however, appeared to shift the balance abruptly back to the tough Nietzsche. Both books bristled with the characteristic phrases of social Darwinism, intended not to caricature opponents but to express Mencken's own beliefs. Agreeing with Tille, Mencken accepted the frank dualism of Huxley's Romanes lecture. "Like Huxley I believe the management of the universe is by no means perfect, but such as it is, we must accept it." Religion and politics, he observed, shared the common delusion that men could suspend or modify the immutable laws of the universe. In religion the result was prayer; in politics, schemes "to combat the eternal and inexorable law that the strong shall prevail over the weak." Nietzsche honored these laws by insisting that the survival of the fittest and natural selection proved the danger and futility of preserving the unfit.[14]

In *Men vs. the Man*, a debate in the form of correspondence with the socialist Robert Rives LaMonte, Mencken again unashamedly translated Nietzsche into Darwinese. Attacking him on this point, LaMonte attempted to distinguish a spiritual and material dimension of the problem. Spiritually (as Mencken really believed) the issue was "better manners, more worthy fiction, higher art and nobler drama." Materially, there need be no struggle for existence because technology provided the necessary abundance.[15]

In response, Mencken first challenged LaMonte's facts concerning technology and abundance, citing data from cigar manufacturing, the Mencken family business. Because there remained a shortage of material wealth, the will to live inevitably entailed a continuing attempt to gain domination over ones' fellow men. "Such is the law of the survival of the fittest and it stands immutable." Pursuing the point, LaMonte then asked bluntly whether Nietzsche's *Ubermensch* was to be a Pasteur or a Rockefeller, a man of genius who conquered nature, or a Pecuniary Magnate who exploited his fellow beings? Although Mencken was torn, he would not concede. "Does the cosmic process prove the millionaire is necessary or beneficient," he asked in return. "I am sure I don't know. But it does prove, I think, that he is inevitable—at least in our present stage of progress. . . . My own private view (the child I must admit of a very ardent wish) is that the idea of truth-seeking will one day take the place of money-making." However, he added, "today the law of natural selection is aiding the man-made laws of artificial selection. Under socialism the unfit would survive."[16]

Mencken, as LaMonte accurately observed, was in fact fighting two battles at once: one for the spiritual and artistic rebirth that produced America's "innocent rebellion";[17] the other for a vanishing order of industrial enterprise in which he only half believed. Nietzsche and Darwin served in both cases. The prophet of a new American literature, Mencken happily enlisted Nietzsche in a "fight against orthodoxy, custom and authority," which was "before the 'Origin of Species' . . . perennially and necessarily a losing one." But Nietzschean individualism also served Mencken the social theorist, son of a Baltimore cigar manufacturer, and third-generation German immigrant, for whom the social tensions of several decades had special meaning. This Mencken recalled his father's battles with labor; stewed over efforts of reformers to regulate; and took perverse comfort in the vision of a universe of toil and struggle. A Robber Baron without a castle, Mencken was determined to "accept the actual forces of existence . . . however ugly these facts may be."[18]

A fundamental confusion in Mencken's allegiance to two concepts of freedom, spiritual and material, complicated this dual concern. Mencken sensed that Nietzsche's Dionysian ideal meant more than garnering to oneself the goods of the earth—that there was an important difference between Darwin's struggle for existence and Nietzsche's *will to power*. But in his version this difference was hopelessly blurred or entirely lost. This was the essence of LaMonte's objections in *Men vs. the Man*. This also was the charge of another critic who noted that Mencken's Nietzsche expounded "a philosophy which might be described as evolutionary or selective utilitarianism, with its roots in Darwinism, but representing a step further than the democratic humanitarianism of Bentham and the English Positivists." The effect, the critic continued, was the absence of the "mysticism in Nietzsche's original conception."[19] In short, what began for Mencken as a struggle for nobility of the soul ended in a material struggle for existence in which "the devil always takes the hindmost."[20] In theory a creative spirit, his Superman seemed remarkably like a Baltimore manufacturer on the way up.[21]

No simple defense of success or *rugged individualism*, Mencken's social Darwinism was thus a peculiar product of his individual temperament. The antithesis of the progressive reformer, he responded to the tensions of the decade by voicing a darker side of middle class concern untempered by humanitarianism: worship of efficiency and strong leadership without democracy (TR seemed to him a Nietzschean crippled by politics); racism and xenophobia unleavened by equalitarianism or internationalism. A Nietzschean social Darwinism, precisely because struggle for existence was the equivalent of a later generation's rat race, provided the ideal rhetoric for expressing rebellion *and* disgust, however confused, with the growing constraints in American life. Mencken's capitalistic Superman was above all a creature of his ambivalence concerning success and capitalism.

Mencken's social Darwinism, like that of Ragnar Redbeard, was thus the exception that proved the rule precisely because both expressed a gospel not articulated in the West "since 300 A.D.!" Both depended on the ability to shock. Concerning *Man vs. the Men*, an ill-fated venture that sold less than 500 copies, Mencken and his critics agreed he spelled out a logic that was *implicit* in all defenses of the existing order. Defenses of capitalism were *really* appeals to jungle force. His individualism, wrote one critic, was the "crass, uncompromising kind that . . . has done so much for the advancement of socialism in England." One American socialist suggested that the ruling classes would be well advised to spread the Nietzsche gospel since, although he disagreed with Mencken, he felt the arguments were the most logical against socialism."However," he added, "they possess one fatal drawback in the fact that the bourgeois dare not publically use them." Mencken had "but pushed to the logical conclusion views which in embryo are held by many bourgeois opponents of socialism, but which, lacking his courage, they dare not develop, and are in consequence forced to occupy a shifty, evasive, and apologetic position."[22] Mencken himself, was also aware of his courage in this regard. America *was* a jungle in practice, he told readers of the *Smart Set:* he thus willingly brought into the house the Darwinian slogans that polite society consigned to the stable.[23] Thus Mencken articulated the peculiar combination of disenchantment with *and* defense of the status quo, such as later characterized grassroots disaffection on the radical right.

Mencken's error, if one accepts the existentialist or gentle version of Nietzsche, also revealed a perennial American tendency to translate dreams of self-realization and *truth-seeking* (to use Mencken's term) into an Algeresque quest for material success. "Self expression and paganism," wrote the critic Malcolm Cowley of this generation, "encouraged a demand for all sorts of products . . . modern furniture, beach pajamas, cosmetics, colored bathrooms with toilet paper to match."[24] From Massachusetts Bay to Woodstock, from the 1630s to the 1960s, the passionate intensity at the heart of Protestant pietism—although promising new life—managed somehow to end in a new lifestyle.

Four

Nietzsche's critics—and these vastly outnumbered his supporters in the progressive era—not surprisingly inflated his image as a prophet of barbarism, and in the process put the stereotype of social Darwinism to yet another use. Two Englishmen, responding directly to Tille, established a pattern that persisted for two decades. F. C. S. Schiller, a pragmatist who admired Darwin, condemned the editor's attempt "to graft Nietzsche's views on the Darwinian conception of the survival of the fittest (as if Darwin would have ignored à la Nietzsche the moral, intellectual, and social qualities in the make-up of fitness)." Reversing the argument, the neo-Kantian philosopher Seth Pringle-Pattison used Nietzsche to damn evolutionism. He had already seen the "logic" of Darwinism in Huxley's Romanes address. "Failure or success in the struggle for existence must . . . be the sole standard," he wrote in 1893, regretting that Huxley would not embrace idealism as the way out. In recognizing this logic, he added in 1898, "Nietzsche stands probably alone among naturalistic thinkers." The German's ethical teaching was "as old as Callicles in the *Gorgias*. . . . And yet he is a phenomenon not without significance at the present juncture, as representing in their most concentrated and logically consistent form [n.b.] ideas which have subtly permeated much of our literature, and which voice themselves today in the Press with a boldness which would have been impossible twenty years ago." A German critic, who himself accepted the neo-Darwinism of Weismann, also found Nietzsche's individualism extreme. "In fact," wrote Conrad Guenther, "he attributes a more energetic action to selection than the social Darwinists do." In short, whether one like or disliked Darwinism, Nietzsche seemed to be the loser.[25]

In the following decades, this pattern persisted. Most Darwinians denied any connection between the *Origin* and Nietzsche. Reform-minded sociologists attacked the Nietzsche-Darwin connection to preface their own correct reading of evolution. In *Democracy and Empire* (1899), F. H. Giddings of Columbia noted that Nietzsche implicitly repudiated Huxley's call to "kick against the pricks." Instead Nietzsche "assumes that Darwinism, in its most radical form of Weismannism, is the only true account of man's place in nature." Giddings, invoking Darwin, then underlined the importance of psychological elements in social development. Similarly (although for different purposes) E. A. Ross of the University of Wisconsin denounced Nietzsche's "ultra-Darwinism"; a contributor to the *International Monthly* condemned the social Darwinism of Nietzsche *and* Tille; and a Spencerian in Chicago censured the "practical Nietzscheanism" evidenced in the "intense struggle for existence" in that city.[26]

As Nietzsche's reputation grew, variations appeared. In 1909 the philosopher James Tufts of the University of Chicago recalled Darwin's stress on sympathy as an antidote to the "present 'reaction' and especially in view of Nietzsche's denunciations." While one writer decried an unholy alliance of Darwin; Nietzsche; individualism; and laissez faire; another welcomed the alliance because he believed that Mendelian genetics, in disproving Darwin, also undermined all forms of Nietzschean conservatism. A Christian socialist blamed Nietzsche *and* Tennyson for making Darwin an apostle of "nature, red in tooth and claw," and cited the Romanes lecture to refute both. Each provided what another termed "a truer interpretation of the facts of evolution."[27]

Opponents of naturalism, reversing the argument, affirmed the connection to discredit one or both thinkers. Some voiced traditional Christian concerns and predicted the adverse affect of Nietzscheanism on religious belief and social conscience. "It is an intensified doctrine of the survival of the fittest that Nietzsche preaches," warned a writer in the *Independent*. "Life was to him simply a struggle for existence," echoed the *Outlook*, charging that Nietzsche wished "to abolish hospital and philanthropic institutions of all kinds which looked to the relief of the weak." The editor of the *Monist* sounded a similar complaint from a philosophic perspective. A second philosopher, an idealist, observed that Nietzsche escaped Huxley's dualism only by retreating to an unabashed positivism of the crudest sort—"Spencer minus the doctrine of the Unknowable."[28]

In similar spirit, several writers found Nietzsche a convenient weapon against eugenics, which, as already noted was becoming by 1910 a bastion of antisocialist sentiment in some quarters. Although in a study of *Nietzsche and Treitschke* (1914) Ernest Barker correctly stressed the differences between Nietzsche and Darwin, he characterized the German as "a sort of combination of Comte and Galton, of Positivism and Eugenics." Less judiciously, a reviewer for *Blackwood's* declared flatly that Nietzsche "was simple enough to pretend that this hero might be produced by some kind of biological process, by the foolish thing that sentimentalists call eugenics." An American lecturer likewise noted that "Nietzsche was the evangelist of aristocracy and eugenics." William English Walling, an American socialist sympathetic to Nietzsche, insisted that his philosophy "has nothing to do with the pitiful fallacy on which eugenics is based." But his caution could scarcely prevail against the growing assumption, as Mencken later put it, that Nietzsche was to Darwin, Spencer, and Huxley "what Beelzebub is to a trio of bad boys."[29]

The image of social Darwinism, as Byran Strong has observed, not only dominated Nietzsche criticism in the prewar years, but itself reflected an American tendency to prize "intelligence over intellect, and the pragmatic mind over the critical mind."[30] Wedded to the assumption that ideas were ultimately plans for action, the progressive generation too easily translated Nietzsche's analysis of the creative potential of intellect into political reactionism and thus rejected it. The presence in his work of such terms as *ubermensch*, slave, and aristocracy—each with overwhelmingly negative connotations—encouraged this translation. Only with the immigration of a later generation of European intellectuals could Americans fully appreciate the tender or existentialist Nietzsche.

If one argues, as has Conor Cruise O'Brien, that the gentle Nietzscheans are blind to anti-Semitism, cruelty, and militarism in Nietzsche's writing, one would conclude that this earlier interpretation of Nietzsche was indeed salutary. Whether or not the image of Nietzsche as social Darwinist was in some sense correct or totally incorrect, however, the point here is that as social myth social Darwinism again served as a vehicle for democratic and humanitarian convictions against readings of Nietzsche which elsewhere helped undermine this faith. Again also, its effectiveness depended on the fact that a social Darwinist was something no one wanted to be.

11. Beyond the Battle
The Literary Naturalists

*Neither the poet nor the novelist, in these days of talk about
"superman," seems to know that in the struggle for
existence the obscure and the feeble tend, very frequently,
to survive.*
"How the Literary Man is Misrepresenting Evolution,"
Current Literature, 43 (1907), 99.

*The idealist, both in politics and in art, almost invariably
assumes that his antagonist is not only wrong, but
immoral. . . . One example of it is to be found in the
article of that college professor (in the* Nation) *who lately
denounced Dreiser for subscribing to a purely animal
theory of behaviour.*
H. L. Mencken to Henry S. Harrison, 25 November
1916, Letters of Henry Louis Mencken ed. Guy J. Forgue
(New York, 1961), p. 98.

One

During the 1890s American novelists also pondered the lessons of biology. In *Caesar's Column* (1892) Ignatius Donnelly treated readers to an unabashedly Darwinian "Sermon of the Twentieth Century." "If Nature, with her interminable fecundity, pours forth millions of human beings for whom there is no place on earth, and no means of subsistence, what affair is that our ours, my brethren?" a new-style clergyman asks his well-to-do congregation. "We did not make them; we did not ask Nature to make them. And it is Nature's business to feed them, not yours or mine." "Nature's attitude toward all life is profoundly vicious, treacherous, and malignant," Mark Twain confided to his notebook soon after reading Huxley's Romanes speech.[1]

In the naturalist novels of Theodore Dreiser and Jack London, Nietzschean Supermen likewise battled their fates in a neo-Darwinian universe. Frank Cowperwood of *The Financier* (1912) and *The Titan* (1914) seemed a direct offspring of Mencken's marriage of Darwin and Nietzsche. Dreiser himself on occasion sounded like the typical social Darwinist. "Until that intelligence that runs this show sees fit to remodel the nature of man," he told a Soviet critic during the 1920s, "I think it will always be the survival of the fittest." In *Martin Eden* (1909) Jack London's autobiographical hero echoed this sentiment. "As for myself, I am an individualist. I believe the race is to the swift, the battle to the strong. Such is the lesson I have learned from biology, or at least think I have learned."[2]

On one level, these Darwinian outbursts, like the reformers' stereotype, merely caricatured positions these authors rejected. Donnelly was a prominent Populist and wrote *Caesar's Column* to promote the cause. Mark Twain at his most cynical remained a bitter critic of the social and industrial status quo. Although Dreiser and London were more complicated cases, both publically espoused socialism at one time or another.

Unlike the reformers' tracts, however, this caricature prefaced predictions of disaster,[3] not confident programs for social reconstruction. In the tradition of romanticism, the heroes of naturalist fiction stormed the universe on behalf of cherished visions. But increasingly their conception of good seemed impossible within the dialectics of the world—from the Connecticut Yankee's utopia of individualism and democracy, to Martin Eden's dream of perfect art.[4] The result characteristically was individual annihilation, social cataclysm, or both, as if their creators could abide neither a world with individualism nor without it. In their use of social Darwinism, the literary naturalists thus completed a pattern that first surfaced in the later work of Herbert Spencer, William Graham Sumner, and others who clung to pre-Darwinian virtues in an increasingly Darwinian world.

Two

Although in *Caesar's Column* Ignatius Donnelly (1831–1901) anticipated the mood and assumptions of later naturalism, his use of social Darwinism differed least from that of his fellow reformers. An antiutopian fantasy in the tradition that later produced Orwell's *1984*, his novel was in part a response to *Looking Backward*, which appeared shortly before Donnelly began to write. In form, the work was a series of letters from one Gabriel Weltstein, a visitor to New York in 1988, to his brother in Uganda in Africa. The model of the moderate reformer, Weltstein chronicles the bloody career of Caesar Lomellini, a drunken demagogue who finally destroys civilization in the process of saving it. This nightmare vision in part reflected Donnelly's own hopes and frustrations: his plan in the late 1880s for a People's party to save America and his own failure in 1889 to win national political office. A modern Jeremiah, Donnelly denounced the picture he drew. "It must not be thought, because I am constrained to describe the overthrow of civilization, that I desire it," he told readers. "I seek to preach into the ears of the able and rich and powerful the great truth that neglect of the sufferings of their fellows . . . and blind, brutal and degrading worship of mere wealth, must . . . eventuate in the overthrow of society and the destruction of civilization."[5]

Weltstein's home in New York is The Hotel Darwin, a symbol at once of the promise and peril of nineteenth-century science. In its ultramodern appointments, The Darwin illustrates the splendors of a technological future. But the faces of its occupants tell another story. Scanning the dining room, Weltstein perceives that "the chief features in the expression of the men were incredulity, unbelief, cunning, observation, heartlessness." The evil spirit prevailing there, he later decides, is the same science that created the wonders of The Darwin. "Science has increased their knowledge one hundred percent, and their vanity one thousand percent," he wrote of the inhabitants. "The acquisition of a few facts about nature had closed their eyes to the existence of a God." To his horror, Weltstein also learns that a ruthless Oligarchy dominates an "underworld" of people without hope. "They seemed to me merely automata, in the hands of some ruthless and unrelenting destiny," he reports. "They knew that tomorrow could bring them nothing better than today—the same shameful, pitiful, contemptible, sordid struggle for mere existence."[6]

Falling in league with members of a revolutionary underground, Weltstein outlines his plan for a "Brotherhood of Justice," based on humanitarianism and Christian love. At a meeting of workingmen, however, his message is drowned in angry calls for force and violence. "A hundred years ago you might have formed your Brotherhood of Justice," a companion lectured. "Now there is but one cure—the Brotherhood of Destruction."[7]

While listening to the "Twentieth Century Sermon"—the most extended statement of the social Darwinist stereotype in reform literature to that time—Weltstein learns that Darwinism sustains the Oligarchy in a similar creed of force. In the "cathedral-like temple" Weltstein sees that the congregation, most of them women, have "a hard and souless look. . . . I could not but notice a sensuality in the full, red-lips and the quick glancing eyes, which indicated they were splendid animals, and nothing more." (The boldness of women in this Brave New World continually reminded Donnelly of its corruptness.) In the "Sermon" Professor Odyard pictures the unmitigated struggle that characterizes all nature, anticipating the message of Huxley's Romanes speech. "The plan of Nature," he tells his audience, "necessarily involves cruelty, suffering, injustice, destruction, death." But might mankind take comfort in some larger hope? Not for a minute. "Let us leave [the poor and suffering] in the hands of Nature. She had made them and can care for them."[8]

Weltstein predictably recoils from this "Nature worship," this "rebirth of Paganism," again noting incidentally that the women snuggled closer to the men with "many a flashing interchange of glances." Taking the floor, he reiterates his gospel of Christian love, only to be driven physically from the temple by the congregation. Again his companion lectures him. Only strength can convert the strong. Caesar, the leader of the Brotherhood of Destruction, can alone convince the Oligarchy. "Caesar is a bigger brute than they are," he observes. "The difference is, they are brutes who are in possession of the good things of this world; and Caesar is a brute who wants to get into possession of them."[9]

The ensuing confrontation between the Oligarchy and Caesar carries the logic of force to its conclusion in a cataclysm that finally engulfs the entire civilized world. Presenting a final analysis, Weltstein's companion predicts a dreary cycle of destruction, rather than unending progress, as the lesson of evolution:

> After about three-fourths of the human family have died of hunger, or been killed, the remainder, constituting, by the law of the survival of the fittest, the most powerful and brutal, will find it necessary, for self-defense against each other, to form squads or gangs. . . . And so, step by step, mankind will re-enact the great human drama, which begins always with a tragedy, runs through a comedy, and terminates in a catastrophe.

Only in the Edenic setting of the mountains of Uganda can Weltstein and his companions at last establish the ideal republic, based on Populist principles, and guided not by a Caesar but the "philanthropy" and "statesmanship" of "a few superior intellects."[10]

One might argue that Donnelly, whose flamboyant career as a land developer partook more than a little of the capitalist ethos, was only half-convinced. While condemning the capitalist Gotham, he never quite hid his admiration for the technological vulgarities of The Darwin or of the "shrewdness and energy," "resolute mouths," and "fine brows" of its residents.[11] The destruction of this world perhaps revealed in Donnelly's case a more complex state of mind, in which one secretly desires social cataclysm as an end in itself, rather than a new order of proletarian brotherhood.

But, these speculations aside, the conclusion of *Caesar's Column* was ostensibly clear. The cult of individual success and material progress, untempered by social justice, would bring suffering and death. Populist reforms would avoid this destructive outcome. Fleeing to Uganda Weltstein reshapes society in line with the Omaha Platform, the Populist program of 1892, which Donnelly also drafted. Unlike the doomed individualists of Dreiser and London, the members of Donnelly's Oligarchy remained symbols of greed, products of the Darwinian logic of the "Sermon of the Twentieth Century."

Between the time he wrote *The Adventures of Huckleberry Finn* (1884) and *What Is Man?* (1906), Mark Twain (1835-1910) lost Donnelly's faith that man might so easily transform his world. In his early work, Twain repeatedly played on the tension between individual character and will, on the one hand, and the determining influences of environment and culture on the other—between Huck Finn's innocence, for example, and the corrupt civilization that threatens to destroy it. In Twain's career, *The Connecticut Yankee* (1888) marked a turning point. In the figure of Hank Morgan, Twain attempted to translate Huck Finn's innocence into a full-blown social theory. Morgan's failure to transform sixth-century England in light of his democratic-industrial dream mirrored Twain's growing pessimism about the course of American society at home and abroad.[12]

In *The Descent of Man*, Huxley's *Evolution and Ethics*, and related works, Twain in the mid-1890s appeared to find new language to express his own and Morgan's disillusionment. It was at this point that he described in his notebook the "vicious, treacherous, and malignant" character of nature. "Man has not a single right which is the product of anything but might," he wrote in a later entry of 1904. "There is no such thing as morality; it is not immoral for the tiger to eat the wolf, or the wolf the cat, or the cat the bird, and so on down; that is their business. . . . It is not immoral for one nation to seize another man's property or life if he is strong enough and wants to take it."[13]

Although Twain, even more than Donnelly, signaled a new mood that would eventually flower in the naturalistic novels of Theodore Dreiser and Jack London, Darwin and Huxley finally left little or no imprint on his work. To be sure, Darwinism may have confirmed a general cynicism concerning man's abilities and convinced Twain that man after all is one of the animals—an influence Sherwood Cummings has argued at length. But the cynicism and pessimism of *The American Claimant* (1892); *Following the Equator* (1897); and *What is Man?* was entirely without benefit of Darwinian rhetoric, even such as surfaced on occasion in the notebooks. The pessimism of *What is Man?* was rooted firmly in the mechanistic determinism of Newtonianism, a conviction Twain expressed years before he read Darwin in declaring, "I believe that the universe is governed by strict and immutable laws."[14] Despite his interest in Huxley's *Evolution and Ethics*, Twain could not or would not see its potential nihilism. Reared on this neo-Darwinian vision, Dreiser and London, in contrast, made it their starting point.

Three

In one of the best known scenes in the novels of Theodore Dreiser (1871-1945) young Frank Cowperwood stands wide-eyed in a fish market before a tank containing a squid and a lobster. "The lobster, it appeared from the talk of the idle bystanders, was offered no food as the squid was considered his rightful prey," Dreiser explained. Fixed by the eye of the lobster, the squid falls finally to its inevitable fate. "That's the way it has to be, I guess," Cowperwood reflects. "That squid wasn't quick enough." The scene also held a more general lesson:

> It answered in a rough way that riddle which had been annoy-
> ing him so much in the past: "How is life organized?" Things
> lived on each other—that was it. Lobsters lived on squids and
> other things. What lived on lobsters? Men of course! Sure,
> that was it! And what lived on men? he asked himself. Was it
> other men? Wild animals lived on men. And there were
> Indians and cannibals. . . . He wasn't so sure about men living
> on men; but men did kill each other. How about wars and
> street fights and mobs? . . . That was it! Sure men lived on men.
> Look at the slaves. They were men. That's what all this
> excitement was about these days. Men killing other men
> —negroes.[15]

Whether Dreiser himself drew this lesson, however, is another matter. In the mid-1890s Spencer and Darwin swept him off his feet. Spencer, he later wrote in an oft-quoted remark, blew him "intellectually to bits." Throughout his life Dreiser ranked the English philosopher among his favorites. But, as Ellen Moers has noted, the lessons he took from these texts concerned religion, not society. "They shifted my point of view tremendously," he wrote to Mencken years later, "confirmed my worst suspicions and destroyed the last remaining traces of Catholicism." *The Descent of Man* confirmed his general faith in evolution and provided fuel for speculation concerning male courtship of females. (In Dreiser's midwest, Darwinism retained its earlier taint, as he learned when in 1897 he paraphrased the *Descent* to his fiancée in Missouri, who refused to believe the theory of evolution.) Dreiser's heroes and heroines were Spencerians first and foremost in being heirs to a tradition of freethought that made them impatient with social conventions and traditional morality, not in being rugged individualists.[16]

When Dreiser praised Spencer it was not the doctrinaire individualist, but the author of *First Principles* and the doctrine of the Unknowable. This doctrine Dreiser translated into a sort of cosmic wonder in the face of inscrutable forces that controlled and often defeated human purpose. Its very contemplation brought a strange sort of calm: "Was it all blind chance or was there some guiding intelligence—a God?" asks the heroine of *Jennie Gehrhardt* (1911):

> Almost in spite of herself she felt there must be something—
> a higher power which produced all the beautiful things—the
> flowers, the stars, the trees, the grass. Nature was so beautiful!
> If at times life seemed cruel, yet this beauty still persisted.
> The thought comforted her.

In the final scene of *The "Genius"* (1915) Eugene Witla finds similar comfort in Spencer's vision of a *universal matrix* completely beyond man's power to comprehend.[17]

The pattern of conflict, transcendence, and awe was especially clear in "McEwen of the Shining Slavemakers," which appeared in *Ainslees's* in June 1901. Written in the first flush of Dreiser's enthusiasm over evolution, the tale was the most explicitly Darwinian of his short stories. While pondering a cluster of ants, Robert McEwen, in Alice-in-Wonderland fashion, finds himself suddenly a member of an ant colony locked in grisly warfare with neighboring tribes. In this neo-Darwinian world, strength and numbers alone decide victory. In a decisive battle against the "Sanguineae," McEwen is finally outnumbered:

> Swiftly they tore at his head and body, endeavoring to dispose
> of him quickly. One seized a leg, another an antenna. A third
> jumped and sawed at his neck. Still he did not care. It was all
> war, and he would struggle to the last shred of his strength,
> eagerly, enthusiastically.

On the brink of annihilation McEwen suddenly awakes from his nightmare, rejoining civilization, as it were, after his taste of savagery.[18]

Although on the surface the tale was a parable of nature's *bellum omnium contra omnes*—and in one reading an evidence of Dreiser's own "social Darwinism"[19]—Dreiser intended something more. To be sure, McEwen, despite the horror of his dream, awakes with an "odd longing" and a "sense of comradeship lost," a reminder of the appeal of struggle and self-sacrifice to Dreiser's generation. But the final lesson is not that life is a battle with victory to the strongest. In the first place, although the vision of nature red in tooth and claw was directly from Huxley, struggle is tempered by mutual aid within each tribe, a fact that tempted Howard Fast to read the story as a plea for socialist brotherhood.[20] More importantly, as Ellen Moers has noted,[21] McEwen in awakening from his dream, transcends the battle to become the detached observer who draws his own lessons. This lesson again is that the universe is infinitely mysterious, careless of individuals, yet joining all in some higher unity. "What a strange world!" McEwen thought. "What worlds within worlds, all apparently full of necessity, contention, binding emotions and unities—and all with sorrow, their sorrow—a vague, sad something out of far-off things which has been there, and was here in this strong bright day, had been there and would be here until this odd, strange thing called *life* had ended."[22]

Sensing an unbridgeable gap between subjective illusion and objective reality, Dreiser like others of his generation, was irresistibly drawn to the notion that the truly creative mind might make its own reality, a view that was the basis of his later interest in Christian Science and spiritualism. "Matter becomes a built-up set or combinations of illusions," he wrote in *The "Genius,"* explaining Christian Science, "which may have evolved or not as one choses, but which unquestionably have been built up from nothing or an invisible, intangible idea, and have no significance beyond the faith or credence, which those who are at base spiritual give them. Deny them—know them to be what they are—and they are gone."[23]

The lesson of the squid in the tank, as Kenneth Lynn has noted,[24] lay not only in the strength of the lobster but in his all-seeing eye, just as Cowperwood and others conquered their lady loves with an almost hypnotic stare. Nietzsche, whom Dreiser first discovered through Mencken, seemed at first to postulate just such a triumph of will. "If the outline of Mr. Nietzsche's philosophy in the introduction is correct," he wrote Mencken in December 1910, "he and myself are hale fellows well met." But a week later he reconsidered. "I am deep in Nietzsche," he again wrote Mencken, "but I can't say I greatly admire him. He seems to [be] Schopenhauer confused and warmed over." Mencken for his part found the Cowperwood of the *Financier* a far cry from Nietzsche's ideal. Dreiser's hero, he wrote, seemed "still little more than an extra pertinacious money grubber and not unrelated to the average stockbroker or corner grocer"—ironically, almost the same complaint that was leveled at Mencken's Superman. Although Eugene Wilta in *The "Genius"* turned to Nietzsche in his hour of need, it was in company with the writings of Schopenhauer and William James "for the mystery of things which they suggest."[25]

The "illusion of beauty" that lured on Cowperwood, Witla, and even Carrie Meeber in *Sister Carrie* (1901) quickly became tangled in a quest for material success. This fact—as Mencken suggested—was a measure of Dreiser's inability to transcend the conventions and values he explicitly rejected. But his individualists nonetheless shunned a Darwinian course. In one of his rare uses of Darwinian rhetoric, Dreiser described the plight of Eugene Witla whose quest for an illusion of beauty (typically in the form of nubile eighteen-year-olds) led him to reject dictates of conscience and convention. To calm his conscience, one of his lovers urges him on an immoral path:

> There was system apparently in society, but also apparently it did not work very well. Only fools were held by religion, which in the main was an imposition, a graft and a lie. The honest man might be very fine but he wasn't very successful. There was a great todo about morals, but most people were immoral or unmoral. Why worry? . . . Don't let a morbid conscience get the better of you.

"Thus she counselled," Dreiser continued, "and he agreed with her. For the rest the survival of the fittest was best." Witla's final rejection of this advice, however, underlined the unacceptability of this Darwinian course, a consensus Dreiser shared with his contemporaries despite his hero's inability to relinquish his illusion of beauty. In the end Witla turns to Spencer's Unknowable, which, as it did for Spencer himself, provides escape from the struggles of earthbound existence. "What a sweet welter life is—how rich, how tender, how grim, how like a colorful symphony," he muses, taking comfort from "those mysterious constellations that make Dippers, Bears, and that remote cloudy formation known as the Milky Way."[26]

Four

For Jack London (1876-1916), peace also lurked behind the struggle and conflict of nature. But it was the peace, not of self-transcendence, but of annihilation and death. The illegitimate child of an itinerant astrologer and the wayward daughter of an Ohio businessman, London was his own best hero. He began his stormy career as an oyster pirate and petty hoodlum along the San Francisco wharves. Better than Dreiser he knew first-hand the realities of struggle. Like Dreiser he found little comfort in the customs and traditions that sustained Huxley's larger hope. Also like Dreiser he turned to Spencer, Darwin, Nietzsche, and finally socialism for help in structuring his world. In *Martin Eden* (1909), a fictional account of his career, he developed the ultimate logic of Darwinism, and in the process sounded a requiem for the optimism of mid-Victorian evolutionism.

In polemical pieces written in the early years of the new century, London evoked the Darwinian stereotype in the conventional way. American society *was* Darwinian. "As long as men continue to live in this competitive society, struggling tooth and nail with one another for food and shelter," he wrote in 1904, "that long will the scab continue to exist." Laissez faire was a creed of the devil take the hindmost in the struggle for existence in which the "strong destroys the weak, and makes a finer and more capable breed of men," he added in a discussion of "The Class Struggle." Describing "How I Became a Socialist" London also gave a Darwinian twist to Nietzsche, concerning his own state before conversion. "I could see myself only raging through life without end," he confessed, "like one of Nietzsche's *blond beasts*, lustfully roving and conquering by sheer superiority and strength." Attacking this former self, London particularly rejected Kidd's view, which he interpreted as a demand that the present generation take less "in order that race efficiency may be projected into a remote future." Workingmen, he wrote, "refuse to be the 'glad perishers' so glowingly described by Nietzsche."[27]

Although London's alternative was not always clear, his socialism was also Darwinian with a vengeance. "The struggle has become, not a struggle between individuals, but a struggle between groups," he wrote. Reluctant to abandon the Alger virtues altogether, he insisted that this group struggle merely translated the individual battle to a higher plane. "Has the individualist never speculated upon this [class struggle] being still a triumphant expression of individualism, of *group-individualism*, if the confusion of terms may be permitted." But this group-individualism differed in one regard from earlier formulations of individualism. No projected efficiency or ethics or any factor other than force would determine the outcome. "It is a question of might," London concluded in his discussion of "The Class Struggle" in the *Independent*. "Whichever class is to win, will win by virtue of its superior strength."[28]

A complex psychology sustained this equivocal position. Calling for "A New Law of Development," London appeared to out-Darwin the severest neo-Darwinist. "The social selection to which [man] is subject is merely another form of natural selection," he wrote. "There is no escaping it, save by the intervention of catastrophes and cataclysms quite unthinkable." Moreover, this law was "inexorable" because "the common man demands it." "Sociology has taught him that m-i-g-h-t spells 'right'. . . . The bourgeoisie, because it was the stronger, dragged down the nobility of the sword; and the proletariat, because it is the strongest of all, can and will drag down the bourgeoisie." Whether the proletariet would at that point demand a "new law" remained uncertain, he concluded.[29]

In *The Iron Heel* (1906) London presented a fictionalized account of "catastropes and cataclysms quite unthinkable," and a vision of the impending struggle. Like *Caesar's Column* the novel was an antiutopian tract, but presented in the form of a manuscript discovered centuries later, after an abortive proletarian revolution had resulted in the triumph of a reactionary Oligarchy and the execution in 1932 A.D. of the leading revolutionary Ernest Everhard. London apparently intended the work to be a warning that the *cult of personality* (to use a later phrase) was fatal to a successful revolutionary movement. Everhard, as his name suggested, was the archetypal London strongman, resembling London himself before his conversion to socialism. "He was a superman, a blond beast such as Nietzsche has described," the narrator wrote, "and in addition he was aflame with democracy." Unbeatable in debate, incomparable in bed, Everhard like London taunted the plutocracy with his creed of might makes right. Just as the trusts crushed small business, so socialism would replace the trusts, he wrote, embroidering a theme from Ghent's *Our Benevolent Feudalism*. "It is in line with evolution," Everhard told an audience of middle-class businessmen, themselves soon to be the victims of the iron heel of the Oligarchy. "We meet combination with greater combination. It is the winning side." The strength of the proletariet, he added, "is in our muscles, in our hands to cast ballots, in our fingers to pull triggers."[30]

This logic, however, leads directly to the bloody annihilation of the revolutionaries and to Everhard's execution. Since the manuscript fragment is discovered after a century of the Rule of Human Brotherhood, and after three-hundred years of the domination of the Oligarchy, readers are left to assume that the movement, purged of Everhard's individualism, finally succeeds.

But this Darwinian scenerio contained more than a simple warning against the cult of personality, as Frederic Jaher has noted:

> By allowing Everhard to taunt the magnates into declaring war, London reconciled the blond beast with the class struggle. Revolution would legitimize the individualist's role in socialism. . . . Violence and destruction, which would be justified in such an uprising, served the double purpose of paranoid revenge and gratification of London's death wish.

This death wish, as Jaher explained further, derived from London's impassioned quest for self-liberation coupled with an inability to accept unequivocally the values either of individualism or socialism. For this purpose the stereotype of Darwinized Nietzscheanism was made-to-order, since at one and the same time it proclaimed the triumph of the individual and his ultimate destruction. Darwinian rhetoric, like the black hats of westerns, distinguished bad guys from the good.[31]

In *Martin Eden* (1909) London pursued this logic to its remorseless conclusion. Like London himself, Martin begins life as a wharf rat and eventually achieves literary fame, but at the price of self-identity and suicide. Restating the perennial American theme of failure-in-success, and anticipating his own suicide less than a decade later, London intended the death of Eden, like that of Everhard, to be a warning against the folly and perils of rugged individualism. Eden is a confirmed social Darwinist; his Nietzscheanism could have convinced the German's severest critics of their suspicions. "The world belongs to the strong—to the strong who are noble as well and who do not wallow in the swine-trough of trade and exchange," Eden lectures Judge Morse, a representative of California's ruling class. Eden's self-destruction, in the tradition of the social Darwinian stereotype, proved the case for socialism.[32]

London admitted that his hero's Nietzscheanism was extreme. Like Huxley, Eden begins with a vision of cosmic chaos, but casts aside the customs and conventions that blinded even Darwinists to the essential truth of this perception. Judge Morse would "make believe" he endorsed the "survival of the strong," Eden charges, but in practice he like other liberals supports a variety of semisocialist measures. "[My] position is incomprehensible to you who live in a veiled lie of social organization and whose sight is not keen enough to pierce the veil," he continues. Freed from the past, Eden would impose his own order upon the universe. Like Mencken, London allowed Eden to bring Darwinism from the stable into the parlor to show the bourgeoisie what they *really* believed.[33]

In piercing the veil, London exploded the notion that the development of civilization is a process of the progressive spiritualization of mankind—a basic premise of most midcentury evolutionism. In her genteel worship of culture, Ruth Morse, whom Martin adores but then rejects, represents the epitome of civilization. But in pursuit of Martin's wealth and fame, she offers finally to live with him "in free love if you will" once he is successful. The fact that her brother secretly escorts her to the rendezvous underscores the shabbiness of the offer. In the world of London's naturalism, men are joined not in spiritual communion, but by the commonest physical drives. The cultivated Miss Morse and Martin's untutored sister equally adore happy endings; Ruth's father and Eden's boorish brother-in-law agree finally in their love of money.

A confusion between spiritual self-liberation and material success similar to Mencken's, leads also to Eden's despair. Seeking the perfect art, Eden desires more than the sordid rewards of business success. His ideal man would not "wallow in the swine-trough of trade and exchange." When Ruth Morse praises a family friend, Charles Butler, for his Algeresque rise from rags to riches, he counters with ridicule: "I feel sorry for Mr. Butler. He was too young to know better; but he robbed himself of life for the sake of thirty thousand a year that's clean wasted upon him."[34]

But Eden's quest for culture through art is similarly flawed. "I love beauty, and culture will give me a fine and deeper appreciation of beauty," he insists. "Rot, and you know it," answers a businessman friend of the Morses. "Martin's after career, not culture. It just happens that culture, in his case, is incidental to career." True to this prediction, Martin reacts angrily after receiving a pittance for his first story. Reports of two-cents a word were "a lie" that had led him astray: "He would never have attempted to write had he known that." For his closest friends, his ideal remains the Alger dream of success, in the laundry business or on a milk-ranch.[35]

Martin Eden's own success, however, brings despair. Seeking salvation through art, he finds only larger pay checks and an eternity of dinner invitations. Seeking self-realization, he loses his sense of self, as an unbridgeable gap separates Mart the hoodlum from Eden the literary lion:

> He drove along the path of relentless logic to the conclusion
> he was nobody, nothing. Mart Eden, the hoodlum, the sailor,
> had been real, had been he; but Martin Eden! the famous
> writer did not exist. Martin Eden, the famous writer, was a
> vapor that had arisen in the mob-mind and by the mob-mind
> had been thrust into the corporeal being of Mart Eden, the
> hoodlum and sailor.[36]

Seeking new life, he finally finds death at the bottom of the ocean into which he plunges while enroute to the South Seas.

For an earlier generation, evolution promised individuality and a rational understanding that allowed man to transcend and control nature. For Martin Eden the final lesson of Darwinism is the identity of man and mob, life and death, knowing and not knowing. "There was a long rumble of sound, and it seemed to him that he was falling down a vast and interminable stairway," Martin reflects as he sinks to the watery depths. "And somewhere at the bottom he fell into darkness. That much he knew. He had fallen into darkness. And at the instant he knew, he ceased to know."[37]

Unfortunately for his plea for socialism, as London later noted, many readers failed to see the point of Eden's death. "One of my motifs in this book was an attack on individualism (in the person of the hero)," he wrote fellow socialist Upton Sinclair. "I must have bungled, for not a single reviewer has discovered it." Even socialists failed to see that *Martin Eden* and even *Sea Wolf* were attacks on Nietzscheanism, he added elsewhere.[38] But this bungle, as several critics have noted,[39] revealed some basic contradictions in London's thought, with the result that his work was shot-through with the same ambivalence as that of Mencken and Dreiser. Rejecting the dream of success, he could not resist its allure. A self-proclaimed socialist, he finally preferred Nietzsche to Marx. A philosophical determinist, he could never relinquish his faith in free will. The aesthetic success of *Martin Eden*, as Charles Walcutt has written of the naturalist novels generally, depended precisely on the tension that resulted from those contradictions. Identifying with Eden's plight, the reader comes illogically to regret a fate he knows could not have been otherwise. As in *The Iron Heel*, Martin Eden's social Darwinian image expressed simultaneously London's unquenchable faith in the individual, perhaps even a lingering hope that sheer force might alone restore ancient virtues, and his reasoned conviction that science through evolution rendered these values obsolete.

If literary naturalism were unequivocally reformist, the social Darwinian stereotype might function exactly as it did in reform literature. If on the other hand it were totally pessimistic or nihilistic, its social Darwinism could be taken at face value. Rather, naturalism was neither and both—a "divided stream" as Charles Walcutt has termed it, in which faith in science joined fear that science ultimately stripped man of purpose and free will. This ambivalence underlay the appeal of individualist heroes who dreamed impossible dreams before being destroyed by the forces of a neo-Darwinian universe. The aesthetic appeal of these novels derived finally from the tension between an overarching faith in human potential and a recognition of the forces that sealed the individual's fate. But this complexity did not change the fact that the naturalists shared their contemporaries' view that social Darwinism—sheer survival in a materialistic struggle—was unworthy of humankind. Lacking the reform Darwinist's faith in control, Dreiser and London in their own way rose above the battle.

12. Imperialism and the Warrior Critique

O Evolution, what crimes are committed in thy name!
C. O. Ovington, "War and Evolution," Westminster, *153 (1900), 411.*

In its last throes the cruel Neo-Darwinian philosophy of nature and man is having one terrible, final, satanic triumph, for it is on no mean measure responsible for this incredible war, and especially for its incredible brutality.
Vernon Kellogg, "War For Evolution's Sake," Unpopular Review, *10 (1918), 146-59.*

The World War was a logical consequence of the idea that you must kill off your competitors in order to survive.
Edgar L. Heermance, Chaos or Cosmos? (1922), p. 53.

One

"The rule of the survival of the fittest applies to nations as well as to the animal kingdom," wrote a prominent Asia watcher in the wake of the Spanish-American War in 1898. Urging annexation of the territories acquired in the conflict, another expansionist argued that "the law of self preservation as well as that of survival of the fittest" demanded a larger American role in the world.[1] Nor apparently were such sentiments entirely new. As early as 1880, John Fiske discussed America's "Manifest Destiny" in evolutionary terms. In *Our Country* (1886) the publicist Josiah Strong invoked Darwin on behalf of expanded missionary efforts. During the 1890s, apostles of a New Navy, notably Stephen B. Luce and Alfred Thayer Mahan, summoned Darwin to what many thought a new and frightening militarism. In the decade before World War I, critics such as Brooks Adams and Homer Lea perfected what one historian has termed the *warrior critique*[2] of American society. By 1914—at least if critics of the "broader policy" are to be believed—imperialism and militarism based on Darwinism had reached epidemic proportions.

No historian has maintained that Darwin fostered these ideas single-handedly. For more than a century Americans developed an arsenal of expansionist arguments, Christian and secular, to justify successive acquisitions.[3] Beginning in the 1860s British and continental theorists showed increasing interest in the *imperial idea*—strictly speaking, the political control of nonsovereign peoples. Crosscurrents of cultural Anglo-Saxonism and biological racism fed the imperial urge, quite independent of Darwinism. *Machtpolitik* also flourished in Europe long before the *Origin of Species*, and its American advocates were in any case timid by comparison with their Old World counterparts.[4]

A minor problem in this interpretation has been the refusal of prominent *dramatis personae* to accept social Darwinian typecasting. Leading Spencerians, notably Carnegie and Sumner, were fervent antiimperialists in 1898.[5] Other international activists—Fiske, Strong, and even Mahan— were conspicuously subdued when it came time to discuss the abandonment of America's historic policy of nonannexation. Aware of this problem, the historian Walter LaFeber suggested that the events of 1898 split the social Darwinists into two camps: one represented by the Spencerians who wanted the fruits of international trade but wished to avoid the "violent climaxes" this policy necessarily involved; and the "more perceptive social Darwinists" like Mahan and Brooks Adams who "especially emphasized this bloody but necessary fact."[6]

By assuming the reality of social Darwinism, with the implication that some theorists welcomed international struggle, these interpretations, despite their qualifications, missed the complex functioning of Darwinism in these debates. In *external social Darwinism*, as it has been called, the pattern was similar to that in discussion of domestic policy. Annexationists, like other social controllers, began with a neo-Darwinian vision of struggle and selection, but then emphasized concentration, cooperation, and control as the means to escape this "natural" outcome among nations. This starting point, as in the case of eugenics and racism, was a peculiar product of the 1890s. It marked a significant departure from the evolutionist assumptions of Fiske, Strong, and others who earlier argued for natural expansion through trade. Antiimperialists and antimilitarists predictably saw new evidence of the sinister impact of Darwinism in all proposals they disapproved.

If the conventional portrait were accurate, it would appear ironic that the United States eventually entered World War I in the name of antimilitarism.[7] But this fact is ironic only if one assumes there was actually "a Darwinized national mentality." In fact, the antiimage of social Darwinism proved a powerful antidote against both imperialist and militarist thought in the United States, serving again as a vehicle for Christian and Enlightenment ideals. As antiimage, the spectre of a social Darwinian *Kultur* galvanized American opinion against the Hun, at the same time preparing the national psyche for a glorious struggle to preserve humanity's ideals.

This complex process of myth-making may be traced by looking in turn at the internationalist evolutionism of Fiske and Strong; the New Navalism and debates over annexation during the 1890s; the warrior critique of Brooks Adams and Homer Lea; and finally the contribution of wartime debates to the image of social Darwinism in American thought.

Two

In his speech on "Manifest Destiny" John Fiske proposed a federation of English-speaking peoples. Delivered on both sides of the Atlantic, the speech was well received, and in 1885 reached an even wider audience through the pages of *Harper's*. Drawing on the Anglo-Saxon school of history, Fiske built directly on Spencer's theory that industrialism would eventually replace militarism in human affairs. In Fiske's colorful version, "dollar-hunters" would then replace "head-hunters." Fiske disliked the term "Anglo-Saxon," which he found too narrow in the scholarly sense and "loose and slovenly" in popular speech. He thus subtituted "English race," but insisted that the latter term was more cultural than biological since as a race the English had "shown a rare capacity" in assimilating others. *Blood* and *language*, as he used the terms, were virtually interchangeable.[8]

More importantly, Fiske insisted on the peaceful nature of the process of world federation. Ironically, a passage sometimes quoted as evidence of his imperialistic tendencies and even his social Darwinism—a reference to the "great and glorious future . . . of the Anglo-Saxon race"—was meant to be a caricature of an expansionist view he did not share. In short, his own proposal for world federation of mankind was, as he insisted, "quite modest, after all."[9]

The following year, Josiah Strong (1847-1916) added missionary Christianity to this vision of an Anglo-Saxon world. Born in Napierville, Illinois, Strong brought the reform fervor of the Middle Border to his many crusades. He originally wrote *Our Country* (1886) for the Home Mission Society of the Presbyterian Church, following a general format secretaries of that organization had used since the 1840s. The work was immensely popular: 175,000 copies were sold by 1916, and individual chapters were widely reprinted.[10]

An active publicist throughout his life, Strong later shifted his emphasis slightly in *The New Era* (1893), from world evangelizing to social Christianity and the creation of an integrated world society of God's kingdom on earth, an international version of the Social Gospel then transforming American Protestantism. Although domestic issues absorbed much of Strong's attention in his later works, he returned to the international situation in *Expansion Under New World Conditions* (1900).

In these writings, as Dorothea Muller has argued persuasively, Strong no more than Fiske was a prophet of imperialist expansionism. Describing "The Anglo-Saxon and the World's Future"—the chapter primarily responsible for his social Darwinist reputation—he explicitly ruled out military conquest. Nor was political control to be the end result of the extension of Anglo-Saxonism, he explained in *The New Era*. Like Fiske he believed in the superiority of Anglo-Saxon culture. But he equally insisted that its basis lay in the twin ideals of civil liberty and spiritual Christianity. Moreover, he was not uncritical of his own race, which, as he wrote in *The New Era*, "will have to answer for many sins against the weaker races and against the weaker of their own race."[11] As appropriate to the religious nature of the work, reviewers hailed *Our Country* as a contribution to the missionary effort: neither then nor later was Strong cited in connection with foreign affairs. During the nineties, Strong personally did nothing to encourage expansionist interest in acquiring Samoa, Hawaii, or the Spanish possessions.[12]

What then of Darwinism in *Our Country* and his later works? In context, Strong's brief references to Darwin and evolution were consonant with the reform Darwinism then emerging in New Liberal circles. Like Spencer, he believed that peace was replacing war permanently. The most "civilized" people, the English-speaking nations, were also the most pacifistic. Strong shared the common assumption that in human evolution intellect and ideals supplanted physical force. Quoting George M. Beard's *American Nervousness* (1881) he embellished Spencer's Lamarckian notion that evolution produced increasingly complex nervous organization, and in turn "the highest civilization."[13]

Strong's single reference to natural selection in *Our Country* cited Darwin's belief that the United States was peopled by "the more energetic, restless, and courageous men from all parts of Europe." Quoting Spencer, Strong added that continued race mixture was the key to the creation of "a type of man more plastic, more adaptable, more capable of undergoing the modifications needful for complete social life"—an ideal of most antiformalists of the 1880s. In this sense only, the spread of Anglo-Saxon peoples would mark the survival of the fittest. To underline the peaceful

nature of the process and the role of culture in it, Strong again quoted
Darwin who in *The Descent of Man* argued that civilized nations replaced
barbarous ones "mainly, though not exclusively through their arts, which
are the products of the intellect."[14]

Strong's words sometimes masked attitudes, which under different conditions and assumptions might produce the ambivalent social Darwinism
of the naturalists or the stridency of some eugenicists. New England seemed
threatened by an influx of aliens. Arable land was rapidly being occupied.
Roman Catholics and Mormons threatened true Christianity. Intem-
perance, mammonism, and socialism weakened the social fabric. But in
the eighties his optimism prevailed. Strong reported that Huxley himself
had discounted rumors that there was a "degeneration of the original
American stock." Strong further predicted that immigration would eventually "add value to the amalgam which will constitute the new Anglo-
Saxon race of the New World."[15]

In *Expansion under New World Conditions* Strong reassessed his earlier
views of America's role and his assumptions concerning evolution after a
decade in which neo-Darwinism transformed the intellectual landscape
almost as dramatically as a brief war altered America's international
situation. Although Strong was critical of administration policy during
the war, and was briefly courted by antiimperialists in 1899, he endorsed
continued American control of the Philippines as the only feasible means,
given the international situation in 1900, to fulfill international respon-
sibilities. But he continued to oppose a general policy of overseas expansion. After 1900, as Dorothea Muller again has pointed out, he criticized
European imperialism; U.S. naval expansion; and the policies of private
corporations overseas.[16]

In the spirit of reform Darwinism, Strong in *The New Era* addressed
issues similar to those that would soon surface in debates over neo-
Darwinism. Social perils seemed more threatening than a decade earlier,
from "deterioration of the Anglo-Saxon stock" by immigration to an increase in urban crime and pauperism. "Ideals" were not separate from
"material conditions" he wrote, quoting William Graham Sumner upon
the importance of the "physical or material." Studies of heredity revealed
its great importance in human affairs. Again turning to *The Descent of
Man*, Strong quoted Darwin's warning that "Christian civilization" tended
to preserve the "defective classes."[17]

For Strong as for other reform Darwinists, this gloomy picture called for
redoubled effort and a conscious, directive social policy. America could not
afford "the survival of the unfittest," he wrote of Darwin's observation:
"the only way to obviate this evil is to raise the lower classes." The new

hereditarianism proved only how responsible men are for the "tendencies" they transmit, he added, again calling for reform. "Cooperation" was a "necessity": for business, churches, and all mankind.[18]

In *Expansion Under New World Conditions* Strong applied these lessons on a global scale. Translating the civilized arts to social efficiency, a term Kidd helped popularize, he now thought a period of intense international competition inevitable:

> Competition means struggle for existence, which so far as we can see has been necessary to the evolution of the higher forms of life; and this principle will no doubt have the same value in the higher development of the world life that it has had in the evolution of national life and lower forms. It will weed out the unfit nations and will discipline and develop not the strongest, but rather the fittest; for survival will depend more on social efficiency than on mere strength.

"However much we may disapprove these tendencies, they will doubtless ignore our disfavor and consumate themselves," he continued. His resignation implied that his earlier Spencerian pacifism had been premature.[19]

Evolution decreed that consolidation would succeed competition, and control replace freedom, he continued. The city dweller must relinquish the countryman's freedom, for example in trash disposal or home construction, he argued, drawing a rather weak analogy between domestic and international affairs. So the emergence of a tightknit world community demanded that "the world Powers . . . assume responsibility for the world's order." In short, the logic of Darwinism demanded, not a Machiavellian policy of struggle, but New Solidarism on a global scale. "There can be no existence without law," he concluded, "and the higher the form of existence, the larger the number of laws to which it owes obedience."[20]

Three

Although Spencerians took comfort in the evolution from militarism to industrialism, proponents of the New Navalism sensed the prospects of unemployment. In "The Benefits of War," which appeared in the *North American Review* in 1891, Rear Admiral Stephen B. Luce met the challenge boldly. The result was an ingenious variation on the Spencerian formula, a variation that made permanent room for peace and a modern, efficient, and well-equipped military.[21]

Luce's career was a distinguished one. Born of a well-to-do family in Albany, New York, he joined the navy at age fourteen. During the Civil War he wrote the standard work on the handling of sailing vessels. As steam replaced sail in the 1870s, he became a vocal critic of America's antiquated and dilapidated navy. Disgusted by polygot crews, and a general lack of training among officers, he helped secure the passage of the Marine Schools Act of 1874, and the establishment of the Naval War College at Newport a decade later.[22]

Opening his article with an appropriate bang, Luce declared: "War is one of the great agencies by which human progress is effected." His target in this case was Francis Wayland's *Elements of Moral Science*, a popular textbook of Luce's generation, in which Wayland affirmed that war was "contrary to the revealed will of God." In rebuttal, Luce combined Spencer with his own belief in human wickedness. "The supreme law of self-preservation compels a man to obtain his daily bread," he wrote. "Strife is continuing and everywhere in this wicked world." But he also agreed with Spencer: "The progressive spirit of the age is leaving the barbarism of war behind." Under these conditions it was imperative that suffering and loss of life be minimized, if war should develop. This result would occur only when war became the business of highly trained specialists—"the few qualified to undertake it"—which scientific schooling alone could provide.[23]

Luce's argument was a study in contradiction. Proclaiming war "an ordinance of God," he insisted he was not ("heaven forbid") "an advocate of war." Venting a neo-Calvinist spleen over "luxuries," the "corruption of morals," and the "cankers of a calm world," he pictured the evolution of a peaceful "civilization."[24] Like the literary naturalists, although making no specific use of Darwinism, Luce combined appeals to science with a nightmare vision of uncontrollable forces, natural and divine. But neither in the nineties nor later did he appeal to laws of struggle and survival to justify military conquest.

The chief strategist of the New Navalism was Alfred Thayer Mahan (1840-1914). In a sense, Mahan was Luce's protégé since it was he who invited Mahan to lecture at the Naval War College in 1885, laying the basis for Mahan's celebrated study of *The Influence of Sea Power* (1890). A brilliant student of geopolitics, Mahan in numerous articles in popular magazines argued the case for increased naval power and a foreign policy attuned to modern technology and the nation's global interests. Like Luce, he combined military advice with attacks on the materialism of our "gain-loving nation," and on socialism. In the spirit of Wordsworth's "Happy Warrior" and in tune with many late Victorians, he found in warfare, if only metaphorically, values of self-sacrifice unknown to "merely utilitarian arguments." "Conflict is the condition of all life, material and spiritual," he observed; "and it is to the soldier's experience that the spiritual life goes for its most vivid metaphors and its loftiest expressions."[25]

Although Mahan, like Strong, once or twice found the language of Darwinism useful in characterizing the international situation, he used it not to urge *machtpolitik* or imperialism. A much quoted remark of his made in 1890[26] concerning the struggle of life exemplified first, that these Darwinian phrases were not in his natural mode of speech (a point confirmed in a recent edition of his letters, which contains no references to Darwin and show no evidence of his having read social evolutionists of any persuasion);[27] and second, that he projected this image as preface to a recommendation that a strong defense could alone impose order on potential chaos.

His reasoning was even clearer on this point in a later discussion of Russia and the "Problem of Asia" (1901), where he developed a similar analogy at length:

> We are confronted with the imminent dissolution of one or more organisms, or with a readjustment of their parts, the results of which, should either come to pass, will be solid and durable just in proportion as the existence and force of natural factors either are accurately recognized, or else reach an equilibrium by free self-assertion, allowing each to find its proper place through natural selection.

But human direction could avert the unpleasant consequence of this "natural" readjustment:

> Such a struggle, however, as implied in the phrase "natural selection," involves conflict and suffering that might be avoided, in part at least, by the rational process of estimating the forces at work, and approximating to the natural adjustment by the artificial methods of counsel and agreement, which seem somewhat more suitable to the present day.

The argument was again that of reform Darwinism: "artificial mechanisms" marked the triumph of the scientific intellect over nature.[28]

In this spirit, Mahan urged annexation of Hawaii in the mid-1890s purely for strategic purposes. Coaling stations were the lifeline of a steam-powered navy, which was for defense only. When war with Spain—which he neither advocated, nor especially welcomed—produced new territories, he supported their retention in the case of the Philippines as a matter of duty, an absolute value he specifically distinguished from sovereign rights or a relativistic expediency.[29] Like Luce, Mahan could be faulted for combining evolutionist relativism with an old-fashioned absolutism that stressed rights and duties. But he was not a social Darwinist in the sense his opponents later charged.

With the end of hostilities in the Spanish-American war in August 1898, debate concerning overseas expansion assumed new urgency. The Republican party, winning a plurality of Congressional seats in the November elections, saw a mandate for retention of the territories acquired from Spain. Debate heightened in early December when President McKinley published details of the Treaty of Paris and called for acquisition of the entire Philippines. Antiexpansionists in both parties generally opposed ratification, although some urged acceptance of the treaty to end the state of war, with independence to be granted later by congressional resolution. In the tangled debates that followed, continuing well beyond the ratification of the Treaty in February 1899, imperialist, or more strictly speaking annexationist, sentiment flowered for a season, more as the result than as the cause of the preceding events. Although Darwinism still played only a minor role in justifying expansionism, these arguments assumed a familiar pattern.

For expansionists, Darwinism provided an appropriate image of a frightening and regrettable international disorder. John Barrett, a well-known writer on Far Eastern affairs, described the law of survival of the fittest as a "cruel, relentless principle." To Charles A. Conant, a banker worried about outlets for "surplus saving" of the developed nations, the same law reflected "profoundly" disturbed economic conditions. A Presbyterian clergyman, Teunis S. Hamlin, warned that struggle was a permanent aspect of the human condition. Behind the war for the Philippines and in the Transvaal "lies the fact that . . . a higher civilization is facing a lower, and the great evolutionary law of the survival of the fittest is at work," he opined. "That is nowhere a gentle law, and civilization seems unable to soften it."[30]

But the point in each case was that dynamic policies could control and contain this neo-Darwinian chaos. Conant proposed that the diplomatic and consular service be highly trained, just as were specialists in "the technical arts," to insure that "the highest efficiency will turn the scale between nations." Hamlin's major concern was the establishment of a court of international arbitration such as then being discussed at the Hague.[31]

Theodore Marburg, a proannexationist, a proponent of arbitration, and later a prime mover behind the League to Enforce Peace, spelled out assumptions implicit in each of these proposals:

In the struggle for existence, amongst lower animals as well as amongst men, the social faculty, the faculty of cooperation, has played a more important part than the individual qualities of fierceness, strength, or cunning. This is what reconciles evolution with the moral law.

International conflict was an indication that "intercourse between the nations and a regard for the interests of mankind as a whole are not old enough to have developed a code of public ethics." Cooperation with Britain to bring order to the world would foster this process. "The spirit of conquest for the sake of merely extending domain has never been rife either in England or America," Marburg added.[32]

Antiimperialists, predictably enough, presented their own readings of evolution. A writer in the *Arena* charged that the imperialist "makes the fatal mistake of overlooking Nature's supremist law: Growth! Evolution! A nation must grow just as an individual—just as a plant. Every effort to *force* its growth is an error and works evil, not good." Condemning administration policy as "un-Christian, un-American, and un-human," another critic saw a common theme in imperialist and business ideology. "The survival of the fittest is seen as truly in the development of nations as in the development of individuals and of species," he lamented. "The analogy of the business world is in the same line."[33]

At issue in this and similar arguments was the question that in more formal terms separated neo-Lamarckians and neo-Darwinians: Was evolution a gradual and cumulative process? Or was it a violent, cataclysmic one? An antiimperialist wrote that annexation involved finally the question of whether we were to be brutes or men:

Selfish fitness to survive has been the inexorable standard, and the law of the survival of the fittest is recognized as the controlling factor in the races of men and in races of brutes alike.

Adding that the "fighting monsters" and the "fighting nations" had gradually disappeared, the author saw the issue now as whether a new standard would replace the "old law of force."[34]

In searching for Darwinian rhetoric in the foreign policy debates of the 1890s, one is struck finally with the paucity of examples, whether among advocates of a New Navy or the annexationists of 1898. In this sense, even these scattered references distort the nature, tone, and complexity of the discussion. Nor do affinities between these scattered arguments and reform Darwinism generally say anything significant on the tangled question of the relation between imperialism and progressivism.[35] But these examples do suggest that, on the few occasions when Darwinism entered the debates, it expressed a deep-seated uneasiness concerning the state of national and international affairs and confirmed the need for new devices to assure stability and order.

Four

From the turn of the century until 1914, the focus of foreign policy discussion shifted from imperialism to the general position of the United States in world affairs. Among the participants, two individuals particularly deserve attention—for supporting a frankly aggressive military posture and for carrying Darwinian arguments to new extremes. One was Brooks Adams, the eccentric scion of the nation's most distinguished family. Even before the advent of "Big Stick" diplomacy Adams addressed global strategies in Rooseveltian terms in *America's Economic Supremacy* (1900), and later in *The New Empire* (1902). The other was Homer Lea, a young Stanford graduate, who, despite severe physical handicaps worked actively in China for revolution. While Theodore Roosevelt advertised the nation's might to Japan by sending the "Great White Fleet" on a world cruise, Lea warned of the "Japanese peril" to California in *The Valor of Ignorance* (1909). In perfecting the warrior critique, Adams and Lea, like Dreiser and London, probed the limits of Darwinian naturalism.[36]

During his early years, Brooks Adams (1848-1927) dabbled in domestic reform, wrote history, and grew increasingly cranky. Whether attacking the Grant administration or chronicling the decline of English Whiggism, he found decay irresistible—a trait he shared with his more illustrous brother Henry. During the seventies and eighties, well before Darwinism helped structure his sentiments, Adams's reading and experience convinced him—as he once wrote, paraphrasing the English rationalist Leslie Stephen—life was "a long struggle in which prizes are to the strong and wise." "What is any election but an appeal to force,—the will of the majority?" he asked in the wake of Grant's victory in 1872. Fascinated by power he did not possess, Adams yearned restlessly for rulers with sufficient strength to arrest the decay of modern life. During the eighteenth century, he wrote of English Whiggery, collapse occurred "because the feeble were in authority, and the weak cannot control the strong." Describing the statesman Pitt, he unwittingly characterized himself and other mugwump types: "By nature and education he was a liberal; he was forced by events to be a reactionist."[37]

In *The Law of Civilization and Decay* (1895), Adams set these sentiments in cosmic perspective. In the background lay the financial crisis of the decade—a blow to the Adams family fortunes—and his growing disgust at a "money-power" he admired almost as much as he despised it. Stated simply, his thesis was that human history followed cycles of dispersion, concentration, and finally dissipation of vital energies. As primitive dispersion led to concentration, "religious, military [and] artistic" values dominated. As fear yielded to greed, commercial instincts triumphed, eventually dissipating social energies in materialism and corruption. "The evidence seems ... to point to the conclusion that, when a highly centralized society disintegrates, under the pressure of economic competition, it is because the energy of the race has been exhausted."[38]

In developing this theory, Adams combined the cyclical view of history with the laws of the survival of the fittest and of thermodynamics. From the original Spencerian perspective, of course, these three principles were contradictory: the laws of matter and motion, of which survival of the fittest was a special case, sustained a faith in linear progress. But in Adams's version, the Darwinian law in effect introduced an ironic comment on conventional wisdom concerning business and businessmen. The concentration of wealth was the result of the "relentless work" of natural selection, he wrote. "Masses of capital were concentrated in the hands of those who were economically the strongest," he wrote of Europe's commercial revolution. In history as in nature this process took time. "Apparently nature needs to consume about three generations in perfecting the selection of a new type," he wrote to explain why the "money-lenders" did not triumph immediately after Waterloo. But this same concentration of wealth, in making "the struggle for life less severe" also initiated social decline. In short, economic survivors were not really the fittest in terms of the total well-being of society. From this special perspective, Adams thus put another peg in the coffin of Spencer's dichotomy between militancy and industrialism.[39]

In *America's Economic Supremacy* Adams, temporarily setting aside his anticommercial bias, called for an active and expansionist foreign policy based on the perfection of trusts and "State Socialism," really a sort of state corporatism. "From the retail store to the empire, success in modern life lies in concentration," he explained. Survival required not brute force but efficiency, he added, echoing the rationale of progressive imperialism. By such reasoning, as Frederic Jaher has shown, Adams moved full circle in his assessment of the Spanish American War, which he had initially described as a "silly business . . . where we can gain neither glory nor profit."[40]

This optimism, perhaps an attempt to capture an elusive public esteem during the Roosevelt years, was short-lived. A critic of democracy *and* the money-lenders, the masses, *and* the nouveau riche, Adams vacillated between the celebration of efficiency (to be achieved through reason and science), and the mourning of chaos and collapse. For Lester Ward and other New Liberals, the cure for science was more science: technology and concentration mandated sociocracy. Despite enthusiam for the development of industrial combination, Adams concluded in *The Theory of Social Revolutions* (1913) that evolution would not produce an adequate controlling intelligence: "the extreme complexity of the administrative problems presented by modern industrial civilization is beyond the compass of the capitalistic mind." Adams's list of the signs of disintegration was a catalog of complaints that progressives had been making for a decade: the "universal contempt for law . . . in the capitalist class itself"; "the chronic warfare between capital and labor"; "the slough of urban politics"; and "most disquieting of all . . . the dissolution of the family." But Adams did not propose industrial regulation, workingman's rights, or the initiative and referendum. Rather, he virtually wallowed in the prospect of social disintegration. "Should Nature follow such a course as I have suggested," he concluded, "she will settle all our present perplexities as she is apt to settle human perturbations." As one of the "Hartford Wits" put it a century earlier: "Death's a cure that never fails."[41]

In *The Valor of Ignorance* tragedy bordered on farce. Born in Denver, Homer Lea (1876-1912) found in the military what was lacking otherwise in life. Physically deformed, short in stature, and so poor in vision he eventually went blind, Lea peered with passionate intensity over the stiff collar of a self-designed uniform he wore as "lieutenant general" in Chinese revolutionary forces fighting the Empress. "As physical vigor represents the strength of man in his struggle for existence," he wrote in poignant if unintentioned self-revelation, "in the same sense military vigor constitutes the strength of nations."[42]

Arguing that Japanese invasion of California could have disastrous effects, Lea hung his largely historical and factual account on Brooks Adams's three-stage-cycle of growth and decay: the first, a struggle for existence when military prowess develops; the second, conquest; and the last, commercialism, a debased form of the original struggle—"without honor or heroism." Like warrior critics since Luce, he mixed social philosophy with military advice. The "mob-mind," he wrote in phrases that would have made Nietzsche blush, was "credulous," "savage," "primitive, hence brutal," "feminine, hence without reason," and "cognisant only of its own impulses and desires." Like Mencken, Lea suspected that the people reciprocated his feelings. "What has been written we realize does not readily find agreement," he wrote in masterly understatement. "The average citizen holds . . . quite the opposite beliefs."[43]

Like the literary naturalists and Brooks Adams, Lea conveyed two messages simultaneously. Taken at face value, *The Valor of Ignorance* was a call for more modern defense and a reasoned "Science of War." The consequence of ignoring this advice, he warned in a final chapter, could be the utter destruction of San Francisco. Yet as Lea plotted the sack of Sausalito, his enthusiasm took over. The fall of San Francisco would trigger the collapse of the entire nation: "dissension throughout the Union, blood rebellions, class and sectional insurrections, until this heterogeneous Republic, in its principles, shall disintegrate, and again into the palm of re-established monarchy pay the toll of its vanity and its scorn."[44] Debased commercialism would then find its reward. With the help of Darwinism, race war on an international scale did duty for class struggle in the topsy-turvy world of liberal reaction. Here, on a global scale, was the cataclysm the literary naturalists pictured in personal and domestic affairs. Again the image of a social Darwinian chaos summoned reason to control an outcome that imagination could not entirely resist.

Five

The fact that Nietzsche was German sealed the connection between Darwinism, militarism, and the Kaiser. Thanks to Bernhardi's *Germany and the Next War* (1911) Nietzsche's connection with German militarism, long suspected, was now "proved." In Weismann, neo-Darwinism also had Germanic roots. By extrapolation, militarism and the elitism of the Junkers shared a common rationale. An English observer parodied this popular logic: "Germany is inundated with the teachings of Treitschke. Treitschke divines his ethical theory from Nietzsche. Nietzsche's philosophy is based on Darwinism: therefore Darwinism is to blame for the moral attitude of Germany." Although this critic found the chain of reasoning highly dubious, three decades of suspicion of Darwinism made it easy for Americans to overlook the gaps. Nietzsche, wrote a Baptist clergyman, summing up the case, had drawn under his banner "artists, plunderers, liberated Jews, epicures and high-livers, materialists scientific and aesthetic, captains industrial and military, crowned heads and financiers, lovers of Nature and the free life."[45]

H. L. Mencken, whose pro-German sympathies made him suspect to American authorities, was aghast at these developments. The English were repaying Nietzsche's scorn "with compound interest," he wrote in 1915. "All things vile are now being ascribed to him over there: the adjective Nietzschean becomes of even more sinister significance than American." Two years later, he felt the sting of these charges personally when agents of the U.S. Department of Justice called upon him, in his words, "to meet the charge that I was an intimate of 'the German Monster,' Nietsky."[46]

As was the case with reform Darwinists in other areas, the indictment of Darwinized *machtpolitik* was not without irony since American progressives meanwhile invoked their own reading of Darwinism in defense of the Anglo-American spiritual struggle against *Kultur*. To John Dewey, whose support of the war made him a special target of antiwar radicals, the peace movement seemed hopelessly blind to the role of force in human affairs. "Is our industrial life other than a continued combat to sift the strong and the weak?" he asked readers of the *New Republic* in 1916. From this fact (which he presumably disapproved) he declared that war might after all accomplish something positive (which in this case he approved).[47]

During the war years the term social Darwinism itself also gained wider circulation. Writing in *The Public* in 1918, David Starr Jordan devoted an entire article to critics of social Darwinism—a doctrine that had developed "in Germany" during the preceding half-century. "The philosophy of 'social Darwinism' involves not merely the facts of struggle, with the elimination of the unadapted or so-called 'unfit', among humanity," he explained. "Its advocates insist that the strong must 'get behind' Evolution by obliterating the weak." A prominent eugenicist, Jordan was a leading spokesman for the view that war had negative eugenic effects. He viewed this social Darwinism as "a vicious and ignorant misinterpretation of Darwin's teachings." As an antidote, he treated readers to a discussion of "Mutual Aid" and "Altruism."[48]

The term social Darwinism also surfaced in several studies of British and American social thought that were more permanent legacies of the wartime debate. "In one book after another—German and English—the reader is bound to notice how such a scientific hypothesis as evolution, properly applicable to biology, is accepted as a genuine law in the improper field of sociology," wrote Columbia historian Carlton Hayes, announcing a view he would develop in the first of many editions of his *Political and Cultural History of Europe* (1916).[49] Works supporting this interpretation included Ernest Barker's, *Political Thought in England* (1915); Lucius M. Bristol's *Social Adaptation* (1915); George Nasmyth's *Social Progress and the Darwinian Theory* (1916); George R. Davies's *Social Environment*; Ralph Barton Perry's *The Present Conflict of Ideals* (1918); and Arthur J. Todd's, *Theories of Social Progress* (1918). With the exception of Nasmyth, an active internationalist and peace advocate, all these authors were academics, mostly social scientists, a fact that doubtless gave weight to their charges. A direct source for a second wave of wartime studies in the1940s, these works brought the term social Darwinism squarely to the public's attention.[50]

Although disagreeing somewhat as to who was and was not a social Darwinist, these authors together delineated the outlines of its influence on domestic and foreign policy thinking: on laissez faire individualism, eugenics, racism, and socialism; and on imperialism and militarism. Wartime concerns were never far in the background. "Racialism" wrote Arthur Tood, a sociologist at the University of Minnesota, "also attracted some men of science and was partly responsible for the false interpretation of Darwin's principles which currently goes by the name Social Darwinism, and which seems to have been financed, in part at least in Germany, by the Krupps, who had everything to gain by the exploitation of chauvinism."[51] Likewise, Nietzsche figured prominently in each account.

In light of the full-dress portraits of social Darwinism two decades later, omissions and inclusions were sometimes curious. All seemed to assume, as Nasmyth stated explicitly, that Darwin, Wallace, and Huxley were innocent since they made "ethical factors" the "chief cause of social progress and human evolution." But among his social Darwinists Nasmyth included Spencer *and* Lester Ward, the latter of whom he attacked at length for the alleged implications of his views for international affairs. Todd found in Sumner's work "an American echo of English and German selectionism," but equivocated in the case of Spencer who in *Man vs. the State* was simply "a very cranky dyspeptic philosopher, imagining a sort of pseudo-science which afflicted more than some of his generation with the disease of Social Darwinism." Although including the socialists among the false Darwinians, Ralph Barton Perry also separated Spencer from their company.[52]

Despite agreement that social Darwinism was widespread, specific examples were sparse. In a preface to Nasmyth's book, the pacifist Norman Angell confessed that one long statement was his own "imagining" of the social Darwinist response. At another point he found evidence of laissez faire Darwinism in a critic's stereotype of the position. Perry found the Darwinian defense of free competition "best represented," not in a Robber Baron or Gilded Age social scientist, but in the economist and fellow Harvard professor Thomas Nixon Carver.[53]

Social Darwinism was not yet a household word. Reviewing Nasmyth's study, the *Nation* found "wearisome" the constant "reiteration of the phrase 'distorted social Darwinism.' ... " Many reviewers of this and the other works ignored the theme entirely. But the final dimensions of social Darwinism were at least in sight. Nor did the authors hide their own disagreement with its many forms. "The superficial appeal to Darwin as though he had taught that evolutionary progress rested on brute animal struggle," wrote another reviewer of Nasmyth in the *Survey*, "needs to be again and again exposed." Before a second wartime generation responded to this challenge, various crosscurrents deepened this conviction.[54]

Epilogue
From Histrionics to History

It was Darwin who at least typified the rigorous logic that wrecked the universe for me and for millions of others.
Gamaliel Bradford, Darwin *(1926), p. 247.*

No doubt Darwinism and the idea of evolution affected men's imaginative outlook; arguments were derived in favour of free competition and also of nationalism.
    Bertrand Russell, *"The Effect of Science on Social Institutions,"* Survey, *52 (1924), 5.*

Unlike many slogans of World War I, social Darwinism continued to flourish in the interwar years. At the Scopes trial in Tennessee no less than in the work of leading sociologists and even literary critics, the suspicion lingered that someone, somewhere was twisting Darwinism for evil purposes. During the 1930s, renewed debate between individualists and collectivists revived charges of brutal Darwinism. The resumption of hostilities with Germany likewise resurrected images of Darwinian *machtpolitik.* By 1941 the burgeoning means of social Darwinism sparked a vigorous exchange in the pages of *Science and Society.* Within a few years the concept was an established part of American historiography.

At Dayton, Tennessee, William Jennings Bryan in 1924 gave a new twist to an apparently inexhaustible theme. The issue, of course, was the teaching of evolution in the schools of the state. For this crime, John T. Scopes attracted national attention and the personal involvement of such notables as Bryan for the prosecution; Clarence Darrow, the Chicago lawyer and civil libertarian, for the defense; and H. L. Mencken as one of many representatives of the national press. Although the context of the trial was the religious implications of Darwinism, the subject of its social consequences soon intruded. Did Bryan actually imagine that the teaching of evolution could harm the young? Darrow demanded. Recalling that Darrow had recently defended the celebrated Chicago murderers, Leopold and Loeb, for the "senseless" killing of young Bobby Franks, Bryan saw his opening. "It is this doctrine that gave us Nietzsche, the only great authority who tried to carry this [doctrine of evolution] to its logical conclusion," Bryan shot back. Was it not well known that Leopold and Loeb cited Nietzsche as the inspiration for their attempt to transcend conventional morality? Had not Darrow, in their defense, stated that the University of Chicago contained more than a thousand volumes of his works? Had the lawyer not then demanded who was to blame: the university? the publishers? or the boys themselves? Darrow, in an excess of environmentalism, had of course intended to say that none were to blame. He now denied that Nietzsche taught any such Darwinian lessons. But for the moment at least Bryan appeared to carry the day with the help of a popular assumption.[1]

No mere courtroom stunt, Bryan's argument reflected a suspicion he had been nurturing for some time. Although he had long defended religious orthodoxy against modernism, he was for many years curiously quiet on the subject of Darwinism. An exception was a brief reference in a popular speech, "The Prince of Peace" (1904), in which he noted that he did "not accept the Darwinian theory" because it denied the spiritual element in man. Although he would "not quarrel" with its scientific truth, he cited its reactionary social implications as *prima facie* evidence of its falsity, that is, it taught "the merciless law by which the strong crowd out and kill of the weak." Although Bryan did not say so explicitly, the implication was that a blow against Darwinism was a strike for both Christianity and democracy.[2]

During the war, anti-Nietzsche propaganda confirmed this conviction. Preaching to a Bible class in Miami in 1916, Bryan told of an American minister in London who asked his congregation not to blame Nietzsche or Germany for the war. A German who was present at the time also defended his country, noting that it was completely untrue that Nietzsche derived his arguments from Darwin. Although both speakers were denying the wartime logic—Nietzsche was not responsible for Junker militarism; he was not a Darwinist—Bryan drew precisely the opposite lesson. "I have found ... that the evolution theory has been often consciously or unconsciously absorbed in a way which has a tendency to paralyse the conscience," he continued. "Whether men know it or not, they have permitted it to become antagonistic to those principles of Christianity which make the strongest the servants of humanity, not its oppressors."[3]

By the 1920s Bryan's conviction matured. Discussing "The Menace of Darwinism" (1921) he cited two instances of Darwinian reactionism. One was eugenics. A champion of this cause, Archdall Reid, had even gone so far as to defend the use of alcohol "on the ground that it rendered a service to society by killing off the degenerate." Darwin himself "by implication" condoned equally brutal policies. The other instance was Nietzscheanism, "the ripened fruit of Darwinism." Bryan admitted he had not made this connection until the war, when he had seen "the doctrine of the 'individual sufficient for himself'—the brute doctrine of the 'survival of the fittest' . . . driving men into a life and death struggle from which sympathy and the spirit of brotherhood are eliminated."[4]

Bryan joined the antievolutionist crusade not to escape politics but, as Lawrence Levine has argued, "in order to combat a force which he held responsible for sapping American politics of its idealism and its progressive spirit." But what has not been noted is that his identification of Darwinism, irreligion, and political reaction was both natural and compelling in light of the popular belief that Darwinism was destroying American ideals. Bryan's "evidence" for this assertion consisted of reform Darwinists' statements to the same effect (for example by E. A. Ross), and the misreading of Archdall Reid's perverse attempt to show where the popular opposition to eugenics led.[5] More revealing were Bryan's own equivocations as he described what some of his countrymen believed "by implication," "consciously or unconsciously," and "whether men know it or not."

By the time he reached Dayton, H. L. Mencken was almost immune to such charges. The Darwinian jungle that once had seemed to demand the domineering presence of a creative Superman, seemed now more like a zoo for his own amusement. Biology for him was now less a vehicle for social philosophy, as in *Men vs. the Man*, than a stick to poke fun at *Homo Neandertalensis*. Attacks on Nietzsche, such as Bryan now launched, seemed "frankly idiotic—the naive pish-posh of suburban Methodists, notoriety seeking college professors, almost illiterate editorial writers, and other such numb skulls." But he had to admit that such anti-Darwinian attacks could be effective. Popular opinion, he noted, held that "Darwin was a scoundrel, and Herbert Spencer another, and Huxley a third—and that Nietzsche is to the three of them what Beelzebub is to a trio of bad boys."[6]

Writing two years after the Scopes trial, a more sober commentator noted in the *Independent* that evolution had come to stand in the minds of the antievolutionists for almost every evil: Leopold and Loeb, communism, and the fact "that the Kaiser started the war because he was an evolutionist." In *The War on Modern Science* (1927) the president of the Science League of America provided further evidence of similar reasoning. In censuring a professor dismissed from a state college for using John Herman Randall's *Mind in the Making*, one Presbyterian congregation observed with relief "that the pupils of Tennessee are to be congratulated that this State institution does not follow in the steps of the German infidels in teaching that man sprang from a lower order of beings."[7]

While fundamentalism kept suspicion of Darwin alive at the grassroots, social Darwinism made its way into American scholarship. Among sociologists, in particular, the concept continued to play an important role in the interwar years. Since the 1890s the idea of misapplied Darwinism had served to delimit the province of the discipline at a time when American "psychological" sociology was differentiating from the "biological" approaches of Spencer; the continental organicists; and the eugenicists who by the beginning of the century dominated British sociology. Quite apart from social conviction, the concept had important implications for choice of subject ("human achievement" in Ward's term) and for approach (the reduction of social institutions and practices to the "interests" of individuals).

During the 1920s the sins of the social Darwinists seemed more than ever methodological. "For certainly social Darwinism in its prevalent mode of interpretation . . . had little to offer that bore encouragingly on the situation," wrote Fay Berger Karpf in *American Social Psychology* (1932), describing psychology on the eve of the arrival of James and Dewey:" . . . traditional psychological and social theory with its individualistic emphasis and association with laissez faire doctrine had little to offer that seemed relevant." The neo-positivist sociologist Read Bain used the term to denounce prewar evolutionism generally, including the work of Albion Small, for its "arm-chair" approach to social analysis. Although Bain confined the term to conservatives who threatened to make sociology a dismal science, he made it clear that Ward's "optimistic, if somewhat esoteric, intellectualism" was no better from the methodological point of view.[8]

Sociologists trained in the prewar years confined the term even more narrowly to the work of Gumplowicz and Ratzenhofer and the racial selectionism of Lapouge, thus preserving Ward's initial usage.[9] The war, however, gave this charge new force. "We are told," wrote Edward Cary Hayes of the University of Illinois in a textbook on *Sociology and Ethics* (1921), "that whether we like it or not, it is useless and foolish to try to repeal a law of nature, and that it is a law of nature that conflict is the method of progress and that for the sane and scientific men the issue of unmitigated conflict is the only right." This so-called social Darwinism, he added, "has not even the support of biological analogy."[10]

As debate over individualism and collectivism revived in the 1930s, other sociologists broadened their definition. In an article on Darwinism in *The Encyclopedia of the Social Sciences* (1931) Frank Hankins provided a lengthy list of *isms* for which Darwin allegedly provided support. In Emory Bogardus's *A History of Social Thought* (1928) and Charles A.

Ellwood's *History of Social Thought* (1939), two studies by leading sociologists, the history of social Darwinism took further shape. "According to [the social Darwinists]," wrote Bogardus, simplifying the issue, "the tooth and fang struggle for existence among animals is the normal procedure among human beings."[11]

The most extensive, and doubtless the most sophisticated treatment, however, appeared in Talcott Parsons's *The Structure of Social Action* (1937), probably the most influential work written by an American sociologist. For Parsons (who drew on the Italian sociologist Vilfredo Pareto on this point) social Darwinism marked the epitome of that "anti-intellectualistic" positivism which, in denying the importance of human intentions and activity, made history an "impersonal process over which [men] have no control." Parsons's targets were both instinct theory (an extreme of hereditarianism) and behaviorism (an extreme of environmentalism). He was less interested in labeling this or that individual a social Darwinist than in showing the position was the *logical* end result of a tradition of empiricism and utilitarianism that stretched finally back to Locke.[12] Despite the complexity of his argument, Parsons's strategy was thus remarkably like that characterizing attacks on social Darwinism since the 1880s. That is, it was the "logical end result" of other positions he wished to attack.

For American sociologists, as for historians, the 1940s marked a coming of age for the concept. The original index to the *American Journal of Sociology*, from its start in 1896 through the 1930s, contained a total of three references to social Darwinism, all explicit uses of the term by Lester Ward and others. However, a revised index for these same years, prepared in light of the growing popularity of the term in sociological circles, contained more than twenty citations.[13]

Among literary critics social Darwinism proved a convenient weapon in the humanist assault on prewar realism and naturalism. In his study *On Contemporary Literature* (1917), initially a series of articles in the *Nation*, Stuart Sherman blasted Theodore Dreiser's "crude and naively simple naturalistic philosophy." Curiously, Sherman, a spokesman for the New Humanism that would flower in the 1920s, found little to fault in Dreiser's depiction of contemporary America:

> In reality our so-called society is a jungle in which the struggle for existence continues, and must continue, on terms substantially unaltered by legal, moral, or social conventions. . . . In the struggles which arise in the jungle through the conflicting appetites of its denizens, the victory goes to the most physically fit and mentally

ruthless, unless the weaklings, resisting absorption, combine against him and crush him by sheer force of numbers.

But taking this "reality" as a starting point, the humanist sought his ideal in opposing nature, a strategy similar to that outlined two decades earlier in Huxley's Romanes address. "The notion that the Darwinian 'survival of the fittest' indicates an aristocratic tendency in nature, he deems a vulgar error based upon a confusion of adaptation to environment with conformity to ideal ends," Sherman lectured. "The line of progress for human society must therefore be in the direction of this human impetus. It cannot possibly lead 'back to nature,' but must steadily show a wider divergence from the path of natural evolution." The war gave the case special urgency. Dreiser's crude naturalism was "such as we find in the mouths of exponents of the new *Real-Politik*." "The application . . . of biological terminology to human institutions—now common among German and other political philosophers—is fraught with confusion and illegitimate inferences," he cautioned.[14]

The critic Lewis Mumford, reviewing several new works on Charles Darwin for the *New Republic* in 1928, contributed another variation of the humanist critique. Darwin, the scientific observer, was a true humanist, Mumford wrote:

Darwin, the man, is one of the most loveable characters in the annals of the nineteenth century: when he is breeding pigeons or meeting with pigeon fanciers, when he is watching orchids or barnacles or experimenting, with the aid of a tender young lady, upon the emotions of an infant, he is like some great earth-god mingling with his own creations: his patience, his singleminded devotion, his tireless communion with nature, put him at the head of that great company of naturalists who have made man at home in a world so long foreign, and have increased the sympathy of human beings with the whole linkage of organic creation.

But Darwin, the theorist of natural selection, was another matter! Regrettably, this Darwin was also human in his desire for applause, which led him to accept credit for reformulating Malthus's dubious law of survival of the fittest, a law that was no more than a "rationalization for the survival of the bourgeoisie." "One might pass over this in silence, were it not for the fact that the Darwin-Malthus myth has played the devil in social apologetics," Mumford continued: "it has been used to defend almost every enormity from the partition of Africa to the Great War; for it gave the sanction of 'science' to all sorts of perverse aims."[15]

A subsequent exchange of letters in the *New Republic* replayed arguments of five decades earlier. A correspondent from Ithaca, New York, noted correctly that Spencer not Darwin coined the phrase survival of the fittest, which in any case meant only the "best fitted to survive in a given environment," for example, the tape worm. From New Mexico a second contributor, defending Mumford, argued that both Darwinism and fundamentalist Christianity were "religions," true only to the faithful and not others. (The idea that science was after all merely another set of superstitions was a prominent part of humanist antiscientism in these years.) The *Origin of Species*—"the Gospel according to St. Charles"—could like the Bible prove anything. At its core, however, was a reactionary social prejudice. "Despite . . . the host of Darwinian apologists, the connotation was just what Mr. Mumford says it was: the 'iron law' and the damnation of the poor."[16]

In the 1930s, New Deal battles moved Darwinian individualism to center stage. In the *Rise of American Civilization* (1927) the historian Charles A. Beard stressed the role of evolution (Darwinism) in undermining the defense of "permanent institutions," and made only passing reference to the fact that Spencer's attacks on socialism were "reassuring to the leaders in the American acquisitive process." Writing in *The Encyclopedia of Social Sciences* three years later, however, he shifted his emphasis to stress the support Darwinism "naturally" gave to the "tooth and claw struggle of Manchesterianism."[17] By the middle of the decade scattered textbooks were incorporating this view of business ideology—for example, Charles C. Chapman's *Business and Banking Thought* (1936) and Edward R. Lewis's *History of American Political Thought* (1937). While acknowledging that it was "difficult to put one's finger" on specific examples of evolutionist conservatism, Lewis observed that "opponents of . . . liberalism . . . continually declared that the measures they opposed would deny the free play of the struggle for existence and the survival of the fittest." This philosophy was expressed "again and again in the Progressive Campaign of 1912."[18]

On the left, the philosopher Sidney Hook revived earlier debate concerning Marx's debt to Darwin. A reviewer, criticizing a work by the socialist Norman Thomas, alleged that socialism was "the result of the reading of the Darwinian hypothesis into social science." Hook argued that Marx himself viewed such misinterpretations of his views "as a form of social Darwinism"—that is, a position that neither Hook nor his mentor accepted.[19]

The outbreak of war in the early 1940s shifted debate back to Darwin's contribution to militarism. Describing "Democracy's Intellectual Fifth

Column," a writer in the *Catholic World* blasted "so-called social Darwinists." Summing up the case, William McGovern's *From Luther to Hitler* (1941) devoted an entire chapter to "Social Darwinists and Their Allies," a group that now inclined Spencer, Gumplowicz, and the eugenicists who were "closely associated." So pervasive was the assumption that natural selection was equivalent to international warfare that a radio announcer concluded a dramatic narration of war news with a plaintive lament, "What a pity that Charles Darwin was ever born!"[20]

The question of the definition of social Darwinism came to a head in an extended exchange in the pages of *Science and Society* during 1941. In the spring issue, Bernhard J. Stern a professor at Columbia attacked Earnest Albert Hooten's *Why Men Behave as Apes* (1940), observing that his "antidemocratic, ruthless, social-Darwinian utterances indicate why Hooten has become the scientific playboy of fascist and neo-fascist groups in this country." In response, the British scientist J. B. S. Haldane attacked the implication that Darwin himself supported such views. He also essayed his own definition of social Darwinism:

> The actual implication of Darwinism to contemporary capitalist society is quite clear. The poor leave more offspring behind them in each generation than the rich. So they are fitter from a Darwinian point of view. . . . If any meaning can be attached to the word Social Darwinism, it should mean the recognition of this fact. . . . If social Darwinism is ruthless, it is ruthless not to the workers, but to the ideals of Professor Hooton and those who agree with him.[21]

Stern, who had employed the concept in his earlier work on American social theory, dissented vigorously. The term social Darwinism was "not of [his] making," but described theorists who ignored the "all important" fact that man's culture distinguished him from the animals. In stressing only physical survival as measured in birth rates, Haldane in effect fell into the same error as the social Darwinists.[22]

As other joined the debate, it was apparent that the issue was more complicated than Stern maintained. While agreeing with his central point, a New York correspondent named Emily Grace quoted Marx and Engels to show that Darwinism had contributed to their social thought. Engels in fact used "Darwinian terms because he is dealing with what is in a sense animal behavior," she noted of a passage in which Engels had described the transference from nature to society of the "Darwinian struggle for individual existence." That is, although she did not make this point, Darwin provided the language for describing social developments of which a theorist did not approve! On the whole, she concluded, it was "perhaps unfortunate that so misleading a term as social Darwinism has become accepted terminology. . . ."[23]

The historical studies of the 1940s built directly on the sources and concerns of the previous two decades. "Although it was meant to be a reflective study rather than a tract for the times," Richard Hofstadter later wrote of his *Social Darwinism in American Thought* (1944), "it was naturally influenced by the political and moral controversy of the New Deal era."[24] His emphasis on eugenics, imperialism, and militarism joined the general debate over fascism in which intellectuals in and around Columbia took such an active part in these years.[25] Similarly, his insistence that the "life of man in society" be explained in the "distinctive terms of cultural analysis" underlined the point Stern and others had been making for some time, and also anticipated the sociological perspective of Hofstadter's later work.

Although Hofstadter's study, the most comprehensive and brilliant of the new works, resembled attacks on social Darwinism since the 1880s, it differed in that the New Liberalism of the progressives no less than the conservatism of their opponents was under indictment. Although Hofstadter muted the point, a clear implication was that, in its allegiance to evolutionism, the New Liberalism ended in racism, eugenics, and militarism, a charge he developed explicitly in *The Age of Reform* (1955). In this analysis the demon was not science per se, but scientism, the false metaphysics that was attached to Darwinism. The solution was to divorce liberal theory from metaphysics, to declare an end to ideology. In contributing to this mood of the 1950s, the assault on social Darwinism, however distorting of the past, thus played one last role in the reorientation of American social thought. Then as earlier, its effectiveness as social myth depended in part on this very distortion.

Notes

Introduction:
The Idea of Social Darwinism

1. Student response on Advanced Placement in American History Examination, May, 1969; *Delaware County* (Pa.) *Times*, 24 January 1970.

2. Richard Hofstadter, *Social Darwinism in American Thought*, rev. ed. (Boston, 1955), p. 202; Eric Goldman, *Rendezvous with Destiny* (New York: Vintage, 1956), pp. 72-81. Textbooks incorporating this account include Dumas Malone and Basil Rauch, *Empire for Liberty* (1960); Thomas A. Bailey, *American Pagent*, 2nd ed. (1961), Dexter Perkins and Glyndon Van Deusen, *The United States of America* (1962); Harvey Wish, *Society and Thought in Modern America* (1962); John Blum et al., *The National Experience* (1963); and John A. Garraty, *The American Nation*, 3rd ed. (1975).

3. Achille Loria, "Darwinisme Social," *Revue Internationale de Sociologie*, 4 (1896) 440-51; Emile de Laveleye and Herbert Spencer, *L'Etat et l'Individu, ou Darwinisme social et christianisme* (Florence, 1885); Oscar Schmidt, "Science and Socialism," *Popular Science*, 14 (1879), 557-91; Jacques Novicow, *La Critique du Darwinisme social* (Paris, 1910); Lester Ward, "Social Darwinism," *American Journal of Sociology*, 12 (1907), 709-10. Other early uses of the term include Emile Gautier, *Le Darwinisme social* (Paris, 1880); G. Vadalà-Papale, *Darwismo naturale e Darwinismo sociale*, (Torino, 1882); Gabriel de Tarde, "Darwinisme naturel et Darwinisme social," *Revue Philosophique* 17 (1884), 607-37; and Gabriel Ambon, "Darwinisme social," *Journal des Economistes*, 5th ser. 39 (1899), 343-52.

4. Floyd N. House, *The Development of Sociology* (New York, 1936), p. 158; Howard Becker and Harry E. Barnes, *Social Thought from Lore to Science*, 3 vols. (New York, 1961), ch. 19; Bernhard J. Stern, "Reply," *Science and Society*, 5 (1941), 374; unnamed Soviet dictionary quoted ibid., 6 (1942), 71.

5. Merle Curti, *The Growth of American Thought*, 2nd ed. (New York, 1943), p. 576; Hofstadter, *Social Darwinism*, 1st ed. (New York, 1944), p. vii.

6. Frank Hankins, review of Hofstadter, *Annals of the American Academy*, 237 (1945), 229; Bert J. Loewenberg, review of Hofstadter, *American Historical Review*, 50 (1945), 820-21; Albert G. Keller, "What Did Darwin Really Say?" *Saturday Review of Literature*, 28 (1945), 8; Edward S. Corwin, "The Impact of the Idea of Evolution on the American Political and Constitutional Tradition," Stow Persons, ed. *Evolutionary Thought in America* (New Haven, 1950).

7. Charles A. Beard and Mary Beard, *The Rise of American Civilization* (New York, 1927), pp. 406-7, 743; Vernon L. Parrington, *Main Currents in American Thought*, 3 vols. (New York, 1927-30), 3: 198-99, 293, 402.

8. Jacques Barzun, *Darwin, Marx, Wagner* (London, 1942), p. viii; Carlton J. H. Hayes, *A Generation of Materialism* (New York, 1941), p. 363; Hofstadter, *Social Darwinism*, 1st ed., p. vii; Thomas Cochran and William Miller, *The Age of Enterprise* (New York, 1942), p. v; Curti, *Growth*, p. 799; John Bartlett Brebner, "Laissez Faire and State Intervention," *Tasks of Economic*

History, 8 (1948), 65. See also Nicholas Pastore, *The Nature-Nurture Controversy* (New York, 1949), pp. 5-10.

9. Edward Corwin, *Constitutional Revolution Ltd.* (Claremont, Ca., 1941), p. 83; Benjamin Twiss, *Lawyers and the Constitution* (Princeton, 1942), pp. 106, 115-16, 154-55; Stow Persons, ed., *Evolutionary Thought in America* (New Haven, 1950). See also Robert G. McCloskey, *American Conservatism* (Cambridge, Mass., 1951), pp. 26-30, 132-33; Philip Wiener, *Evolution and The Founders of Pragmatism* (Cambridge, Mass., 1949); and Daniel Aaron, *Men of Good Hope* (New York, 1951).

10. Irvin G. Wyllie, *The Self Made Man* (Rutgers, 1954), p. 86; "Social Darwinism and the Businessman," *Proceedings of the American Philosophical Society*, 103 (1959), 629-35. For social theory see Kenneth E. Bock, "Darwin and Social Theory," *Philosophy of Science*, 22 (1955), 123-34.

11. Wyllie, "Social Darwinism," p. 635.

12. Joseph F. Wall, *Andrew Carnegie* (New York, 1970); Milton Berman, *John Fiske: The Evolution of a Popularizer* (Cambridge, Mass., 1961); Dorothea Muller, "Josiah Strong and American Nationalism," *Journal of American History*, 53 (1966), 487.

13. Raymond J. Wilson, ed., *Darwinism and the American Intellectual* (Homewood, Ill., 1967), p. 93. See also Cynthia Eagle Russett, *Darwin in America* (San Francisco, 1976), ch. 4.

14. Wyllie, "Social Darwinism," p. 635.

15. Robert C. Bannister, " 'The Survival of the Fittest Is Our Doctrine': History or Histrionics" *Journal of the History of Ideas*, 31 (1970), 377-98.

16. Cf. Hofstadter, *Social Darwinism*, rev. ed., p. 4: "England gave Darwin to the world, but the United States gave to Darwinism an unusually quick and sympathetic reception." All subsequent references to Hofstadter, unless otherwise noted, are to the revised 1955 Beacon Press edition.

17. Robert C. Bannister, "William Graham Sumner's 'Social Darwinism,' " *History of Political Economy*, 5 (1973), 89-109.

18. Commenting on my article in the *Journal of the History of Ideas*, Michele I. Aldrich, "United States: Bibliographical Essay," in Thomas F. Glick, ed., *The Comparative Reception of Darwinism* (Austin, Tex., 1974) wrote: "Bannister believes that the reform thinkers were not inspired by Darwin's own work but went back to it after rejecting the conservatives in order to strengthen their case." On the contrary: reformers were doubly inspired by the *Origin of the Species*. Despite the ambivalence of their reaction, they were from the start *the* Darwinian social theorists.

19. Herbert Spencer, *Man vs. the State* (London, 1892: bound with *Social Statics*, abridged and revised), p. 366.

20. Hofstadter, *Social Darwinism*, p. 204.

21. Cf. the first edition of Samuel E. Morison and Henry Steele Commager, *The Growth of the American Republic* (New York, 1930) with the 4th ed. of 1950, esp. 2: 269-70, 274-75.

22. Edward C. Kirkland, *Dream and Thought in the Business Community* (Ithaca, N.Y., 1956).

23. See John Buenker, "The Progressive Era," *Mid-America*, 51 (1969), 175; and David Thelen, *The New Citizenship* (Columbia, Mo., 1972).

24. Robert Wiebe, *The Search for Order* (New York, 1967); and "The Progressive Years," in William H. Cartwright and Richard L. Watson, *The Reinterpretation of American History and Culture* (Washington, 1973).

25. Michael Zuckerman, "The Nursery Tales of Horatio Alger," *American Quarterly*, 24 (1972) 191-209.

26. Samuel C. T. Dodd, *Combinations* (New York, 1888), p. 14; Henry D. Lloyd, *Man the Social Creator* (New York, 1906), pp. 218-220.

27. Quotations from Wilson Smith, *Professors and Public Ethics* (Ithaca, 1956), pp. 63-4, 65-6.

28. Ibid., p. 73.

Chapter 1
The Scientific Background

1. Francis Darwin, ed., *The Life and Letters of Charles Darwin*, 3 vols. (London, 1887), 2: 262 [Darwin to Charles Lyell, 4 Jan., 1860], quoted in James A. Rogers, "Darwinism and Social Darwinism," *Journal of the History of Ideas*, 33 (1972), 269; Marx to F. Engels, 18 June 1862 in Marx and Engels, *Gesamtausgabe* (Frankfurt, 1927), quoted in Conway Zirkle, "Commentary," *Critical Problems in the History of Science*, ed. Marshall Clagett (Madison, 1959), p. 456; Friedrich Engels, *Dialectics of Nature* (New York, 1940), p. 19, quoted in Gerald Runkle, "Marxism and Charles Darwin," *Journal of Politics*, 23 (1961), 108-26; Nietzsche, *The Joyful Wisdom*, p. 290, quoted in Gertrude Himmelfarb, *Darwin and the Darwinian Revolution* (London, 1959), 345. See also Chapter 6, note 57 below.

2. Barzun, *Darwin, Marx, Wagner*, pp. 69, 103; Hofstadter, *Social Darwinism*, p. 201.

3. Rogers, "Darwinism and Social Darwinism," pp. 265-80. See also John C. Greene, "Darwin as a Social Evolutionist," *Journal of the History of Biology*, 10 (1977), 1-27.

4. Howard Gruber, *Darwin on Man* (London, 1974), p. 24.

5. Walter F. Cannon, "The Uniformitarian-Catastrophist Debate," *Isis*, 51 (1960), 39.

6. Ibid. pp. 39, 44. The original sources for the quotations are Roderick Murchison, *The Silurian System*, 2 vols. (London, 1839), 1: 576; and Charles Lyell, *Life, Letters and Journals*, ed. Katherine Lyell, 2 vols. (London, 1881), 2: 376. On Lyell's resistance to evolution see Michael Bartholomew, "Lyell and Evolution," *British Journal for the History of Science*, 6 (1973), 261-303.

7. Maurice Mandelbaum, "The Scientific Background of Evolutionary Theory," *Journal of the History of Ideas*, 18 (1957), 342-61.

8. Cannon, "Uniformitarian-Catastrophist Debate," p. 55.

9. Alfred North Whitehead, *Science and the Modern World* (New York: Mentor, 1948), ch. 6.

10. John C. Green, "The Concept of Order in Darwinism," *The Concept of Order*, ed. Paul G. Kuntz (Seattle, Wash., 1968).

11. J. Walter Wilson, "Biology Gains Maturity," *Critical Problems*, ed. Clagett, pp. 401-18.

12. Asa Gray, *Darwiniana*, ed. A. Hunter Dupree (Cambridge, Mass., 1963).

13. *Methodist Quarterly Review*, 53 (1871), 348; Burr quoted in "Recent Works on Evolutionism," *Princeton Review*, ser. 2, 3 (1874), 170-71.

14. Arthur Lovejoy, *The Great Chain of Being* (Cambridge, Mass., 1936). The following analysis draws heavily on Wilson, "Biology Gains Maturity."

15. Conway Zirkle, "Species Before Darwin," *Proceedings of the American Philosophical Society*," 103 (1959), 636-44.

16. Charles C. Gillispie, "Lamarck and Darwin in the History of Science," *Forerunners of Darwin*, ed. Hiram Bentley Glass et al. (Baltimore, 1959), 265-90.

17. See Loren Eiseley, *Darwin's Century* (New York, 1961), pp. 187-204; and Peter J. Vorzimmer, *Charles Darwin: The Years of Controversy* (Philadelphia, 1970), ch. 4; and Frank N. Egerton, "Darwin's Early Reading of Lamarck," *Isis*, 67 (1976), 452-56.

18. On the relations between science and literature in the 1850s see Lionel Stevenson, "Darwin and the Novel," *Nineteenth Century Fiction*, 15 (1960-61), 29-38; James Harrison, "Tennyson and Evolution," *Durham University Journal*, 64 (1971), 26-31; and Susan Gliserman, "Early Victorian Science Writers and Tennyson's 'In Memoriam,'" *Victorian Studies*, 18 (1974-

75), 437-59. Erasmus Darwin quoted in Barry G. Gale, "Darwin and the Concept of the Struggle for Existence," *Isis*, 63 (1972), 325, 328.

19. Lyell and Darwin quoted ibid. pp. 332-33.

20. Charles Darwin, *Autobiography*, ed. George G. Simpson (New York: Collier, 1961), p. 58. Darwin's debt to Malthus is questioned in Loren Eiseley, "Charles Darwin, Edward Blyth, and the Theory of Natural Selection," *Proceedings of the American Philosophical Society*, 103 (1959), 94-158; and reaffirmed in Joel S. Schwartz, "Charles Darwin's Debt to Malthus and Edward Blyth," *Journal of the History of Biology*, 7 (1974), 301-18. See also Sandra Herbert, "Darwin, Malthus, and Selection," ibid., 4 (1971), 209-17; and Robert M. Young, "Malthus and the Evolutionists," *Past and Present*, no. 43 (1969), 109-45.

21. Peter J. Bowler, "Malthus, Darwin, and the Concept of Struggle," *Journal of the History of Ideas*, 37 (1976), 644.

22. Asa Gray, *Darwiniana* (Cambridge, Mass.: John Harvard Library, 1963), p. 30; Ward quoted in James C. Welling, "The Law of Malthus," *American Anthropologist*, o.s. 1 (1888), 1-23.

23. Darwin, *On the Origin of Species* (London, 1859), p. 62, quoted in Gale "Darwin and the Concept of a Struggle for Existence," p. 322.

24. Conway Zirkle, "Natural Selection before Origin of Species," *Proceedings of the American Philosophical Society*, 84 (1941), 71-123; and "Species Before Darwin," pp. 637-38. On Matthew see Kentwood A. Wells, "The Historical Context of Natural Selection," *Journal of the History of Biology*, 6 (1973), 225-58.

25. See Derek Freeman, "The Evolutionary Theories of Charles Darwin and Herbert Spencer," *Current Anthropology*, 15 (1974), 211-21; and Walter F. Cannon, "The Basis of Darwin's Achievement," *Victorian Studies*, 5 (1961), 109-34.

26. Greene, "The Concept of Order," p. 99. See also Philip P. Wiener, *Evolution and the Founders of Pragmatism* (Cambridge, Mass., 1949), p. 81.

27. Vorzimmer, *Darwin*, pp. 11, 76.

28. Eiseley, *Darwin's Century*, ch. 9; and Joe D. Burchfield, "Darwin and the Dilemma of Geological Time," *Isis*, 65 (1974), 301-21.

29. See Mandelbaum, "Scientific Background," pp. 357-58.

30. Garland Allen, "Thomas H. Morgan and the Problem of Natural Selection," *Journal of the History of Biology*, 1 (1968), 113-39. See also Alvar Ellegard, *Darwin and the General Reader* (Goteberg, Sweden, 1958), ch. 12. For a detailed discussion of the broader problem see Gerald L. Geison, "Darwin and Heredity," *Journal of the History of Medicine*, 24 (1969), 375-411.

31. Peter J. Bowler, "The Changing Meaning of Evolution," *Journal of the History of Ideas*, 36 (1975), 95-114.

32. Darwin quoted in Rogers, "Darwinism and Social Darwinism," p. 272.

33. Ibid.

34. Ibid., pp. 273-74.

35. Charles Darwin, *The Descent of Man*, 2nd ed. (New York, 1874), pp. 151-52.

36. Ibid., pp. 161-62. Cf. 1st ed., 2 vols., (London, 1872), 1: 173.

37. Thomas H. Huxley, "Administrative Nihilism," *Works* (New York, 1915), 1: 272, 277.

38. Leonard Huxley, ed. *The Life and Letters of Thomas Henry Huxley*, 2 vols. (New York, 1901), 2; 284 quoted in Rogers, "Darwinism and Social Darwinism," p. 272.

39. Alfred R. Wallace, *Contributions to the Theory of Natural Selection*, 2nd ed. (London, 1871), pp. 311-12. For the relation between Wallace's religious, scientific, and social views see Roger Smith, "A. R. Wallace: Philosophy of Nature and Man," *British Journal of Science*, 6 (1972), 177-99; Malcolm J. Kottler, "Alfred R. Wallace, the Origin of Man, and Spiritualism," *Isis*, 65

(1974), 145-92; and Wilma George, *Biologist Philosopher* (London, 1964).

40. Ibid., pp. 333, 329-30.

41. Nathaniel S. Shaler, "Wallace on Natural Selection," *Nation*, 10 (1870), 422-23; Brace, "Darwinism in Germany," *North American Review*, 110 (1870), 284-99.

42. Edward Bellamy, *Looking Backward* (New York: Modern Library, 1951). pp. 218-20; Wallace, "Human Selection," *Popular Science*, 38 (1890), 100-01; Maurice Burritt, notes on "Evolution and the Modern State" (ca. 1904-08) Burritt Papers, Cornell University.

Chapter 2
Hushing Up Death

1. John E. Cairnes, "Social Evolution," *Fortnightly*, o.s. 23 (1875), 64-65; James Martineau, "The Place of Mind in Nature," *Contemporary Review*, 19 (1872), 618-19; Emile de Laveleye, "State vs. the Man," ibid., 47 (1885), 492. The translation was subtitled "Darwinisme social et christianisme" (Florence, 1885). See also David Ritchie, *Darwinism and Politics* (London, 1891), p. 37; Edward Bemis, "Socialism and State Action," *Journal of Social Science*, 21 (1886), 57; George W. Julian, "Is the Reformer Any Longer Needed?" *North American Review*, 127 (1878), 237-60; William C. Owen, *The Economics of Herbert Spencer* (New York, 1891), p. 119; and Achille Loria, *The Economic Foundations of Society* (New York, 1899), pp. 66-67.

2. Spencer, *Various Fragments* (New York, 1910), pp. 116-17. Unless otherwise noted, references to all of Spencer's works are to this Appleton edition of 1910. David Duncan, *Life and Letters of Herbert Spencer*, 2 vols., (New York, 1908), 1: 325; *Various Fragments*, p. 128.

3. Frank Fairman, *Herbert Spencer on Socialism* (London, 1884), p. 1; Hamlin

Garland, "A New Declaration of Rights," *Arena* 3 (1891), 167; Hayes, *A Generation of Materialism* (New York, 1941), p. 11; Hofstadter, *Social Darwinism*, p. 47.

4. Henry George, *A Perplexed Philosopher* (London, 1937), pp. 100-20; Laurence Gronlund, *The Cooperative Commonwealth* (Boston, 1884), p. 88; Hofstadter, *Social Darwinism*, p. 41. See also Bernhard E. Fernow, "Providential Functions of Government," *Science*, n.s. 2 (1895), 252-65.

5. The best recent study of Spencer's life and thought is John D. Y. Peel, *Herbert Spencer: The Evolution of a Sociologist* (London, 1971).

6. Ibid., ch. 4; Spencer, *Social Statics* (New York, 1865), pp. 22-24.

7. Peel, *Spencer*, p. 83.

8. *Social Statics*, pp. 39, 40.

9. Ibid., p. 517.

10. Ibid., p. 51.

11. Ibid., p. 121.

12. Ibid., p. 27.

13. "Reviews," *Atlantic Monthly*, 13 (1864), 777.

14. Borden P. Bowne, *Kant and Spencer* (Boston, 1912), p. 14.

15. *Social Statics*, pp. 353, 355-56, 415-16.

16. Ibid., pp. 454-55.

17. Ibid., pp. 357, 449, 456.

18. Ibid., pp. 349-57. For Spencer's debt to idealism see Ernest Barker, *Political Thought in England*, 2nd ed., (London, 1928), pp. 70-80.

19. Spencer, "A Theory of Population," *Westminster Review*, 57 (1852), 468-501; and *Principles of Biology*, 2 vols. (New York, 1910), 2: 530. Cf. John C. Greene, "Biology and Social Theory," *Critical Problems*, ed. Clagett, p. 435 who comments that "the logical implication of Spencer's argument was that the progress of humanity had been accomplished by a competition of races." Spencer's ability to resist this logic was consistent with his muting of all struggle.

20. Talcott Parsons, *The Structure of Social Action* (New York, 1937) quoted in Cynthia Eagle Russett, *The Concept of Equilibrium in American Social Thought* (New Haven, 1966), p. 38.

21. Spencer, *First Principles*, pp. 497, 461, 467.

22. Ibid., p. 448. See also Russett, *Concept of Equilibrium*, ch. 3.

23. Ibid., pp. 38-39.

24. *First Principles*, pp. 55, 57, 175-76, 206.

25. Ibid., p. 510. The issue of Spencer's "materialism" versus the "idealism" was debated, for example, in the journal of the Boston Free Religious Association. See the *Index*, n.s., 1 (1880), 230-32; 2 (1881), 195-96, 285, 321; and 3 (1882), 145, 195-96. The English rationalist Leslie Stephen made this point in commenting: "Darwinism has enabled the empirical school to annex history; for they are no longer frightened by the bugbear of *a priori* principles and absolute rights. They are no longer forced to choose between a fixed order, imposed by supernatural sanction, and accidental combination capable of instantaneous and arbitrary reconstruction. . . . The evolutionist admits that a truth may be *a priori* relatively to the individual without having therefore a transcendental character. . . . " "An Attempted Philosophy of History," *Fortnightly*, 27 (1880), 679-80.

26. Spencer, *Essays*, 3 vols. (New York, 1910) 1: 9, 60. As Harold Sharlin has argued, Spencer went beyond "analogy" but stopped short of arguing total "identity" in the different spheres, thus shuttling unsatisfactorily between the two. See Harold I. Sharlin, "Spencer, Scientism, and American Constitutional Law," *Annals of Science*, 33 (1976), 457-80.

27. *Principles of Biology*, 2 vols. (New York, 1910) 1: 104, 494, 410. Where the first edition is the same as the 1910 edition, the latter is cited.

28. For an extended discussion see Freeman, "The Evolutionary Theories of Darwin and Spencer."

29. Spencer, "The Survival of the Fittest," *Nature*, 5 (1872), 263-64.

30. *First Principles*, 1st ed. (New York, 1865), p. 404; Spencer to his father, 9 June 1864, quoted in Freeman, "Evolutionary Theories," p. 216.

31. *The Principles of Biology*, 1:2, 522, 548.

32. Ibid., 1: 530.

33. *Principles of Biology*, 1st ed., 2 vols. (New York, 1866-67), 2: 508.

34. *Principles of Biology*, 2 vols. (New York, 1910), 1:548, 535; Goldwin Smith, "Has Science Yet Found a New Basis for Morality?" *Contemporary Review*, 45 (1882), 770.

35. *Principles of Biology*, 1st ed., 1:468-69.

36. For Darwin's opinion of Spencer see Freeman, "Evolutionary Theories," p. 219.

37. *Study of Sociology*, pp. 20-23; Duncan, *Life and Letters*, 1: 211; *Principles of Sociology*, 2, pt. 5.

38. Spencer revised *First Principles* in 1867, 1875, and 1880. For changes in his emphasis see Greene, "Biology and Social Theory," pp. 437-39.

39. Henry H. Howorth, "A New View of Darwinism," *Nature* 4 (1871), 161-62; Martineau, "The Place of Mind in Nature."

40. Spencer, *Essays*, 1: 379; "The Survival of the Fittest," p. 264.

41. Spencer, *Study of Sociology*, pp. 315, 399. Such statements, which Spencer made frequently, reflected the awkwardness that resulted from his desire to appear to accept Darwin but to avoid drawing to himself the widespread criticism the *Origin* had aroused. To view such statements simply as attempts to share the "prestige" of a theory that Spencer and his contemporaries unequivocally approved is to oversimplify a more complex situation.

42. Ibid., pp. 366-67.

43. *The Principles of Ethics*, 1, pt. 1, chs. 11-12.

44. Henry Calderwood, "Herbert Spencer on the Data of Ethics," *Contemporary Review*, 37 (1880), 67; Smith, "Has Science Yet Found a New Basis for Morality?" The latter was reprinted in *Popular Science*, 20 (1882), 753-78.
45. Spencer, *Man vs. the State* (bound with *Social Statics, Abridged and Revised*), chs. 1, 2.
46. Ibid., pp. 364-65.
47. Ibid., p. 366.
48. Laveleye, "State vs. the Man," Letter to the Editor, *Contemporary Review*, 47 (1885), 759-60; Spencer, *Various Fragments*, p. 116.
49. Spencer, *Essays*, 1:397.
50. Ibid., pp. 428-30, 462.
51. Huxley, *Evolution and Ethics* (New York, 1898), pp. 80, 18, 82-83.
52. Spencer, *Essays*, 3: 222, 224; *Various Fragments*, pp. 121-29.
53. Cf. *Social Statics* (1865), pp. 454-55, and *Social Statics, Abridged and Revised*, p. 238.
54. Cf. *Principles of Biology*, 1st ed., (1866-67), 2:506-7, and ibid., 2nd ed. (1910), 2: 537.
55. Cf. *Principles of Biology*, 1st ed., 2: 508 and ibid. 2nd ed., 2: 538; *First Principles* (New York, 1865), p. 486 and ibid. (1910), p. 473.
56. *Principles of Ethics*, 2: 393-94.
57. Ibid., 2: 394; *Principles of Biology*, 2: 532-33, cf. 1st ed. (1866-67), 2: 504; *Principles of Sociology*, 3: 608.
58. *Various Fragments*, pp. 115-16. The critic was the positivist Frederic Harrison. *Principles of Sociology*, 3: v; *Facts and Comments*, pp. 172-88, 200, 11.

Chapter 3
Philanthropic Energy
and Philosophic Calm

1. Burton J. Hendrick, *The Life of Andrew Carnegie*, 2 vols. (New York, 1932), 1: 35.
2. Quoted in James H. Bridge, "Work and Play with Herbert Spencer,"
Unpartizan Review, 14 (1920), 1-13.
3. Spencer, *Essays*, 3 vols. (New York, 1910), 3:476, 486. Unless otherwise noted references to Spencer's work are to the New York edition of 1910.
4. New York *Tribune* quoted in Bridge, "Work and Play," p. 13; Hofstadter, *Social Darwinism*, pp. 48-49; Wyllie, "Social Darwinism and the Businessman."
5. Henry Holt, *Garrulities of an Octogenarian Editor* (Boston, 1923), p. 298 quoted in Hofstadter, *Social Darwinism*, p. 34.
6. Higginson and Emerson quoted in John Fiske, *Edward Livingston Youmans* (New York, 1894), pp. 503-4, 544.
7. *Methodist Quarterly Review*, 46 (1864), 690-93; Emma Brace, ed., *The Life of Charles Loring Brace* (New York, 1894), pp. 445-46; see also Brace, "Darwinism in Germany," *North American Review*, 110 (1870), 284-99.
8. On Harvard, see George P. Winston, *John Fiske* (New York, 1972), ch. 2; on the Porter-Sumner controversy, see Burton J. Bledstein, "Porter versus Sumner," *Church History*, 43 (1974), 340-49; Elisha Mulford, *The Nation* (New York, 1870), pp. 26-27.
9. Chauncey Depew, *My Memories of Eighty Years* (New York, 1922), pp. 383-84 quoted in Hofstadter, *Social Darwinism*, pp. 44-45, who adds that "No doubt there were many to applaud the assertion. . . . "
10. Depew, *Orations and After Dinner Speeches* (New York, 1890), pp. 320, 522-23.
11. Edward Atkinson, "Political Economy," *Index*, 3 (1872), 50; and "The Recent Failures and their Lessons," *Commercial and Financial Chronicle*, 19 (1874), 361-62.
12. Henry Holt, "Herbert Spencer's Reputation," *Nation* 8 (1869), 394-95; Fiske, "Herbert Spencer and the Experts," ibid., p. 439.
13. Spencer, *Social Statics* (New York, 1865), p. 457; Fiske, *Youmans*, pp. 178-79;

Ethel F. Fisk, *The Life and Letters of John Fiske* (New York, 1940), p. 93 quoted in Winston, *Fiske*, p. 3; Edward L. Youmans. ed., *Herbert Spencer on the Americans* (New York, 1883) p. 41.

14. *Atlantic Monthly*, 16 (1865), 383.
15. Edward L. Youmans, "Introduction," *Illustrations of Universal Progress* (New York, 1864), pp. vi-vii.
16. Ibid., p. xiii. See also *Atlantic Monthly*, 13 (1864), 775-77. For a dissent from Youman's interpretation see a review of *First Principles* in the *Methodist Quarterly Review*, 46 (1864), 690-93.
17. David Duncan, *Life and Letters of Herbert Spencer* (New York, 1908), 1: 168. Cf. the interpretation of this statement in Hofstadter, *Social Darwinism*, p. 31; *Atlantic Monthly*, 16 (1865), 383; and Chauncey Wright, *North American Review*, 100 (1865), 437.
18. John Spencer Clark, *The Life and Letters of John Fiske*, 2 vols. (Boston, 1917), 1: 237. On Fiske's intellectual development see Milton Berman, *John Fiske: The Evolution of a Popularizer* (Cambridge, Mass., 1961).
19. Berman, *Fiske*, pp. 32-33.
20. Fiske to his mother, 13 November 1873, quoted in Berman, *Fiske*, pp. 103-4.
21. Ibid., p. 100.
22. Youmans quoted ibid., p. 101.
23. Fiske, "The Progress from Brute to Man," *North American Review*, 117 (1873), 280-82. For a discussion of Fiske's alleged "imperialism" see ch. 12 below.
24. Henry W. Holland, "Fiske's Cosmic Philosophy," *Nation*, 20 (1875), 135-37; unsigned review, "Recent Literature," *Atlantic*, 35 (1875), 619.
25. *Dial*, 5 (1884), 177.
26. On the Social Science movement, see Luther Bernard, *The Origins of American Sociology* (New York, 1940); Thomas Haskell, *The Emergence of Professional Social Science: The American Social Science Association* (Urbana, Ill., 1977); and Mary O. Furner, *Advocacy and Objectivity* (Lexington, Ky., 1975).

27. Quoted in Bernard, *Origins*, p. 466.
28. On DelMar and Sterne see Bernard, *Origins*, pp. 461-76; Joseph Dorfman, *The Economic Mind in American Civilization*, 5 vols. (New York, 1946-1959), 3: 98-101; John Foord, *Simon Sterne* (New York, 1903); and *Dictionary of American Biography*, s.v. "DelMar, Alexander."
29. See esp. "Herbert Spencer," *New York Social Science Review*, 1 (1865), 67-82; "Sociological Record," ibid., 2 (1866), 97-104; and "The Progress of Social Science," ibid., 1 (1865), 104.
30. Ibid., pp. 97-109.
31. "Law and Lawyers in the United States," ibid. 1 (1865), 246-47; Sterne, *The Constitutional and Political Development of the United States*, 4th ed. (New York, 1888), p. xvi.
32. DelMar, "Historical Aspects of the Monetary Question," *Fortnightly*, o.s. 63 (1895), 565-72.
33. Fiske, *Youmans*, p. 39.
34. Youmans quoted in ibid., pp. 68, 95.
35. Greeley quoted ibid., p. 300.
36. Youmans, "The Centennial Celebration," *Popular Science*, 5 (1874), 237-40.
37. Youmans, "The Recent Strikes," ibid., 1 (1872), 623-24; "A Case of Swindling," ibid., 10 (1877), 235; and "Man as an Object of Scientific Study," ibid., 1 (1872), 366-68.
38. Youmans, "The Social Science Association," ibid., 5 (1874), 369; Youmans to Spencer, 27 May 1881, in Fiske, *Youmans*, pp. 369-70. In *Nation* editorials, I could locate only one example of an implicit appeal to Darwinism to support the laissez faire position. In this case the writer, who is not identified in the *Nation Index*, argued that there should be no confiscation of large fortunes since their owners "may be said, as a general rule, to be the best men fitted to discover public wants and supply them. The great capitalist is, in other words, generally a man who has been appointed by natural selection to take charge of a portion of the sav-

ings of the community and use them to the best advantage in producing and exchanging." "The Great Economic Difficulty," *Nation*, 27 (1878), 78-79. This exception, the sort of phrase reformers seized upon, suggests that while some laissez faire theorists were doubtless tempted to invoke these new "laws" of nature, their failure in general to do so reflected not ignorance of Spencer or Darwin but an awareness that such analogies were extremely vulnerable.

39. John E. Cairnes, "Social Evolution," *Popular Science*, 6 (1875), 604-12; Youmans, "Cairnes on Social Evolution," ibid., pp. 617-18.

40. *Nation*, 10 (1870), 89-90; Youmans, "The Literature of Evolution," *Popular Science*, 6 (1875), 745-48; "The *Nation* on German Darwinism," ibid., 8 (1875), 235-40. For an early expression of Wright's views on Spencer see the *Nation*, 2 (1866), 724-25.

41. Youmans, "Science in Relation to War," *Popular Science*, 14 (1879), 817-19.

42. Smith, "Has Science Yet Found a New Basis for Morality?" p. 760.

43. Ibid., p. 761.

44. Youmans, "Goldwin Smith on Scientific Morality," *Popular Science*, 20 (1882), 884-87; Louisa S. Bevington, "The Moral Colour of Rationalism," *Fortnightly*, o.s. 36 (1881), 183-84.

45. Van Buren Denslow, *Modern Thinkers* (Chicago, 1882), pp. 211-55; and *The Principles of Economic Philosophy* (New York, 1888), pp. 22-23.

46. Youmans, "DeLaveleye on Socialism," *Popular Science*, 27 (1885), 270-272.

47. George, *A Perplexed Philosopher* (London, 1937), p. 119.

48. Ibid.

49. Youmans, "Forces of Human Progress," *Popular Science*, 18 (1881), 553-56.

50. Youmans, ed., *Spencer on the Americans*, pp. 22-25.

51. Ibid., p. 28.

52. Ibid., pp. 35-50, 58-67; Fiske to Spencer, 3 September 1883 in Fiske, *Youmans*, p. 379.

53. Youmans, ed., *Spencer on the Americans*, p. 83.

54. Spencer, *Essays*, 3: 486.

55. For example see William J. Ghent, *Our Benevolent Feudalism* (New York, 1902), p. 88.

Chapter 4
Amending the Faith

1. Lester Ward in Youmans, ed., *Spencer on the Americans*, p. 79. On the "antiformalist" revolt see Morton G. White, *Social Thought in America* (New York, 1949).

2. Lewis G. Janes, "The Brooklyn Ethical Association," *Popular Science*, 42 (1893), 671-78; Spencer quoted in ibid., p. 674. Vols. in the Brooklyn Ethical Association series were: *Evolution* (Boston, 1889); *Sociology* (Boston, 1890); *Evolution in Science* (New York, 1891); *Man and the State* (New York, 1892); *Factors in American Civilization* (New York, 1893); and *Life and the Conditions of Survival* (Chicago, 1895).

3. Janes, "Brooklyn Ethical Association," p. 671; and *The Scope and Principles of the Evolution Philosophy* (Boston, 1889), p. 23; Robert G. Eccles, "The Labor Question," *Popular Science*, 11 (1877), 607.

4. Eccles, "The Study of Applied Sociology," *Man and the State*, p. 33; and "The Atmosphere and Life," *Popular Science News* (July 1894), p. 105.

5. Eccles, "The Study of Applied Sociology," pp. 23-52.

6. Janes, *Scope and Principles*, p. 24.

7. Eccles, *Popular Science News* (September 1894), p. 141.

8. Andrew Carnegie, "Wealth," *The Gospel of Wealth*, ed. Edward C. Kirkland (Cambridge, 1962), p. 16; and *The Autobiography of Andrew Carnegie* (New York, 1924), p. 338.

9. Joseph F. Wall, *Andrew Carnegie* (New York, 1970), p. 365.

10. Carnegie, *Autobiography*, p. 327.

11. Carnegie, *Notes of a Trip Around the World* (New York, 1879), pp. 17, 21. If this reading is correct, it would appear that Wall, *Carnegie*, pp. 365, 374, despite its revisionism, overstates the case in noting that Carnegie set sail "determined to see the world as an operating laboratory for Herbert Spencer."

12. Carnegie, *Autobiography*, p. 333; Wall, *Carnegie*, p. 386.

13. Carnegie, "Business Success," *The Empire of Business* (New York, 1933), p. 13; "An Employer's View of the Labor Question," *The Gospel of Wealth*, pp. 107-23; and *Triumphant Democracy* (New York, 1886), p. 23 and also pp. 13, 94, 359, 433.

14. Robert G. McCloskey, *American Conservatism* (New York, 1951), ch. 6. Carnegie quoted in Wall, *Carnegie*, p. 812. For a discussion of ideology and role strain, see Francis X. Sutton et al., *The American Business Creed* (Cambridge, Mass. 1956).

15. Carnegie, *Gospel of Wealth*, p. 138; and *Miscellaneous Writings of Andrew Carnegie*, ed. Burton J. Hendrick, 2 vols. (New York, 1933), 2: 203.

16. Edward Kirkland, "Divide and Ruin," *Journal of American History*, 43 (1956), 3-17; Carnegie, "The Common Interest," *The Empire of Business*, p. 67; and *Autobiography*, p. 333.

17. Carnegie, "Wealth," *Gospel of Wealth*, p. 16. The critic was Hugh P. Hughes, "Irresponsible Wealth," *Nineteenth Century*, 28 (1890), 890-91. During the 1880s Carnegie's secretary was James Howard Bridge, an Englishman and admirer of Spencer, who may well have influenced Carnegie's choice of words in "Wealth." Cf. "Harold Brydges" [James H. Bridge], *Uncle Sam at Home* (London, 1888), p. 240, describing international economic competition as "a struggle keener than Waterloo. . . . The victory, like that of military encounters, will be survival of the fittest; but the fittest here is the one possessing the most efficient and economic industrial system." See also Bridge, "Trusts As Their Masters View Them," *World's Work*, 5 (1902), 2782-5; and *The Inside Story of the Carnegie Steel Company* (New York, 1903), pp. vii-viii.

18. Carnegie, "Wealth," p. 29.

19. See William E. Gladstone, "Mr. Carnegie's Gospel of Wealth," *Nineteenth Century*, 28 (1890), 677-93; and a symposium on "Irresponsible Wealth," ibid., pp. 876-900. Also William J. Tucker, review in *Andover Review*, 15 (1891), 631-45.

20. Hughes, "Irresponsible Wealth," pp. 893-94; Tucker, *Andover Review*, p. 633.

21. Carnegie, "Summing up the Tariff Question," *Miscellaneous Writings*, 1: 306-50; "Pennsylvania Industry," ibid., pp. 298-303; *Mr. Andrew Carnegie on Socialism* (1891) quoted in Wall, *Carnegie*, p. 392; Carnegie, "Popular Illusions," p. 89.

22. Charles Francis Adams, Jr., *The Federation of The Railroad System*, (Boston, 1880), p. 10; United States Senate Select Committee on Interstate Commerce, *Testimony*, 49 (18 January 1886), 819, quoted in Gabriel Kolko, *Railroads and Regulation* (Princeton, 1965), pp. 38-39.

23. William Letwin, *Law and Economic Policy in America* (New York, 1965); Gabriel Kolko, *The Triumph of Conservatism* (New York, 1963).

24. Samuel C. T. Dodd, *Combinations* (New York, 1888), p. 14; Charles R. Flint et al., *The Trust* (New York, 1902), p. 173.

25. David S. Cowles, *Corporations and Competition* (New York, 1908), p. 173; Arthur J. Eddy, *The New Competition* (New York, 1912), p. 15; George W. Perkins, *The Worker's Fair Share* (New York, 1916).

26. Brandeis quoted in "The Third Party and The Trusts," *Nation*, 95 (19 September 1912), 253-54.

27. *The National Cyclopedia of American Biography*, 51 vols. (New York, 1898-1969), 2: 466; and Frank L. Mott, *A History of American Magazines*, 5 vols. (New York, 1930-68), 3: 495-99.

28. William J. Youmans, "The Fight

Against Poverty," *Popular Science*, 31 (1887), 414.

29. W. J. Youmans, "Altruism and Egoism," ibid., 34 (1889), 560.

30. W. J. Youmans, "Human Selection," ibid., 38 (1890), 270-71. See Henry Dwight Chapin, "Social and Psychological Inequality," *Popular Science*, 30 (1887), 757-65; "The Struggle for Subsistence," *Journal of Social Science*, 25 (1888), 93-97; "The Survival of the Unfit," *Popular Science*, 41 (1892), 182-87.

31. W. J. Youmans, "Science and Civilization," ibid., 38 (1891), 704-5; "The Bearing of the Doctrine of Evolution on Social Problems," ibid., 44 (1893), 122.

32. W. J. Youmans, "The Unemployed," *Popular Science*, 44 (1894), 842-43.

33. W. J. Youmans, "The Duke of Argyll on Evolution," ibid., 51 (1897), 411-13.

34. Ibid., p. 413.

35. The quotation is from Youmans, "External and Internal Aggression," ibid., 56 (1900), 386-87. For discussion of the theme of cataclysm, see Frederic C. Jaher, *Doubters and Dissenters* (Glencoe, Ill. 1964), and chs. 5, 10, 11, 12 below.

36. Henry Holt, *Sixty Years as a Publisher* (London, 1923), p. 47.

37. Holt, "The Social Discontent," *Forum*, 19 (1895), 79; *Sixty Years*, pp. 282, 53.

38. Holt, "The Social Discontent," p. 78.

39. Ibid., pp. 177-81.

40. Ibid. On Kidd, see ch. 7 below.

41. Holt, *Morals in Modern Business* (New Haven, 1909), p. 54.

42. Statement of principles on inside cover of each issue; "Devil and the Deep Sea," *Unpopular Review*, 6 (1916), 223-30.

43. Preston W. Slosson, "The Conservation of Competition," ibid., 3 (1915), 269-80; Holt, "Competition," ibid., pp. 281-97.

44. Ibid.; see also *Sixty Years*, pp. 373-402. If Holt needed reminding, another contributor to the *Unpopular Review* soon warned readers of the perils of "Darwinian" nature. See Paul Elmer More,

"Justice," *Unpopular Review*, 4 (1915), 81-95.

45. Holt, *On the Civic Relations* (Boston, 1907), p. 630.

46. John Dewey, *Character and Events*, 2 vols. (New York 1929), 1: 57-61.

Chapter 5
William Graham Sumner

1. *Nation*, 40 (1885), 526-27; Lucius M. Bristol, *Social Adaptation* (Cambridge, Mass., 1915), pp. 153-55; Arthur J. Todd, *Theories of Social Progress* (New York, 1918), p. 246; Upton Sinclair, *The Goose Step* (Pasedena, Ca., 1923), pp. 123-24; Hofstadter, *Social Darwinism*, p. 51.

2. Ibid., pp. 45, 63, 65. See also Hofstadter, "William Graham Sumner: Social Darwinist," *New England Quarterly*, 14 (1941), 457-77.

3. Although Hofstadter, ibid., pp. 464-65, was aware of the fact that Sumner drew this distinction and of the problems it posed in labeling him a "social Darwinist," he attempted to avoid them in several ways. Sumner, he suggested, "was *perhaps* [emphasis mine] inspired to minimize the human conflict in the struggle for existence by a desire to dull the resentment of the poor toward the rich." Moreover, he charged, Sumner sometimes ignored the distinction. (Hofstadter, as it turned out, quoted virtually every such instance in Sumner's voluminous writings when this may have been the case.) As further evidence, Hofstadter stated that Sumner's student, Albert Keller, later ignored it. At any rate, Hofstadter added, "it was easy" for conservatives of Sumner's generation "to argue by analogy from natural selection to social selection of fitter men." In the book version of *Social Darwinism*, p. 224, note 17, Hofstadter omitted the reference to Keller.

4. Youmans, ed., *Spencer on the Americans*, pp. 35-40; *Popular Science*, 35 (1889), 261-68. For attacks by two mem-

bers of the Brooklyn Ethical Association see James A. Skilton, Skilton to *Brooklyn Times*, 25 February 1885; and Lewis G. Janes, *Our Nation's Peril* (New York, 1899), p. 13.

5. Merwin A. Sheketoff, *William Graham Sumner: Social Christian 1869-72* (Ph.D. diss., Harvard, 1961); Bruce E. Curtis, *The Middle Class Progressivism of William Graham Sumner* (Ann Arbor, Mich.: University Microfilms, 1964), and "William Graham Sumner' 'On the Concentration of Wealth,'" *Journal of American History*, 55 (1969), 823-32; Harry V. Ball, "Law and Social Change: Sumner Reconsidered," *American Journal of Sociology*, 67 (1962), 532-40. See also Dominick T. Armentano, *The Political Economy of William Graham Sumner* (Ann Arbor, Mich.: University Microfilms, 1967).

6. Harris Starr, *William Graham Sumner* (New York, 1925), pp. 66, 71-72. Sumner's Sermons are in the William Graham Sumner Papers, Yale University Library.

7. Sumner to Jennie Elliott, 8 August 1870; "The Authority of Conscience," 10 December 1870; "Individualism," 11 May 1871, mss. in the Sumner Papers, Yale; Starr, *Sumner*, p. 167.

8. Sumner, "Rationalism," Sermon no. 72, 1871; "Church's Law," 3 April 1872; The Solidarity of the Human Race," 11 January 1873; "Ill Gotten Wealth," 1 October 1869; "Individualism," 11 May 1871, mss. in the Sumner Papers, Yale.

9. Roger B. Salomon, "Realism as Disinheritance," *American Quarterly*, 16 (1964), 532-44; Sumner, *The Challenge of the Facts*, ed. A. G. Keller (New Haven, 1914), pp. 347-48, 394-95.

10. Sumner, "Is the War Over?" *New York World*, 9 October 1876.

11. Sumner, "Have We had Enough?" (1874); "Lesson of the Panic," (1874), mss. in the Sumner Papers, Yale.

12. Charlton T. Lewis, comment on Sumner paper, *Journal of Social Science*, 6 (1874), 24.

13. Sumner, *The Forgotten Man*, ed. Albert G. Keller (New Haven, 1919), pp. 224-25. Among these economists were Richard Ely, John Bates Clark, and Simon Patten, who in 1885 joined in founding the reform-oriented American Economic Association.

14. One apparent exception is "The Predicament of Sociological Study," *Challenge*, pp. 415-25, which Keller dated ca. 1900. The text, however, suggests that this was but another version of essays on sociology which Sumner wrote in the early 1880s. Specifically, it was probably a speech before the Nineteenth Century Club reported in the *New York Times*, 7 March 1883.

15. Sumner, "Socialism," *Scribner's*, 16 (1878), 887-93.

16. Sumner, review of *Progress and Poverty, New York Times*, 6 June 1880; *Forgotten Man*, p. 225; *War and Other Essays*, ed. Albert G. Keller (New Haven, 1911), pp. 167-92.

17. Sumner, Misc. ms. no. 2, (ca. 1878), Sumner Papers, Yale; "The Survival of the Fittest," *Index*, n.s. 4 (1884), 567; "Survival Again," ibid. pp. 603-4.

18. Isaac L. Rice, comment, *New York Times*, 7 March 1883, p. 5; "The Selfish Sciences," ibid. 9 March 1883; "Cornering a Professor," (n.d., n.p., ca. 1883), clipping in the Sumner Papers, Yale.

19. Charles Frederic Adams, " 'Sentiment' and 'Sociology,' " *New York Times*, 18 March 1883; William J. Potter, "Prof. Sumner on the Survival of the Fittest," *Index*, n.s. 4 (1884), 578. See also William M. Salter, "Darwinism in Ethics," *Open Court*, 1 (1887), 77-79.

20. Alfred Jaretzki, "Social Classes," *Index*, n.s. 6 (1885), 294-96; Lester Ward, *Glimpses of the Cosmos*, 6 vols. (New York, 1913-18), 3: 301-5, 365.

21. *Nation*, 40 (1885), 526-27.

22. Lewis Mumford, *The Golden Day* (New York, 1926), ch. 4; Kirkland, "Divide and Ruin"; John Stuart Mill, *Essays on Some Unsettled Questions*, esp. Essay 5; Harvey G. Townsend, *Philosophical*

Ideas in the United States (New York, 1934), ch. 7.

23. Sumner, *War*, p. 191; *What Social Classes Owe to Each Other* (New York, 1911), p. 156.
24. See *Index* ref. in notes 17 and 19 above.
25. Sumner, misc. ms. no. 2, p. 24, Sumner Papers, Yale; *War*, p. 173; *Folkways*, (New York: Mentor, 1960), pp. 18, 30, 31, 45.
26. Sumner, *War*, p. 10.
27. Ibid., p. 170.
28. Starr, *Sumner*, p. 386.
29. Sumner, *War*, p. 14; *Folkways*, pp. 64-65.
30. Sumner, "Bequests of the 19th Century to the 20th," *Yale Review*, n.s. 22 (1933), 732-54, (written ca. 1900).
31. Sumner, *Forgotten Man*, pp. 249-53.
32. Curtis, "Sumner 'On the Concentration of Wealth.'"
33. Sumner, *War*, pp. 271-344.
34. Frederic C. Jaher, *Doubters and Dissenters* (Glencoe, Ill., 1964).
35. Sumner, "Bequests"; *Folkways*, pp. 27-28; *War*, pp. 163-64.
36. Charles C. Walcutt, *American Literary Naturalism* (Minneapolis, 1956), pp. 25-29.
37. Sumner, *Folkways*, p. 71.
38. Ibid., pp. 527-39.
39. Ibid., pp. 534-39.
40. Armentano, *Political Economy*, ch. 8.
41. Robert G. McCloskey, *American Conservatism* (Cambridge, Mass., 1951), chs. 2, 3.

Chapter 6
The Survival of the Fittest
Is Our Doctrine

1. Henry George, *Progress and Poverty* (New York, 1942), pp. 101, 480; Edward Bellamy, *Edward Bellamy Speaks Again!* (1937), p. 34; Lloyd, *Man the Social Creator* (New York, 1906), pp. 218-20; Lester F. Ward, "Politico-Social Functions [1881]," *Glimpses of the Cosmos*, 6 vols. (New York, 1913-18), 2:

336; and "Mind as a Social Factor [1884]," ibid., 3: 364.
2. Minot J. Savage, *The Religion of Evolution* (Boston, 1876), p. 131; Rudolf von Schmid, *The Theories of Darwin*, trans. G. A. Zimmerman (Chicago, 1882), p. 391. For Savage's repudiation of laissez faire using a similar argument, see "The Effects of Evolution on the Coming of Civilization," in *Evolution* [Brooklyn Ethical Association] (Boston, 1889), pp. 367-87. See also William Graham, *The Creed of Science* (London, 1881), pp. 407-12, by a philosophical idealist.
3. Abraham D. H. Kaplan, *Henry Charles Carey* (Johns Hopkins University Studies in Historical and Political Science, XLIX, no. 4, 1931), p. 82; Ralph H. Gabriel, *The Course of American Democratic Thought* (New York, 1940), pp. 80-86.
4. Kaplan, *Carey*, p. 61.
5. Henry C. Carey, *The Unity of Law* (Philadelphia, 1872), pp. xvii, 157, 183, 295.
6. Ibid., pp. xviii-xix, 59, 370-72. Cf. C. Darwin, *The Descent of Man*, 2 vols., New York, 1872, 1: 161-63.
7. John L. Peck, *The Ultimate Generalization* (New York, 1876); *The Political Economy of Democracy* (Philadelphia, 1879), pp. 3-29. Peck, a faculty member of the University of Pennsylvania, represented, as did Carey, the prevailing protectionist sentiment in Philadelphia. See also Joseph Wharton, "International Industrial Competition," *Journal of Social Science*, 4 (1871), 51.
8. Francis Bowen, *Gleanings of a Literary Life, 1838-80* (New York, 1880), pp. 199-231, 247-87; *Modern Philosophy* (New York, 1877), chs. 15-16, 21-22.
9. Bowen, "Malthusianism, Darwinism, and Pessimism," *North American Review*, 129 (1879), 450-51, 456, 470-72.
10. Cf. Hofstadter, *Social Darwinism*, p. 88.
11. In *The Kingdom of the Selfish* (New York, 1889), pp. 221, 242 ff. Peck singled out Sumner and Spencer; his authority

was Lester Ward discussed below.
12. Washington Gladden, *Working People and Their Employers* (Boston, 1976), pp. 42-43.
13. George mentioned Carey in *Progress and Poverty*, pp. 35, 227-28; in *Protection or Free Trade* (New York, 1941), pp. 9, 79; and in *The Science of Political Economy* (New York, 1941), pp. 93-94, 196.
14. George, *Progress and Poverty*, pp. 99-102, 480-81, 558.
15. Charles A. Barker, *Henry George* (New York, 1955), pp. 376; George, *Progress and Poverty*, pp. 508, 526, 560.
16. George, *Progress and Poverty*, p. 476; Barker, *George*, pp. 339, 359-60; George, *A Perplexed Philosopher* (London, 1937), pp. 105-6.
17. George, *Progress and Poverty*, p. 514; also *Free Trade*, p. 160, and *Social Problems* (New York, 1949), p. 1.
18. The four are Winwood Reade, William Graham Sumner, Herbert Spencer, and Edward L. Youmans. Although George made only a minor contribution to Sumner's and Spencer's reputations as "conservative Darwinists," his criticisms of Reade and Youmans appear to have directly influenced later accounts. For Reade, see Barzun, *Darwin, Marx, Wagner*, p. 108, and Goldman, *Rendezvous*, pp. 91-92. For Youmans see Hofstadter, *Social Darwinism*, p. 34; Commager, *American Mind*, p. 202; Goldman, *Rendezvous*, p. 85; and Sidney Fine, *Laissez Faire and the General Welfare State* (Ann Arbor, 1956), p. 136. In *Progress and Poverty*, pp. 100-1, Henry George also identified a fifth individual—the pre-Darwinian economist John R. McCulloch. Making his case, George first quoted a statement by Louis Agassiz, the vehemently anti-Darwinian geologist, to the effect that Darwinism was "Malthus all over," and then rendered a Darwinian paraphrase of McCulloch.
19. Barzun, *Darwin, Marx, Wagner* p. 108; Goldman, *Rendezvous*, pp. 91-92.

20. Winwood Reade, *The Martyrdom of Man*, 22nd ed., (London, n.d.), pp. xlvii-1, 502-44. Cf. John F. Stasny, "W. Winwood Reade's The Martyrdom of Man: A Darwinian History," *Philological Papers*, 13 (1961), 37-49.
21. George, *Progress and Poverty*, pp. 480-81.
22. Reade, *Martyrdom*, pp. 543-44. See Barzun, *Darwin, Marx, Wagner*, p. 108; and Goldman, *Rendezvous*, pp. 91-92.
23. For the Sumner-George exchange, see Sumner's review of *Progress and Poverty* in the New York Times, 6 June 1880, *What Social Classes Owe to Each Other* (New York, 1911), esp. pp. 22, 48-52, 68; and George, *Social Problems*, pp. 63, 67, 72. George also attacked Sumner in *Free Trade*, pp. 250-52.
24. Hofstadter, *Social Darwinism*, pp. 56-57. See ch. 5 n.3 above.
25. George, *Progress and Poverty*, pp. 359-60, 364, 404, 480, 487, 504.
26. Spencer, "Letter to the *St. James's Gazette*," cited in *A Perplexed Philosopher*, pp. 52-61; George to Edward R. Taylor, March 1882, in Henry George, Jr., *The Life of Henry George, Works of Henry George* (New York, 1911), 10: 370; *A Perplexed Philosopher*, pp. 58, 67, 97.
27. George, *A Perplexed Philosopher*, pp. 101-3.
28. Ibid., pp. 118-20.
29. See Ch. 3, above.
30. Henry D. Lloyd, *Notebook* 9 (1888), 215, H. D. Lloyd Papers, Wisconsin Historical Society; *Wealth Against Commonwealth* (New York, 1894), pp. 3-4.
31. Bellamy, *Looking Backward* (New York, 1951), pp. 213-27; Arthur Morgan, *Edward Bellamy* (New York, 1944), p. 262; Jesse Cox, "Objections to Nationalism," *Nationalist*, 3 (1889), 325-30.
32. Lloyd, *Wealth against Commonwealth*, pp. 494-95.
33. Martha Avery, "The Curse of Charity," *Nationalist*, 1 (1889), 184-87. See also

Solomon Schindler, "What Is Nationalism?" *New England Magazine*, n.s. 7 (1892), 53-61.

34. Lloyd, *Notebook* I (eye) (1887), 122, Lloyd Papers.

35. Bellamy, *Looking Backward*, pp.213-27.

36. Lloyd, *Notebook* G (1888), 112; *Notebook* 18 (1890), 475; Kidd's 'Social Evolution,'" Mss. Additional (1896), 1-3, Lloyd Papers; *Wealth against Commonwealth*, pp. 494-95.

37. Herbert Birdsall, "Professor Harris's Discovery," *Nationalist*, 2 (1890), 61-63. Cf. William T. Harris, "Edward Bellamy's Vision," *Forum*, 8 (1889), 207-8; Francis A. Walker, "Mr. Bellamy and the New Nationalist Party," *Atlantic Monthly*, 65 (1890), 261-62; and John S. Cobb, "General Walker and the Atlantic," *Nationalist* 2 (1890), 135-38. Harris and Walker in fact illustrate the Hegelianism and classical economics, respectively, that sustained two varieties of "conservatism" during the period.

38. James C. Welling, "The Law of Malthus," *American Anthropologist*, o.s. 1 (1888), 12; Franklin B. Sanborn, "The Social Sciences," *Journal of Social Science*, 21 (1886), 5. See also John W. Powell, "Competition as a Factor in Human Evolution," *American Anthropologist*, o.s. 1 (1888), 297-323; and Thomas Davidson, "Property," *Journal of Social Science*, 23 (1887), 111.

39. Henry Carter Adams, "Lecture on the Transportation Problem," (1894), p. 16, ms., H. C. Adams Papers, Michigan Historical Collections; John Bates Clark, "Non-Competitive Economics," *New England Magazine*, n.s. 5 (1882), 846.

40. On Ward, see Samuel Chugerman, *Lester Frank Ward, The American Aristotle* (Durham, N.C., 1939); John Burnham, *Lester Ward in American Thought* (Washington, D.C., 1956); and Clifford H. Scott, *Lester Frank Ward* (Boston, 1976).

41. Ward, "Cosmic and Organic Evolution," (1877), *Glimpses*, 2; 148-63; "The Scientific Basis of Positive Political

Economy," (1882), ibid., 3; 32-35.

42. Ward, "Political-Social Functions," ibid., 2; 336-37; "Scientific Basis," ibid., 3: 47; *Dynamic Sociology*, 2 vols. (New York, 1883), 1: 7-8; E. L. Youmans, ed., *Herbert Spencer on the Americans* (New York, 1883), p. 79.

43. Ward, "Professor Sumner's Social Classes," (1884), *Glimpses*, 3: 301-5; "Mind as a Social Factor," ibid., 3: 365; "False Notions of Government" (1887), ibid., 4: 70.

44. Ward, "Neo-Darwinism and Neo-Lamarckism" (1891), *Glimpses*, 4: 290-95.

45. Ibid., p. 291; "Psychologic Basis" (1893), ibid., 4: 345-66; "Political Ethics" (1894), ibid., 5: 38-66; "Plutocracy" (1895), ibid., 5: 228-40. Quoted from "Psychologic Basis," p. 350.

46. Quoted ibid., 4: 347.

47. Ward, "Political Ethics," ibid., 5: 38-66. Spencer's *Principles of Biology*, 2 vols. (New York, 1910), 1: 553, affirmed that "social arrangements" nullified the "survival of the fittest" in the case of modern man. Progress in modern times might thus be "ascribed almost wholly" to adaptation on the Lamarckian model. See ch. 2 above.

48. See index ref. to Schopenhauer in Ward, *The Psychic Factors of Civilization* (Boston, 1892).

49. See "Neo-Darwinism," *Glimpses*, 4: 294-95; "Social Darwinism," *American Journal of Sociology*, 12 (1907), 709-10; "Eugenics, Euthenics, and Eudemics" (1913), *Glimpses*, 6: 382-97.

50. Esp. Ward, "Contemporary Sociology," *American Journal of Sociology*, 7 (1902); *Pure Sociology*, 2nd ed., (New York, 1907), pp. 193-200; "Evolution of Social Structures," *American Journal of Sociology*, 10 (1905), 589-605; "Social and Biological Struggles," ibid., 13 (1907), 289-99; "Motives in Social Conflict," ibid. (1908), 646; and "Social Integration through Conflict," ibid. (1908), 806-7.

51. John Collier, "The Struggle for Existence in Sociology," *Current Literature*,

35 (1903), 323-26.

52. For discussion of Kropotkin see ch. 7 below.

53. Jacques Novicow, *La Justice et l'Expansion de la Vie* (Paris, 1905), discussed in Ward, *Glimpses*, 6: 269-71; *Les Luttes entre les Sociétés Humaines* (Paris, 1893); George Nasmyth, *Social Progress and the Darwinian Theory* (New York, 1916).

54. Hofstadter, *Social Darwinism*, chs. 8, 9.

55. Ward, "Social and Biological Struggles," pp. 290-93; "Social Darwinism."

56. Ward, "Social and Biological Struggles," pp. 291-92. For other examples in the writings of younger social scientists and philosophers involved in the pragmatic or "antiformalist" revolt see C. S. Peirce, "Evolutionary Love," *Monist*, 3 (1893), 176; and Charles Horton Cooley, *The Social Process* (New York, 1924) pp. 226-28.

57. See Gerald Runkle, "Marxism and Charles Darwin," *Journal of Politics*, 23 (1961), 108-26; Ralph Colp, "The Contacts between Karl Marx and Charles Darwin," *Journal of the History of Ideas*, 35 (1974), 329-38; and Valentino Gerratana, "Marx and Darwin," *New Left Review* 82 (Nov./Dec. 1973), 60-82. Complexities of motive and evidence are considered in Shlomo Avineri, "From Hoax to Dogma," *Encounter*, 28 (1967), 30-32; Lewis S. Feuer, "Is the 'Darwin-Marx Correspondence' Authentic?" *Annals of Science*, 32 (1975), 1-12, and "On the Darwin-Marx Correspondence," ibid., 33 (1976), 383-94; and Margaret A. Fay, "Did Marx Offer to Dedicate *Capital* to Darwin?" *Journal of the History of Ideas*, 39 (1978), 133.

58. Frederick Engels, *The Dialectics of Nature* (New York, 1940), p. 19, quoted in Runkle, pp. 109-10.

59. Karl Marx, *Letters to Dr. Kugelman* (New York, 1934), p. 30, quoted in Colp, "Marx and Darwin," p. 333.

60. Rudolf Virchow quoted in Ernst Haeckel, *Freedom in Science and Teaching* (New York, 1879), pp. 89-90.

61. Haeckel, ibid., pp. 91, 94. On Haeckel's later reputation as a "conservative Darwinist" see Ernest Untermann, *Science and Revolution* (Chicago, 1905), p. 144; Nasmyth, *Social Progress*, p. 6; and August Bebel, *Woman: her position in the Past, Present, and Future*, translated H. B. Adams Walther (London, 1893), 126-29. Cf. Daniel Gasman, *The Scientific Origins of National Socialism: Social Darwinism in Ernst Haeckel and the German Monist League* (London, 1971). Challenging earlier portraits of Haeckel as liberal or socialist, Gasman argues that he contributed to "social Darwinist" defenses of aristocracy and individualism, racism, and German nationalism. Haeckel and his associates in the Monist League thus allegedly constituted a link between nineteenth-century evolutionism and Nazi ideology. So viewed, Haeckel's response to Virchow in 1878 was a reaffirmation of "his oft-stated position" (p. 112), although Gasman offers no other examples of similar "Darwinian" defenses of aristocracy or individualism. Regrettably, however, Gasman's definition of "social Darwinism" compounds every confusion in the literature of the subject. Failing to distinguish "individual" from "collectivist" versions he remains puzzled (significantly) that Haeckel, the aristocrat-individualist, who stressed "the universality of struggle," should also have stressed social "harmony and cooperation." (pp. 83 and 100, note 5). While not attempting to settle the larger question of Haeckel's political views, I am arguing only that his response to Virchow was tongue-in-cheek, and that Haeckel meant what he said about not dragging politics into discussions of Darwinism. Nor do I rule out the possibility that members of the Monist League, with or without Haeckel's inspiration, later fashioned Darwinian defenses of racism or aggressive nationalism that diverged from the Anglo-American experience.

In Haeckel's case I would suggest, however, that images of unmitigated struggle prefaced an emphasis, as Gasman himself finally argues, on "bonds of community and the mutual obligation of every individual in society" (p. 83). This interpretation of Haeckel is affirmed in Niles R. Holt, "Liberal Social Darwinism in Germany and France, 1870-90," unpublished paper read at American Historical Association annual meeting, December 1978.

62. Huxley, "Preface," *Freedom in Science* by Haeckel. William K. Clifford, *Lectures and Essays* (London, 1879), pp. 421-23 also took Virchow's prediction at face value, but dismissed as improbable the prospect in England of "a socialist revolution founded on the doctrine of descent." See also John Tyndall, "Virchow and Evolution," *Popular Science*, 14 (1879), 266-90.

63. William H. Mallock, "Poverty, Sympathy, and Economics," *Forum*, 5 (1888), 400; Richard Ely, *Socialism* (New York, 1894), p. 74.

64. Untermann, *Science and Revolution*, p. 148.

65. Enrico Ferri, *Socialism and Modern Science*, trans., Robert Rives LaMonte (New York, 1900), p. 5. For LaMonte's later connection with H. L. Mencken's "social Darwinism" see ch. 10 below.

66. Untermann, *Science and Revolution*, p. 150.

67. Quoted in Vladimir G. Simkhovitch, *Marxism vs. Socialism* (New York, 1913), p. 188.

68. Herman Whitaker, "Weismannism and Its Relation to Socialism," *International Socialist Review*, 1 (1901), 519.

69. William J. Ghent, "Why Socialists are Patisans," *Independent*, 59 (1905), 969-70; Gaylord Wilshire, "The Mutation Theory," *Socialism Inevitable* (New York, 1907); Robert R. LaMonte, "Science and Revolution," *Social Democrat*, 13 (1909), 105-13.

70. Ferri, *Socialism and Modern Science*, p. 371; and Ghent, *Our Benevolent Feudalism* (1902), p. 29. Irvin Wyllie,

"Social Darwinism and the Businessman," noted that the junior Rockefeller was the source of the statement concerning the "American Beauty rose." See also Raphael Buck, "Natural Selection under Socialism," *International Socialist Review*, 2 (1902), 784-85. For uses of the stereotype by British socialists see John Arnott, *The Mending of Mankind: Darwinism and Socialism* (Manchester, Eng., n.d.), p. 9; Robert Blatchford, *Merrie England* (London, 1894), pp. 144-51; Thomas Kirkup, "Darwinism and Socialism," *Economic Review*, 1 (1891), 531, and *A History of Socialism* (1888), pp. 294-310; and George Lacy, *Liberty and Law* (London, 1888), p. 41. These sources were of course known to American reformers. For example, Henry D. Lloyd quoted Kirkup in *Notebook* D (1887), 50, Lloyd Papers.

71. David Goldstein, *Socialism: The Nation of Fatherless Children* (Boston, 1903), p. 60.

72. Simkhovitch, *Marxism vs. Socialism*, p. 187; Ward, "Social Darwinism," pp. 709-10, and "Social and Biological Struggle," pp. 289-90, the latter also quoted in Simkhovitch, p. 188.

73. See McCloskey, *American Conservatism*, chs. 4-5; Louis B. Wright, "Franklin's Legacy to the Gilded Age," *Virginia Quarterly Review*, 22 (1946), 268-79; Perry Miller, "Introduction," *American Thought* (New York, 1954); and Donald Meyer, *The Positive Thinkers* (New York, 1965).

Chapter 7
Neo-Darwinism and the Crisis
of the 1890s

1. Edward P. Foster, "Behind the Mask," *Arena*, 2 (1890), 588-91; Peter Grant, "Song of the Trusts," *By Heath and Prairie* (Chicago, 1900), pp. 89-90; New Jersey Labor Commission quoted in Alfred R. Wallace, "The Social Quagmire," *Arena*, 7 (1893), 526. See also Rodney Welch, "Horace Greeley's Cure

for Poverty," *Forum*, 8 (1889), 586. Although critics had characterized American society in "Darwinian" terms since the 1870s, the conviction grew from the nineties onward that the situation was growing worse and was perhaps hopeless. For example see John D. Works, "Man's Inhumanity to Man," *Twentieth Century Magazine*, 2 (1910), 331. This attitude provided the background for the work of H. L. Mencken and the literary naturalists discussed in chs. ten and eleven below.

2. Hamlin Garland, *Main Travelled Roads* (New York, 1954), p. 73; editorial in *Scientific American*, 77 (1897), 186. For professionals, Darwinian phraseology expressed at once a disdain of commercialism ("money-grubbing") and fear that organizational routine was destroying individuality. See William B. Hornblower, "Has the Profession of Law Been Commercialized?" *Forum*, 18 (1895), 679-85.

3. See Frederick Churchill, "August Weismann and a Break from Tradition," *Journal of the History of Biology*, 1 (1968), 91-112.

4. Samuel Garman, "Weismann on Heredity," *Nation*, 50 (1890), 357-58. On neo-Lamarckianism see Edward J. Pfeifer, "The Genesis of American neo-Lamarckianism," *Isis*, 56 (1965), 156-67.

5. Joseph LeConte, "The Factors of Evolution," *Monist*, 1 (1891), 334; Herbert E. Cushman, "Professor August Weismann," *Outlook*, 55 (1897), 253; Charles S. Peirce, "Evolutionary Love," *Monist* 3 (1893), 176-200; Morgan to Wallace, 8 February 1892, cited John C. Burnham, "Instinct Theory and the German Reaction to Weismannism," *Journal of the History of Biology*, 5 (1972), 321-28.

6. Alexander Japp, *Darwin* (London, 1901), pp. 74, 98-99, 110; George Paulin, *No Struggle for Existence, No Natural Selection* (Edinburgh, 1908), p. 249.

7. Edward A. Ross, "Turning Towards Nirvana," *Arena*, 4 (1891), 739.

8. LeConte, "The Factors of Evolution," p. 335; Edward S. Morse, "Natural Selection and Crime," *Popular Science*, 41 (1892), 443-46. For sharper distinctions between biological and social inheritance see Henry Calderwood, *Evolution and Man's Place in Nature* (New York, 1893), p. 20; and Leslie Stephen, *Social Rights and Duties*, 2 vols. (London, 1896), 2: 30-54. Burnham, "Instinct Theory" suggests important differences between the Anglo-American and German responses on this issue.

9. Karl Pearson, *The Chances of Death*, 2 vols., (London, 1897), 1: 222, 175.

10. George Stocking, "Lamarckianism in American Social Science 1890-1915," *Journal of the History of Ideas*, 23 (1962), 239-56. Henry Drummond, *The Ascent of Man* (New York, 1894), p. 43.

11. On Huxley, see Cyril Bibby, *Scientist Extraordinary: The Life and Scientific Work of Thomas Henry Huxley* (New York, 1972); Albert Ashforth, *Thomas Henry Huxley* (New York, 1969); and Michael S. Helfand, "T. H. Huxley's Evolution and Ethics: The Politics of Evolution and the Evolution of Politics," *Victorian Studies*, 20 (1977), 159-77.

12. Huxley, *Evolution and Ethics* (New York, 1898), pp. 83, 75, 31.

13. Ibid., pp. 14, 36.

14. Ibid., pp. 11, 12.

15. Ibid., p. 40.

16. Ibid., pp. 85-86.

17. Helfand, "Huxley's Evolution and Ethics."

18. Huxley, *Evolution and Ethics*, p. 197, quoted ibid. p. 168.

19. Huxley, "On The Natural Inequality of Man," *Methods and Results* (New York, 1897) quoted in Helfand, p. 171. In my view, Helfand makes too much of Huxley's "logical" inconsistencies on this point and overemphasizes his "veiled" attacks on Wallace (and George) rather than his opposition to Spencer.

20. John Dewey, "Evolution and Ethics," *Monist*, 8 (1898), 321-41; Spencer, "Evolution and Ethics," [5 August 1893], *Various Fragments* (New York, 1910),

pp. 121-29; Bibby, *Scientist Extraordinary*, p. 146.

21. For reaction in "Administrative Nihilism," see Thaddeus B. Wakeman, "Public Administration," *Nationalist*, 1 (1889), 100-5; William C. Owen, *The Economics of Herbert Spencer* (New York, 1891), p. 119; John W. Powell, "Human Evolution," Anthropological Society of Washington, *Transactions* (1883), 206-8; Frederick M. Willis, "The Sphere of the State," *Nationalist*, 2 (1890), 155-62; and editorial, "Nationalism and Evolution," ibid., 3 (1891), 416-17.

22. Huxley, "The Struggle for Existence," *Nineteenth Century*, 23 (1888), 161-80; Spencer to Huxley, 6 February 1888 in David Duncan, *Life and Letters of Herbert Spencer*, 2 vols. (New York, 1908), 1: 374-76.

23. Huxley, *Evolution and Ethics*, p. 80.

24. Ibid., pp. 18-19, 23.

25. Huxley to George Romanes, quoted in Bibby, *Scientist Extraordinary*, p. 136.

26. Oma Stanley, "T. H. Huxley's Treatment of 'Nature,'" *Journal of the History of Ideas*, 18 (1957), 120-27. Huxley's translation of Goethe quoted ibid., p. 120; Huxley, *Crayfish* (1879), quoted Bibby, *Scientist Extraordinary*, p. 138.

27. Huxley, "Prologue," *Science and Christian Tradition* (1892), quoted in Stanley, "Huxley," p. 126.

28. Huxley, *Evolution and Ethics*, p. 3.

29. Huxley, "On the Advisableness of Improving Natural Knowledge," (1866), quoted Ashford, *Huxley*, p. 162.

30. Huxley, *Evolution and Ethics*, pp. 51-52.

31. St. George Mivart, "Evolution in Professor Huxley," *Nineteenth Century*, 34 (1893), 193, 198-211; Spencer, "Evolutionary Ethics," *Various Fragments*, p. 121; editorial, "Ethical Seriousness," *Nation*, 56 (1893), 440-41; Huxley to Farrer, quoted in Bibby, p. 138. Leslie Stephen, "Ethics and the Struggle for Existence," *Contemporary Review*, 64 (1893), 159, commented: "War is evidently immoral, we think; and a doctrine which makes the whole process of evolution a process of war must be radically immoral too. The struggle, it is said, demands 'ruthless self-assertion,' and the hunting down of all competitors."

32. Kelly, review of W. W. Willoughby's, *Social Justice* in *Political Science Quarterly*, 16 (1901), 171-73. In a later article "Kidd's View on Evolution," ibid., 17 (1902), 515-18, Kelly judged Huxley more favorably as showing that "it is upon man's wisdom and morality that the whole future depends."

33. Herbert L. Stewart, "Criticisms on the Nietzsche Revival," *International Journal of Ethics*, 19 (1909), 440.

34. Arthur M. Lewis, *Evolution Social and Organic* (Chicago, 1908), p. 99.

35. Dewey, "Evolution and Ethics," p. 326; Leo S. Rowe, "American Political Ideas and Institutions," *Municipal Affairs*, 1 (1897), 323-24; Henry C. Vedder, *Socialism and the Ethics of Jesus* (New York, 1912), p. 371. See also Hartley Withers, *Poverty and Waste* (London, 1914), pp. 142-44.

36. Lewis G. Janes, "Ethics in Natural Law," *Popular Science*, 46 (1895), 323; and *Our Nation's Peril* (Boston, 1899), p. 13. See also John C. Kimball, "From Natural to Christian Selection," *Life and the Conditions of Survival* [Brooklyn Ethical Association] (Chicago, 1895), pp. 333-60.

37. Arthur J. Eddy, *The New Competition* (New York, 1912), pp. 13-14.

38. Leonard Huxley, *Progress and the Unfit* (London, 1926), pp. 10, 30. For an earlier example see Caleb W. Saleeby, *Evolution* (New York, 1906), pp. 282-3. Weismannism was also a stimulus to eugenics. See David Starr Jordan, review of Weismann in *Dial*, 13 (1892), 242-44; and Martin L. Holbrook, *Stirpiculture* (New York, 1897), p. 74.

39. Andrew Seth, "Prof. Huxley on Nature and Man," *Blackwood's*, 154 (1893), 823-34. Although Seth noted that few readers would rest content in this

posture, Huxley's sentiments later found a direct echo in Ambrose Bierce, "Nature as a Reformer," *Cosmopolitan*, 45 (1908), 1. Describing the painful nature of progress, Bierce concluded: "Through all her works and ways 'one increasing purpose runs': to 'weed out' the incompetent, the unthrifty, and alas! the luckless—all the 'unfit.' Doubtless an omnipotent power could have accomplished the end without the means, but the situation is as we see it, and not otherwise. The method is cruel unthinkably, but the soul in this body of death is hope."

40. Charles M. Bakewell, "Nietzsche: A Modern Stoic," *Yale Review*, n.s. 5 (1915), 73.

41. On Kidd see Clarence Crane Brinton, *English Political Thought in the 19th Century* (London, 1933).

42. Benjamin Kidd, *Social Evolution* (London, 1894), pp. 34-35, 43, 62, 63.

43. Ibid., p. 82.

44. Ibid., p. 22.

45. Ibid., pp. 3-5, 93-94.

46. Theodore Roosevelt, "Degeneration and Revolution," *North American Review*, 161 (1895), 94-109.

47. William D. LeSueur, "Kidd on 'Social Evolution,'" *Popular Science*, 47 (1895), 38-48.

48. *Critic*, o.s. 22 [n.s. 25] (1894), 94, 419; Ely, "Religion as a Social Force," *Christian Quarterly* (July 1897), 321; Bliss quoted in Franklin M. Sprague, *The Laws of Social Evolution* (Boston, 1895), p. 12; Drummond, *The Ascent of Man*, p. 54; Harold Laski, "Sociological Romance," *New Republic*, 9 (1916), 235-37.

49. LeSueur, "Kidd on 'Social Evolution,'" p. 41.

50. Ibid., pp. 46-48.

51. "Literary Notes," *Popular Science*, 45 (1894), 557-58.

52. Kidd, *Social Evolution*, pp. 29, 75, 288, 28, 113.

53. Ibid., pp. 10-11, 69-70.

54. *Nation*, 68 (1894), 294; *Popular Science*,

45 (1894), 558; LeSueur, "Kidd on 'Social Evolution,'" p. 39.

55. Henry D. Lloyd, "Kidd's Social Evolution," ms. 1896, Lloyd Papers; Edward Cummings,"Charity and Progress," *Quarterly Journal of Economics*, 12 (1897), 31; William J. Bryan, "The Menace of Darwinism," *Commoner* (April 1921). See also Lucius M. Bristol, *Social Adaptation* (Cambridge, 1915), ch. 5: "He pictures the misery of the exploited classes in industrial centers and seems to feel [n.b.] that all this is natural and necessary"; Richard Ely, "Social Progress," ms. (ca. 1897), Ely Papers, Wisconsin Historical Society; R. Didden, "Individualism or Collectivism?" *Westminster Review*, 149 (1898), 655-66; and Henry C. Thompson, *A New Reading of Evolution* (Chicago, 1907), p. 322.

56. Kidd, *Social Evolution*, pp. 5, 11. Cf. William Dean Howells, *A Traveler from Altruria* (1894), p. 164: "The struggle of life has changed from a free fight to an encounter of disciplined forces, and the free fighters are ground to pieces between organized labor and organized capital"; and Ray Stannard Baker, "Capital and Labor," *McClure's* 21 (1903), 463: "Is there any doubt that the income of organized labor and the profits of organized capital have gone up enormously, while the man-on-a-salary and most of the great middle class . . . have had no adequate increase in earnings?" Both quoted Richard Hofstadter, *The Age of Reform* (New York, 1955), p. 214.

57. Ibid., pp. 215, 289. See also Bernard Semmel, *Imperialism and Social Reform* (London, 1960), p. 32.

58. Kidd, *Social Evolution*, pp. 233, 237.

59. Benjamin Kidd, *Individualism and After* (Oxford, 1908), pp. 12, 13, 25, 36.

60. Farrer, "Kidd's 'Social Evolution,'" *Contemporary Review*, 65 (1894), 769-80; Heinz Maus, *A Short History of Sociology* (London, 1962), p. 44.

61. For two contemporary accounts see

Edith Sellers, "Our Most Distinguished Refugee," *Contemporary Review*, 66 (1894), 537-49; and Robert E. Ely, "Prince Kropotkin," *Atlantic Monthly*, 82 (1898), 338-46.

62. Peter Kropotkin, *Mutual Aid* (London, 1902), p. x.

63. Kropotkin, *Mutual Aid*, p. xiv; "The Scientific Bases of Anarchy," *Nineteenth Century*, 21 (1887), 238-52.

64. Vladimir G. Simkhovitch, *Political Science Quarterly*, 18 (1903), 702-5; and David M. Means, *Nation*, 76 (1903), 217.

65. *Athenaeum*, 1 (1903), 41.

66. Cuthbert Lennox, *Henry Drummond* (London, 1901), pp. 5, 19.

67. Ibid., chs. 3-4.

68. Drummond, *Natural Law in the Spiritual World* (New York, 1884), pp. 11, 97-120.

69. Ibid., pp. xiii, 203.

70. Ibid., pp. xi, 35, 37, 40, xxiii.

71. Lennox, *Drummond*, p. 76; Drummond, *The Ascent of Man*, p. 43.

72. Drummond, *The Ascent of Man*, pp. 13, 19, 13, 34.

73. Ibid., pp. 22-23, 28, 53.

74. Spencer to E. L. Youmans, 17 May 1883, in David Duncan, *Life and Letters of Herbert Spencer*, 2 vols. (New York, 1908) 1: 309; Spencer to Mrs. Lynn Linton, 6 June, 3 September 1894, ibid., 2: 72-73; Linton, "Professor Drummond's Discovery," *Fortnightly* n.s. 56 (1894), 448-57.

75. On Wood and New Thought see Donald Meyer, *The Positive Thinkers* (New York, 1965).

76. Henry Dyer, *The Evolution of Industry* (New York, 1895), p. 55; Lyman Abbott, *The Industrial Problem* (Philadelphia, 1905), pp. 40-1.

Chapter 8
A Pigeon Fanciers' Polity

1. On Ross see Julius Weinberg, *Edward A. Ross and the Sociology of Progres-sivism* (Madison, Wis., 1972). In *The Foundations of Sociology* (New York, 1905) Ross wrote: "This process of modifying a species Darwin called 'natural selection,' and showed that it applied to man as well as to the lower species. But soon the thought arose, Does not *society* impose decisive conditions as well as *nature*? Along side of natural selections are there not . . . social selections?" In *The Descent of Man*, Darwin encouraged such speculation by remarking that "excepting in the case of man himself, hardly any one is so ignorant as to allow his worst animals to breed" (p. 152). But, as noted in ch. 1 above, he insisted that man must exercise philanthropy and left the stockbreeding analogy undeveloped. This chapter discusses the emergence of such reasoning and the role of the "social Darwinian" stereotype in it.

2. Roosevelt's comments reprinted in Ross, *Sin and Society* (Boston, 1907), pp. ix-xi. For different meanings of "social control" among social scientists see Georges Gurvitch, "Social Control," *Twentieth Century Sociology*, ed. G. Gurvitch (New York, 1945).

3. On eugenics, see Field, "Progress of Eugenics"; Mark H. Haller, *Eugenics* (New Brunswick, N.J., 1963); Rudolph Vecoli, "Sterilization: A Progressive Measure?" *Wisconsin Magazine of History*, 43 (1960), 190-202; Donald K. Pickens, *Eugenics and The Progressives* (Nashville, 1968); and Kenneth M. Ludmerer, *Genetics and American Society* (Baltimore, 1972). Although this chapter deals only with eugenics, the movement was closely related to that for immigration restriction. See esp. Ludmerer, *Genetics*, pp. 26-33, 87-119.

4. James A. Field, "The Progress of Eugenics," *Quarterly Journal of Economics*, 26 (1911), 62. Don S. Kirschener, "The Ambiguous Legacy: Social Justice and Social Control in the Progressive Era," *Historical Reflections*, 2 (1975), 69-88, notes that social justice and social con-

trol were not necessarily incompatable. Nor did these two ideals pit one group of humanitarians against another of technocrats. Rather individual reformers "were moved by a tenderminded wish to liberate the downtrodden from the shackles of society," and "a tough minded desire to protect society from the threat of the downtrodden." For a clear recognition of the two impluses in the writing of a leading American eugenicist, see Roswell H. Johnson, "The Evolution of Man and Its Control," *Popular Science*, 76 (1910), 49-70.

5. Hofstadter, *Social Darwinism*, p. 161. Richard J. Halliday, "Social Darwinism," *Victorian Studies*, 14 (1971), 389-405, argues for limiting the term to eugenics and related programs.

6. Noyes quoted in Haller, *Eugenics*, p. 37; Ridgeway, *Proceedings of the British Association* (1908), p. 45, and Davenport, *Heredity in Relation to Eugenics* (1912), p. 5, both quoted in G. Spiller, "Darwinism and Sociology," *Sociological Review*, 7 (1914), 233-34.

7. Charles V. Drysdale, *Neo-Malthusianism and Eugenics* (London, 1912), p. 6.

8. Haller, *Eugenics*, p. 40; William Noyes, "The Criminal Type," *Journal of Social Science*, 24 (1887), 31.

9. Francis Galton, *Memories of My Life* (reprint ed., London, 1908) pp. 287-88.

10. Derek W. Forrest, *Francis Galton: The Life and Work of a Victorian Genius* (London, 1974), p. 85. On Galton as eugenicist, see also Constance Corning, "Galton and Eugenics," *History Today*, 23 (1973), 724-32. Ruth Schwartz Cowen, "Nature and Nurture: The Interplay of Biology and Politics in the Work of Francis Galton," *Studies in the History of Biology*, 1 (1977), 133-208, which I read after writing the above, supports the conclusion that Darwin had little impact on Galton, while describing other social concerns that shaped Galton's work.

11. Galton, *Hereditary Genius* (London, 1962), p. 392.

12. Ibid., p. 406; *Inquiries into Human Faculty and Development* (New York, 1883), p. 305.

13. Francis Galton, *Memories*, p. 290.

14. William R. Greg, "NonSurvival of the Fittest," *Enigmas of Life*, quoted in Field, "Progress of Eugenics," pp. 9, 64.

15. Albert V. Dicey, review of *Enigmas of Life* in *Nation*, 16 (1873), 371-73; and Drysdale, *Neo-Malthusianism*, p. 6.

16. Richard L. Dugdale, *The Jukes* (New York, 1877), pp. 55, 119.

17. George Iles, "Heredity," *Popular Science*, 14 (1879), 356-64.

18. Alexander G. Bell, "Upon the Formation of a Deaf Variety of the Human Race," National Academy of Science, *Memoir* (1883), 179-80. Bell's uncertainty was echoed in a review of his work by W. K. Brooks, "Can Man Be Modified by Selection?" *Popular Science*, 27 (1885), 15-25.

19. Loring Moody and Elizabeth Thompson, *Heredity. Its Relation to Human Development* (Boston, 1882), p. 117.

20. Bellamy, *Looking Backward*, pp. 218-20.

21. Hiram M. Stanley, "Our Civilization and the Marriage Problem," *Arena*, 2 (1890), 94-100.

22. Amos G. Warner, *American Charities* (1894) quoted in Haller, *Eugenics*, p. 60; A. Mansfield Holmes, "Heredity and Environment," *Arena*, 9 (1894), 581; Wesley Mills, "Heredity in Relation to Education," *Popular Science*, 44 (1894), 472-80; James C. Browne, "Biology and Ethics," *Popular Science*, 44 (1894), 671-77.

23. A. R. Wallace, "Human Selection," ibid., 38 (1890), 100, 106; originally published in the *Fortnightly*, o.s. 54 (n.s. 48) (1890), 325-37.

24. Ludmerer, *Genetics*, p. 18.

25. Annie Besant, *The Law of Population* (New York, 1878), p. 42; Samuel J. Holmes, "The Decadence of Human Heredity," *Atlantic Monthly*, 114 (1914), 308; Roswell Johnson, "The Evolution of Man," *Popular Science*, 76 (1910), 59.

26. Martin L. Holbrook, *Stirpiculture* (New York, 1897), p. 3; Edward Isaacson, *The Malthusian Limit* (London, 1912), p. 25.
27. Albert Wiggam, *The New Decalogue of Science* (New York, 1923), p. 220.
28. William Duncan McKim, *Heredity and Human Progress*, (New York, 1899), pp. 191-93.
29. Ludmerer, *Genetics*, pp. 83-86.
30. John B. Haycraft, *Darwinism and Race Progress* (London, 1895), p. 170; George Archdall Reid, *Present Evolution* (London, 1896), p. 370. See also Reid, "Heredity and Social Problems," *Independent*, 60 (1906), 379-83, and "Biological Foundations of Society,"*American Journal of Sociology*, 11 (1906), 532-54. Since Reid wanted artificial selection by penalizing procreation of alcoholics, he was really parodying natural selection. Discovering that he was taken seriously, he later attempted to explain away this bit of hyperbole. See Reid, *Alcoholism* (London, 1901), pp. 167-68.
31. James White, "Darwinism and Malthus," *Journal of the Victoria Institute*, 42 (1910), 222-40; and C. T. Ewart, "Social Science," *Westminster Review*, 174 (1910), 637-43. See also Charles Walker, "Dangers of Socialistic Legislation," *Science Progress*, 7 (1913), 460-71; "The Interpretation of Fact in the Study of Heredity," ibid., 8 (1913-14), 324; and Harold Laski, "The Scope of Eugenics," *Westminster Review*, 174 (1910), 25-34.
32. Edwin E. Slosson, "Survival of the Unfittest," *Independent* 107 (1921), 24-25; Frederick William Inman, *Biological Politics* (Bristol, Eng., 1935), pp. 48-49.
33. Frederick W. Headley, *Darwinism and Modern Socialism* (London, 1909), pp. 1, 16.
34. Charles P. Blacker, *Eugenics: Galton and After* (London, 1952) p. 139; Field, "Progress of Eugenics," p. 64; Ludmerer, *Genetics*.
35. Arthur Mitchell, *The Past in the Present* (Edinburgh, 1880), p. 313; Franklin Giddings, "Race Improvement Through

Civilization," *Independent*, 60 (1906), 383; the Reverend J. Tuckwell, comment on White, "Darwinism and Malthus," p. 240. See also John Arthur Thomson, *Darwinism and Human Life* (London, 1909), p. 217, who specifically attacked the callous "Darwinism" of Haycraft's *Darwinism and Race Progress*.
36. Edward T. Devine, *The Family* (New York, 1912), p. 17; and Samuel Z. Batten, "Redemption of the Unfit," *American Journal of Sociology*, 14 (1908), 236-39. See also Herman Whitaker, "Natural Selection," *Arena*, 24 (1900), 130-37; and in Great Britain C. B. Kent-Roylance, "Evolution in Human Society," *Fortnightly*, 99 (1913), 1165; and W. R. MacDermott, "Darwinolatry," *Westminster Review*, 173 (1910), 495.
37. David Collin Wells, "Social Darwinism," *American Journal of Sociology*, 12 (1907), 697-98.
38. Herbert W. Conn, "The Individual and the Race," quoted at start of this chapter; Leonard Hobhouse, *Social Evolution and Political Theory* (New York, 1911), pp. 9-22.

Chapter 9
The Scaffolding of Progress

1. Darwin quoted in George Fredrickson, *The Black Image in the White Mind* (New York, 1971), p. 230.
2. Hofstadter, *Social Darwinism*, p. 172; Thomas F. Gossett, *Race: The History of an Idea in America* (Dallas, Tex., 1963); Fredrickson, *Black Image*, chs. 7-10. See also Gertrude Himmelfarb, *Darwin and the Darwinian Revolution* (London, 1959), ch. 19.
3. See John C. Greene, "Some Early Speculations on the Origins of Human Races," *American Anthropologist*, 56 (1954), 31-41, and "The American Debate on the Negro's Place in Nature, 1780-1815," *Journal of the History of Ideas*, 15 (1954), 384-96.

4. Benjamin Rush "Observations," (1799), quoted in Greene, "American Debate," p. 389.
5. Winthrop Jordan, *White Over Black* (Chapel Hill, N.C., 1968), pp. 287-94, 308-311.
6. See William S. Stanton, *The Leopard's Spots* (Chicago, 1956) and Joseph S. Haller, Jr., *Outcasts from Evolution* (Urbana, Ill., 1971).
7. Josiah C. Nott, *The Negro Race* (Mobile, Ala., 1866), pp. 12-3, quoted in Fredrickson, *Black Image*, p. 233; Darwin to W. Graham, 3 July 1881, Francis Darwin, ed., *Life and Letters of Charles Darwin* (London, 1887), 1: 316, quoted in Himmelfarb, *Darwin and The Darwinian Revolution*, p. 343.
8. Himmelfarb, *Darwin and the Darwinian Revolution*, pp. 342-43.
9. Ibid., pp. 340-41.
10. Charles Darwin, *The Descent of Man*, 2nd ed., (New York, 1874), pp. 201-5.
11. Ibid., pp. 206-227.
12. A. R. Wallace, *Contributions to the Theory of Natural Selection*, 2nd ed., (London, 1871), pp. 301, 312, 321, 317.
13. Ibid., pp. 322-331.
14. T. H. Huxley, "Man's Place in Nature," [1863] *Evidences as to Man* (New York, 1871), pp. 189-202; Bibby, *Scientist Extraordinary*, p. 143.
15. Huxley, "Emancipation . . . Black and White," [1865] *Collected Essays*, 9 vols. (New York, 1896-1902), 7: 67-75.
16. Benjamin Moran, *The Journal of Benjamin Moran*, 2 vols. (Chicago, 1948), 1: 78-79. Cf. the interpretation in Himmelfarb, *Darwin and the Darwinian Revolution*, p. 343.
17. Fredrickson, *Black Image*, p. 238.
18. John William DeForest, *A Union Officer in the Reconstruction*, ed., James H. Croushore and David Potter (New Haven, 1948), p. 117.
19. Ibid., pp. 131, 158.
20. Fredrickson, *Black Image*, ch. 7.
21. For a summary of Spencer's views see Haller, *Outcasts*, ch. 5.
22. Spencer quoted ibid., p. 131.

23. John Fiske, "The Progress from Brute to Man," *North American Review*, 117 (1873), 259, 253.
24. Joseph LeConte, "The Genesis of Sex," *Popular Science*, 16 (1879), 167; Nathaniel Shaler, "Science and the African Problem," *Atlantic Monthly*, 66 (1890), 36-45:
25. C. Vann Woodward, *The Strange Career of Jim Crow*, 2nd ed., rev. (New York, 1957), p. 64.
26. Frederick L. Hoffman, *Race Traits and Tendencies of the American Negro*, American Economic Association, *Publications*, 11 (1896), 1, 142.
27. Ibid., pp. 326-27.
28. Hoffman to Jerrmiah W. Jenks, 20 January 1896, Papers of the American Economic Association, Northwestern University; Hoffman, *Race Traits*, p. 328.
29. Ibid., p. 328.
30. Hollis B. Frissell to J. W. Jenks, 29 October 1896, A.E.A. Papers; DuBois, *Annals of the American Academy*, 9 (1897), 127-33; Washington to Jenks, 7 September 1896, A.E.A. Papers.
31. Davis R. Dewey, "Memorandum with Regard to Paper Submitted by F. L. Hoffman," [1895], ms. in A.E.A. Papers; Hoffman to Jenks, 11 January 1896; 10 December 1895, A.E.A. Papers.
32. Frederick Starr, "The Degeneracy of the American Negro," *Dial*, 22 (1897), 18; William G. Sumner to Hoffman, 15 December 1896, A.E.A. Papers.
33. Joseph A. Tillinghast, *The Negro in Africa and America*, American Economic Association, *Publications*, 3rd ser., 3 (1902), 228.
34. William B. Smith, *The Color Line* (New York, 1905), pp. 12-13; William E. B. DuBois, review in *Dial*, 38 (1905), 317.
35. Myrta L. Avary, *Dixie After the War* (1906), p. 393; John S. Williams, "The Negro and the South," *Metropolitan Magazine*, 27 (1907), 137-51; Benjamin R. Tillman, "The Race Question," *Van Norden's Magazine*, 2 (1907), 25, quoted in Fredrickson, *Black Image*, pp. 257-

58; Daniel Tompkins, "National Expansion," [ca. 1900], quoted in George T. Winston, *A Builder of the New South* (Garden City, N.Y., 1920), pp. 303-4.

36. William Hannibal Thomas, *The American Negro* (New York, 1901), p. xii.

37. Ibid., pp. 418, 430.

38. "The American Negro," *Independent*, 53 (1901), 393-94; and DuBois, "The Storm and Stress in the Black World," *Dial*, 30 (1901), 262-64.

39. Ibid.

40. Fredrickson, *Black Image*, p. 284.

41. Carl Kelsey, *The Negro Farmer* (Chicago, 1903), p. 66; William Elwang, *The Negroes of Columbia Missouri* (Columbia, Mo., 1904), p. 64; Jerome Dowd, *The Negro in American Life* (New York, 1926), p. 396. See also Dowd, *The Negro Races*, 2 vols. (New York, 1907, 1914), 2: 69-70.

42. Kelsey, *Negro Farmer*, pp. 6, 70, 78; Elwang, *Negroes of Columbia*, p. 66; Dowd, *Negro Races*, 1: 446.

43. Charles A. Ellwood, preface to Elwang, *Negroes of Columbia*; and *Sociology and Modern Social Problems* (New York, 1910), pp. 233, 235, 246.

44. Ibid., pp. 246-47, 250-52.

45. Ray S. Baker, *Following the Color Line* (New York, 1964), pp. 12, 147, 296.

46. Ibid., pp. 86, 274, 147.

47. Ibid., p. 305.

48. Baker, *Journal* J, pp. 170-71, ms. in Baker Papers, Library of Congress.

49. DuBois, "Relations of the Negroes to the Whites in the South," *Annals of the American Academy*, 18 (1901), 121; Ellwood, *Sociology and Modern Social Problems*, p. 251; and U. G. Weatherly, "World Wide Color Line," *Popular Science*, 79 (1911), 485. See also an unsigned article "Influence of Heredity upon Success in Life," *Current Literature*, 44 (1908), 439-42.

50. William E. Walling, "Science and Human Brotherhood," *Independent*, 66 (1909), 1319.

51. Charles A. Ellwood, *Christianity and*

Social Science (New York, 1923).

Chapter 10
The Nietzsche Vogue

1. Ragnar Redbeard, *Might is Right* (Chicago, 1896), p. 13; Henry Louis Mencken and Robert R. LaMonte, *Men vs. the Man* (New York, 1910), p. 69.

2. Friedrich Nietzsche, *The Works of Friedrich Nietzsche*, ed. Alexander Tille, 2 vols. (London, 1896-97). The initial volumes of this uncompleted edition were numbered 10 and 11. Nietzsche, *The Complete Works*, ed. Oscar Levy, reprint ed., 18 vols. (New York, 1964), appeared between 1909 and 1913. Much of the early debate concerning Nietzsche and Darwin in the English-speaking world thus occurred before his views were widely or accurately known.

3. Conor Cruise O'Brien, "The Gentle Nietzscheans," *New York Review of Books*, 5 (November 1970), 14. A leading proponent of the "tender" Nietzsche is Walter A. Kaufmann, *Nietzsche* (New York, 1956). See also Bryan Strong, "Images of Nietzsche in America 1900-1970," *South Atlantic Quarterly*, 70 (1971), 575-94.

4. Paul Carus, *Nietzsche and Other Exponents of Individualism* (Chicago, 1914), ch. 4.

5. Nietzsche, *Works*, ed. A. Tille, 10: 248 [written 1887]; *The Complete Works*, ed., Levy, 6: 208 [written 1878]; and *Works*, ed. Tille, 11: 173 [written 1889]. The reference to "learned cattle" is from *Ecce Homo*, quoted in William M. Salter, *Nietzsche the Thinker* (New York, 1917), p. 402.

6. Nietzsche, *The Complete Works*, ed. Levy, 10: 338.

7. Ibid., 14: 45; see also ibid., pp. 51, 330, 357.

8. A. Tille, "Preface," *Works*, 10: x-xv. On Tille's alleged contributions to National Socialism see Daniel Gasman, *The Scientific Origins of National*

Socialism (London, 1971), pp. 149-50, which draws on the more extended study of Hedwig Conrad-Martius, *Utopian der Menschenzuchtung* (Munich, 1955).

9. Ragnar Redbeard, *Might is Right*, pp. 99, 2, 166. Although this work is not listed in the catalog of the Library of Congress, a copy may be found in the Cornell University Library. It was apparently reissued in 1910 in a fifty-cent paperback edition in Chicago by G. Engelke.

10. The author's name was Arthur Desmond. See Charles A. Stonehill, *Anonymns and Pseudonyms*, 2nd edn., (New York, 1927).

11. Ragnar Redbeard, *Might is Right*, p. 2.

12. Generalizations concerning Nietzsche's reception in the United States are based on examination of virtually all books and articles about Nietzsche in the period 1896-1920 listed in the catalog of the Library of Congress, *The Reader's Guide*, and *The International Guide*.

13. *Popular Science*, 57 (1900), 668; Sigmund Zeisler, "The Philosophy of Nietzsche," *Dial*, 29 (1900), 219-21; Salter, *Nietzsche the Thinker*, pp. 2, 401-2; George B. Foster, *Friedrich Nietzsche* (New York, 1931), pp. 71, 96-98, 108-12, a collection of lectures written during World War I; William E. Walling, *Larger Aspects of Socialism* (New York, 1913), p. 205.

14. Mencken and LaMonte, *Men vs. the Man*, pp. 31-32; Mencken, *Friedrich Nietzsche* (Boston, 1908), p. 311. For LaMonte's earlier views on Darwinism see his *Socialism Positive and Negative* (New York, 1907).

15. Mencken and LaMonte, *Men vs. the Man*, pp. 14-15.

16. Ibid., pp. 63-69, 204-8.

17. Henry May, *The End of American Innocence* (New York, 1959), pp. 206-9 discusses the Nietzsche vogue.

18. Mencken, *George Bernard Shaw* (Boston, 1905), p. x; *Happy Days* (New York, 1940), pp. 252-62; *Nietzsche*, p. 107.

19. Ernest Boyd, *H. L. Mencken* (New York, 1925), p. 27.

20. Mencken, *Nietzsche*, pp. 124, 164, 93.

21. Two additional factors that shaped Mencken's Darwinian rendering of Nietzsche were his belief that the Germans, who were irrationally anti-British, did not see his true relation to Darwin; and Mencken's personal difficulties in translating German. See *Nietzsche*, p. 261; and Mencken to E. Stone, 1 March 1937. *Letters of H. L. Mencken*, ed. G. Forgue (New York, 1961), p. 414.

22. Edgar Kemler, *The Irreverent Mr. Mencken* (Boston, 1950), p. 41; *Political Science Quarterly*, 25 (1910), 570; and *Wilshire's Magazine*, quoted in "Will Nietzsche Come Into Vogue in America?" *Current Literature*, 49 (1910), 67.

23. Mencken, "Prophet of the Superman," *Smart Set*, 36 (1912), 154.

24. Malcolm Cowley, *Exile's Return* (New York, 1956), p. 62.

25. Ferdinand C. S. Schiller, "A Philosophic Mr. Hyde," *Nation* (London), 62 (1896), 459-60; Andrew Seth Pringle-Pattison, *Man's Place in the Cosmos* (London, 1897), p. 24; Pringle-Pattison, "The Opinions of Friedrich Nietzsche," *Contemporary Review*, 73 (1898), 749-50; Conrad Guenther, *Darwinism and the Problems of Life* (London, 1906), p. 417.

26. Franklin H. Giddings, *Democracy and Empire* (New York, 1899), p. 346; Edward A. Ross, *The Foundations of Sociology* (New York, 1905), p. 330; Alfred Fouillée, "Nietzsche and Darwinism," *International Monthly*, 3 (1901), 134-35; Victor Yarros, "Theoretical and Practical Nietzscheanism," *American Journal of Sociology*, 6 (1901), 682-94. See also Otto Heller, *Prophets of Dissent* (New York, 1918), p. 120.

27. James H. Tufts, "Darwin and Evolutionary Ethics," *Psychological Review*, 16 (1909), 204; Sidney Low, "Darwinism and Politics," *Fortnightly*, n.s. 86 (1909), 519-32; L. Smith, "Ibsen, Emerson, and Nietzsche," *Popular Science*, 78 (1911),

152-57; Henry C. Vedder, *Socialism and The Ethics of Jesus* (New York, 1912), pp. 368-71; and P. Meyers, *History as Past Ethics* (Boston, 1913), p. 356.

28. Thomas S. Baker, "What is the Superman?" *Independent*, 65 (1909), 613-16; *Outlook*, 66 (8 September 1900), 94; Paul Carus, "Immorality as a Philosophic Principle," *Monist*, 9 (1899), 572-616; Charles M. Bakewell, "The Teachings of Nietzsche," *Ethics*, 9 (1899), 329. Max Nordau employed a similar tactic in his *Degeneration*, American ed. (1895), and in "The Philosophy and the Morals of War," *North American Review*, 169 (1899), 794-95. See also William Barry, *Heralds of Revolt* (London, 1904), pp. 366-67; and Paul Elmer More, *Nietzsche* (Boston, 1912), p. 68.

29. Ernest Barker, *Nietzsche and Treitschke* (London, 1914), pp. 8, 12; Foster, *Nietzsche*, p. 71; Walling, *Larger Aspects*, p. 192; Mencken, *Prejudices*, 3rd ser. (New York, 1922), p. 129. See also John Arthur Thomson, *Darwinism and Modern Life* (London, 1909), p. 219.

30. Strong, "Images of Nietzsche," p. 576.

Chapter 11
Beyond the Battle:
The Literary Naturalists

1. Ignatius Donnelly, *Caesar's Column* (Cambridge, Mass.: John Harvard Library, 1960), p. 184; and Mark Twain, *Mark Twain's Notebook*, ed. Albert B. Paine (New York, 1935), p. 288, quoted in Sherwood Cummings, "Mark Twain's Social Darwinism," *Huntington Library Quarterly*, 20 (1956-57), 167.

2. Theodore Dreiser to Sergei Dinamov, 5 January 1927, quoted in William A. Swanberg, *Dreiser* (New York, 1965), p. 319; Jack London, *Martin Eden*, ed. Sam S. Baskett (New York, 1956), p. 237.

3. For discussion of the "cataclysmic vision" see Frederic C. Jaher, *Doubters and Dissenters* (Glencoe, Ill., 1964).

4. Charles Walcutt, *American Literary Naturalism* (Minneapolis, 1956).

5. Donnelly, *Caesar's Column*, p. 3. For background see the introduction to the John Harvard Library edition by Walter B. Rideout.

6. Ibid., pp. 15, 176-77, 38.

7. Ibid., p. 174.

8. Ibid., pp. 178-90.

9. Ibid., pp. 187, 190.

10. Ibid., pp. 291, 302.

11. Ibid., p. 15.

12. See Henry Nash Smith, *Mark Twain's Fable of Progress* (New Brunswick, 1964).

13. Quoted in Cummings, "Twain's Social Darwinism," p. 168.

14. Quoted in Cummings, *"What Is Man?":* The Scientific Sources," *Essays on Determinism*, ed. S. J. Krause (Kent, O. 1964), p. 110.

15. Theodore Dreiser, *The Financier* (New York, 1946), pp. 3-5.

16. Ellen Moers, *Two Dreisers* (New York, 1969), pp. 134-41; Dreiser to H. L. Mencken, 13 May 1916, Robert H. Elias, *The Letters of Theodore Dreiser*, 3 vols. (Philadelphia, 1959), 2: 211; Swanberg, *Dreiser*, p. 73.

17. Dreiser, *Jennie Gerhardt* (Cleveland, 1946), p. 17; and *The "Genius"* (Cleveland, 1946), p. 735.

18. Dreiser, *The Best Short Stories of Theodore Dreiser*, ed. Howard Fast (Cleveland, 1947), p. 113.

19. See Robert H. Elias, *Theodore Dreiser: Apostle of Nature* (New York, 1949), pp. 104-5.

20. Howard Fast, "Introduction," *Short Stories of Theodore Dreiser*, p. 9.

21. Moers, *Two Dreisers*, pp. 144-145.

22. Dreiser, *Short Stories*, p. 115.

23. Dreiser, *The "Genius"*, p. 689.

24. Kenneth S. Lynn, *The Dream of Success* (Boston, 1955), p. 24.

25. Dreiser to Mencken, 6 December 1909,

ed. Elias *Letters*, 1: 97, 98; Mencken, "Theodore Dreiser," *A Book of Prefaces* (New York, 1917), p. 114; Dreiser, *The "Genius,"* p. 734.

26. Dreiser, *The "Genius,"* pp. 361, 736. Two articles, which came to my attention after writing the above, take a parallel view of Dreiser: Joe D. Thomas, "The Natural Supernaturalism of Dreiser's Novels," *Rice Institute Pamphlets*, 44 (1957), 112-25; and "The Supernatural Naturalism of Dreiser's Novels," ibid., 26 (1959), 63-69. Cf. Randall Stewart, "Dreiser and the Naturalistic Heresy," *Virginia Quarterly Review*, 34 (1958), 100-16.

27. Jack London, "The Scab,"*Atlantic Monthly*, 93 (1904), 63; "The Class Struggle," *Independent* 55 (1903), 2603-10; and "How I Became a Socialist," *War of the Classes* (London, 1905), p. 48.

28. London, "The Class Struggle," pp. 2605, 2610.

29. London, "Wanted: A New Law of Development," *War of the Classes*, pp. 217-64.

30. London, *The Iron Heel* (London: Everett Library, n.d.), pp. 5, 103, 119.

31. Jaher, *Doubters and Dissenters*, p. 204. London's novel triggered debate among American Socialists concerning the meaning of evolution. Writing in the *International Socialist Review* of April 1908, John Spargo called *The Iron Heel* "unfortunate" in that "it gives new impetus to the old and generally discredited cataclysmic theory." Robert Rives LaMonte defended London in "Science and Revolution," *The Social Democrat*, 13 (1909), 105-13.

32. London, *Martin Eden*, p. 297.

33. Ibid., pp. 296-97.

34. Ibid., pp. 296, 67.

35. Ibid., pp. 104-5, 196.

36. Ibid., p. 357.

37. Ibid., p. 381.

38. London to Upton Sinclair, 23 November 1909, photocopy in the Papers of Upton Sinclair, Indiana University; King

Hendricks and Irving Shepard, ed., *Letters from Jack London* (London, 1965), pp. 306-8, 367-68, 463.

39. Walcutt, *American Literary Naturalism*; Lynn, *Dream of Success*.

Chapter 12
Imperialism and the Warrior Critique

1. John Barrett, "The Problem of the Philippines," *North American Review*, 167 (1898), 267; Charles A. Conant, "The Economic Basis of 'Imperialism,' " ibid., p. 327.

2. See James P. Mallan, "The Warrior Critique of the Business Civilization," *American Quarterly*, 8 (1956), 216-30.

3. For a discussion of changing "secular" arguments see Albert K. Weinberg, *Manifest Destiny* (Baltimore, 1935); and for the Christian strain in American expansionism, Ernest L. Tuveson, *Redeemer Nation* (Chicago, 1968).

4. Hofstadter, *Social Darwinism*, p. 184. Historians have nonetheless insisted that Darwin's contribution was important. "Darwin had been talking about pigeons," wrote Richard Hofstadter, referring to the subtitle of the *Origin of Species*, "but the imperialists saw no reason why his theories should not apply to men" (p. 171). "While the biological argument for militarism was hardly the dominant note among American leaders," he added, "it did give them a cosmic foundation that appealed to a Darwinized national mentality" (p. 192). Qualifying this view still further, Walter LaFeber wrote: "Perhaps social Darwinism was not the primary source of the expansionist ideology, but, as Mahan wrote, the 'struggle for life,' 'the race for life,' are phrases so familiar that we do not feel their significance till we stop to think of them." Convinced that "social Darwinism" was in the air, LaFeber gave prominent place to Strong, Mahan, et al. as proto-

imperialists in his study *The New Empire* (Ithaca, N.Y. 1963). See also Ralph D. Bald, "Development of Expansionist Sentiment in the United States 1885-1895," Ph.D. thesis, University of Pittsburgh, 1953.

5. Hofstadter, *Social Darwinism*, p. 195 expressed mock surprise at Sumner's defense of the nation's "democratic" heritage, and attributed his antiimperialist stand to personal integrity and a slightly old-fashioned sense of patriotism.

6. LaFeber, *New Empire*, pp. 97-98.

7. Hofstadter, *Social Darwinism*, p. 196.

8. John Fiske, "Manifest Destiny," *American Political Ideals* (New York, 1885), pp. 98-99.

9. Ibid., pp. 143, 94. A similar use of the terminology of "natural selection" to parody the views of expansionists appeared at roughly the same time in the following poetic description of the westward thrust of European civilization:

Where peoples in process of selection,
  By virtue of "survival of the fittest,"
On islands developed by accretion
  Still live, notwithstanding their
    condition,
And that evolution by its latest
  Consigns them to extinction.

See Sextus P. Goddard, *Buds, Briers, and Berries* (Worcester, Mass., 1880), pp. 109-14.

10. On Strong see Jurgen Herbst, "Introduction" to Josiah Strong, *Our Country* (Cambridge, Mass., 1963), pp. ix-xxvi; and Dorothea Muller, "Josiah Strong and American Nationalism," *Journal of American History*, 53 (1966), 487.

11. Strong, *Our Country*, pp. 214, 200-1; and *The New Era* (New York, 1893), pp. 68, 54-55.

12. Muller, "Strong," pp. 490-91, 503.

13. Strong, *Our Country*, p. 209.

14. Ibid., pp. 201, 211, 214-15.

15. Ibid., pp. 209, 211.

16. Muller, "Strong," pp. 497-501.

17. Strong, *New Era*, pp. 34-35, 80, 282-83, 228, 346.

18. Ibid., pp. 36, 346.

19. Strong, *Expansion Under New World Conditions* (New York, 1900), pp. 238-39.

20. Ibid., pp. 246, 284-85.

21. Stephen B. Luce, "The Benefits of War," *North American Review*, 153 (1891), 672-83. For evidence that militarists were already suspected of misusing Darwinism see Calvin Thomas, "War and Evolution," *Open Court*, 2 (1888), 1355-59.

22. On Luce's battle for efficiency in naval administration, see Albert Greaves, *Life and Letters of Rear Admiral Stephen B. Luce* (New York, 1925).

23. Luce, "Benefits," pp. 677-81.

24. Ibid., p. 671.

25. Mahan, "A Twentieth Century Outlook," *Harper's* 95 (1897), 532-33. On Mahan see John W. Pratt, "Alfred Thayer Mahan," in *The Marcus Jernegan Essays in American Historiography* (Chicago, 1937); Peter Karsten, "The Nature of 'Influence': Roosevelt, Mahan, and the Concept of Sea Power," *American Quarterly*, 23 (1971), 585-600.

26. Cf. LaFeber, *New Empire*, note 4 above.

27. Robert Seager and Doris Maquire, eds. *The Letters and Papers of Alfred Thayer Mahan*, 3 vols. (Annapolis, Md., 1975).

28. Mahan, "The Problem of Asia," *Harper's*, 100 (1900), 545. See also "A Twentieth Century Outlook," p. 529.

29. Mahan, "The Merits of the Transvaal Dispute," *North American Review*, 170 (1900), 313.

30. Barrett, "The Problem of the Philippines," p. 267; Conant, "The Economic Basis of 'Imperialism,'" p. 327; and Teunis S. Hamlin, "The Place of War in the 20th Century," *Independent*, 52 (1902), 531-32.

31. Conant, "The Economic Basis of 'Imperialism,'" p. 225; Hamlin, "The Place of War," p. 531.

32. Theodore Marburg, *Expansion* (Balti-

more, 1900), pp. 5, 77.

33. Albert H. Coggins, "The Menace of Imperialism," *Arena*, 24 (1900), 345-50; Raymond L. Bridgman, "The Body Politic of Mankind," *New England Magazine*, n.s. 21 (1899), 27. See also David Starr Jordan, *Imperial Democracy* (New York, 1899), pp. 94-96.

34. Raymond L. Bridgman, "Brute or Man?" *New England Magazine*, n.s. 19 (1898), 84. See also George H. Shibley, "Is the Republic Overthrown?" *Arena*, 22 (1899), 443-53.

35. See William Leuchtenburg, "Progressivism and Imperialism," *Journal of American History*, 39 (1952), 483.

36. The following analysis builds directly on Mallan, "The Warrior Critique," and Frederic C. Jaher, *Doubters and Dissenters* (Glencoe, Ill., 1964).

37. Brooks Adams, review of L. Stephen's *Liberty, Equality, Fraternity* in *North American Review*, 118 (1874), 445; and "The Last Stage of English Whiggery," *Atlantic Monthly*, 47 (1881), 569-70. On Adams see Arthur F. Beringause, *Brooks Adams* (New York, 1955); Thornton Anderson, *Brooks Adams: Constructive Conservative* (Ithaca, N.Y., 1951); and Jaher, *Doubters and Dissenters*.

38. Brooks Adams, *The Law of Civilization and Decay* (New York, 1895), p. xi.

39. Brooks Adams, "The Gold Standard," *Fortnightly*, o.s. 62 [n.s. 56] (1894), 242; and *Civilization and Decay*, pp. 352, 249.

40. Brooks Adams to Henry Adams, 27 February 1898, quoted in Jaher, *Doubters and Dissenters*, p. 173.

41. Brooks Adams, *The Theory of Scientific Revolutions* (New York, 1913), pp. 226-27.

42. Homer Lea, *The Valor of Ignorance* (New York, 1909), p. 11.

43. Ibid., pp. 138, 149.

44. Ibid., pp. 254-55.

45. John E. Mercer, "Nietzsche and Darwinism," *Nineteenth Century*, 77 (1915), 421-23; W. C. A. Wallar, "A Preacher's Interest in Nietzsche," *American Journal of Theology*, 19 (1915), 74. For other examples see Otto Heller, *Prophets of Dissent* (New York, 1918), p. 120; "What Might Makes Right," *Independent*, 80 (1914), 79-80; Vernon Kellogg, "War for Evolution's Sake," *Unpopular Review*, 10 (1918), 146-59, and *Headquarter Nights* (Boston, 1917), pp. 22-29; William R. Thayer, *Volleys from a Non Combatant* (New York, 1919), pp. 20-21; and Louis More, *The Dogma of Evolution* (Princeton, 1925), p. 345. The latter observed of Germany: "Unfortunately, they did what no other people were willing to do; they put this fallacious doctrine [of Darwin-Nietzsche] into practice."

46. H. L. Mencken, "The Sawdust Trail," *Smart Set*, 46 (1915), 156; and "Introduction" to Nietzsche, *AntiChrist* (New York, 1920), p. 15.

47. John Dewey, "Force," *New Republic*, 5 (1916), 295-97. See also John Burroughs, "Arrival of the Fit," *North American Review*, 201 (1915), 197-201.

48. David Starr Jordan, "Social Darwinism," *Public* (1918), 400-1.

49. Carlton J. H. Hayes, "The War of the Nations," *Political Science Quarterly*, 29 (1914), 702-5.

50. Richard Hofstadter, *Social Darwinism* cited all these works except Todd and Davies. In the *Annals of the American Academy*, 73 (1917), 245, a reviewer of Davies's *Social Environment* praised the author for noting that "the biological view, with its concept of struggle and natural selection, has led to extreme individualism, conflict, and war."

51. Arthur J. Todd, *Theories of Social Progress* (New York, 1918), p. 275. See also William E. Ritter, *War, Science and Civilization* (Boston, 1915), pp. 14-18.

52. George Nasmyth, *Social Progress and the Darwinian Theory* (New York, 1916), pp. 269, 250; Todd, *Social Progress*, p. 250; Ralph Barton Perry, *The Present Conflict of Ideals* (New York, 1918), p. 124. See also Perry, *Philoso-*

phy of the Recent Past (New York, 1926), p. 28.

53. Nasmyth, *Social Progress*, pp. viii-ix, 329.

54. Reviews in the *Nation*, 102 (1916), 650, and the *Survey*, 37 (1916), 92.

Epilogue: From Histrionics to History

1. This exchange is quoted in John C. Long, *Bryan, the Great Commoner* (New York, 1928), pp. 391-94.

2. Bryan, *The Prince of Peace* (Chicago, 1909), p. 13.

3. Bryan, "Mr. Bryan in the Bible Class," *Commoner* (March 1916), p. 18.

4. Bryan, "The Menace of Darwinism," *Commoner* (April 1921), pp. 5-8.

5. Lawrence Levine, *Defender of the Faith* (New York, 1968), p. 270; Edward A. Ross, *Seventy Years of It* (New York, 1936), p. 88 describes a dinner meeting with Bryan in 1905.

6. Mencken, *Notes on Democracy* (New York, 1926), p. 57; *Prejudices*, 3rd ser. (New York, 1922), p. 129.

7. Duncan Aikman, "Ape Laws as Political Medicine," *Independent*, 116 (1926), 543; Maynard Shipley, *The War on Modern Science* (New York, 1927), p. 191.

8. Fay Berger Karpf, *American Social Psychology* (New York, 1932), p. 214; Read Bain, "Trends in American Sociological Theory," *Trends in American Sociology*, ed. George Lundberg (New York, 1926), pp. 76-79. See also Erville B. Woods, "Heredity and Opportunity," *American Journal of Sociology*, 26 (1920), 3; and Hope Tinsdale, "Biology in Sociology," *Social Forces*, 18 (1939), 29-40.

9. For example see Floyd N. House, *The Range of Social Theory* (New York, 1929), pp. 98-99, 398-99; Harry E. Barnes and Howard Becker, *Social Tought From Lore to Science*, 2 vols. (New York, 1938), ch. 19.

10. Edward Cary Hayes, *Sociology and Ethics* (New York, 1921), p. 269. See also

Albert B. Wolfe, *Conservatism, Radicalism, and Scientific Method* (New York, 1923), pp. 42-47, by a professor of economics at Ohio State.

11. Emory Bogardus, *A History of Social Thought* (Los Angeles, 1922), p. 300.

12. Talcott Parsons, *The Structure of Social Action* (New York, 1937), pp. 110-20. See also ibid. pp. 219-28. For Pareto's views see his *The Life of Mind and Society*, ed. A. Livingston, 4 vols. (New York, 1935), 1: 492-3 and 4: 1481.

13. Cf. the *Index* to the *American Journal of Sociology* published in 1947 and 1966.

14. Stuart P. Sherman, *On Contemporary Literature* (New York, 1917), pp. 91-92, 13-15.

15. Lewis Mumford, "The Critics of Darwin," *New Republic*, 53 (1928), 301-2.

16. Charles E. Edgerton, "Congress, Poverty, and the Tapeworm," *New Republic*, 53 (1928), 351; C. E. Ayres, "The Gospel According to Darwin," *New Republic*, 54 (1928), 100.

17. Charles A. Beard, *The Rise of American Civilization* (New York, 1927), p. 407; *The Encyclopedia of the Social Sciences*, 1 (1930), 162; and "The Myth of Rugged Individualism," *Harper's*, 164 (1931), 20-21.

18. Edward R. Lewis, *A History of American Political Thought* (New York, 1937), pp. 381, 270. See also Thomas C. Cochran, "The Faith of Our Fathers," *Frontiers of Democracy*, 6 (1939), 17-19.

19. Sidney Hook, "Marx and Darwin," *New Republic*, 67 (1931), 290-91.

20. Thomas P. Neill, "Democracy's Intellectual Fifth Column," *Catholic World*, 155 (1942), 151-55; William McGovern, *From Luther to Hitler* (Boston, 1941); and Robert E. Coker, "What Are the Fittest?" *Scientific Monthly*, 55 (1942), 488. See also Edwin G. Conklin, "Does Science Afford a Basis for Ethics?" ibid., 49 (1939), 295-303; F. Ashley Montagu, "Nature of War," ibid., 54 (1942), 342; Edmund W. Sinot, "The Biological Basis of Democracy," *Yale Review*, n.s. 35 (1945), 61-73; [unsigned],

"War Is Not Necessary or Inevitable Biologically," *Science News Letters,* 33 (1938), 195; and Carl Becker, "Some Generalities that Still Glitter," *Yale Review,* 29 (1940), 658-61.

21. Bernhard J. Stern, review in *Science and Society,* 5 (1941), 181; John B. S. Haldane, "Concerning Social Darwinism," ibid., pp. 373-74.

22. Stern, "Reply," ibid., 374-75. For earlier uses of the term by Stern see his sketch of William Graham Sumner in *The Encyclopedia of the Social Sciences,* 14 (1934), 463-64: "His was a stark, drastic, social Darwinian philosophy." Also *Social Forces,* 12 (1935), 164.

23. Emily R. Grace et al., "More on Social Darwinism," *Science and Society,* 6 (1941), 71-78.

24. R. Hofstadter, "Author's Note" to 1955 reissue of *Social Darwinism in American Thought* (Boston).

25. Viewed in the context of the broader debate concerning "totalitarianism," these characterizations of "social Darwinism" constituted what might be termed a left-liberal variant of the indictment of "scientism" found from a Hegelian-Marxist position in Herbert Marcuse, *Reason and Revolution* (New York, 1941).

Index

Abbott, Lyman, 76, 163
Adams, Brooks, 226, 236-38
Adams, Charles F., Jr., 87
Adams, Henry B., 110
Adams, Henry Carter, 126
Adler, Felix, 80
Agassiz, Louis, 64, 69, 120 n.18, 139, 140
Aikman, Duncan, 245 n.7
Alger, Horatio, Jr., 3, 6-7, 12, 221, 224
Allen, Garland, 28
Ammon, Otto, 190, 200
Angell, Norman, 241
Argyll, George J. D. C. (8th Duke of), 91
Atkinson, Edward, 60-61
Atlantic Monthly, 73; on Fiske, 65; and Spencer, 59, 62, 63, 70
Avary, Myrta L., 194 n.35
Aveling, Edward B., 34
Avery, Martha, 124 n.33

Baer, Karl Ernst von, 27, 43
Bagehot, Walter, 48, 109, 119, 120
Bain, Read, 246
Baker, Ray Stannard, 155 n.56, 180, 198-99
Baker, Thomas S., 210 n.28
Bakewell, Charles M., 150 n.40, 210 n.28
Balfour, Arthur James, 140, 141
Barker, Ernest, 210 n.29, 240
Barrett, John, 226 n.1, 234
Barzun, Jacques, 6
Batten, Samuel Z., 178
Beard, Charles A., 6, 11, 249
Beard, George M., 229
Beecher, Henry Ward, 63, 76, 77
Bell, Alexander Graham, 171
Bellamy, Edward, 112, 119; and Donnelly, 213; and eugenics, 90, 171-72, 173, 174; and Kidd, 154, 156; and social Darwinian stereotype, 114, 124-25, 127; and Wallace, 33; and Ward, 128
Belmont, August, 76
Bentham, Jeremy: and Kidd, 157; and

Mencken, 207; reception in U.S., 13; and Spencer, 34, 36-40, 62-63
Bernhardi, Friedrich von, 202, 239
Besant, Annie (neé Wood), 174
Bevington, Louisa S., 73-74 n.44
Bierce, Ambrose, 150 n.39
Biological analogy. *See* Organic analogy
Birdsall, Herbert, 125 n.37
Blacker, Charles P., 177 n.34
Bliss, William Dwight Porter, 152
Blumenbach, Johann F., 182, 183, 186
Bogardus, Emory, 246-47
Botta, Anne Lynch, 83
Bowen, Francis, 115, 117-19, 120, 124
Bowler, Peter J., 24, 28
Bowne, Borden Parker, 39
Brace, Charles Loring, 33, 59
Bradford, Gamaliel, 243
Brandeis, Louis D., 88
Brebner, John Bartlett, 6
Brentano, Lujo, 103
Bridge, James H., 85 n.17, 87
Bridgman, Raymond L., 235 n.33
Bristol, Lucius M., 98, 155 n.55, 240
Brooklyn Ethical Association, 79-82, 89
Browne, James C., 173 n.22
Bryan, William Jennings, 155, 201, 243-46
Büchner, Friedrich Karl Christian Ludwig, 159
Buckle, Henry Thomas, 63, 99, 100, 118, 119
Buffon, Georges de, 17, 21, 22, 182
Burckhardt, Jakob, 112
Burr, Enoch, 20
Burritt, Maurice, 33 n.42
Bushnell, Horace, 63, 160

Cairnes, John Elliott, 34, 71-72, 74
Calderwood, Henry, 49
Cannon, Walter, 17, 18
Carey, Henry Charles, 74, 115-19, 120, 124
Carnegie, Andrew, 79, 89, 137; anti-imperialism of, 227; and Gospel of